Honoring God and Family

*A Christian Response to Idol Food
in Chinese Popular Religion*

Chuck Lowe

Evangelism and Mission Information Service
Wheaton, USA

Theological Book Trust
Bangalore, India
2001

Honoring God and Family

A Christian Response to Idol Food in Chinese Popular Religion

© 2001 by Billy Graham Center

Published by
Theological Book Trust
P.O. Box 9529, Bangalore 560 095, India.

and

Evangelism and Missions Information Service (EMIS), publishing division of the Billy Graham Center at Wheaton College, 501 College Ave., Wheaton, IL 60187-5593 USA

ISBN 1-879089-35-1 (EMIS)

For information about other publications or resources of TBT
Theological Book Trust
P.O. Box 9529, Bangalore 560 095, India.

For information about other publications or resources of EMIS or the Billy Graham Center, phone (630) 752-7158,
E-mail: EMIS@wheaton.edu
or visit the website: www.billygrahamcenter.org

Table of Contents

The shenist practice of offering food to the ancestors, and then including those offerings in a family meal, has long posed an obstacle to the evangelization of traditional Chinese and a dilemma for converts in shenist homes. How can Christians honor God without offending family?

Ancestor veneration is a central element in shenist family life and populist Chinese culture. The rituals still retain a large measure of their historic vitality and traditional meanings, despite the onslaught of modernity.

The Roman Catholic and Protestant rites controversies arose out of conflicting stances toward participation in ancestral rites and meals. The alternatives reflect the influence of social location on both missionary and national: the intellectual elite tended toward rationalistic interpretations; the bureaucratic elite, toward pragmatic interpretations; and the masses, toward spiritistic interpretations.

107924

The Chinese classics confirm that ancestral rites serve both social and religious functions. The classics also reflect the effects of social location, with the intellectual elite adopting rationalistic interpretations, the masses tending more toward spiritistic explanations, and the bureaucratic elite advocating observance of the rites on pragmatic grounds.

The cultural and religious context in ancient Corinth is similar in important respects to contemporary shenism. First, the offering of food to gods and ancestors—and the consumption of food offerings in communal meals—pervade life within the home, and social relations outside the home. Secondly, these meals inseparably unite religious and social functions. Thirdly, the effects of social location on ritual interpretation are readily apparent: the philosophical elite tended toward rationalism; the bureaucratic elite, toward pragmatism; and the masses, toward spiritism.

The Hebrew Bible and rabbinic traditions insisted on scrupulous avoidance of anything remotely associated with idolatry or idol offerings. At the same time, some evidence remains to suggest that at least a portion of the Jewish social elite reached a degree of accommodation with pagan rites, and that the Jewish philosophical elite sought rapprochement with Greco-Roman philosophical interpretations of religion.

In 1 Corinthians 8–9, Paul is not setting out his own position, but is refuting the Corinthian justification for participating in cultic feasts. Their argument reflects the effects of social location on ritual interpretation. When read as indirect communication, his reply harmonizes naturally with his argument in chapter 10.

In 1 Corinthians 10 Paul renders his verdict on the consumption of idol offerings. He distinguishes two contexts: feasts held in conjunction with an offering, and meals with no apparent ceremonial component. The former are prohibited as idolatrous; the latter are generally permissible.

Paul's stance on idol food is essentially in harmony with Acts 15 and Revelation 2, though the latter are stricter due to their social contexts. The mainstream of the early Church maintains that stricter stance, due again to its social context.

Paul's teaching on idol offerings requires Christians to differentiate cultic and non-cultic celebrations. The distinction is largely feasible, and is assisted by recent developments within shenism.

Dedication

To Leon Morris

Acknowledgments

My interest in the issue of food offerings within Chinese culture was kindled in 1984, when I began teaching New Testament in the Master of Divinity program at Singapore Bible College. The then Dean of English Studies, Dr. E. N. Poulson, designed an extraordinary program integrating exegesis, theology, and homiletics. As a result, for one semester per year over the next decade, I devoted the greater part of my time to researching and teaching 1 Corinthians.

Thanks are due also to successive classes of students, for teaching me about Chinese (and Hindu) practices regarding food offerings. Together we mulled over the application of Paul's teaching to contemporary Asia. In my third year, I was privileged to supervise the M.Div. thesis of Rev. Wong Fong Yang. His research sharpened my thinking, and identified areas of remaining ambiguity needing further investigation. I count my years at SBC as a high privilege, especially the opportunity to teach and to learn from its extraordinary candidates for ministry.

I researched and wrote the bulk of this book during 1998, while serving as Missionary Scholar in Residence at the Billy Graham Center, Wheaton College, Wheaton, IL.

Special thanks are due to its associate director, Dr. Ken Gill, for overseeing my appointment; to Mrs. Dotsey Welliver, for her patient editorial hand; to Mrs. Betty Woodard, for extraordinary service with interlibrary loans; and to Mrs. Vonnie Albert, for general good humor and helpful bass fishing tips.

Several scholars and friends consented to read early drafts of this book, including Dr. Andrew Hwang, Singapore Bible College; Dr. Simon Chan, Trinity Theological College, Singapore; Dr. David Pao, Trinity Evangelical Divinity School; and Drs. Chuck Weber, Gene Green, Scott Moreau, and Brent Fulton of Wheaton College.

More personal debt is due my family: Irene, my partner in life and in ministry, who first 'shanghai-ed' me to serve in Asia; and our sons, Benjamin the fisherman, and Nathaniel the sportsman. Together, while this book was in progress, we moved halfway around the world on three separate occasions, faced the scourge of cancer, and overcame numerous less challenging bumps and bruises.

Finally, I acknowledge my debt to Dr. Leon Morris, of Melbourne, Australia, in gratitude for his supervision of my doctoral research many years ago. It is small compensation for your efforts, kind fellow, but comes with warm affection.

Synopsis

Ancestor veneration presents a significant hindrance to evangelism and a cause of controversy for the Church throughout much of Asia, including Korea, Japan, and various southeast Asian Chinese communities. The tension is not only between the Church and its social environment, but also between various perspectives within the Church.

Under the wider rubric of ancestor veneration, the consumption of idol offerings is especially problematic. Christianity is widely known to be monotheistic and exclusivistic. Consequently, after some initial resistance, shenist families commonly release converts from the obligation to make offerings to their ancestors. Having granted this significant concession, however, they typically find it incomprehensible and insolent when Christians refuse even to participate in the family feast which is the focus of every celebration, simply because the food was previously offered to ancestors.

Caught between the competing demands of faith and family, and of God and culture, the Church polarizes into two camps:

(1) those who join feasts with family and friends in order to retain relationships, even though it involves eating food offered to idols

(2) those who avoid any food known (or sometimes even strongly suspected) to have been offered to idols.

Contrary to widespread perception, the opposing positions are not essentially theological, as though the alternatives were liberal syncretism or conservative ethnocentrism. Rather, each stance commonly reflects the social location of its proponents. From ancient China to modern Asia, from shenist practitioner to foreign missionary and national Christian, a basic typology emerges: the intellectual elite consistently lean toward rationalistic interpretations of the rites; the bureaucratic elite, toward pragmatic interpretations; and the populist masses, toward spiritistic interpretations.

Greco-Roman domestic ritual and interpretation display remarkable parallels to the Chinese ancestral cult, including the consumption of idol offerings, and the effects of social location on ritual interpretation. Consequently, Paul's treatment of idol food in 1 Corinthians 8–10 is directly applicable to the contemporary Asian context.

Unfortunately, despite numerous attempts, the light of this passage has not properly shone on the Asian context, because its rhetoric is subtle, and its argument, complex. Populist interpretation resorts to proof-texting, subordinating the argument of the text to the agenda of pragmatics: "May we eat idol food, or should we abstain?" Scholarly interpretation also tends to pay insufficient attention to the argument of the text, due to a preoccupation with an agenda of systematics: "Is Paul's position coherent or contradictory?"

Careful attention to the development of the argument in 1 Corinthians 8–10 is crucial to accurate interpretation. In chapters 8 and 9, Paul raises and refutes the Corinthian rationale for their position. In chapter 10, he sets out his own. Essentially, he reconfigures the presenting issue from one of eating idol food to one of participating in cultic feasts: idolatry is the issue, not idol food. At the same time, idolatry extends beyond the ritual of offering food or drink to gods and ancestors, to participation in the feasts held in conjunction with such rituals. Even if they abstain from worship and deny the existence of the gods, those who join a cultic feast are guilty of idolatry by virtue of their participation in the meal. On the other hand, where there is no worship, the prior history of the food is inconsequential, and Christians may eat freely.

By configuring the issue in this way, Paul takes a slightly different tack from the Apostolic Council (Acts 15:20,29) and from the elder John (Rev. 2:14,20), who each categorically prohibit the consumption of idol food. It would be presumptuous, however, to assume an irreconcilable conflict here. In a context comparable to that facing the Council, Paul advocates similar restrictions (1 Cor. 9:20). Similarly, he likely would be more concerned about the prehistory of meat if the church in Corinth were facing political harassment, as in Pergamum and Thyatira. Theological consistency does not entail uniformity of practice in widely divergent contexts.

Of the three biblical contexts, 1 Corinthians 8–10 most closely parallels the situation confronting converts in shenist cultures. From Paul's teaching, it is evident that Christians must not participate in cultic meals, though they should join non-cultic meals. This principle does not resolve every ambiguity, but it does cover most situations. Significantly, recent developments in local shenism facilitate the proposed distinction between cult and culture.

Honoring God without Dishonoring Family: The Gospel and Chinese Popular Religion

Summary: The shenist practice of offering food to the ancestors, and then including those offerings in a family meal, has long posed an obstacle to the evangelization of traditional Chinese and a dilemma for converts in shenist homes. How can Christians honor God without offending family?

"This practice of placing food upon the graves of the dead seems to be beyond any charge of sacrilege and perhaps also free from any taint of superstition" (Matteo Ricci, sixteenth-century Jesuit missionary to China).[1]

"If I were called on to name the most serious impediment to the conversion of the Chinese, I should without hesitation point to the worship of ancestors" (William Martin, nineteenth-century Protestant missionary to China).[2]

"It is constantly repeated and we believe with much truth that Ancestral Worship still presents one of the greatest obstacles to the progress of Christianity" (James Jackson, Chairman of the Committee on Ancestor Worship for the Centenary Conference of Protestant missionaries in China, 1907).[3]

"Ancestor veneration is the greatest obstacle to the Christian mission among the Chinese...It prevents the great majority of the Chinese from coming to Christ" (Daniel Hung, national pastor in Taiwan, 1983).[4]

"Ancestor worship has been one of the most important traditional practices among Chinese, Japanese, and Koreans in Asia and has been a continuing obstacle to Christian evangelism and missions" (Bong Rin Ro, Korean missionary and convener of a 1983 Asian conference on the Christian response to ancestor practices).[5]

From the sixteenth-century Roman Catholic mission to China, through the nineteenth-century Protestant mission, and up to the present time, ancestral rites have proved an enormous obstacle to the conversion of traditional Chinese, and a ground for fierce contention among both missionaries and national Christians.[6]

Offerings to ancestors are a central element of traditional Chinese culture. The practice is taken for granted in the earliest extant literary sources and predates all the formal Chinese religions, whether Confucianism, Buddhism, or Taoism. Moreover, where ancestral practices were at odds with the beliefs and practices of these later religions, it was largely the latter, not the former, which made the necessary adjustments.[7] Among religions practiced by Chinese, Christianity stands alone in its steadfast prohibition against the offerings.

The making of offerings also transcends differences of interpretation. Some practitioners consider the ancestors to be spiritual beings in dire need of food; some make offerings largely as an expression of respect for the deceased; others emphasize the role of the rites in unifying the culture and stabilizing the society; some deny any special ritual significance to the offerings at all. Whatever differences exist in interpretation, however, the vast majority of adherents are united in practice. Except, that is, for Christians.

Due in significant measure to its prohibition against ancestral rites, Christianity appears foreign to a community that values its ethnic superiority, disruptive and intractable to a society that aims for harmony, and unfilial in a culture where filial piety is the primary virtue. In short, despite opposition to characteristic cultural vices of 'second-wives,' drunkenness, and gambling, the refusal of Chinese Christians to participate in the veneration of ancestors marks them as fundamentally, blatantly, and distinctively immoral.

Ironically, it is the very desire to avoid immorality that motivates the prohibition in the first place. No tenet is more fundamental to Christianity, or more often reinforced in Scripture, than the prohibition against idolatry. From the Decalogue to the post-exilic prophets, idolatry is expressly, repeatedly, and forcefully forbidden. The New Testament also prohibits idolatry, from the beginning of the Gentile mission, when Christianity first came into contact with idolatry (Acts 15:1–29), to its final page (Rev. 21:7–8).

Chinese Christians are thus caught between the pull of their culture and the push of their faith. To be Chinese and filial requires the practice of ancestral rites. To be Christian and faithful has traditionally required abstention from the rites. How can Chinese be both filial and Christian? How can they honor both God and family?

Gods, Ghosts and Ancestors

Anthropologists commonly classify Chinese preternatural beings into three categories: gods, ghosts, and ancestors.[8] The typology is attractive because it corresponds to the social structure of everyday life: gods are equivalent to government bureaucrats; ghosts to brigands (during times of civil disorder in rural, imperial China) or to beggars (commonly today); and, ancestors to family members. Whatever the merits of this typology, the present study cuts across these boundaries.[9] The focus here is on ancestral practices—encompassing the categories of ghost and ancestor—but with scant regard for gods.

Ancestors versus Gods

Gods are a lower priority for the simple reason that they pose less a source of contention between Christian converts and their shenist families. There are two reasons for this. For one, Christianity is sufficiently established and consistent that its exclusive monotheism and opposition to idolatry are widely known, while offerings to gods and to tutelary spirits are widely perceived to be fundamentally and explicitly religious. For the other, the worship of particular gods is not the chief concern of shenism. Within a single family, it is not uncommon for each sibling to frequent a different temple. Parents commonly oppose the conversion even of their adult children. However, once those children are baptized, they generally no longer expect them to attend the temple or to participate in domestic worship of the gods.

The veneration of ancestors, however, is not so easily reconciled, either for converts or for non-Christian family members. The Chinese concept of family is fundamentally lineal, not nuclear or even extended; 'family' includes at least three or four generations of deceased and extends to yet unborn generations. Ties to ancestors are an integral part of both family and individual identity. Moreover, in Confucian ethics and in Chinese culture as a whole, filial piety is indisputably the core ethical value, and is expressed toward deceased ancestors no less than toward living parents and grandparents. To neglect the veneration of ancestors is to be unfilial; to be unfilial is to be immoral and un-Chinese.

Yet for a great many converts, the line separating veneration of ancestors from worship of gods is not clear. Academic anthropologists fasten on the ritual distinctions, for instance, in the types and preparation of food offerings. But for most converts, these differences cannot offset the portrayal of ancestors as preternatural beings with the power to convey blessing and to inflict punishment. The parallels between the rituals used in worship of gods and in veneration of ancestors are commonly deemed sufficient justification to prohibit both as idolatrous. This conviction brings the convert into direct conflict with family, lineage, and culture.

Food Offerings in the Ancestor Cult

Ancestral practices taken in their entirety are many, varied, and sometimes ambiguous.[10] The breadth of practices, the variety of meanings assigned them, and the lack of detailed biblical teaching on many of the typical Chinese practices allows for limited progress in evaluation. For such reasons, this study focuses more narrowly on the place of food offerings within the ancestral cult.

Of all the ancestral practices, the food offerings pose the greatest problem, both because of implicit meaning and because of subsequent use. Many ancestral customs are ambiguous. Bowing to the deceased, for instance, is often defended with a measure of success as a cultural sign of respect: Chinese also bow to living elders. But food offerings seem inherently to portray the deceased as in need of ongoing sustenance, and with this comes a wide range of beliefs, including the ability of deceased ancestors to bless or afflict, depending on the treatment accorded by their descendants.[11]

Moreover, of all the offerings (including incense, mock money, and paper replica of consumer goods, such as clothes, cars, and homes), only the food is put to subsequent use. The other offered items are burned to convey them to the spirit world. But the food is not. Ancestors come to partake of its spiritual essence. Once they have finished, the food is carried back to the kitchen for final preparation, and then served to the family. Every important family celebration or cultural holiday includes a feast, and no feast can begin until appropriate portions are offered to the ancestors.

For shenists nothing is more offensive than the typical Christian refusal to join in the family feast. After initial and sometimes vigorous resistance, the older generation will generally grudgingly permit their children to be absent from the rites venerating ancestors. That significant concession makes it all the more infuriating when their

Christian children refuse even to eat with the family on festive occasions.[12] The focus of this monograph is here: neither on the vast topic of ancestor veneration, nor on the making of offerings to the ancestors, but on participation in feasts that include food previously offered to ancestors (or to gods).[13]

A Geographic and Ethnic Focus

Beyond narrowing the scope from ancestor veneration as a whole to the consumption of food offerings in particular, a geographic and ethnic focus is also necessary. In one form or another, ancestral offerings and feasts characterize most Asian cultures, including the Japanese, Korean, Javanese, Chinese East Asian, and even post-Maoist mainland Chinese (especially in the rural areas and in the southern provinces). Similar practices also appear in sub-Saharan Africa and Latin America. Yet the need for detailed description—not to mention the impossibility of competence across so many cultures—requires that discussion be limited to a single context. Consequently, this study focuses ethnically on Chinese customs, and geographically, on Singapore and Malaysia. Nevertheless, informed readers should be able to compare the details of their contexts with practices sketched here, in order to draw out the implications of these conclusions for their own cultural milieu.

Social Location and Ritual Interpretation

Any discussion of Chinese religion immediately faces two ambiguities: terminology and description.

'Folk Religion,' 'Popular Religion,' and 'Shenism'[14]

No label proves entirely satisfactory. 'Chinese folk religion' or 'Chinese popular religion' are both common in anthropological literature, but ethnic Chinese do not use such terms to describe themselves. Adopting an emic perspective, some social anthropologists prefer to speak of 'shenism' (for the ritual and belief system) and 'shenist' (for the practitioner), from the standard Chinese terms for the central practice, *'bai shen'* ('venerate spirits'). This is admittedly more accurate, but also communicates less, except for those within the academic guild or for those familiar with Mandarin. In this study I shall use all three terms interchangeably.

Of course, content is more critical than terminology, and not surprising, it is more problematic as well. Two distinctions are crucial, and both can be implied in the term 'Chinese popular religion.'

'Popular Religion' and Common Practice

At times 'popular religion' emphasizes continuity, the form of religion that characterizes the 'populace' as a whole. At least in Chinese religion, continuity primarily encompasses practice, rather than meaning. Across centuries, across classes, across socio-political positions, the chief continuity has been in forms and symbols, rather than in meaning and interpretation. The intellectual elite and lower-class illiterates, political leaders and peasants, ancients and moderns, tend to assign different meanings to the same ritual acts. But by and large they engage in basically the same rituals (though the elite generally take the lead and the political leadership may be under obligation to perform additional rites). This continuity is noted here, and will be assumed throughout. It is not the focus of this investigation, nor the sense in which 'popular religion' generally appears here.

'Popular Religion' and Elite Interpretation

In its second sense, 'popular religion' highlights certain discontinuities. The existence of discontinuities has been recognized for centuries, though attempts to pin them down precisely have prompted considerable debate in the last several decades.[15] Whatever their differences, each taxonomy tends to accept—with a variety of qualifications—a basic distinction between 'populist' interpretations that endorse the existence and potency of spirits, on the one hand, and 'elite' interpretations that emphasize the moralistic and social functions of the rites, on the other. Weller explains:

> [The populist interpretation tends to] talk about these spirits, and behave toward them, as if they were embodied beings who really affect the world…
>
> The elite stresses the moral and psychological functions of religion, but generally dismisses the possibility of using active spirits to achieve real empirical results. Passive interpretations encouraged the elite to use religion as a political tool.[16]

The role of social location is fundamental in all that follows, so it bears brief elaboration.

The distinction mainly concerns the interpretation—more than the practice—of rites. Strikingly, from the ancient Chinese classics, through the sixteenth-century Catholic mission to China and its nineteenth-century Protestant counterpart, up to contemporary East Asia, interpretations of Chinese rites can be differentiated into three basic perspectives: the masses tend toward spiritism; the intellectual elite, toward rationalism; and the bureaucratic elite, toward pragmatism.[17]

Social location accounts for a considerable amount of the controversy over the proper Christian response to ancestral rites. Commonly Christians seek to distinguish legitimate from illegitimate practices by asking, "What does this rite or practice signify? Is it religious or cultural?"

For example, is offering food to ancestors nothing more than a sign of respect for the deceased, just as the younger generation serves their elders at table and invites them to eat first? Or is it an attempt to appease spirits so that they will reciprocate with blessing rather than causing misfortune? Arguably, if the former is right, then Christians could both make and subsequently eat the offerings without qualm. In the latter, at least the offering—if not also the meal—would be deemed cultic. The answer, it turns out, depends on who asks the question, and whom they ask.

When Western academics interview Chinese intellectuals, for example, they are more likely to expect, to receive, and to accept, a naturalistic response. Evangelical missionaries, on the other hand, typically do not come from—nor do they commonly reach—the elite. When they inquire about the meaning of the rites, they are more likely to hear—and to believe—that the offerings provide for the ongoing needs of ancestral spirits who reciprocate or take revenge, depending on whether they are appeased or neglected. Consequently, intellectuals are more inclined to interpret the offerings as commemorative and to offer no objection to the meals. Mainstream evangelicals, however, tend to interpret the offerings as cultic, and to prohibit participation in the meals.

Shall we conclude, as the various disputants often have, that the one side is theologically liberal, or the other, culturally ethnocentric? With the benefit of hindsight, and with no intention of equivocation, it is evident that both those who affirm the religious character of the rites and the accompanying meals, and those who affirm their social function, are correct. The rites and meals are religious in character, especially in populist imagination and practice. The rites and meals perform important socio-political functions, and often exclusively socio-political functions from the perspective of the bureaucratic and intellectual elite.

At the same time, each side in this dispute is wrong, and in a similar way: each tends to overemphasize one dimension of the rites and meals. Each attempts to make sense of multiple meanings through a reductionistic focus on one set of meanings to the exclusion of the other. This is understandable, as the alternative appears to be indecision or endless qualification. A blanket approval or disapproval is much easier to implement. But it is much less fair to the nuance of daily life.

So the operative question is, When function and meaning vary according to social location, which interpretation is definitive? The shenist, because it represents the majority of the populace? The intellectual elite, because it is more reflective and rational? The bureaucratic elite, because it represents the dominant power structure? This is not a theoretical query concerning an abstract issue. Must Christians abstain from the rites and the accompanying meals because they have religious significance for many practitioners? Or may they participate, on the grounds that the meals—if not also the rites—are predominantly (or even exclusively) social and cultural, at least according to the bureaucratic elite? Or may they take part, so long as they concur with the intellectual elite, that spirits do not exist and offerings are purely commemorative?

The effect of social location on ritual interpretation is a thread weaving throughout the breadth of this study, from the survey of ancient Chinese classics, through the history of Christian missions to China, up until the present time. Remarkably, several ancient Roman social commentators noted the same trifurcation about the time Paul wrote 1 Corinthians.[18] This fact gives rise to the hope that the biblical text may resolve the conundrum.

A Modest Contribution

Whether or not Christians may participate in meals including offered food is determined in large measure by the significance of the offering. Historically, two methods have been employed to assess meaning: interpretation of contemporary practice, and research in Chinese classics. On these grounds, many argue that the rites have recently become—or that they have always been—fundamentally social and cultural. Evaluating these claims is the task of chapters two through four. The three chapters move progressively further back in time: from contemporary analyses, to the sixteenth and nineteenth centuries, and ultimately to the early Chinese classics and philosophers.

Three millennia of commentary and analysis encourage a sense of modesty and also contribute to the research agenda: What interpretations have been considered, and which preferred? By whom? With what consequences? A historical survey reduces the risk of two common errors: repeating the mistakes of history and reinventing the wheel. It also uncovers an instructive link between interpretation and social location running throughout the entire period, and identifies unresolved issues.

Once the shenist practice of ancestor veneration is laid out, the focus shifts to the biblical text, in the search for a parallel context and relevant guidance. The context is supplied by the Greco-Roman domestic cult, which included offerings of food and drink to deceased ancestors, spirits, and gods, followed by communal meals (chapter five). The Old Testament and Jewish response to gentile domestic cult (chapter six) is also instructive because it sheds light on the background and context of the New Testament teaching.

The relevant biblical teaching comes to the fore in chapters seven through nine. Paul's instruction in 1 Corinthians 8–10 is the center of attention (chapters seven and eight), for the simple reason that it provides the most direct and relevant discussion on the consumption of food offerings in all of Scripture. Chapter nine briefly examines two other relevant texts (Acts 15:1–35, and Rev. 2:12–29), to assess whether the New Testament is monolithic or whether it reflects a range of responses on this issue. The chapter includes a brief survey of early Church Fathers, to assess how they applied biblical teaching in the face of often virulent hostility.

By way of conclusion, chapter ten fuses the two horizons of Christian ethics, synthesizing the biblical data and applying it to the modern context. The proposals are intentionally modest in ambition. If this controversy has not been settled over the last four hundred years, it is unlikely to be settled by the present monograph. If evangelical theologians from various Asian countries have not yet reached a consensus, a resident foreigner is unlikely to resolve the impasse. But it may be possible to establish biblical and cultural parameters to exclude fastidiousness on the one end, and relativism on the other.

Finally, a comment is in order concerning the intended audience of this monograph. In the past decade, upwards of ten doctoral dissertations have been written on this topic. Given the requirements of that genre, most take a unique position on some aspect of the issue, and argue it at great length and in minute detail. The first draft of this monograph responded to each in some detail. As a result, it was dense and impenetrable to all but scholars. My editor—not to mention, my wife—objected that to be useful, a book must be intelligible. The revision, which you hold in your hands, still remains far from scintillating. I do not expect to see it for sale in airport bookstores. Given the history and complexity of the controversy, the discussion is unavoidably lengthy and detailed. But it is my hope that it is accessible to pastors, Bible college and seminary students, and to highly motivated lay people.

This investigation seeks to make a modest but significant contribution to easing the confrontation between Christianity and traditional Chinese culture. This, in turn, may increase the prospects for harmonious and successful evangelization of traditional Chinese, and for the formation of a distinctly traditional Chinese Church. Through the medium of a semi-technical monograph, I hope to raise a proposal for discussion among the leadership of the Church, including the combined communities of theologians, pastors, and lay leaders. My intent is to encourage discrete discussion and critique, in order to preserve public harmony and avoid disruptive controversy. Popularization remains the eventual goal, but only if—and when—a considerable measure of consensus is reached.

Endnotes

[1] Ricci 1953 (1615): 96.

[2] Martin 1890: 619.

[3] Jackson 1907: 215–16.

[4] Hung 1983: 32.

[5] Ro 1985: preface.

[6] At the same time, while widely overlooked, Christianity's stance against ancestral rites has recently stimulated its growth, and in two respects.

The first is noted in a report arising from the 1990 national census in Singapore. Observing the substantial increase in converts to Christianity and to secularism, at the expense of Taoism, the authors conclude that the well-educated are leaving traditional ritual practices that they perceive to be 'illogical' and 'superstitious' for belief systems which appear to be more 'rational' (Kuo and Tong 1995: 22, 32, 38).

A second respect in which Christian opposition to ancestral practices facilitates its growth can be inferred from Western sociological analyses of rapidly growing (and shrinking) Christian denominations and sects. The basic principle to emerge from these studies is that the groups which tend to grow are those that place high expectations on adherents and demand high commitment from them (Kelley 1977; Finke and Stark 1992). Similarly, Kim (1985) attributes the rapid growth of the Church in Korea at least in part to its absolute refusal to participate in the worship of ancestors, even in the face of persecution and death.

Nonetheless, the overall effect of the Christian opposition to ancestral rites continues to be negative. This is evident in two statistics from the 1990 Singapore census; the former rarely noticed, the other axiomatic. Among the well-educated, it is the English-speaking who tend more toward Christianity, while the Chinese-educated more often opt for secularism. More widely recognized—and more problematic because it involves the bulk of the populace—the less educated, the working-class, and the older adults tend to persist in the traditional religions (Kuo and Tong 1995: 32, 41).

The 1990 census quantifies what has long been apparent to sociologists and anthropologists working within a variety of cultures: it is those who have already abandoned traditional religions who are most likely to convert. (This is also the group in the West that is most likely to embrace new religions, although there it involves moving away from nominal Christianity, often into Eastern religions or Christian cults [Stark 1996: 37–47]). Christianity has succeeded spectacularly in reaching those have been 'de-culturated' through modernization, urbanization, and English-medium education. But its relative failure both among the Chinese-educated elite as well as among the working classes confirms what is evident to anyone who visits a local worship service. By and large Christianity has not been enculturated into traditional Chinese culture. Consequently, traditional Chinese are not easily converted to Christianity.

At one point Kuo and Tong are in danger of repeatedly conventional wisdom: they warn that Chinese who convert run the risk of losing their traditional culture (1995: 33). Generally, however, they succeed in putting the horse before the cart: it is those who have already abandoned their traditional culture that are likely to convert to Christianity (or to secularism) in the first place (1995: 17, 19, 21). Thus conversion may well exacerbate culture dislocation (or, actually, accelerate cultural relocation), but conversion is more a result, than a cause, of the process (Lowe 1997).

   [7] At its first attempt to enter China, Buddhism was widely rejected due to its family-disavowing ethic of celibacy and monastery. Subsequently ancestral offerings were incorporated into Buddhist mythology, and from there into practice. Offerings were permitted, either as gifts to the Buddha which accrued merit for deceased ancestors, or simply as direct offerings to ancestral spirits. Many temples even arrange to make offerings to the deceased as a service to busy patrons.

   [8]   See, e.g., Jordan 1972.

   [9]   The schema arguably forces the parallel between the supernatural and natural realms. 'Ghosts' and 'ancestors' might better be combined as sub-divisions of one over-arching category: both are spirits of deceased humans. 'Ghosts' are the spirits of those who died prematurely or violently, or of those whose needs are not supplied by descendants.

Gods, on the other hand, are commonly differentiated into three categories. Celestial deities are powerful but remote. Earth deities are tutelary, ruling over various geographical regions and topographical, ecological, or meteorological phenomena. Chthonic deities govern the underworld (Wee 1977: 142–85). While some of these deities may also be deceased humans, they lived in the distant past, and have long since been divinized. By virtue of their history, and their power they are distinguished from either sort of ancestral spirit.

[10] The Asia Theological Association monograph (Ro, ed. 1985) offers a broad survey of the issues involved in ancestor veneration as a whole. Chua (1998) provides detailed guidance concerning ritual practice and interpretation.

[11] Often the story is told of a Chinese and a Westerner at a grave site. Seeing the Chinese offer food, the Westerner mockingly asks, "Will your ancestor come to eat the food you have provided?" The Chinese retorts, "Yes, when your ancestor comes to smell the flowers you have brought."

The anecdote is amusing, but overlooks the crucial distinction: no one in the West believes that the dead come back to smell the flowers.

In the end, this is another manifestation of cultural imperialism, as though the Western practice and interpretation of floral bouquets can be imposed on the Asian custom of food offerings. It also reeks of class bias, as though because some Chinese reject the belief in spirits consuming food, all do so.

[12] An analogy might help Western readers more fully appreciate the truma caused the family by the common Christian approach to food offerings. Many Christian families in the West have experienced deep distress when adolescent or adult children renounced the parental faith. Yet even those who no longer believe the cardinal doctrines of the faith may continue to join their families in church on major holidays, such as Thanksgiving, Christmas, or Easter, or for major family celebrations, such as baptisms, weddings, and funerals. It is unlikely that any would refuse to eat Christmas or Easter dinner simply because the holiday has religious overtones or because the meal begins with grace. Yet Chinese Christians are commonly advised to maintain such rigorous standards: not simply refusing to participate in the actual rituals, but also being absent while the ritual is performed, and abstaining from any meal where offered food is served (or, at the very most, joining the feast but accepting only unoffered food).

[13] In much of the first half of this study, the focus necessarily extends beyond the consumption of food offerings to ancestral rites in general. Thus, for instance, the historic controversy involving the Roman Catholic and Protestant missions to China took in the entirety of the ancestral cult; it did not focus narrowing on the consumption of food offerings. Similarly, the Chinese classics typically comment on the rites generally, not on cultic feasts in particular. Consequently, surveys of this material are necessarily broader. Even in these cases, however, the aim is to gather materials which shed light on the consumption of ancestral offerings.

[14] 'Popular religion' may be distinguished from that curious abstraction existing predominantly in Western university classrooms, 'world religions.' The focus of this study is Chinese religion not in the abstract, but as it is practiced and interpreted in concrete socio-historical contexts.

[15] A great many taxonomies appear in the literature. Sociologist Max Weber (1964) distinguishes between 'traditional' and 'rational' religions. Anthropologist Robert Redfield (1956) proposes a bifurcation between 'great' and 'little' traditions. From the Chinese context, C. K. Yang (1961) distinguishes between 'institutional' and 'diffused' religion. Weller (1987) proposes three categories: popular, specialist, and elite. Bell (1989) provides a helpful survey.

[16] Weller 1987: 145.

[17] This trifurcation is admittedly inadequate as a comprehensive analysis of Chinese — or any other—religion. It seeks to capture only discontinuities, and, for that matter, only typological discontinuities. It does not incorporate—nor does it deny—universal continuities across the categories, or various discontinuities within each category.

Johnson, Nathan, and Rawski (1985: xi, xiii) capture the complexities inherent in any distinction between elite and popular culture:

> There were many varieties of popular culture, non-elite sub-cultures as it were, reflecting differences of power, prestige, education, and wealth, and of region, dialect, and occupation. Elite culture, too, displayed significant internal variations. And, of course, popular and elite cultures were very different from each other. But—and this is much harder to account for— these diverse elements were integrated into a single complex cultural system. The intellectual and spiritual world of the scholar or official in late imperial times was not utterly alien to the peasant or laborer, nor was the reverse true.

Gratefully, the purpose and scope of this study does not require the construction of a comprehensive typology capable of incorporating the various levels of continuity and discontinuity within Chinese religion.

Johnson (1985) attempts to construct such a typology, and ends up with a grid of nine categories, comprising two axes (education and dominance), with three gradations of each. Nine distinctions certainly provide more precision than three. But twenty-seven would provide more than nine, and so on.

My objective is to establish three basic propositions: (1) Chinese rituals are interpreted differently by various practitioners; (2) these interpretations tend to coalesce into at least three basic types; and, (3) these types tend to correlate with the social location of the practitioners

[18] Lest Western readers adopt a supercilious stance toward primitive cultures, it should be noted that social location has largely comparable effects in modern Western society. See, for example, Hunter 1983: 49–60; Johnstone 1983: 142–62; Finke and Stark 1992; Stark 1996.

CHAPTER 2

Ties That Bind:
Ancestral Rites and Meanings

Summary: Ancestor veneration is a central element in shenist family life and populist Chinese culture. The rituals still retain a large measure of their historic vitality and traditional meanings, despite the onslaught of modernity.

Ancestral ties 'bind' in two opposing respects. In a positive sense, they unite a family and its entire lineage for as many generations as the family tracks its history.[1] In traditional Chinese conception, family is neither merely nuclear, nor even extended, but lineal, incorporating both ancestors and descendants. Filial piety is the fundamental ethical value, and is expressed toward the deceased no less than toward the living.[2] Ties to ancestors are thus an integral part of individual, family, and cultural identity. Precisely because of their centrality, however, filial piety and ancestor veneration also 'bind' in a negative sense: they constrict potential and actual converts.

Over the last four hundred years of Christian missions, however, a chorus of voices has consistently proclaimed the imminent demise of shenism.[3] Four hundred years ago, Jesuit missionary Matteo Ricci counseled patience with the traditional rites, expecting them to be replaced gradually by Catholic rituals. One hundred years ago Protestant missionaries William Martin and Timothy Richard assured their colleagues that 'superstitious' customs would fall before the onslaught of science. From time to time today, an interpreter claims that the long heralded era has now arrived, that the practice of rites has decreased, and their meanings and functions have been sanitized of all spiritistic features.

To establish a frame of reference, this chapter begins with a brief summary of the most common ritual occasions and offerings, with special attention to the consumption of the offering in a communal meal. It then surveys contemporary levels of practice and the range of meanings currently assigned to the rites. Granted the historic challenge posed by the rites, are they still an obstacle to evangelization and conversion? Or has their deterrent largely been nullified, either through decreased practice or through revisionist interpretation?

Chinese Ancestor Veneration

The focus for the rites is the ancestral tablet. This tablet typically stands on the family altar in the main communal room of the eldest son's home.

Altars range in size from a narrow shelf hung on the wall to a massive marble structure taking up an entire side wall of the main front room, from floor almost to ceiling. Normally the left side of the altar (the worshipper's right side) is reserved for the gods.

The most commonly worshipped deities in Singapore are Guanyin (50 percent of Chinese religionists) and Dabegong (48 percent of worshippers). Gautama Buddha ranks third (22 percent), just ahead of Guangong (18 percent). None of the other dozens of deities receives the devotion of more than 10 percent of Singaporean shenists.[4] Usually the gods are depicted on a scroll at the back of the altar, though statues of deities are also common. A single incense pot serves for all the gods.

The right side of the altar, the subordinate position, is reserved for the ancestors. There may be one tablet for each recent ancestor, or a collective tablet representing them all. Generally the tablet contains the name of the deceased, birth and death dates, and the names of descendants. Tablets are commonly from seven to twelve inches high, and are made of carved hardwood, typically painted red and gilded. In imperial China or in rural Taiwan, wealthy families or clans used to construct a separate ancestral hall, where the lineage tablets would be kept, with their place on the family altar taken by a paper replica or by a photo of the deceased. There are relatively few ancestral halls in land-scarce Singapore; those that do exist are commonly attached to older temples.

Ancestral rites feature in three sorts of occasions: routine offerings, annual festivals, and life-cycle celebrations.

Routine Offerings

The day begins with ancestors as with living family members: with a respectful greeting and breakfast. In the case of ancestors, the greeting takes the form of a bow and the burning of incense. 'Breakfast' consists of several pieces of fruit placed on the altar in front of the ancestral tablet. Mandarin oranges are the most common offering, since they last well in the heat and are also propitious (in Cantonese the word for 'mandarin orange' is a homonym of the word for 'gold'). But apples, pears, and a variety of other fruits are widely offered as well, especially those preferred by the ancestor when alive. Various other small food items, such as steamed bread or buns, may also be offered.

The most fastidious families change the fruit daily, but more commonly it remains on the altar for two or three days. Once removed, it is placed in the refrigerator. From then on it is treated like any other piece of fruit, to be eaten as desired or served to guests. As needed, the fruit may even be taken directly from the altar and served to visitors.

In addition to these modest daily offerings, there are more ample bimonthly celebrations marking the first and fifteenth days of each lunar month (full moon and new moon). Practices vary widely at this time. Some people accord the days little special attention; the more religious—or the less busy—will offer multicourse meals to the ancestors. However much food is supplied, once the ancestor is deemed to have finished, the food is collected for later consumption by the family.

The first and fifteenth are also special days for temple services, with chanting for the remission of sins and the accumulation of merit. At this time fruit, buns, dried noodles, and uncooked rice are commonly brought to the temple and placed before the deities. After the chanting service, the food may be left behind for the use of the temple attendants, or it may be brought home for family consumption.

Annual Festivals

Given the size of China, as well as its ethnic and linguistic diversity, holidays and customs inevitably differ in detail from family to family. But through all the diversity, basic continuities exist both in the occasions observed and in the major features of each celebration.[5]

The first and most important calendrical celebration is 'Lunar New Year' (*Chun Jie*). This is a time of great festivity: firecrackers (where not illegal), door posts draped in red cloth, lion dances, family reunions, visits to and from extended family and friends, exchange of mandarin oranges and *hongbao* (red envelopes containing small monetary gifts).

The celebrations begin on the eve, with the most important meal of the entire year: 'reunion' dinner. Family members make special effort to return to the patriarchal home. Even the deceased are included: before the family sits down to eat, representative portions of the food are first set out on a table before the ancestral altar. After some time, the food is returned to the kitchen, where it is chopped into serving portions, mixed with the rest of the food, and brought to the table for family consumption.

The next major festival in the calendar is *Qing Ming* (pronounced 'Ching Ming'). This occurs roughly two months later (while originally scheduled for the third day of the third lunar month, it is now generally celebrated on April 5th). The focus is on the deceased, and the rituals are traditionally located primarily at the gravesite. Early in the morning family members travel to the cemetery, where they spend some time tidying the grave, pulling weeds, and cleaning the tombstone. Following this, they burn incense and 'hell money' (mock money in denominations of millions of dollars). They also make food offerings, including pork, chicken, duck, wine, fruits, buns, and tea. After half an hour or so, the family may sit around and consume the food in a picnic (more common in years past), or bring it home for a meal later in the day. Now that land scarcity has made cremation the norm, increasing numbers are traveling to columbaria for simplified rites.

The 'Dragon Boat festival' (*Duan Wu Jie*)—also known as the 'Rice Dumpling festival'—commemorates the protest suicide of ancient patriot and poet Qu Yuan. Held on the fifth day of the fifth lunar month, its main features are dragon boat races and steamed rice dumplings. Food offerings with a communal meal do not feature prominently in this festival, though shenists may offer rice dumplings to their ancestors.

'Hungry Ghost festival' (*Zhong Yuan Jie*) is the most conspicuously occultic celebration in the Chinese calendar.[6] Those deceased who have no one to provide them food, money, and clothing in the afterlife (either because they have no descendants or because their descendants neglect them), suffer hunger, thirst, cold, and homelessness in a sort of purgatory for eleven months of the year. But during the seventh lunar month, the god of the underworld releases them to find satisfaction and to take revenge.

The object of their vengeance is meant to be their own negligent offspring; but prudence is the better part of valor. Consequently, as well as taking special pains to make sure that their own relatives' needs are met, shenists commonly make special offerings of hell money and food along the wayside to satisfy any malignant spirits that might be lingering in the area. A measure of the seriousness with which this custom is observed is found in the tens of thousands of dollars which the government spends annually to re-seed the grass in public housing areas where people have burned their offerings.

In addition to private familial offerings, temples organize special rituals and a communal feast around the fifteenth day of the month. Giant paper incense candles burn for several days. *Wayang* (Chinese opera) entertains both worshippers and ghosts. A large tent covers a vast array of food offered to the spirits. On the feast day, the temple auctions off items ranging from cognac to electrical appliances, donated by shopkeepers and blessed by the spirits. A large communal meal follows, distributing and sharing the food which has been offered to, and blessed by, the ghosts. The celebration ends with the burning of an effigy of the god of hell, symbolically returning him and the spirits to purgatory for the next eleven months.

The fifteenth day of the eighth month marks the 'Mid-Autumn festival' (*Zhong Qiu Jie*), more commonly known by the two most prominent aspects of its celebration, mooncakes and lanterns. Originally probably a harvest festival linked with the moon goddess Chang-E, it took on nationalistic overtones in the fourteenth century. At that time, the Chinese rebelled against the Mongolian Yuan dynasty, beginning the Ming dynasty. The timing for the rebellion was secretly distributed, hidden on slips of paper baked into mooncakes.

The contemporary festival is marked by the gift of mooncakes—pastries molded in a variety of symbolic shapes, such as fish, rabbits, or pagoda, and filled with a variety of sweet fillings, such as sugar, melon seeds, or almonds. Pomelo, reminiscent of the shape of a full moon, is also popular. For the children, evening is a time to play with lighted decorative lanterns.

While some still worship and make offerings to the moon, for the vast majority the holiday is a time to enjoy a much-loved and rather expensive delicacy, and to recall the innocent days of youth, playing with lanterns. Shenists typically offer mooncakes not only to their senior relatives and their friends, but also to their ancestors.

The 'Double-Ninth festival' (*Chong Yang Jie*) is named after its designated day, the ninth day of the ninth month. It functions largely as the autumnal equivalent of Qing Ming, with offerings of food and clothing at the gravesite. Originally in China the festival was prompted by the ancestors' need for heavier clothing as winter approached, but in Singapore today, it is not so widely celebrated as its spring counterpart (perhaps in large measure due to the consistency of tropical climate). Where celebrated, the food offerings form the basis of a communal meal at gravesite or home, just as during *Qing Ming.*

The traditional Chinese calendar includes several other festivals, and there are a host more specifically religious occasions celebrated by shenists, such as the birthday of particular gods (Guanyin, for example, typically has three major celebrations per year). But the festivals described above are the most popular, and are representative with respect both to variety and to significance.

Life-Cycle Celebrations

Every major family event is formally announced to the ancestors. The birth of a child is celebrated on its first-month anniversary. At this time the parents give relatives and friends red eggs and cakes, and sometimes also chicken and glutinous rice. Shenists also burn incense and offer food to the ancestors and to the deities worshipped in the home.

Wedding engagements are customarily announced not only to friends, but also to ancestors. Friends commonly receive cakes; ancestors receive offerings. A central component of the wedding itself is the tea ceremony. Shenists first bow and offer tea to Buddha or to the god of heaven (or whatever other deities are worshipped in the home), and then to the ancestors, before bowing to and serving senior members of the family. At the wedding dinner, traditional shenists may set an extra place for any deceased parents of bride or groom, and serve them throughout the meal.

Of all the family-life celebrations, funeral rites incorporate the largest number of rituals, and culminate in the transformation of the deceased into an ancestral spirit. Specific customs vary considerably, due to differences in geographical origin, dialect group, or family practice. But through all the diversity, certain commonalities emerge. Among the customary features are the gathering of the family unit, the wearing of mourning garments, the holding of a funeral wake over several days, the performance of rituals to help the deceased pass into the afterlife, burial or cremation, and finally the installation of the deceased as an ancestral spirit.

Traditional Chinese beliefs affirm that the deceased must undertake a perilous journey before reaching a resting place in heaven. Personal effects are placed in the coffin for use on the journey. Food is offered for sustenance, and 'hell money' as bribes to the gatekeepers in the underworld. Taoists priests lead the family, especially the eldest son, in rituals designed to expedite the passage of the deceased through the various stages of Hades and to facilitate the transformation from ghost to ancestor.

The last stage of this process comes with the dotting of the ancestral tablet, signifying that the spirit has taken up residence there. Generally the process is completed on the forty-ninth day after death, and is commemorated with a memorial service, the burning of joss-sticks and 'hell money,' the offering of food, and a communal feast for family and close friends. The tablet is placed on the domestic altar (or, less commonly, installed in an ancestral hall adjoining a temple), where it joins the company of those venerated with offerings of incense and food during the usual calendrical celebrations, and individually on the death anniversary.

In each of these life-cycle celebrations food is offered to the ancestors and subsequently consumed by the family, but generally as a matter of economy, to avoid throwing out edible food. Communal feasts are a major part of wedding celebrations, but there the focus is on the living, though deceased immediate relatives may also be invited to join the meal. Only during the funeral feast does the ancestral spirit play a prominent role: this marks the last time that the deceased routinely eats with family.

Cult and Culture

Even from a rapid survey, the dilemma confronting converts and their families is plain. Traditional Chinese culture—as with traditional cultures typically—is characterized by an intermingling of religious and social elements. The spirits of deceased ancestors participate in the routines of daily life, and all the more so during festive occasions and life-cycle celebrations. Some festivals, such as Lunar New Year, have their roots in animistic agrarian society. Others, such as Qing Ming, Hungry Ghost, and Double Ninth, serve explicitly to provide for the needs of spirits. It is not surprising, therefore, that many Christians avoid all traditional festivals—including the associated family feasts—because of possible religious undertones.[7]

Nor is it surprising that shenists should be offended by such a stringent ethic. Family plays a large part in each calendrical festival and life-cycle ritual. Many celebrations honor deceased family members; most include the deceased alongside living celebrants. Shenists certainly do not appreciate Christians' refusal to participate in the explicitly and distinctly religious rituals, but at least they find this understandable. They find it inexplicable and offensive, however, when Christians withdraw from family feasts on the grounds that the food was previously offered to ancestors.

This impasse might conceivably be broken in either of two ways. Perhaps as some Christian analysts have long anticipated, the practice of the rites will soon fade under the withering assault of modern science and philosophy. If so, the problem will resolve itself as food is no longer offered to gods and ancestors or served at meal to family and friends. Or perhaps the practice of the rites will persist while their spiritistic meanings and functions erode. If so, the tension will dissipate as Christian converts feel progressively more freedom to participate in family feasts which have lost their former cultic significance.

Both developments have been invoked to justify Christian participation in shenist feasts. Recent evidence, however, indicates that ancestral rites still retain a large measure of their traditional vitality and their spiritistic significance.

Trends in Shenist Practice and Interpretation

Until recently, it was an axiom of Western sociology of religion that modernization breeds 'secularization,' that is, a weakening of the vitality and significance of religion. Through scientific and technological advance, traditional beliefs appear to lose credibility. Through urbanization, mass communication, and frequent migration, religious communities lose the stability on which their vigor depends. For both reasons, religion slips from the center of life and society to its periphery.[8]

In recent decades, though, religious revival and invention in the West have cast doubt on the inevitability of secularization. Whatever the conclusion to the grand debate, research in Singapore documents the continued vitality of shenist rituals and spiritistic interpretations.

The Vitality of Ritual Participation

In 1988, the Singapore Federation of Chinese Clan Associations commissioned a survey of Chinese families in high-rise public housing estates, to assess changes in the practice of traditional Chinese festivals and rituals.[9] Overall, the report confirms the continuing vitality of shenist practices, despite a discernible decrease in adherents and a simplification in observance.

The proportion of Chinese informants who profess traditional Chinese religions has decreased from 97.1 percent in the 1931 census to 77.5 percent in the 1988 survey. Nonetheless, among the remaining 77.5 percent, home-based activities remain high: over 90 percent continue to burn joss-sticks and offer fruit. More than 60 percent still offer food and visit the temple.[10]

In addition to home-based rituals, Chinese festivals remain popular, though participation levels differ markedly between those festivals perceived to be predominantly cultural, and those seen to include a significant admixture of religion. Lunar New Year, with its strong cultural role, is celebrated in some way by 99 percent of the sample (for example; reunion dinner, family visitation, exchanging *hong bao*).

Qing Ming, on the other hand, with its considerable spiritistic undertones, still receives substantial—but significantly less—support: 81 percent observe in some manner or another. At the same time, there is considerable variation in practice between what are widely perceived to be the cultural and the religious aspects of the celebration: 82 percent of informants visit the graveyard or columbarium; only 63 percent pray to ancestors at home. Hungry Ghost festival fares considerably worse due to its largely spiritistic associations: only 73 percent of informants participate.[11]

These statistics document a significant reduction in participation, a noticeable simplification in ritual, and a reserve on the part of growing numbers of secularists and Christians toward spiritistic festivals and rites. Nonetheless, given the extravagant predictions of modernization and secularization, what is more striking is the continued strength and vitality of traditional rites.

The Vitality of Spiritistic Interpretation

Apart from lower rates of ritual observance, secularization may also lead to more rationalistic, less spiritistic interpretations among those who continue to observe the rites.[12] Again the data indicates some trend in that direction, but the process is not so rapid, nor so far developed, as some advocates propose.[13]

Several lines of evidence confirm the durability of spiritistic interpretations. First, the survey by the Singapore Federation of Chinese Clan Associations reveals that religious commitment is the most effective predictor of ritual participation. Eighty-five percent of shenists observe more than four traditional festivals a year; 74 percent of 'orthodox' Buddhists do likewise. With secularists, devotion drops to 28 percent; and with Christians, it bottoms out at 9.6 percent.[14] In other words, those open to spiritistic practices and meanings observe more rituals; those opposed observe the fewest.

To assuage Christian qualms, the Federation proposed sanitized versions of traditional rites, omitting characteristically religious features.[15] In contrast to recent Christian analyses advocating accommodation, the manual makes no attempt to deny the cultic significance of various festivals and celebrations, especially funeral rites, Qing Ming, and Hungry Ghost festival.[16]

Additional evidence comes from a recent Buddhist critique of shenist practice.[17] Writing on behalf of the Buddhist Missionary Society of Malaysia, Tan Teik Beng faults shenism for its animistic corruptions, including the beliefs that ancestral spirits dwell in tablets, that spirits of the deceased are present at graveside offerings, that unattended spirits become hungry ghosts, that the dead are to be feared and appeased, and that the deceased reciprocate their benefactors.[18] He equally criticizes populist rituals, such as worshipping gods, making offerings to secure protection from disaster, burning paper money and consumer goods in order to send them to heaven, offering food lest ancestors go hungry, and asking favors from the deceased.[19] In contrast to disavowals from some Christian analysts, this Buddhist intellectual shows no hesitation in ascribing spiritistic interpretations to shenism.[20]

Local anthropological and sociological studies also support spiritistic interpretations of Chinese festivals and rites. In his dissertation on funeral rites, for instance, Tong Chee Kiong observes a belief in reciprocity between ancestors and descendants.[21] He also notes the function of funeral rites in bounding the soul released by death, lest it otherwise wander and inflict harm.[22] Overall, his portrait of the spiritistic dimension to the rites is remarkably similar to exclusivistic Christian analyses.[23] The same is true of other sociological and anthropological analyses of Chinese religion in Singapore.[24]

Modernization and Secularization

This data requires significant qualification of the thesis that modernization breeds secularization. Overall, the decrease in the practice of Chinese traditional religion is not as drastic as the secularization theory would anticipate, especially given the rapid social and economic changes in Asia.

In Singapore, even among the younger generation, 69 percent of Chinese still observe traditional shenist festivals and rituals. Among those who claim no religion, many still pray to ancestors and visit temples on occasion.[25] In a recent survey in Hong Kong, only 14 percent claimed never to sacrifice to ancestors. When asked about their practice over the preceding five years, 26 percent acknowledged a decrease, 9 percent an increase, and 65 percent, no change.[26] The practice of the rituals is likely to persist for the foreseeable future.[27]

Spiritistic interpretations of the rites also remain widespread. Even one of the most ardent advocates of Christian participation in the rites concedes that over 70 percent of his shenist informants consider the deceased to be dependent on the living for food, assistance, and comfort.[28] Of his Christian informants, only 2 percent participate fully in household ancestral rites; most refuse to offer food, incense, paper money, or other provisions.[29] The spiritistic significance of the rites is the obvious explanation both for shenist observance and for Christian resistance.[30]

Despite the effects of modernization and secularization, then, ritual participation remains strong, and spiritistic interpretation, widespread. Shenist rituals and beliefs are in no imminent danger of either cessation or rationalization.[31] The problem of ancestral rites is not going to fade away within the foreseeable future.

The Social Location of Shenism

One other feature of shenism warrants comment: its social location. Or rather, its differing character according to social location. Many surveys of Chinese religion—including those mentioned above—stumble across this phenomenon somewhat unaware, and consequently give it little attention. Yet in adjudicating between the cultural and religious character of shenism, social location is the pivotal factor in explaining the conflicting reports and contradictory conclusions.

In an analysis of ancestral practices in Hong Kong, for example, Henry Smith observes that apart from religious affiliation, the two factors most influencing practice and interpretation are level of education and place of origin (urban Hong Kong or rural China).

These factors condition a wide range of behaviors, including frequency of participation and motives for participation. They also correlate with a wide range of interpretations, including the need of the deceased for nourishment, the obligation on ancestors to reciprocate, the willingness and ability of ancestors to do so, the belief in the existence of hungry ghosts, and the importance of having a son to perpetuate the sacrifices.[32] In effect, then, when he argues that the rites are predominantly cultural, and that Christians may participate freely, Smith is—apparently unwittingly—siding with the elite against the populists, with the educated against the masses, with urbanites against ruralists, and with modernists against traditionalists.

Anthropologist Robert Weller explicitly observed a similar phenomenon in Taiwan. In his analysis of Chinese religion, he differentiates three social locations, each with a distinctive outlook: populist masses, specialist religious workers, and bureaucratic elite.[33]

Populist interpretations are the least ideologized, systematized, and explicit; they also tend to be the most spiritistic. The interpretations of religious specialists—Buddhist and Taoist clergy who perform the rites—differ markedly from populist understandings in each respect. The bureaucratic elite, for their part, tend to manipulate the festivals for political ends. All three groups join together in observing the rites; "unified participation, however, need not imply unified interpretations."[34]

Malaysian Buddhist Tan Teik Beng offers a similar distinction in his critique of shenism. At least from the time of Confucius, he notes, intellectuals sought to reform populist superstitions, including the worship of gods, nature, spirits, and ancestors. The elite continued to practice the rites, but reinterpreted ancestor veneration in terms of filial piety. Despite their best efforts, however, they could not eradicate populist interpretation. The masses have consistently retained their spiritistic beliefs and practices.[35] As an intellectual, Tan unsurprisingly sides with the intellectual elite and against the 'superstitious' masses, thus confirming his own analysis of social location.[36]

Similarly, in justification of simplified and rationalized rites, the Singapore Federation of Chinese Clan Associations notes that "in the context of a highly educated and sophisticated Singapore traditional practices based on superstitions will not be acceptable by and large."[37] In so characterizing the alternatives, the authors reflect their own social location as much as that of the populists. Traditional beliefs are 'superstitious;' only more rational beliefs and practices are acceptable to the highly educated. In any event, the basic distinction is consistent: populist spiritism and elite rationalism.

At the same time, the Federation inadvertently illustrates a third social location, bureaucratic pragmatism. Its aim in sanitizing shenist rituals is that all Chinese might be able to participate, whatever their religious convictions, because

> the preservation of such customs and rituals is crucial to social stability and cohesion because these traditional practices reflect the basic Chinese virtues of loyalty, filial piety, humanism, and righteousness. These are moral values that hold a nation together and help ensure a stable and peaceful society.[38]

This is a characteristically bureaucratic response to religion.[39]

The 1990 national census indicated that the effect of social location on ritual practice and interpretation is widespread in Singapore.
In their analysis of the spread of Christianity and secularism, at the
expense of Taoism, Kuo and Tong conclude:

> A social class cleavage is particularly evident, with the higher-
> income, better educated Singaporeans becoming Christians
> or non-religionists and the lower-income, less-educated
> Singaporeans staying in their traditional faith.[40]

The well-educated are leaving traditional ritual practices which they
perceive to be 'illogical' and 'superstitious' for belief systems which
appear to be more 'rational.'[41] Here too, then, the masses tend toward
the spiritism of shenism, and the elite toward the rationalism of
Christianity and secularism.

Conclusion

In none of these respects is the current Asian context novel. The
rites exist now in much the same way as when modern Christian
missions first penetrated China. Within every generation of foreign
missionaries or national Christians, a minority has proclaimed the
imminent cessation or progressive rationalization of the rites. The
evidence cited to support these expectations has consistently been
misconstrued in chronological terms (ancient spiritism versus modern rationalism), when it has consistently better fit a sociological
framework (populist spiritism, elite rationalism, bureaucratic pragmatism).

A survey of the history of the Chinese rites controversies substan-
tiates this historical continuity, reinforces the analysis of the contemporary state of affairs as presented here, and sheds light on previous
attempts to resolve the impasse between Christian exclusivism and
shenist rites.

Endnotes

¹ This varies considerably, and in part according to class and wealth. Historically elite lineages may keep track of eighteen or twenty generations. The poorer classes often honor only those ancestors known from living memory.

² Traditionally, the chief obligation of each family member is to bring honor to, and maintain the longevity of, the lineage. Thus, in a well-known and oft-cited saying, Mencius writes, "There are three things which are unfilial, and to have no posterity is the greatest of them" (4.1.26).

³ Recently a Buddhist source has joined the hopeful chorus: "The abandonment of traditional funeral rites is gradually being accepted by the Chinese Buddhists and there is good prospect of seeing its complete disappearance by the next generation" (Tan 1988: 53).

⁴ Tong, Ho and Lin 1992:83. The syncretic character of Chinese religion is evident from the derivation of these popular deities: the female Guanyin originated as a male Indian deity; Dabegong is indigenous to Southeast Asia; Guangong is Taoist; and Gautama Buddha is meant to be a boddhisattva rather than a deity.

⁵ The material on Chinese festivals is vast. See, for example, Committee on Chinese Customs and Rites 1989; Wong 1987; Latsch 1985; Bloomfield 1983.

⁶ Cf. Bloomfield 1983:53.

⁷ See, for example, Tong 1988.

⁸ The literature is vast. For introductions, see Berger 1969; Luckmann 1967; Martin 1978.

⁹ The results were published in two articles Lin, Ho and Tong 1990; Tong, Ho and Lin 1992. For present purposes, the 1988 survey is more helpful—even if the sample is considerably smaller and less representative—than the 1990 census. This is because the former focuses on the Chinese population.

The different focus makes it difficult to correlate the details of the survey and the census, and thus to confirm the findings of the former. Nevertheless, at least on the level of overall trends, the conclusions are comparable (Kuo and Tong 1995: 57–59; cf. Tong, Ho and Lin 1992: 97–100).

The 1988 survey probably understates the move away from shenism, as its sample is drawn solely from public housing estates (Tong, Ho, and Lin 1992:80). Residents of private housing tend to be those of higher socio-economic status, which correlates positively with switching away from Chinese traditional religion (Tong, Ho and Lin 1992:85–87; Kuo and Tong 1995: 51–56). Nonetheless, distortion would be reduced by the fact that 85 percent of the populace lives in public housing (Tong, Ho and Lin 1992: 80, n2).

[10] Tong, Ho and Lin 1992: 82, 84, 97. The 1995 census report measures overall frequency rather than breaking down rates of participation by activity, but the results also attest to the continued vitality of Chinese traditional religions. Only 14.5 percent of self-identified Buddhists, and 11.1 percent of Taoists, never participate in home-based worship (as compared with 25.7 percent of Protestants). Higher numbers forgo temple worship (16.9 percent of Buddhists, and 18 percent of Taoists), but this does not necessarily signify a lack of religious devotion, as Buddhism and Taoism do not require regular temple visits. Shenists may worship at the temple only on special occasions and at times of crisis (Kuo and Tong 1995: 43–45).

[11] Tong, Ho and Lin 1992: 88.

[12] In a recent doctoral dissertation and a series of spin-off academic articles, Henry Smith justifies Christian participation in shenist meals on these grounds (1989a, 1989b, 1987). His argument is vitiated by three methodological flaws.

First, he assesses religious import over against cultural significance, as though the stronger nullifies the weaker (1987:233). As a result, only rites that are predominantly religious are counted as religious.

Secondly, the data confirms that shenists are committed to—and Christians along with secularists, oppose—the religious dimensions of the rites. Smith understates the significance of each by averaging the widely disparate scores (1987: 85–87).

Thirdly, he groups twelve motivators in three clusters: 'commemoration' (respect, love, and gratitude for the deceased), 'religious' (need and fear), and 'assistance' (to comfort, to assist the deceased in the afterlife, and to inform the deceased of significant family events) (1987: 49–52). Thus, by definition, he understates religious significance, restricting it to 'fear of the dead and selfish craving for material blessings' (1987: 233–34 cf. 227).

[13] In this century, three sorts of evidence have been adduced to demonstrate that the rites are no longer religious: political, ecclesiastical, and social-scientific. Of these, only the third is particularly germane to this monograph.

The political argument arose in both Protestant and Catholic circles in pre-war and war-time Japan. After considerable and persistent resistance, both communions accepted the claim of the Japanese government that State Shinto was political in intent and therefore permissible for Christians (see, e.g., Holtom 1963).

The ecclesiastical argument arose within Roman Catholic circles through Vatican II. Three of the documents are particularly relevant to ancestral rites: the Declaration on the Relationship of the Church to Non-Christian Religions *(Nostra Aetate),* the Decree on the Church's Missionary Activity *(Ad Gentes),* and the Constitution on the Sacred Liturgy *(Sacrosanctum Concilium).* Beyond permitting Catholics to participate in traditional indigenous rituals, Vatican II advocates incorporation of such rites into Catholic liturgy (see Abbott, ed. 1966a, 1966b, 1966c; Butcher 1996).

Since political pressure to participate is minimal in Singapore (except perhaps for Christian politicians), and since this monograph is written for the Protestant communions, neither of these arguments is sufficiently relevant to override space restrictions in this book.

[14] Lin, Ho and Tong 1990: 82.

[15] Committee on Chinese Customs and Rites 1989: 9.

[16] Committee on Chinese Customs and Rites 1989: 49, 67, 129, 135–37.

[17] Tan 1988.

[18] Tan 1988: 2, 8–9, 50–55, 64–66, 66–69.

[19] Tan 1988: 3, 52–53, 55, 64–65.

[20] He freely acknowledges, for example, that for the masses: their ancestors are present as spirits or souls during their sacrificial offerings at the graveyard when they perform the Qing Ming ceremony. Thus the ceremony is not only an occasion for showing filial piety and remembering their ancestors, but also for the purpose of asking for favors and giving thanks for blessings bestowed. The ancestral tablets in the family altar are also believed to be the place where the ancestors' spirits or souls reside (Tan 1988: 64–65).

[21] Tong 1987: 9–20.

[22] Tong 1987: 23.

[23] In an important collateral observation, Tong (1987: 20) cautions against accepting informant reports at face value, a tendency that often weakens the accommodationist argument:

Reasons given by the Chinese informants for performing death rituals emphasize ethical and moral values…The calculated self-interest or egocentric motivation is almost never made public but is masked by ethical and moral values im-

portant to the Chinese, such as filial piety and duty. These
are often the reasons given for the necessity of performing
the rituals. But an examination of the things requested and
expected from the dead will reinforce [the fact that] the conception of death rituals has also to do with giving of gifts to
the dead and the obligation of the deceased to reciprocate
with larger gifts.

[24] See, for example, Wee 1977; Leo and Clammer 1983.

[25] Tong, Ho and Lin 1992: 97–100; Kuo and Tong 1995: 32;
Clammer 1985: 52, 54.

[26] Smith 1987: 16–17, 35; 1989a: 31–32. These figures are roughly
comparable to those reported for Singapore (Kuo and Tong 1995).

[27] In partial defense of the secularization thesis, however, modernization has led to an increase in the rationalization of religion. This
is evident not only in the rise of secularism, but also in the switch to
Buddhism and Christianity, both of which are perceived to be more
'rational' than shenism or Taoism (Kuo and Tong 1995: 32, 38; Lowe
1997). The effects of secularization are also apparent in the Federation attempt to boost participation by simplifying the rites and by
rationalizing their traditional spiritistic elements (Committee on Chinese Customs and Rites 1989). Yet at all points, it should be noted that
the secularizing effects of modernity are evident predominantly among
those who turn from shenism, rather than among those who remain.

[28] Smith 1987: 49–54. He attempts to reduce this percentage by
distinguishing 'religious' and 'assistance' motivations. But that leads
to some curious discrepancies. For instance, feeding hungry ancestors is not religious, while bribing them is. Offering food to one's own
ancestors is not religious, but offering to someone else's ancestors is.
The belief that the living can provide for the continuing needs of the
deceased is not religious, but the belief that the deceased can provide
for the living is. Offering food and beverage to the deceased is not
religious, but offering 'hell money' and clothing is.

[29] Smith 1987: 176, 180–83, 204–6.

[30] This deduction is borne out by the survey. Smith tabulates the
reasons Christians give for abstaining: 66 percent, because shenists
motives are primarily religious; 48 percent, because demons are the
actual recipients of the offerings; 30 percent, because the rites are
religious (1987: 194–200).

Unfortunately, Smith discounts these convictions as "a residual
dependence upon the missionaries' theological, ethical, and social
standards," and hopes that through his research local Christians will

"come to terms with their Christian identity from within their Chinese socio-religious context in a way that has not been necessary under a state of foreign dependence" (Smith 1987: 169–70).

At the same time, his informants report receiving little teaching about ancestral rites from the church (Smith 1987: 200). If their convictions cannot be attributed to church indoctrination, can they be ascribed to dependence upon the much less numerous and influential foreign missionary force? It is no less imperialistic for foreign missionaries today to champion participation against the better judgment of national Christians, than for their forebears to have prohibited participation a century ago.

[31] Smith himself concedes:

> Among those respondents who identified themselves as adherents of traditional religions—Buddhism, Taoism, and ancestor worship—many expressed moderate to strong approval even of the religious items...Obviously, popular religious ideas and customs related to ancestors claim a sizeable following in Hong Kong (1987: 85, cf. 234–35).

This is a more nuanced and accurate picture than his claims that "ancestor-related beliefs and practices have been largely drained of their popular religious associations" (1987:i) or that "ancestor worship carries little religious significance among contemporary Hong Kong Chinese" (1987: 5, cf. 83–84, 233–34).

[32] Smith 1987: 34, 42–44, 55n2, 56n1, 59n1, 61, 63n1, 65n1, 73, 81, 84.

[33] Weller 1987: 14–21. Given the limited influence that the clerical elite have over the ancestral cult, I do not give this social location particular attention. In its place, I focus on the practices and especially the beliefs of the intellectual elite.

[34] Weller 1987: 20.

[35] Tan 1988: 6–10. Concerning ancient practice, he writes:

> While the more sophisticated Chinese regarded this Ancestor Worship as a kind of respect for the dead and a way of showing their love of continuing tradition, for the average Chinese, it indicated a fear of the dead—a terror that the spirits of the dead might return to harm the living if they were not accorded proper care and attention (p2; cf. pp 9–10).

He characterizes Chinese funerals especially as spiritistic in populist imagination (pp 51–52).

To [Confucius}, the rite performed in ancestor worship should be in the form of an expression of gratitude, devotion, remembrance, and love. However, in the common people's practice of ancestor worship, superstitious elements are introduced. To them, their ancestors are present as spirits or souls during their sacrificial offerings at the grave-yard when they perform the Qing Ming ceremony (pp 64–65).

[36] Tan 1988: 51–52, 66.

[37] Committee on Chinese Customs and Rites 1989: 23. This assessment reflects the conclusions of the Federation survey. It is the young, English-educated, graduate professional elite who are most likely to leave shenism for either secularism or Christianity (Tong, Ho and Lin 1992: 99).

[38] Committee on Chinese Customs and Rites 1989: 9; cf pp 19, 21.

[39] For example, on the role of Buddhism in legitimizing political structure in Thailand, see Suksamran 1993; Jackson 1989.

[40] Kuo and Tong 1995: 32, 41, 57–58.

[41] Kuo and Tong 1995: 22, 38.

CHAPTER 3

The Chinese Rites Controversies: Ancestral Rites and the Christian Missions to China

Summary: The Roman Catholic and Protestant rites controversies arose out of conflicting stances toward participation in ancestral rites and meals. The alternatives reflect the influence of social location on both missionary and national: the intellectual elite tended toward rationalistic interpretations; the bureaucratic elite, toward pragmatic interpretations; and the masses, toward spiritistic interpretations.

Twice in previous centuries the Church has sought to accommodate some elements of traditional Chinese ancestral customs.[1] The first experiment began four hundred years ago with the Jesuit mission to China, though it was eventually overturned by papal edict, resulting in the expulsion of Catholic missionaries in 1706. The second began some one hundred and fifty years ago with the Protestant mission to China, before it was largely overtaken by fundamental changes, both within the missions movement and within the socio-political environment of China, around the turn of the twentieth century.

The focus of this historical survey is the continuity that links these two encounters between Christianity and Chinese ancestral practices.[2] Each period was characterized by tension between essentially two positions: accommodation and radical disjunction. Significantly, the opposing positions consistently correlated with the social location of both missionary and target audience. Accommodation was commonly the preferred strategy of intellectualist missionaries seeking to reach the Chinese ruling elite. Aversion was consistently the reflexive response of mainstream missionaries reaching out to the masses.

In the course of research, one pastor advised me not to bother with the historical overview: "It is all so long ago. What relevance does it have today?" Quite simply this: the current debate reflects the same basic alternatives, and each still largely correlates with social location. Any new proposal that ignores earlier attempts at a solution is likely only 'to reinvent the wheel,' at its best moments, and to repeat the mistakes of history, at its worst. So this chapter surveys the earlier attempts to reconcile Christianity and ancestral rites in order to gain insight into the strategies and their social locations, as well as their advantages and drawbacks.

The Roman Catholic Rites Controversy

As conventional wisdom would have it, the hero of the Catholic mission to China was the Jesuit Matteo Ricci, and the villain was Charles Maigrot, Vicar Apostolic of Fukien [Fujian] and member of the Paris Foreign Mission Society. Recent studies tend to portray Ricci and his successors among the Jesuits as paragons of sensitive enculturation, reproaching Maigrot and the Mendicants as cultural imperialists. Unsurprisingly, the historic realities were considerably more nuanced.

Ricci and Maigrot certainly represent opposing ends of the historic continuum. Juxtaposing these two mission leaders also highlights the bitter irony of the Catholic mission. In 1692, Ricci's accommodationist approach bore fruit in the Edict of Toleration from the Kangxi emperor, declaring Christianity to be a *religio licita,* permissible within the empire. The very next year, Maigrot published what was in effect an 'Edict of Intolerance,' setting in motion a process which led ultimately to the Catholic repudiation of the Jesuit rapprochement and the imperial expulsion of Catholic missionaries from China.

Nonetheless, it is gross oversimplification to portray the one as a model of culturally sensitive missions, and the other as a villain. On the one hand, from his own writings it is clear that Ricci knowingly and intentionally understated the spiritistic implications of the rites. On the other, from the Mendicant queries to Rome, and from the response of the Congregation for the Propagation of the Faith, it is clear that the Jesuits' opponents were motivated not by cultural imperialism, but by a concern for the purity of the faith.[3]

In essence, both sides sought to enculturate Christianity in China. Given the circumstances, this required a relative weighting to be granted to cultural integration on the one hand, and to purity of the faith on the other. Where the Jesuits differed from the Dominicans and Franciscans was in the relative emphasis placed on each value. The Jesuits rightly recognized that to oppose the rites would be politically and culturally explosive, and would result in the expulsion of the Church from China. History proved them right. The Mendicants worried that the Jesuit approach would result in syncretism. The history of the mission in China did not permit the opportunity for them to be proved right or wrong. But clearly the decision between these alternatives was much less obvious than contemporary wisdom allows.

Ricci and the Jesuit Strategy in China

In keeping with established Jesuit practice, Ricci's strategy had two principal objectives: the one, to enculturate Christianity; and the other, to gain the acceptance, or at least the tolerance, of the ruling authorities. Only when both objectives were attained, he realized, would conversion to Christianity be a realistic prospect for Chinese. Only then would there be any hope of a viable national Church.

Chinese Rites in the Sixteenth Century

In Ricci's time, rites played a central role in three separate contexts. At the highest level, the emperor made obeisance to Heaven biannually, with animal sacrifices. This served a largely civil and political function, legitimizing his rule and reinforcing his claim to be the 'son of Heaven.' To oppose these rites—or to offer them—would signal rejection of the emperor's claim to authority and would thus be an act of direct rebellion.

Regional and local magistrates, on their part, made regular offerings both to Confucius and to the regional tutelary deities. All successful candidates at civil service exams were obliged to make obeisance to Confucius in the hall attached to the examination center, with bowing, candles, and incense. Those who subsequently took up appointments as magistrates were required as an official part of their duties to make solemn sacrifice to Confucius twice a year, offering animals, wine, flowers, and incense. In addition, they presented less elaborate offerings twice a month, at new moon and full moon. The magistrates also made seasonal offerings to the tutelary deities purportedly ruling over each region. To oppose these rites would alienate the local and regional bureaucrats, depriving the Church of political influence or recognition.

At the lowest level, the populace offered veneration to ancestors daily, and more elaborately twice a month, rites largely similar to those practiced still. Twice a year additional major offerings were presented at the grave site. Funeral offerings were the most elaborate of all. To oppose these rites would be to reject a central element of Chinese culture.

Enculturation would require Christians to reach some accommodation with filial piety, the core value of Chinese culture and Confucian ethics. Political toleration would require rapprochement with the imperial system and its administrative structure of Confucian mandarins. Both forced Ricci to develop a formal response to traditional Chinese rites.

Ricci the Strategist

Ricci was not a relativist, much less a syncretist. He simply recognized the necessity of working within existing political and social realities. He was well-aware of the imperial requirements laid on Buddhism, Taoism, and Confucianism:

> Humvu, the founder of the present reigning family, ordained that these three...sects, should be preserved for the good of the kingdom. This he did in order to conciliate the followers of each sect. In legislating for their continuance, however, he made it of strict legal requirement that the cult of the Literati [Confucianism] should have preference over the others, and that they alone should be entrusted with the administration of public affairs.[4]

Ricci realized that the most he could hope was for Christianity to be granted equal status with the traditional Chinese religions, on equal terms. That would require Christians to co-exist peaceably with competing religions, and to function within the socio-political framework of Confucianism.

Ricci accepted these parameters. At the same time, he sought to turn them to his advantage, by entering the culture through Confucianism, which was not only politically dominant, but also religiously ambiguous and pliable. To justify this rapprochement, he argued that Confucianism was rationalistic, neither prohibiting nor commanding beliefs concerning a future or transcendent life.[5] From a Christian perspective this may be inadequate, but for those determined to work through existing cultural structures, ambiguity certainly counts as a marked advance on the idolatry and spiritism of populist Buddhism and Taoism. Moreover, the sixteenth century was a time of great intellectual foment within Confucianism. A great number of revisionist interpretations of Confucius' teaching were in circulation. Ricci grasped the opportunity to add another, promoting a theistic interpretation of the Confucian classics, in order to serve as a foundation for Christianity.[6]

The characterization of Confucianism as rationalistic and originally theistic—rather than spiritistic—permitted Ricci to endorse participation in the politically and culturally mandated rites. Speaking of
the mandarins, he insisted:

> They do not believe in idol worship. In fact they have no
> idols. They do, however, believe in one deity who preserves
> and governs all things on earth.[7]

Similarly, he described the annual memorial rites as "an honor bestowed upon their departed ancestors, just as they might honor them
if they were living."[8] He explained at greater length:

> They do not really believe that the dead actually need the
> victuals which are placed upon their graves, but they say that
> they observe the custom of placing them there because it
> seems to be the best way of testifying their love for their dear
> departed...This practice of placing food upon the graves of
> the dead seems to be beyond any charge of sacrilege and
> perhaps also free from any taint of superstition, because they
> do not in any respect consider their ancestors to be gods, nor
> do they petition them for anything or hope for anything from
> them.[9]

Ricci interpreted the rites in honor of Confucius in like manner:
"They do not recite prayers to Confucius nor do they ask favors of
him or expect help from him. They honor him only in the manner
mentioned of honoring their respected dead."[10]

For Ricci, then, the decisive factor in interpreting the rites is the
intention of the participants. Acts are not idolatrous, he reasoned, so
long as they seek merely to honor the ancestors, without providing
for their material needs in the afterlife or seeking their help to overcome obstacles in this life. Confucian teaching and practice adheres
to these parameters, he insisted; so ancestral rites were permissible
within a Confucian framework. On these grounds, he considered it
possible to be both Confucian and Christian, both to venerate ancestors and to worship God.

An Evaluation of Ricci's Strategy

There can be little doubt that Ricci underestimated the religious
dimensions in the memorial and funeral rites. He implicitly acknowledges this by the tentativeness of his evaluation: "This practice of
placing food upon the graves of the dead *seems to be* beyond any
charge of sacrilege and *perhaps* also free from any taint of superstition."[11]

In addition, his distinctions are inconsistent. Food offerings are purportedly not intended to supply the needs of the dead, while offerings of clothing are![12] Offerings to Confucius and ancestors are not intended to appease or to invoke assistance, yet offerings to tutelary spirits are.[13] Statues of gods should be destroyed, while ancestral tablets are to be preserved.[14] In short, Ricci deemed rites honoring deities to be idolatrous, yet comparable rites venerating Confucius and ancestors to be purely honorific. The logic is less than compelling.

Ricci is on even thinner ground when he describes the beliefs of the masses with regard to their gods. He proposes:

> It is quite certain that comparatively few of these people have any faith in this unnatural and hideous fiction of idol worship. The only thing they are persuaded of in this respect is, that if their external devotion to idols brings them no good, at least it can do no harm.[15]

Nonetheless, he acknowledges that:

> the number of idols in evidence throughout the kingdom of China is simply incredible. Not only are they on exhibition in the temples, where a single temple might contain thousands of them, but in nearly every private dwelling...In public squares, in villages, on boats, and through the public buildings, this common abomination is the first thing to strike the attention of a spectator.[16]

The required sacrifices were never cheap, especially for rural laborers or peasant farmers. Is it likely that their extravagance reflects agnosticism?

Apparently not even Ricci or his subordinates were convinced by his logic, for they encouraged converts to destroy their idols.

> When the Chinese became Christians, they stripped the rooms of their homes of the statuette idols with which they were adorned and, when there was nothing to replace them, their pagan friends said the Christian religion was empty and bare because it had no God.[17]

If the removal of idols signifies the renunciation of belief in the gods, must not their presence signify belief?

Similarly, at New Year, when shenists hung statues of their gods over the door to the home, the Jesuits encouraged converts to substitute tablets bearing the name of Jesus and Mary "as a profession of faith and an indication of their household patrons."[18] If shenists did not really have confidence in their idols, why did the Jesuits recommend functional substitutes for Christians? If tablets of Jesus and Mary signified Christian faith, does this not indicate that the statues of gods signified shenist faith?

The point of this evaluation is not to uncover glaring inconsistencies in Ricci's approach to the rites, but to demonstrate that his approach was basically pragmatic. Ricci sought a thin crack in the wall of Chinese culture and religion, where the seed of the gospel might take root and slowly expand, creating a fissure wide enough for the Church to thrive. He explains the strategy underlying his rapprochement with Confucianism:

> Even though the *literati* do not set out to speak of supernatural things, in morals they are almost completely in accord with us. And so I commenced in the books I wrote to praise them and to make use of them to confute the others, not directly refuting but interpreting the places in which they are contrary to our faith...since we would have much more to do if we had to fight against all three sects.[19]

Elsewhere he freely acknowledged that this strategy necessitated a tendentious use of Confucian sources:

> I make every effort to turn our way the ideas of the leader of the sect of the literati, Confucius, by interpreting in our favour things which he left ambiguous in his writings. In this way our Fathers gain great favour with the *literati* who do not adore the idols.[20]

Thus, Ricci appealed to Confucian rationalism against the spiritism of Buddhism and Taoism, yet reinterpreted that same rationalism when it undermined the gospel. His intention was less to understand Confucianism in its own right, and more to use it as a bridge for bringing the gospel into Chinese society, and as an ally in the fight against idolatry.

Ricci was a Christian apologist, not a disinterested sinologist. On the foundation of an absolutist theology, he constructed an accommodationist methodology. His response to the rites demonstrates both, for he advocated only temporary toleration. His long-term goal was the replacement of ancestral offerings with the giving of funds for care of the poor and for the work of evangelism.[21] In short, Ricci was a pragmatic absolutist; not a philosophical relativist.

The Influence of Social Location on the Jesuit Strategy

The Jesuit affinity for the *literati* over the masses reflects the effects of social location on both practitioner and interpreter. With regard to practitioner, Ricci noticed very early in his ministry that "the religious beliefs of the lettered class [Confucianists] had nothing in common with idol worship," while the "enormous and monstrous idols of brass and marble" were popular among "the common horde."[22] Spiritism was characteristic of the masses; rationalism and pragmatism, of the literati:

> The ultimate purpose and the general intention of this sect, the Literati, is public peace and order in the kingdom...The Literati deny that they belong to a sect and claim that their class or society is rather an academy instituted for the proper government and general good of the kingdom.[23]

Ricci the intellectual missionary adopted a rationalistic interpretation of the rites in order to appeal to the pragmatic bureaucrats against the spiritistic masses.

The Mendicant Rejection of the Jesuit Strategy

To preserve unity of mission and consistency in methodology (and perhaps also for other, less noble reasons), Pope Gregory XIII was induced in 1585 to assign the Jesuits exclusive rights to ministry in Japan and China. But the Franciscans and Dominicans could not be denied for long. Their first members entered China in the 1630s, and other orders followed in succeeding decades. Controversy was not far behind.[24]

In 1643, the Dominican Juan Bautista de Morales challenged the Jesuit approach to ancestral rites before the Vatican's missions commission, the Sacred Congregation for the Propagation of the Faith. After deliberating for two years, the Propaganda prohibited "intrinsically illicit and superstitious" rites, while permitting the sanitizing of rites considered to be only contextually religious.[25] Most rites fell under the latter category, and could be adapted by the simple expedient of adjusting their context slightly. Thus, for example, provided a crucifix were hidden on the altar, Christian mandarins could participate in obligatory civic rites to tutelary spirits (proposition 7). Similarly, Christians could venerate their ancestors with incense, flowers, candles, bowing, tablets and pictures, provided the objects were placed on an ordinary table, not on an altar (proposition 12). Among the prohibited rites were idolatrous sacrifices to Confucius (proposition 8) and solemn sacrifices to ancestors (proposition 9).

At first glance, the distinction seems astute, but it quickly proved problematic. For instance, the Propaganda permitted mandarins to participate in what was indisputably public worship of tutelary deities, so long as they concealed a crucifix on the altar and directed their attention toward God (proposition 7). At the same time, it prohibited them from employing the same stratagem in an effort to sanitize comparable rites to Confucius or to the ancestors (propositions 8–10). The basis for distinguishing those rituals which are intrinsically religious from those which are only contextually and remediably religious is not readily apparent.

Feeling that their position—and the rites—had been misrepresented, the Jesuits sent a representative, Martino Martini, to present their case before the Propaganda Fide. He offered no objection to Morales' account of the ritual activities, but disputed the purported intention of the worshipper, and thus the significance of the actions.

Morales had spoken of 'sacrifices,' 'worship,' 'deities,' 'temples,' 'altars,' 'offerings,' 'priests,' 'blessings,' 'idolatry,' and 'prayers'; Martini dismissed these terms as tendentious.[26] His defense of Jesuit strategy drives home the ambiguity of ritual symbolism. What distinguishes an altar from a plain table, a sacrifice from a memorial, an offering from a presentation, a priest from a celebrant, a temple from a memorial hall, worship from honor, cultural rituals from idolatry, idolatrous feasts from communal celebrations, or religion from culture? Apparently only the intention of the participant and the interpretation of the observer.

The ritual did not change; just the intention and the interpretation. But that made all the difference. At first the Congregation had prohibited the rites, including meals involving food offerings, "as the case is presented" by Morales.[27] The same Congregation, a few years later, approved the rituals, including meals incorporating food offerings, "according to what was explained" by Martini.[28] Were the two decrees contradictory, Dominican Juan Polanco asked subsequently. Not at all, replied the Vatican in 1669. Each is binding "keeping in mind the circumstances, etc., as outlined in the questions presented."[29]

That being so, the decisive question is, "Whose intention counts? Whose interpretation is authoritative?" It is unnecessary and probably fallacious to assume that, where the Mendicants and Jesuits differed in matters of apparent fact, one must be right and the other wrong. Chinese religion then as now was decentralized and diverse. Practice would have been relatively consistent, but intention and meaning would have varied widely between informants.

Still, in the diversity, one trend is again apparent. The Mendicants, ministering predominantly to the lower classes, described the practices and beliefs of 'the people' and 'the Chinese' generically. The scholarly Jesuits, following in the path of their mentor Ricci, repeatedly appealed to the *literati:* 'scholars,' 'students,' and 'philosophers.' Social location and intellectual orientation played a significant role both in the intention of the practitioner and in the understanding of the interpreter.

A Reflection on the Catholic Controversy

The Jesuits and the Mendicants sought the same end: the Christianization of China. Where they differed was in the means to that end, especially in the short-term. Specifically, they assigned different respective weight to the competing priorities of enculturation and purity of faith.

In the current postmodern climate of religious and philosophical relativism, the final Vatican verdict receives short shrift. An Instruction from the Propaganda Fide dating from 1659 helps to redress this imbalance:

> Do not try to persuade the Chinese to change their rites, their customs, their ways, as long as these are not openly opposed to religion and good morals. What would be sillier than to import France, Spain, Italy, or any other country of Europe into China? Don't import these, but the faith. The faith does not reject or crush the rites and customs of any race, as long as these are not evil. Rather, it wants to preserve them.[30]

One could hardly hope for a more positive assessment of culture, even from the twenty-first century.

Noll dismisses the statement with the off-hand comment that, "Had the guidelines presented here been followed throughout the China mission in the years following, there may very well never have been a Chinese Rites Controversy."[31] Admittedly this noble ideal was not always followed. Yet it must be insisted that both Mendicants and the Propaganda Fides were motivated not by an sense of cultural superiority but by an abhorrence of idolatry:

> All sacrifices except those that are offerd [sic] to God, are illicit. Worship of demons and idols must be abandoned.[32]

> These sacrifices or oblations are tainted with superstition.[33]

> The Chinese Rites, as being tainted with superstition, were forbidden.[34]

So the decrees expressly avoided prohibiting Chinese rites *in toto*, seeking instead to distinguish cult from culture:

The same answers are not opposed to other things being performed in honor of the dead, if they are in keeping with the culture of those pagans, if they are not really superstitious, and do not look superstitious, but are within the limits of civil and political rites.[35]

The Propaganda Fides may well have been excessively scrupulous in their determination that "every appearance, every hint of pagan superstition, as Tertullian advised, be avoided from afar,"[36] and in prohibiting not only flagrant idol worship, but even the "taint" of idolatry.[37] But if they erred on the side of excessive scruples, they did at least take seriously the danger of syncretism and the need to preserve the purity of monotheism from the corruption of idolatry.

This is the same problem confronting the Church still: achieving equilibrium between the often competing concerns for purity and for enculturation. Those who show more tolerance toward the rites should not—at least not on these grounds—be dismissed as syncretists or liberals. Conversely, those who largely reject participation in the rites should not—at least not on these grounds—be dismissed as ethnocentric or imperialistic. The tension between cult and culture virtually guarantees that differing emphases will persist even among those who rightly reject the unbiblical and unconscionable extremes of syncretism and ethnocentrism.

The Protestant Rites Controversy

When the Protestant missionary movement penetrated China in the nineteenth century, the controversy over ancestral rites and food offerings erupted again. While the Protestant mission lacked a centralized body to promulgate binding edicts, a series of General Conferences of the Protestant Missions held in Shanghai addressed common problems and strategies in the China mission, including the issue of ancestor veneration. The first conference, in 1877, was largely hostile toward Chinese religions and ancestral rites.[38] The 1890 Conference, however, was more diverse and controversial.

Admitting some differences in detail, essentially the same two opposing positions recurred.[39] As in the Catholic controversy, all parties were opposed to outright idolatry. More starkly than in the Catholic controversy, all parties conceded that the rites as practiced were in large measure idolatrous. The main dispute was whether the idolatrous elements were central and the rites irremediable, or whether cultic elements were peripheral and the rites salvageable.

The motives of the two factions corresponded to their respective Catholic counterparts. Those categorically opposed to the rites were driven primarily by a concern for purity. Those more sympathetic to adapting the rites emphasized the obstacle to conversion posed by any prohibition. Significantly, as with the Jesuits and Mendicants, the perspectives were socially located: mainstream missionaries reaching out to the masses tended to be exclusivistic, while intellectual missionaries reaching out to the literati leaned toward accommodation. The divergence thus reflected the social location not only of the target audience, but equally of the missionaries.

Accommodating the Rites[40]

The subtitle of William Martin's paper at the conference of 1890 captures his sentiments better than the title proper: "The Worship of Ancestors—A Plea for Toleration."[41] Read in his absence by a sympathizer, Gilbert Reid, Martin counseled an approach largely in line with Ricci's, though he was less sanguine—or more realistic—about the actual meaning of the practices.

Martin recognized that in the ancestral tablets "according to popular belief, dwell the spirits of the dead."[42] In the case of food offerings, he admitted also that "the souls of the departed are invited to partake of the finer essences of viands."[43] Nevertheless, he advised against prohibiting the rites, both on pragmatic and on moral grounds.

Pragmatically, trying to put an end to the rites is like a man who finds the view from his house blocked by a mountain, and decides to move the mountain rather than the house. The rites spring from filial devotion; they are deeply rooted in Chinese society, both historically and functionally; they are promoted by the government; and they are thoroughly integrated into the daily life of the populace.[44]

Morally and religiously, the rites contain "much that may claim our approving sympathy."[45] They strengthen the family bond, act as a restraint against evil, and support a belief in the afterlife. Due to these benefits, he counseled that the rites not be swept away, but be modified or reinterpreted.

> I maintain that its objectionable features are its excess, not its
> essence. To prune off such excrescences, preserving the good
> and eliminating the evil, I believe to be altogether feasible;
> and if so, is that not preferable to the quixotic attempt to
> destroy the system root and branch?[46]

This, of course, raises a practical question: Which elements would need to be changed?

Not so many as some critics suppose, according to Martin.[47] Bowing, invocation, or offerings are not irretrievably worship: bowing is used to express respect toward the living; the invocation can be modified to address God; even the food offering could be reinterpreted as a Chinese equivalent to the Western custom of offering flowers at a grave site. The only objectionable feature he finds in the rites is the tendency to transform the ancestor into a tutelary deity.[48] This can be rectified through teaching, and the practices reinterpreted without being prohibited.[49]

> In conclusion, I respectfully suggest that missionaries refrain from any interference with the native mode of honoring ancestors, and leave the reformation of the system to the influence of the divine truth, when it gets a firmer hold on the national mind.[50]

This conclusion was to be the cause of considerable controversy. But first Rev. H. Blodget presented a scheduled paper on the same topic from the alternative viewpoint.

Opposing the Rites

Blodget began with a thorough survey of Chinese classics to demonstrate that ancestor veneration has always assumed reciprocation between the living and the spirits of the deceased.[51] Following this, a survey of current practices might have seemed appropriate, but since that had been thoroughly undertaken by M.T. Yates at the 1877 conference, Blodget merely defended Yates from the claim that he had presented only the negative aspects of ancestral veneration:

> Setting aside all partisan views, it is quite possible that those who have lived more in books, and less among men, should fail to see the darker shades of this subject. The statements of Dr. Yates must be verified, or shown to be incorrect, by impartial comparison with the facts of daily life. That a student in his study has not seen such things will not be regarded as sufficient proof that they do not exist.[52]

Here there is a hint, if only that, of social location: for intellectuals the rites are innocuous; in 'real life,' they are idolatrous.

Two further details in his presentation are especially instructive. For one, in urging that conviction be coupled with discretion, he cites 1 Corinthians:

> 'The things which the Gentiles sacrifice, they sacrifice to devils, and not to God.' 'Ye cannot drink the cup of the Lord and the cup of devils.'[53]

For the other, Blodget notes that there is a continuum of convictions motivating food offerings and prayers to the dead. These range from belief in, and fear of, the spirits; to agnosticism or atheism, coupled with a desire to show filial piety; to unreflective compliance with ethnic custom. Nonetheless, he insists, whatever the beliefs of a given participant, the practice inherently implies communication between dead and living. Consequently, "entire severance from the evil is the only safe course."[54]

Here lies the essence of the difference between the two sides in the dispute: Martin justifies participation on the grounds that the rites require only a little sanitizing, which is easily done. Blodget considers them intrinsically and irremediably cultic.

The Ensuing Controversy

The sentiment of the majority was quickly evident. The *Report* remarks laconically—and unprecedentedly—that Blodget's paper "was greeted with great applause."[55]

A heated discussion followed. Those objecting to the rites pointed to the expectation of reciprocation between the living and the dead. Those in favor of participation focused on the obstacle that prohibition would present to conversion, and the possibility of sanitizing the rites. The issue proved so controversial that further discussion had to be postponed until the evening session, and then broke out again on the morning of the next—and concluding—day of the Conference.[56]

Three contributions to the debate are particularly notable. The first is the now infamous incident involving Hudson Taylor. After three statements in a row commending Martin's paper (by J. Ross, Timothy Richard, and Gilbert Reid), Taylor apparently could tolerate no more. He stood, and breaking the protocol of parliamentary procedure, declared:

I trust that all those who wish to raise an indignant protest against the conclusion of Dr. Martin's paper will signify it by rising.

The *Records* tersely records: "Almost the whole audience did so."[57] After a protest by Gilbert Reid, the discussion was deferred until the evening session.

The second notable contribution came from the one Chinese participant in the conference. Rev. Y. K. Yen argued that Martin's view was undermined by a fundamental fallacy; namely, the attempt to distinguish the veneration of ancestors as human beings from their worship as deities, coupled with the assertion that the former is the essence, and the latter, an excrescence. "Both are part and parcel of the same thing."

The association has become so hereditary among the Chinese, that to prostrate and to make offerings bring up in their minds the feeling that the spirits are present, hear their prayers, accept their gifts, and in return will care for them; in short, do for them what Christians believe God over all can do. I think every missionary ought to tell the Chinese to reverence their ancestors, but at the same time let it be without those forms which are current among them. There are new forms which can be adopted.[58]

The rites cannot be sanitized, he insists.

The evening session ended without reaching a definite conclusion, but reading between the lines, it seems likely that the discussion continued informally after hours. First thing the next morning, and to the surprise of some participants, Rev. C. W. Mateer moved a resolution opposing Martin's conclusion, and proposing that the Conference affirm "that idolatry is an essential constituent of ancestral worship."[59] The motion was immediately seconded by Hudson Taylor.

Repeated, rapid, and transparently heated exchanges ensued. One hundred years later, it is not evident that the two sides were debating the same issue. Essentially, proponents argued for retaining only so much Chinese custom as possible without endorsing idolatry. This is clearly the thrust of Martin's article. Nevertheless, his conclusion undeniably goes far beyond this, urging without qualification that missionaries tolerate present practices. So does the title, advocating tolerance not of ancestral *rites* or *veneration,* but of *worship.*[60]

It is too optimistic to suppose that both sides actually agreed in substance, or that consensus could have been reached had Martin only been present to clarify whether the body of his essay—or the title and conclusion—more accurately reflected his intentions. In any event, the conference chose to make a decisive, but not drastic, response. The motion that "idolatry is an essential constituent of ancestral worship" was carried; a subsequent motion to delete Martin's paper from the Conference *Records* was not.

Conclusion

The dispute continued as long as the mission to China. But after the 1890 conference, the debates mostly rehearsed old arguments. Beyond the details, two lessons arise out of the centuries of controversy.

For one, history drives home the need for a sense of moderation and a degree of tolerance. For the most part, the alternatives are not polar opposites. While there may be occasional exceptions, generally this has never been a conflict between religious syncretists and cultural imperialists. Both Jesuit and Mendicant, Hudson Taylor and William Martin, sought to present the gospel to China in an authentically biblical and Chinese way. Where Scripture and culture were in tension, the missionaries differed—sometimes strenuously—over the relative weight to be accorded religious purity, on the one hand, and cultural propriety, on the other. But these are differences in emphasis more than in substance, and in strategy more than theology.

Contemporary discussions will proceed more smoothly if they begin with explicit disavowal of both religious inclusivism and cultural ethnocentricism. Establishing inviolable theological and sociological parameters may increase trust among advocates of various perspectives, and facilitate respectful disagreement over practice. Within these parameters, differences are likely to persist, but they should be recognized as disagreements over the details of implementation, not over theology or culture. For all that, the differences may still be crucial, even where they are subtle.

The second lesson from the history of the rites controversy concerns the significance of social location. Those missionaries sympathetic toward the rites, from Matteo Ricci to William Martin and Timothy Richard, were generally intellectuals engaged in elite ministries designed to reach the educated class. Those opposed, from Juan Bautista de Morales to Hudson Taylor, tended to be less scholarly and engaged in evangelizing the masses.

As time went on, the missionary movement increasingly recognized the effects of social location, at least on the Chinese. The 1907 Conference was especially clear on this point:

> The essence of Ancestral Worship is filial piety. What it has become among the superstitious multitude does not militate against this.

> This memorial view of Ancestral Worship is a very common one amongst the educated even when belief in some sort of existence after death is still retained.

> A skeptical view about the existence of God and spirits—is but too common among the educated classes today.

Whether idolatrous or not, this cult of ancestors undoubtedly occupies the place in heart and life which God himself should fill. In its less superstitious forms as practiced among scholars it usurps the place of the Creator, and in its popular forms as practiced by the masses it is a positive evil.[61]

The 1907 committee paper also ascribes much of the controversy among missionaries to the failure to pay heed to the effects of social location on the Chinese:

Many of the differences of opinion and views of Ancestral Worship which have manifested themselves in discussion upon the subject, and some of the misunderstanding in regard to each other's position, have arisen from neglecting to remember the difference between the worship described in the classics and perhaps to some extent still practiced amongst some few educated people and the ordinary popular practices of the masses...We must bear this in mind in our discussions of the subject, or else we shall not find ourselves talking about the same thing.[62]

Those missionaries who championed the rites had in mind the ways in which the rites were practiced and interpreted by the literati among whom they ministered. Those engaged in ministry among the masses, however, heard an endorsement of the idolatry and superstition prevalent among the lower classes. The gulf that separated both missionaries and nationals was as much social as theological.[63]

This phenomenon raises a fundamental question: Which interpretation of the rites is authoritative? Accommodationists have often supported their position by appeal to Chinese literary sources, preeminently Confucius, but also a number of other writings, both earlier and later. The argument proposes that the rites were traditionally rationalistic and moralistic—expressions of filial piety—and that populist conceptions reflect animistic corruptions. These sources, and this argument, warrant a closer look.

Endnotes

[1] Lin (1985: 149–50) cites evidence of Nestorian and Jewish accommodation with ancestor veneration in China. Unhappily, the extant evidence is too sparse to elucidate either the interpretation assigned to the rites or the rationale for participation in them.

[2] While the consumption of food offerings is the focus of this monograph, this chapter is necessarily broader because the controversies in China encompassed the rites as a whole (including both the making and the consumption of offerings). The broader controversy is no less relevant, both because it originally encompassed the consumption of food offerings, and also because it involves the same general principles as the current controversy over consumption.

[3] This is not to deny that the Dominicans and Franciscans were imperialistic. The point is simply that their stance on ancestral offerings should not be attributed facilely to imperialism or ethnocentricity. They had serious concerns for purity of theology, worship, and lifestyle.

[4] Ricci 1953: 104.

[5] Ricci 1953: 97.

[6] Rule 1986: 24; Ross 1994: 130, 144–45. In contrast to contemporary Confucianism, which was monistic, Ricci appealed to an 'original' theistic Confucianism. He argued that it was only the influence of Buddhism which distorted Confucianism in the direction of philosophical monism (Ricci 1953: 94–95).

[7] Ricci 1953: 94–95.

[8] Ricci 1953: 96.

[9] Ricci 1953: 96.

[10] Ricci 1953: 97.

[11] Ricci 1953: 96 *emphasis added.*

[12] Ricci 1953: 73, 96. Ricci writes: "It is a custom also, in imitation of their minor sacrifices to the idols, to burn pieces of paper or of white silk. By doing this they imagine that they are offering a robe to the departed in memory of his kindness and generosity" (p 73).

[13] Ricci claims that "viands are offered to these spirits of the cities and incense burned for them but not for the same purpose as this is done for Confucius or for ancestors. The difference is that in these spirits they do recognize the power of a deity who can punish the wicked and reward the good" (1953:97).

[14] Ricci 1953: 462.

[15] Ricci 1953: 105.

[16] Ricci 1953: 105.

[17] Ricci 1953: 460.

[18] Ricci 1953: 460.

[19] Cited in Rule 1986: 31.

[20] Cited in Rule 1986: 1.

[21] Ricci 1953: 96.

[22] Ricci 1953: 399, 100–1. Of the three Chinese religions, Ricci could tolerate only Confucianism. He disparaged Buddhism as "noisome mendacity," with "enormous and monstrous idols," whose priests had a "natural bent to evil" and were "given to sexual indulgence" (pp 99–101). Taoism he characterized as "low and dishonest," "ravings," "deceit" and "delirium" (pp 102–3). Ricci needed a bridge into traditional Chinese society: Confucianism was culturally feasible, politically necessary, and religiously the least objectionable.

[23] Ricci 1953: 97–98.

[24] The disputes centered on three issues: (1) 'terms' (i.e., the proper Chinese terms to use in translating spiritual realities, especially the appropriate word for God); (2) rites (including ancestral, Confucian and tutelary rituals); and, (3) ecclesiastical practices (such as baptism, the use of the crucifix, and plaques honoring the emperor within a church). Of these, only the second is immediately relevant to present purposes.

[25] The Sacred Congregation for the Propagation of the Faith, September 12, 1645; cited in Noll, ed. 1992: 3, cf. 1–5.

[26] The Sacred Congregation of the Holy Office, March 23, 1656; cited in Noll, ed. 1992: 5–6.

[27] The Sacred Congregation for the Propagation of the Faith, September 12, 1645; cited in Noll, ed. 1992: 2–3.

[28] The Sacred Congregation of the Holy Office, March 23, 1656; cited in Noll, ed. 1992:5–6.

[29] The Sacred Congregation of the Holy Office, Nov. 13, 1669; cited in Noll, ed. 1992: 7.

[30] The passage continues:

Generally speaking, men prize and love their own ways, and especially their own nations, more than others. That is the way they are built. There is no more effective cause of hatred and estrangement than to change a country's customs, especially those people have been used to from time immemorial. This is particularly true if, in place of the customs that have been suppressed, you substitute the practices of your own country. Do not disdain Chinese ways because they are different from European ways. Rather, do everything you can to get used to them.

Admire and praise what is deserving of praise. What is not praiseworthy need not be heralded with flattery. The prudent thing would be either to withhold judgement, or at least not to condemn hastily and rashly. What is evidently evil should be removed more by signs of disapproval than by words. Eliminate evils gradually, seizing the opportunity when minds are ready to receive the truth (Sacred Congregation for the Propagation of the Faith, 1659; cited in Noll, ed. 1992: 6–7).

[31] Noll, ed. 1992: 6.

[32] Sacred Congregation for the Propagation of the Faith, September 12, 1645; cited in Noll, ed. 1992: 4.

[33] The Sacred Congregation of the Holy Roman and Universal Inquisition, November 20, 1704; cited in Noll, ed. 1992: 22.

[34] *Ex quo singulari,* July 11, 1742; cited in Noll, ed. 1992: 48.

[35] Sacred Congregation of the Holy Roman and Universal Inquisition, November 20, 1704; cited in Noll, ed. 1992: 22; cf. p52.

[36] Sacred Congregation of the Holy Roman and Universal Inquisition, November 20, 1704; cited in Noll, ed. 1992: 23.

[37] The Sacred Congregation of the Holy Roman and Universal Inquisition, November 20, 1704; cited in Noll, ed. 1992: 22, 48, 55. They were also naive in assuming that Chinese could be content with rites which originated in the West:

Meanwhile, however, these should take care, with all the zeal and diligence they can, to do away with pagan ceremonies, so that gradually those rites may become the practice established in this matter by Christians and for Christians, which the Catholic Church has piously prescribed for the dead (pp 22; cf 52, 57).

[38] The one exception was a controversial paper on Confucianism written by James Legge. Resolution 8 of the report contains the official Conference decision to omit both the paper and the summary of the discussion which followed (Lewis, ed. 1878: 20). On the surface, the issue concerned the proper term to be used for God, but the dispute actually centered on the rationale for choosing the term. Legge, like others who preferred the designation 'Shang-di,' argued that the ancient Confucianists were theists, that they worshipped the

Christian God and were thus saved, and that Confucius was a man 'sent by God.' He did allow, however, that Confucianism had since been corrupted by animism, Buddhism, and Daoism, and these accretions needed purging (Legge 1852; 1877).

Despite the consistently negative tone of other essays, however, each participant cautioned against imposing Western customs on Chinese converts. Thus, their objections to the rites were religious, rather than cultural, and whatever their degree of success, they did try to make the distinction.

[39] Both sides in the debate knew of the Catholic precedent and appealed to it: exclusivists cited the final Catholic decision; accommodationists noted the disastrous consequences of that decision. The controversy recurred for the simple reason that the rites were still a vital feature of Chinese culture, and the dilemma facing the Christian mission was no less acute, with the hazards of idolatry on the one hand, or terminal persecution on the other. These factors ensured that a new generation of missionaries would never be content with a second-hand solution, reached by rivals, almost two centuries earlier (cf. Covell 1986: 69, on the Protestant antagonism toward Catholicism in general, and toward Catholic missionary strategy in particular).

[40] Prior to the two papers addressing ancestral practices in particular, the 1890 Conference first heard two papers on ethnic customs in general. Each of the latter explicitly opposed both Western cultural imperialism and Chinese ancestor veneration (cf. Ohlinger 1890: 605–7; Noyes 1890: 610).

[41] Martin 1890; cf. 1901: 264–77.

[42] Martin 1890: 623.

[43] Martin 1890: 624.

[44] Martin 1890: 620–23.

[45] Martin 1890: 623.

[46] Martin 1890: 625.

[47] Martin 1890: 625–27.

[48] Thus, he later suggested, converts could keep tablets, visit the cemetery on the appointed day, bow before the coffin, and make food offerings, provided that they did not seek any blessings from the ancestors or intend to worship them (Martin 1901: 276–77).

[49] Martin 1890: 629.

[50] Martin 1890: 631.

[51] Blodget 1890: 631–36.

[52] Blodget 1890: 637; referring to Yates 1878.

[53] Blodget 1890: 653; citing 1 Cor 10:20–21. Blodget is one of the few disputants in the history of the discussion to make direct reference to 1 Corinthians 8–10. As well as citing Paul's interdiction (1 Cor 10:20–21), he also alludes to the apostle's earlier attempt at gentle persuasion:

> If the disciple is weak in faith, and still retains 'a conscience of the idol,' it will become a snare to him to lead him into sin. If he be strong in faith, and knows that his tablet is 'nothing in the world,' still it will be offensive to him, as bringing him into remembrance of his former idolatry, and he will wish to put it out of the way on his own account, as well as on account of his weak brother, and on account of the heathen also, who still worship it, and would suppose it to be retained by him, if retained, for the same purpose (p 650; cf. 1 Cor 8:9–13).

Though citing Paul, Blodget is more radical than the apostle, supposing that the strong, who in Corinth advocated participation in rites, would in China be repelled by them.

[54] Blodget 1890: 651.

[55] Lewis, ed. 1890: 654.

[56] Lewis, ed. 1890: 654–60, 690–99, 699–702.

[57] Lewis, ed. 1890: 659.

[58] Lewis, ed. 1890: 690–92.

[59] Lewis, ed. 1890: 699.

[60] That the word 'worship' was particularly grating is confirmed in the 1907 paper on ancestor worship. Rev. James Jackson comments, "The title of Dr. Martin's paper, 'Ancestor Worship: a plea for toleration' gave great offence to many" (Jackson 1907: 217).

[61] Jackson 1907: 220, 224, 232, 233.

[62] Jackson 1907: 216–17.

[63] A third lesson from history is that the rites have proved far more resilient than foreigners ever anticipated. From the mission of Ricci, through the ministry of Richard and Martin, missionaries regularly proclaimed the imminent demise of ancestral practices, or at least of spiritistic interpretations. As modernity spread into China at the beginning of the twentieth century, this expectation heightened into the conviction that social, educational, and economic development would soon dispel all belief in spirits.

In 1913, at the regional Continuation Committee conference held in Canton, it was noted that

> great numbers of thinking Chinese, especially those of the
> student class, have discarded their former worship, not only
> abandoning but even destroying idols and temples, and are
> already fairly conversant with the principles of Christianity
> (Mott, ed. 1913: 190).

The contrast is again socially located, with idolatry in disfavor among
the educated; at the same time, the expectation was that the elite
would lead the entire nation away from idolatry.

The mood of the 1922 Conference was considerably less
triumphalistic, acknowledging that worship at the temples continued
unabated (Hodges 1922: 27). Nonetheless, there were signs that
animism was loosening its hold on the people. A paper on "Non-
Christian Religious Movements in China" noted

> an indifference to idolatry, which is the reaction of the intel-
> lectual or the industrial worker entangled in the machinery
> of modern life, but not of the peasant attached to the soil
> (Hodges 1922: 27).

Belief in the spirits is still socially located, but the expectation is that
through industrialization, skepticism would spread beyond the
philosophical rationalism of intellectuals to include the functional
rationalism of urban factory workers: "The railway, the schools, the
renaissance, and the preaching of the Church are undermining the
confidence in the power of the gods" (Hodges 1922: 28). Faith in the
old ways persisted, but purportedly only among peasant farmers.

Yet the disfavor into which animism was falling did not encompass ancestral customs. Hodges describes ancestor veneration as "still
the fundamental and universal religion of the Chinese" (p 28). He
forthrightly acknowledges the three motivations commonly underlying ancestor veneration: (1) the sincere belief that the deceased need
the provisions offered; (2) the belief that ancestors have the power to
bless or punish; and, (3) the commitment to the moral and social
values undergirding the practices. Hodges remains guardedly hopeful:

> Ancestor worship is destined to change from the magical
> relationship between ancestors and descendants to a moral
> relationship. The old forms of worship will continue for many
> years, but the crass magical ritual will be sloughed off and a
> moral connotation given to the current forms. This is already
> taking place among the intellectual classes and will slowly
> permeate all classes. We need not expect a sudden change,
> however. The popularity of the services for the dead and the

elaborate funerals even among the Christians testifies to the great hold which ancestor worship still has over all classes of the people (p 28).

That expectation has yet to be realized.

CHAPTER 4

Sage and Shen:
Ancestor Rites in the Chinese Classics

Summary: *The Chinese classics confirm that ancestral rites serve both social and religious functions. The classics also reflect the effects of social location, with the philosophical elite adopting rationalistic interpretations, the masses tending more toward spiritistic explanations, and the bureaucratic elite advocating observance of the rites on pragmatic grounds.*

From the time of the Jesuit mission up to the present, those who perceive the rites as primarily cultural rather than cultic have typically sought support in the Chinese classics, and especially in the sayings of Confucius. Ricci, for example, argued that Confucian sources demonstrated the rites to be an expression of filial piety, in honor of the deceased. He attributed the religious overtones of the rites to subsequent corruption by populist Buddhism and Daoism.

Since that time, archaeological discoveries and literary studies have established that animistic interpretations of the rites predated Confucius, so Ricci's chronology receives little support today. But a modified line of argument still appears regularly: Confucius turned Chinese folk beliefs in a rationalistic direction, from which they never retreated.[1]

In actual fact, there is no simple historical trajectory from animism to rationalism, from rites as religious to rites as cultural. The literary sources do reveal a basic line of development from animism to anti-spiritism to monism. Nevertheless, there are clear indications of a range of perspectives at any one time, defying any simple historical trajectory.

Given that literary sources tend to originate from and to be preserved by the intellectual class, they are not representative of the full range of views present within the culture. Populist beliefs must be reconstructed by inverting literary polemic. Overall, there is ample indication that the literati generally sought to rationalize popular beliefs and to stifle spiritistic interpretations. There is evidence, too, that they never fully succeeded. The literary sources also support the existence of a third position: the pragmatism of the bureaucratic elite, who showed less interest in the existence of supernatural realities than in strengthening the social order through continued practice of traditional rites.

The Rites in Pre-Confucian Literary Sources

Among the earliest extant Chinese writings are the 'Book of History' *(Shu Ching),* a collection of historical narratives, and the 'Book of Odes' *(Shih Ching),* a collection of poems (dating from the Chou period, possibly as early as the eighth century BCE.). These works provide valuable insight into pre-Confucian Chinese religion.

The Book of History *(Shu Ching)*

During this period, ancestral veneration clearly held simultaneous political, social, and religious significance.

Politically, an emperor would resign in the ancestral temple, and his successor would be appointed with sacrifices of wine and food to deceased predecessors (2.1.4.4; 4.4.1; 5.22.26). The ancestors, along with Heaven and Earth and the titular spirits, guided the emperor in his exercise of authority:

> The former king kept his eye continually on the bright requirements of Heaven, and served and obeyed the spirits of heaven and earth, of the land and the grain, and of the ancestral temple;—all with a reverent veneration. Heaven took notice of his virtue, and caused its great appointment to light on him (4.5.1.2).

In this role ancestors punish, but not capriciously. Instead of angrily attacking anyone who neglects them, they punish those who act immorally, whether emperor or commoner (4.7.2.11–14).[2]

The worship of ancestors is also a sign and expression of morality. A corrupt ruler is accused of all manner of evil, including cruelty, nepotism, oppression, greed, and torture. Included in this list of wickedness is neglect of God and the spirits: "He abides squatting on his heels, not serving God or the spirits of heaven and earth, neglecting also the temple of his ancestors, and not sacrificing in it" (5.1.1.4–6; cf. 5.1.3.3). Specifically, ancestor veneration is an aspect of filial piety. An advisor exhorts the king, "When honoring your ancestors, think how you can prove your filial piety" (4.5.2.7). The lack of filial piety is considered the greatest of evils, worse than treason, robbery, and violence (5.9.15–17).

Alongside its civil and ethical functions, ancestor veneration is also spiritistic. It is not simply that the memory of the virtuous deceased is a moral influence on descendants. The dead are actually conceived of as present at the sacrifices: "When the sounding-stone is tapped or strongly struck; when the lutes are swept or gently touched; to accompany the singing;—the imperial progenitors come to the service" (2.4.2.9).

This data provides an important corrective to the common tendency to bifurcate rites into either social or religious functions. Are the rites religious, moral, or civil? These are false alternatives. As in traditional societies generally, family, community, morality, and religion were interwoven and inextricable in pre-Confucian China.

The Book of Odes *(Shih Ching)*

The *Odes* more strongly emphasize the religious dimension of the rites, without minimizing their social and political functions. Three features are especially noteworthy.

First, offerings are part of a reciprocal system between ancestors and descendants.

When our barns are full,
And our stacks can be counted by tens of myriads,
We proceed to make spirits and prepare viands,
For offerings and sacrifice;
We seat the representatives of the dead, and urge them to eat:—
Thus seeking to increase our bright happiness[3] (2.1.5.1).

The ancestors bless with abundant harvest; the descendants present thanksgiving offerings.

The relationship bordered on contractual. One king lamented that though he fulfilled all his responsibilities, the spirits did not reciprocate.

I have not ceased offering pure sacrifices;
From the border altars [to Heaven & Earth] I have gone to the ancestral temple.
To the (Powers) above and below I have presented my offerings...
There is no Spirit whom I have not honoured.
How-tseih [ancestor of the king] is not equal to the occasion;
God does not come to us (3.3.4.2).

Nonetheless, reciprocation was not purely mechanical; virtue was a necessary prerequisite for effective sacrifice.

Secondly, the spirits are portrayed as attending the sacrifices and partaking of the food.

> Grandly come our progenitors;
> Their spirits happily enjoy the offerings;
> Their filial descendant receives blessing:—
> They will reward him with great happiness,
> With myriad of years, life without end (2.6.5.2).

The spirits enjoy the aroma, the liquor, and the food:

> Fragrant has been your filial sacrifice,
> And the Spirits have enjoyed your spirits and viands (2.6.5.4).

This obliges them to bless those who made the offerings: "They confer upon you a hundred blessings...They will ever confer on you the choicest favors" (2.6.5.4).

Thirdly, once the ancestral spirits have finished with the food, they depart and the worshippers join together in a feast.

> The great representative of the dead then rises,
> And the bells and drums escort his withdrawal,
> (On which) the Spirits tranquilly return (to their place).
> All the servants, and the presiding wives,
> Remove (the trays and dishes) without delay.
> The (descendant's) uncles and cousins
> All repair to the private feast (2.6.5.5).

The worshippers eat and drink to the full, and greet one another with the joyous refrain, "The Spirits enjoyed your spirits and viands, And will cause you to live long" (2.6.5.6).

Summary

Sinologist Chan Wing-tsit draws three conclusions from the pre-Confucian evidence. First, in the earliest period of Chinese history, folk religion predominated, including

> the belief in all sorts of gods, in the spirits of ancestors, in a
> supreme power called the Lord on High or Heaven...Heaven
> was regarded as anthropomorphic in character and spiritual
> beings could bring blessings or calamities.[4]

This, and not Ricci's theism, is the earliest recorded form of Chinese religion.

Secondly, as early as the Chou period (1111–249 BCE), humanism shaped the rites. Belief in Heaven and in the spirits persisted, but their actions were rendered moral. Punishment or reward was no longer capricious, but was thought to be determined by human behavior. In this context, the religious dimension of sacrifice was imbued with ethical—rather than shamanistic—significance. Given the risk of artificial disjunctions, it bears emphasizing that the ethical element was not opposed to—much less did it displace—the spiritistic. Rather, it added a moral overtone to populist beliefs.

Thirdly, Chan makes an important observation with respect to social location:

> Whereas common folk continued to believe in the immortal-ity of the soul, a belief later to be enhanced by the Taoist belief in immortals and the Buddhist promise of Paradise, the enlightened were convinced that immortality consisted of everlasting virtue, accomplishment, and wisdom.[5]

To the extent that rationalism eventually supplanted animism, it did not do so evenly across the board, but primarily among the intellec-tual and political elite.

Ancient Chinese Philosophers

Confucius is only the most famous among a multitude of philoso-phers teaching in China during the period between the sixth and fourth centuries BCE. Their writings—and especially their views of ancestral spirits and rites—reflect the rationalistic bias characteristic of intellectuals. But there are indications that animistic views of the rites persisted throughout this period, especially, but not exclusively, on the folk level.

Confucius

In the *Analects* Confucius professes ignorance toward the super-natural, including the rites.

> Someone asked the meaning of the great sacrifice. The Mas-ter said, "I do not know. He who knew its meaning would find it as easy to govern the kingdom as to look on this;"—pointing to his palm (3.11).

As a result he was noticeably reluctant to speak on such matters: "The subjects on which the Master did not talk, were—extraordinary things, feats of strength, disorder, and spiritual beings" (7.20).

For all this, Confucius treated the rites with utmost seriousness. He never failed to offer a portion to the ancestors soberly (10.18), even of humble fare and a simple meal (10.8). He would receive even as expensive a gift as a carriage and horses nonchalantly, but would bow when given food from a sacrifice (10.15). When a disciple advo-cated doing away with the sacrifice of a sheep on the first of each month, Confucius retorted, "You love the sheep; I love the ceremony" (3.17).

For Confucius filial piety was the foundation of all morality: "Filial piety and fraternal submission!—are they not the root of all benevolent actions?" (1:2). Devotion is due the dead no less than the living:

> That parents, when alive, should be served according to propriety; that, when dead, they should be buried according to propriety; and that they should be sacrificed to according to propriety (2.5 cf. Mencius 3.1.2).

From this perspective, to refuse to perform ancestral rites is a flagrant violation of the most fundamental moral virtue.

As goes the family, so goes society. Social disorder is attributable to the neglect of ancestral rites.

> The philosopher Tsâng said, "Let there be a careful attention to *perform the funeral rites* to parents, and let them be followed when long gone *with the ceremonies of sacrifice*;—then the virtue of the people will resume its proper excellence" (1.9).

Confucius can think of no higher praise for an admired ruler than to say that of all his stellar moral and political qualities, "what he attached chief importance to, were the food of the people, the duties of mourning, and sacrifices" (20.1; cf. 8:21).

At first glance this professed ignorance of the spirit world, coupled with a strong emphasis on ancestral rites, seems contradictory. But Confucius was a moralist, preoccupied with social order and leery of unproductive cosmic speculation. Thus, when a disciple asked about serving the spirits of the deceased, Confucius retorted, "While you are not able to serve men, how can you serve their spirits?...While you do not know life, how can you know about death?" (11.11).

Similarly, in reply to the aphorism that 'one should sacrifice to a spirit as though the spirit was present,' Confucius responded, "If I am not present at the sacrifice, it is as though there were no sacrifice" (3.12).[6] The important element, from Confucius' perspective, was not the presence of the spirit, but the devotion of the worshipper. These statements do not express agnosticism so much as they repudiate speculation. Worshippers should focus on what is within their grasp, namely, reverent ritual; rather than on something over which they have no control, that is, the presence or absence of the spirit.[7]

Another ambiguous saying has a similar thrust: "To give one's self earnestly to the duties due to men, and, while respecting spiritual beings, to keep aloof from them, may be called wisdom" (6:20). Confucius here assumes the existence of the spirits, but calls people to concentrate on their social obligations, rather than on speculation about—or manipulation of—spirits. In this respect, his bureaucratic pragmatism is evident. Confucius was a social philosopher. For him what mattered was the role of the rites in stabilizing the family and thus the society. He showed little concern about the ontological reality of the spirit world.

This reticence, though, was distinctive, rather than representative of the times. In fact, each saying shows Confucius admonishing his inquirer to give less attention to speculation about the supernatural and more to the practice of the rites. Coupled with this reserve is a condescension toward the masses:

> The common people can be made to follow a path but not to understand it (8.9).[8]

> Those who are born with knowledge are the highest. Next come those who attain knowledge through study. Next again come those who turn to study after having been vexed by difficulties. The common people, in so far as they make no effort to study even after having been vexed by difficulties, are the lowest (16.9).[9]

Again social location is at work: the intelligentsia are superior and tend toward rationalism; the masses are inferior and superstitious.

The strongest evidence of populist superstition and folk religiosity is seen in the subsequent fate of Confucius. Though he refused to speculate about spirit beings, he was quickly transformed into one within shenism. No sooner was he dead, Legge notes, than a local ruler erected a temple for him and ordered sacrifice four times a year. By CE 57, national decrees required that sacrifices to Confucius be held in colleges throughout China. By CE 609, temples were regularly constructed alongside examination halls, with offerings on the first and fifteenth of each month, and solemn offerings twice a year, just as for the gods and ancestors. Legge noted the irony: "He [Confucius] was unreasonably neglected when alive. He is now unreasonably venerated when dead."[10]

The irony spreads beyond ritual practice to its meaning. Sociologists Leo Juat Beh and John Clammer insist:

> It is often argued that Confucianism is not a 'religion,' but that it is rather a moral code or a philosophical system. In fact throughout Southeast Asia Confucianism frequently takes on the attributes of a religion in that Confucius himself *(Kong-zi* or *Kong-fu-zi)* and the teachings that have come down from him become venerated as supernatural entities.[11]

In Singapore, Confucius is venerated both as one *shen* among many within syncretic Chinese religion, as well as in temples devoted exclusively to him.[12]

Often religion is forced into an historic trajectory, contrasting ancient, superstitious practices with modern rational beliefs. In Confucius, however, we find an ancient rationalistic philosopher and pragmatic bureaucrat in the midst of a sea of populist spiritism. Much the same trend persists still. Social location certainly cannot explain every variation in ritual interpretation, but at the very least a social continuum encompasses the data far more adequately than a historical continuum.

'One Hundred Philosophers'

The centuries immediately following Confucius are known as the period of '100 philosophers,' for its proliferation of philosophers and schools of thought. Yet much of this teaching merely repeats or elaborates themes already familiar from Confucius.

Mencius, for example, repeats the aphorism about serving parents when alive, burying them when dead, and then sacrificing to them (3.1.2). He also affirms the supreme importance of filial piety, including the veneration of deceased ancestors (4.1.27; 5.1.4; 4.2.13). At the same time, he notes the utilitarian aspect of religious devotion, declaring that when the ruler neglects sacrifices, the spirits arrange for him to be deposed. When spirits do not respond to sacrifice, the ruler changes them for others (7.2.14). Mencius thus combines a rationalistic focus with spiritistic assumptions.

The Doctrine of the Mean also offers little that is new to the discussion. Filial piety remains central to ethics, and includes offerings to the ancestors (17.1–2; 18.2; 19.3). Significantly, the sacrifices to Heaven and to ancestors are juxtaposed:

> By the ceremonies of the sacrifices to Heaven and Earth they
> served God, and by the ceremonies of the ancestral temple
> they sacrificed to their ancestors (19.6).

It is tempting to conclude that the parallel reference assumes a parallel significance between the two ceremonies, but this supposition is undermined by the Confucian profession of ignorance which immediately follows:

> He who understands the ceremonies of the sacrifices to
> Heaven and Earth, and the meaning of the several sacrifices
> to ancestors, would find the government of a kingdom as
> easy as to look into his palm! (19.6).

Rites are more commonly performed than understood.

Also significant for the debate over the meaning of ancestral rites is the statement: "They served the dead as they would have served them alive; they served the departed as they would have served them had they been continued among them" (19.5). This was a key text for the Jesuits in their efforts to prove that ancestral veneration has no significance beyond perpetuating the filial piety shown to living parents.

Yet the saying does not purport to explain the significance of rites and offerings to ancestors. It merely commends continued devotion to the values and goals of the deceased: "Filial piety is seen in the skillful carrying out of the wishes of our forefathers, and the skillful carrying forward of their undertakings" (19.2; cf. Confucius *Analects* 1.11; 4.20).

The parallel constructed is not between living family members and deceased ancestors, or even between the meaning of serving each. Rather, the explicit continuity relates only to the devotion of the descendants: their service does not end with the death of their ancestors (cf. Confucius *Analects* 2.5; Mencius 3.1.2). So the saying would permit any interpretation of the rites, from the purely moral to the explicitly spiritistic.

Among the ancient philosophers, Mo Tzu and Hsün Tzu are especially significant. In particular, the contrast between their views demonstrates the ongoing ambiguity concerning the reality of the supernatural realm and the meaning of the rites. Their differences also serve to reinforce the significance of social location for the interpretation of rites.

Mo Tzu on the Rites

Little is known of Mo Tzu beyond what is available in his writings. He probably lived in the period between Confucius and Mencius; thus sometime in the late fifth or early fourth centuries BCE. His sayings reflect dependence on the *Book of History* and the *Book of Odes,* and were probably compiled by his disciples.[13]

Mo Tzu, like Confucius, is deeply concerned about social chaos, and looks to the rites as a stabilizing influence. But in contrast to Confucius, he argues that the rites cannot be sustained without an underlying belief in the spirits, and thus castigates those who deny their existence.

> Now why do we have this [disordered] state of affairs? It all comes about because people are in doubt as to whether ghosts and spirits exist or not, and do not realize the ghosts and spirits have the power to reward the worthy and punish the

wicked. If we could only make all the people in the world believe that the ghosts and spirits have the power to reward the worthy and punish the wicked, then how could there be any disorder in the world?[14]

He seeks to instill a healthy fear of the spirits as regulators of human morality.

The ghosts and spirits will invariably spy you out and know what you have done. Before the punishment of the ghosts and spirits, wealth, honor, strength of numbers, bravery, might, strong armor, and sharp weapons are of no avail, for the punishment of the ghosts and spirits will overcome all these.[15]

He directs his attention at two levels: rulers and the common people.

If the fact that the ghosts and spirits reward the worthy and punish the evil can be made a cornerstone of policy in the state and impressed upon the common people, it will provide a means to bring order to the state and benefit to the people...The officials and heads of bureaus will not dare to be corrupt. When they see good, they will not dare to withhold reward, and when they see evil, they will not dare to withhold punishment. And the people who give themselves up to evil and violence, thievery and rebellion, using weapons, knives, poison, fire, and water to assault innocent persons on the roads and byways and seize their carriages, horses, robes, and furs for their own benefit—all these people will as a result cease their activities, and the world will be well ordered.[16]

The only problem is to prove that spirits actually do exist.

To prove the existence of the spirits, Mo Tzu argues from the premise that if spirits exist people will have seen them; since many people through the ages claimed to have seen spirits, he concludes, they must exist.[17] He also argues pragmatically that belief in spirits strengthens social order:

Because the ancient sage kings believed that it was through the ghosts and spirits that the worthy were rewarded and the evil punished, they invariably conferred rewards in the ancestral temple and meted out punishments at the altar of the soil.[18]

Moreover, he insists that nothing is lost by such a belief—not even the money spent on the sacrifices—if it turns out that spirits do not exist:

Now when we prepare pure wine and millet and offer them
with reverence and circumspection, if ghosts and spirits really exist, then we are thereby providing food and drink for
our fathers, mothers, elder brothers, and elder sisters. Is this
not a great benefit?

Of course if ghosts and spirits do not really exist, then it
would seem that we are wasting the materials we use, the
wine and millet. But though we expend them, it is not as
though we were simply pouring the wine in a sewage ditch
and throwing the millet away. For the members of the family
and the people of the community can all gather to drink and
eat them. Therefore, though no ghosts or spirits existed at all,
we would still have the opportunity to gather together a
pleasant group and make friends with the people of the
community.[19]

Rites thus have both social and religious functions.

Apart from the multiple functions of ancestral veneration, two
other conclusions follow. First, his analysis confirms that the rites
were originally animistic, and that the rationalistic reinterpretation of
ancestral offerings appeared early, but not uniformly. Though per-
manently entrenched, there is no evidence that rationalism supplanted
spiritism. Watson comments similarly:

In the centuries following Mo Tzu's death…a growing atmo-
sphere of sophistication and rationalism led men to reject or
radically reinterpret the ancient legends and religious beliefs
that Mo Tzu had so fervently affirmed. The common people
probably continued to hold fast to the old beliefs, and indeed
the idea of the retribution of the spirits reappears, as vigorous as ever, among the tenets of popular Taoism in the second century CE. But educated men of the Ch'in and Han no
doubt cast a skeptical eye on Mo Tzu's tales of vengeful
ghosts.[20]

His statement requires one qualification, however. The process of
rationalization began before Mo Tzu, and at least as early as Confucius.

Secondly, like Confucius, Mo Tzu reflects the pragmatic orientation of a social philosopher and bureaucrat. Of course, by insisting on
the ontological reality of ancestral (and other) spirits, he distances
himself from the non-committal Confucius. But even that shows the
similarity of their underlying values: belief in the spirits is to be
preferred because it facilitates social control over both ruler and
subject. If, in fact, spirits do not actually exist, social order is nonetheless maintained; and nothing is lost.[21]

Hsün Tzu on the Rites

Hsün Tzu (313-238 BCE) lived long enough after Mo Tzu to be familiar with his writings, and soon enough to be vehemently opposed to his views.[22] He abruptly dismisses a variety of his predecessor's teachings, including his argument purportedly proving the existence of spirits:

Always when people see ghosts, it is at times when they are aroused and excited, and they make their judgments in moments when their faculties are confused and blinded. At such times they affirm that what exists does not exist, or that what does not exist exists, and then they consider the matter settled (section 21).[23]

For him, 'spirits' and 'Heaven' are simply terms used for natural processes that people observe but cannot account for, such as the orderly movement of the sun, the change of seasons, or the weather (section 17).[24]

Ironically, Hsün Tzu denies the existence of spirits for the same reason as Mo Tzu insists on it: both are motivated by pragmatic concern for social order. Without fear of the spirits, Mo Tzu worries, neither ruler nor subject will act morally. Yet if people believe that success or failure comes only through the spirits, Hsün Tzu fears, they will not work diligently. Thus he insists that success or failure are "merely the natural result of your own actions" (section 17).[25] As a result, there is no need to fear celestial portents, carefully watched and superstitiously interpreted in ancient China.[26] Instead, what is truly to be feared are what Hsün Tzu calls 'human portents': mismanagement, laziness, incompetence, corruption, and violence.[27]

Hsün Tzu's view of funeral ceremonies and ancestral rites illustrates his overall perspective.

To be generous in the treatment of the living but skimpy in the treatment of the dead is to show reverence for a being who has consciousness and contempt for one who has lost it... The rites of the dead can be performed only once for each individual, and never again. They are the last occasion upon which the subject may fully express respect for his ruler, the son express respect for his parents (section 19).[28]

Sacrifices do not worship the spirit—but honor the memory—of the deceased.[29]

Given that spirits do not exist, the rites serve not the material needs of the deceased, but the emotional needs of the living:

> When they deal with the living, their purpose is to ornament
> joy, when they deal with the dead, to ornament grief, when
> they pertain to sacrifices, to ornament reverence, and when
> they pertain to military affairs, to ornament majesty (section
> 19).[30]

Consequently, to omit the rites would bring not the wrath of 'hungry
ghosts' but the frustration of pent-up emotions:

> The sacrificial rites originate in the emotions of remembrance
> and longing for the dead. Everyone is at times visited by
> sudden feelings of depression and melancholy longing...If
> they come to him and he is greatly moved, but does nothing to
> give them expression, then his emotions of remembrance and
> longing will be frustrated and unfulfilled, and he will feel a
> sense of deficiency in his ritual behavior. Therefore, the former
> kings established certain forms to be observed on such occa-
> sions (section 19).[31]

The funeral rites "have no other purpose than...to send the dead man
away with grief and reverence" (section 19).[32]

In actual fact, though, the rites have at least one other purpose:
they reinforce the social order. Different customs are mandated for
each rank in the social order. Generally speaking, whatever the lower
classes do, the upper classes do and then some: increased coffin
thickness, more and better quality clothes and food offerings, more
elaborate decorations (section 19).[33] Even in the absence of a religious
role or a spiritistic framework, the rites are not redundant, for they
still serve crucial psychological and social functions.

Hsün Tzu was not so naive as to expect that everyone would
embrace his views. Specifically, he recognized that his rationalism
would be more acceptable to intellectuals than to the masses. He ends
his discussion of sacrificial rites by describing their different functions according to social location:

> The sage understands them, the gentleman finds comfort in
> carrying them out, the officials are careful to maintain them,
> and the common people accept them as custom. To the gentle-
> man they are a part of the way of man; to the common people
> they are something pertaining to the spirits (section 17).[34]

Ancestor veneration is socially located. The practice of the rites transcends social context; the meaning assigned them reflects it. For the
social elite, the rites are memorials; for the bureaucrats, they reinforce
the social order; for the masses, they pacify the spirits.[35]

Institutionalized Confucianism

During the Han dynasty (206 BCE–CE 220), Confucianism diffused throughout Chinese society, as its sense of social propriety and filial piety spread throughout the culture.[36] Two prominent works from this period, the *Book of Filial Piety (Hsiao Ching)* and the *Book of Rites (Li Chi)*, approach ancestral veneration from different angles, but concur in ascribing both cultural and religious functions to the rites.

The Book of Filial Piety

The title of this book provides a concise statement of its focus. As Chan Wing-tsit remarks, "In concentrating on the doctrine of filial piety and in stressing the expression of it in religious rites, it has made filial piety itself a religion."[37]

Filial piety is the pre-eminent moral and social value, the fundamental obligation upon all people.

> Filial duty is the constant doctrine of Heaven, the natural righteousness of Earth, and the practical duty of man. Every member of the community ought to observe it with the greatest care (ch 7).[38]

It serves as the source from which all other ethical and social values issue.

> The duty of children to their parents is the fountain whence all other virtues spring…The first duty of a son is to pay a careful attention to every want of his parents. The next is to serve his government loyally; and the last is to establish a good name for himself (ch 1).[39]

Properly observed, it is a panacea for whatever ails the world: "By the principle of filial duty the whole world can be made happy and all calamities and dangers can be averted" (ch 9).[40]

In such a context, it comes as little surprise to find that the function of ancestral offerings is to express filial devotion.

> In memory of our deceased parent we build a shrine. For the purpose of showing our remembrance we offer sacrifices every spring and autumn (ch 18).[41]

Those who do not offer sacrifices violate the most fundamental of all moral obligations.

> There is nothing so great in the world as man, and there is nothing so great in a man as filial piety. The first duty of a son is to venerate his parent, and in order to show reverence for his dead father he has to offer him sacrifice when he offers sacrifices to Heaven (ch 9).[42]

Despite all else they may do for their parents, only those who make such offerings can be considered filial.

> A filial son has five duties to perform to his parents: (1) He must venerate them in daily life. (2) He must try to make them happy in every possible way, especially when the meal is served. (3) He must take extra care of them when they are sick. (4) He ought to show great sorrow for them when they are dead. (5) He must offer sacrifices to his deceased parents with the utmost solemnity. If he fulfills these duties, then he can be considered as having done what ought to be done by a son (ch 10).[43]

Wearing the label 'unfilial' is no small matter. It is the most heinous crime, worse than any of the three thousand offenses penalized in the criminal law (ch 11).

Ancestral rites are thus fundamentally ethical, and derivatively social and civil. Yet despite this overwhelming emphasis, the *Book of Filial Piety* never excludes a spiritistic dimension to the rites. The sacrifices are offered not simply in memory of the ancestors, but to their spirits, and for their spirits.

> While alive, parents reposed in (the glory of) their sons; and, when sacrificed to, their disembodied spirits enjoyed their offerings (ch 8).[44]

Similarly, the demonstration of filial piety prompts the spirits to manifest themselves.

> When the utmost reverence is shown in ancestral temples, spiritual beings will (come to enjoy the sincere offerings) and manifest themselves. Perfect filial piety and brotherly respect penetrate spiritual beings (ch 16).[45]

The question, "Is ancestor veneration spiritistic or filial?" constructs a false dichotomy. In this most familial of texts, the rites retain a spiritistic dimension. In fact, it may not be going too far to insist that the rites are filial precisely *because* spirits exist.

The Book of Rites

The *Book of Rites,* with its emphasis on rituals and their meaning and purpose, helpfully complements the *Book of Filial Piety,* with its focus on underlying motive. Despite the different orientation, the overall perspective is strikingly similar: the rites express respect for the deceased, reinforce the social and political structure, and simultaneously include a spiritistic dimension.

Filial piety and spiritistic interpretations are not mutually exclusive alternatives. Rites are indeed memorial:

> Sacrificing means directing one's self to. The son directs his thoughts (to his parents), and then he can offer his sacrifice (so that they shall enjoy it) (21.1.6).

At the same time, the spirits of the deceased are expected to attend the sacrifice:

> In presenting the sacrifice (of repose) in the ancestral temple, (the son) offered it (to his parent) in his disembodied state, hoping that his shade would peradventure return (and enjoy it) (32.3).

The spirit enjoys not just the honor, but also the offering:

> [The descendant] declares his mind and wish, and in his lost abstraction of mind seeks to have communion with the dead in their spiritual state, if peradventure they will enjoy his offerings...Such is the aim of the filial son (in his sacrifices) (21.1.9)!

So the use of sacrifices to express filial piety in no way precludes a belief in the continued existence of the spirit. To the contrary, the express purpose of the sacrifice is "to please the souls of the departed" and thus to promote "a union (of the living) with the disembodied and unseen" (7.1.11). The objective is "to have communion with the spirits" (9.2.14 cf. 9.2.16).[46]

Similarly, the role of the rites in strengthening the social order is coupled with a belief in the actual existence of the spirits. Sacrificial regulations reflected the bureaucratic structure, with rulers making offerings to the highest spirits and deities, and to the greatest number of ancestral spirits (20.1–9). Yet even in acknowledging the political function of the rites, the text accepts the spiritual reality: "The mass of ordinary officers and the common people had no ancestral temple. Their dead were left in their ghostly state" (20.5).[47]

Traditional societies are commonly characterized by a unity of politics, religion, and family. The *Book of Rites* explicitly finds all three combined in the ancestral rituals:

> The object of all the ceremonies is to bring down the spirits from above, even their ancestors; serving (also) to rectify the relations between ruler and ministers; to maintain the generous feeling between father and son, and the harmony between elder and younger brother; to adjust the relations between high and low; and to give their proper places to husband and wife. The whole may be said to secure the blessing of Heaven (7.1.10).

The rites function comprehensively to establish communion with the spirits, to strengthen political control, to unify the family, and to support the existing social structure.

Three other features of this work are relevant to current discussions. Firstly, those interpreters—from Ricci to the present—who seek to minimize the religious significance of the rites find Confucian ambiguity conducive to their aims. Three particular sayings have been widely cited as evidence of agnosticism.

> While respecting spiritual beings, keep aloof from them (Confucius *Analects* 6.20).

> When your parents are alive, comply with the rites in serving them; when they die, comply with the rites in burying them; comply with the rites in sacrificing to them (Confucius *Analects* 2.5).[48]

> They served the dead as they would have served them alive; they served the departed as they would have served them had they been continued among them (*Doctrine of the Mean* 19.5).

Notably, each of these sayings reappears in the *Book of Rites,* where it includes an explicit or implicit recognition of the reality of the spirits (21.1.1,5,7).

"To respect spirits but to keep one's distance from them" is taken to mean that spirits should neither be neglected nor barraged with selfish demands (21.1.1).[49] Similarly, 'to comply with the rites in sacrificing to the deceased' is attributed to the desire that "the departed should enjoy the service" (21.1.6). So also, 'to serve the dead as though they were living' establishes the proper demeanor for communion with the spirits, it does not deny their continued existence in spirit form (21.1.8-12). Whatever Confucius may have meant, these sayings clearly can be interpreted in a way conducive to belief in the reality of ancestral spirits.

The *Book of Rites* addresses a second aspect of the current debate; namely, the expectation that spirits will reciprocate for the offerings they receive. According to the *Book of Rites,*

> The sacrifices of such [sincere] men have their own blessing;—not indeed what the world calls blessing. Blessing here means perfection;—it is the name given to the complete and natural discharge of all duties...
> It is only the able and virtuous man who can attain to this perfection; and can sacrifice when he has attained to it...Thus intelligently does he offer his sacrifices, without seeking for

anything to be gained by them;—such is the heart and mind of
a filial son (22.2).

Clearly a counter-cultural, purist streak is manifest here. 'The world'
(i.e., the masses) practice the rites in search of reciprocation and
blessings, such as success, longevity, and the protection of spiritual
beings.[50] The 'able and virtuous man' (i.e., the Confucian gentleman)
seeks only the perfection of virtue, achieved through propriety, and
manifest in the selfless performance of rites. Once again, the intent of
the rites—and thus, their meaning—varies according to social location.

A third relevant feature in the *Book of Rites* is its understanding of
the food offering. "At sacrifices there are the provisions that are left.
The dealing with these is the least important thing in sacrifices, but it
is necessary to take knowledge of it" (22.10). The guiding principle
here is propriety: the food is distributed in a 'trickle-down' fashion
from emperor through the civil service hierarchy to commoners. In
this way the sacrifice again reinforces the social order: reminding
emperors and senior bureaucrats to share with those lower in the
hierarchy, and reminding the commoners to wait patiently to receive
their share, not merely of the sacrifice, but of all social benefits (22.11).[51]

Yet the decidedly social and political function of the rites does
not negate their religious implications.

In sacrifice there is a recognition of what belongs to ten
relationships. There are seen in it the method of serving
spiritual Beings; the righteousness between ruler and subject;
the relation between father and son; the degrees of the noble
and mean; the distance gradually increasing between relatives; the bestowment of rank and reward; the separate duties
of husband and wife; impartiality in government affairs; the
order to be observed between old and young; and the boundaries of high and low (22.13).

Once again the unity of religion, politics, society, and family is apparent, as is characteristic of undifferentiated, traditional societies. Rites
involve both other-worldly and this-worldly relationships.

Neo-Confucianism

While something of an ambiguous term, 'neo-Confucianism' generally refers to the recovery of Confucianism around the end of the
first millennium CE. After its role as state religion during the Han
dynasty (206 BCE–CE 220), Confucianism was largely supplanted by
Buddhism and, to a lesser extent, Taoism. By the Sung dynasty (CE
960–1279), Confucianism had returned to political favor, but it was a

revised Confucianism, incorporating a metaphysic designed to compete with its distinctly religious rivals.[52]

Given that space constraints permit inclusion of only one representative neo-Confucianist, there is no doubt that it must be Chu Hsi (CE 1130–1200). Chu addresses the question posed to Confucius, rejects the same two opposing answers, yet comes up with a more definitive third alternative to rationalism or spiritism: monism.

> Question: In sacrificing to Heaven, Earth, and the spirits of mountains and rivers with offerings of meat, silk, and wine, is it merely to express one's sincerity or is there actually some force that comes to receive the sacrifice?

> Answer: If you say that nothing comes, then why sacrifice? What is it that is so solemn about it that causes people to make offerings with awe and reverence? But if you say that there are really spiritual beings riding in high chariots and coming in a group, that is just wild talk (51:50b).

His solution, the neo-Confucian solution overall, postulates the existence of material forces, in the place of spiritual powers.

> *Kuei* [malevolent spirits] and *shen* [benevolent spirits] are but force. What expands or contracts, comes or goes, is force. In the universe there is nothing which is not force (51.2b–3a).

Gods (whether Heaven or Earth, or spirits of mountains or rivers) and ancestral spirits are also material force. But while the force of deities is always expanding, the material force of the deceased gradually dissipates and eventually disperses (51:21a).

In Chu's view, the rites cannot be restricted to ethical, social, and political functions without rendering them meaningless; pragmatism provides an inadequate foundation for the rites.

> Take the case of sacrifice. Many vessels with fruit and meat are arrayed and many ceremonies have been instituted. It won't do if there is no communication with the spirit to perform the sacrifice in order to deceive people (51:40b–41b).

At the same time, conceptualizing *shen* in terms of material force evades popular superstitions.

Two features of his exposition are worth noting. For one, even at this late date, alternative views persist.

> Those in the world who believe in spiritual beings all say that they really exist in the world. Those who do not believe in them are decidedly sure that there are no spiritual beings. But then

some have actually seen them...These people do not realize
that what they see are but something like rainbows (51.4b–5a).

Chu then offers his theory as an alternative, in order to justify con-
tinuance of the rites (contra materialism) without descending into
spiritism (contra shenism).

For the other, he again confirms what has been evident at each
stage, that beliefs about the spirits are socially located, with an affirmation of their existence being characteristic of the lower class:

The principle of *kuei* and *shen* and life and death is definitely
different from what the Buddhists say (the soul in transmigra-
tion) or what the popular masses understand (like spirits of the
dead) (51.3b).

Similarly, he laments the propensity of the masses to seek "from the
spirits what they don't deserve [so that] there is no limit to what they
would do" (53a).

Conclusion

This chapter makes no pretense to offering a comprehensive
analysis of the meaning of Chinese rites, either within the time periods covered, or across the breadth of the history of Chinese philosophy. But perhaps enough has been said to establish two propositions.

First, at no point in Chinese history, at least not from the time of
Confucius onwards, is there unanimity concerning the meaning of
the rites or the reality of the spirit world. Even during the height of
neo-Confucianism (the most rationalistic of the Chinese schools of
philosophy), belief persisted in the reality, power, and presence of
the spirits.

Secondly, throughout the entirety of the historical period surveyed, the interpretation of the rites is socially located. In particular,
the belief that it is possible and necessary to provide for ancestral
spirits, in order to secure their assistance and ward off malevolence,
is characteristic of the less educated masses. The literate elite, in
contrast, seek less spiritistic alternatives, from the humanism of
Confucius to the monism of neo-Confucianism. Where a belief in the
spirits is preserved among intellectuals, as in the case of Mo Tzu, it is
promoted for pragmatic reasons. By and large, though, it is rejected
by the *literati* as unsubstantiated speculation or silly superstition.

This has obvious ramifications for understanding the historic
rites controversies and potential ramifications also for present debates. It illustrates, and thus indirectly confirms, the same sort of
social factors at work in the contrasting perceptions of Jesuit and

Mendicant, of Protestant educator and evangelist, of Chinese *literati* and commoner. Perhaps social location—both of the Christian inter-preter and of the Chinese practitioner—accounts for a large measure of the debate persisting still.

Significantly, this conclusion offers little contribution to the study of Chinese philosophy. To the contrary, it serves more as cursory documentation for, and minor adjustment of, what is virtually a truism among specialists:

> Students of Chinese religion should sharply distinguish the religion of the masses and that of the intellectuals. The former worship all kinds of gods and spiritual beings, engage in divination and similar practices, and believe in superstition of many sorts whereas the enlightened shun all of these.[54]

Nonetheless, the relevance of social location—and the conflicting views of the rites evident in the history of Chinese thought—is widely neglected by theologians, missiologists, and historians seeking either to condemn the rites as spiritistic, or to justify them as purely filial. Ancestral rites have long served both functions simultaneously, though generally more of one than of the other, according to the social class of the practitioner.

Endnotes

¹ The relevance of this survey to the topic at hand bears restatement, lest the point be lost in the course of discussion. The focus of this monograph is the consumption of food offerings. But due to the nature of the ancient literary sources, this chapter discusses the significance of the ancestral cult as a whole. Despite this broader focus, the historical analysis still contributes directly to the thesis of the monograph. If the rites are merely commemorative, as has often been claimed, then there would likely be no barrier to the consumption of food offerings (or even to full participation in ancestral rites).

² Thus, in an effort to convince his reluctant subjects to move to a new region, the king invokes his ancestors and theirs:

Were I to err in my government, and remain long here, my High sovereign, the founder of our House, would send down great punishment for my crime…If you, the myriads of the people, do not attend to the perpetuation of your lives, and cherish one mind with me, the one man, in my plans, my predecessors will send down on you great punishment for your crime…Your ancestors and fathers will cut you off and abandon you, and not save you from death…Your ancestors and fathers urgently represent to my High sovereign, saying, "Execute great punishments on our descendants" (4.7.2.11– 14).

Ancestors thus function as an instrument of political and social control.

³ This passage refers to the early custom of selecting a descendant, generally a grandchild, as a stand-in to receive the offerings and issue blessings on behalf of a deceased ancestor.

⁴ Chan 1969: 99.

⁵ Chan 1969: 99–100.

⁶ Citing Waley 1938: 97.

⁷ Cf. Waley 1938: 97 n2.

⁸ Citing Lau 1979.

⁹ Citing Lau 1979.

¹⁰ Legge 1960: 1.92.

¹¹ Leo and Clammer 1983: 175.

¹² In the Long Shan Shi temple in Race Course Road, pride of place in the entrance belongs to a gilded Buddha. He is flanked on the left by the Earth Goddess and the Goddess of fishermen; on the right, by Confucius. This is reputed to be one of the most powerful images

of Confucius among all the temples within Singapore, according to Leo and Clammer. In the specialist religion which is folk Buddhism, Confucius is the *shen* of education, to whom students pray for success in exams in a highly competitive academic environment.

> It is clear in Singapore that Confucianism does not only function as a philosophico-moral system, but spills over into folk religion where Confucius joins the pantheon of heaven as a specialist in education which justifies his appearance on most temple altars throughout the republic (Leo and Clammer 1983: 178).

Confucius' own fate confirms his disparaging remarks about the 'common people.'

[13] All quotes below come from Section 31 of his writings. Since the section is long and is not further sub-divided, citations identify the page number in the translation by Watson 1963b.

[14] Watson 1963b: 94.

[15] Watson 1963b: 94.

[16] Watson 1963b: 104–5.

[17] Watson 1963b: 95–96

[18] Watson 1963b: 104

[19] Watson 1963b: 108.

[20] Watson 1963b: 13.

[21] With respect to the debate whether the ancestral rites are religious (like rites honoring deities) or merely honorific and cultural (in contrast to rites honoring deities), it is worth noting that Mo Tzu both links and distinguishes ancestors and gods:

> The ghosts and spirits of past and present are of three kinds only: the *spirits* of Heaven, the *spirits* of the mountains and rivers, and the *ghosts* of men who have died (Watson 1963b: 107 *emphasis added*).

Ancestors are linguistically, and thus presumably conceptually, distinguished from deities; but it would be precipitous to conclude from this that ancestral rites are solely an expression of filial piety. At least this much is clear: Mo Tzu conceives of ancestors as having the same tutelary function, and the same power to bless or afflict, as do Heaven and Earth, and the various nature spirits.

[22] Since the writings of Hsün Tzu are divided into lengthy sections, with no subdivisions, for ease of reference I cite them according to page number in the translation of Watson 1963a.

[23] Watson 1963a: 135.

[24] Watson 1963a: 80.

[25] Watson 1963a: 79. Hsün Tzu elaborates:

If you encourage agriculture and are frugal in expenditures, then Heaven cannot make you poor. If you provide the people with the goods they need and demand their labor only at the proper time, then Heaven cannot afflict you with illness. If you practice the Way and are not of two minds, then Heaven cannot bring you misfortune...But if you neglect agriculture and spend lavishly, then Heaven cannot make you rich. If you are careless in your provisions and slow to act, then Heaven cannot make you whole. If you turn your back upon the Way and act rashly, then Heaven cannot give you good fortune (Section 21, Watson 1963a: 79).

[26] Section 17, Watson 1963a: 83–84.

[27] Section 17, Watson 1963a: 84.

[28] Watson 1963a: 97. He even cites the offerings as evidence against the continued existence of ancestral spirits:

Articles that had belonged to the dead when he was living are gathered together and taken to the grave with him, symbolizing that he has changed his dwelling. But only token articles are taken, not all that he used, and though they have their regular shape, they are rendered unusable...All this is done to make clear that these things will not actually be used. The dead man is treated as though he had merely changed his dwelling, and yet it is made clear that he will never use these things (Section 19, Watson 1963: 104).

[29] Strikingly, Hsün Tzu insists that he is not teaching anything new; to the contrary, he finds this meaning in the pre-Confucian aphorism, "Serve the dead as though they were present."

When conducting a sacrifice, one divines to determine the appropriate day, fasts, and purifies oneself, sets out the tables and mats with the offerings, and speaks to the invocator *as though the spirit of the dead were really going to partake* of the sacrifice. One takes up each of the offerings and presents them *as though the spirit were really going to taste* them ...The sacrificer himself presents the wine vessel, *as though the spirit were really going to drink* from it. When the guests leave, the sacrificer...weeps *as though the spirit had really departed* along with them. How full of grief it is, how reverent! One serves the dead *as though they were living,* the departed as though present (Section 19, Watson 1963a: 110–11).

Confucius the conservative humanist sought to shift the focus from speculation concerning the spirit realm, to character development in the moral sphere (Analects 3.12); in the hands of a radical rationalist, the same saying denies the existence of that spirit realm altogether.

[30] Watson 1963a: 104.

[31] Watson 1963a: 109–10.

[32] Watson 1963a: 105.

[33] Watson 1963a: 97.

[34] Watson 1963a: 110. Similarly, when describing divination and ceremonies designed to influence the weather he comments:

They are done merely for ornament. Hence the gentleman regards them as ornaments, but the common people regard them as supernatural. He who considers them ornaments is fortunate; he who considers them supernatural is unfortunate (Section 17, Watson 1963a: 85).

[35] Hsün Tzu actually describes four social contexts rather than three, as he distinguishes the philosopher (sage) from the social elite in general (gentleman). The difference is minor. What is remarkable is the measure of concord: both schema recognize the effect of social location; both agree on the characterizations of elite rationalists, populist spiritism, and bureaucratic pragmatism; neither claims its categories to be exhaustive.

[36] Chan 1969: 124.

[37] Chan 1969: 124.

[38] Citing Chen 1908: 20.

[39] Chen 1908: 16–17.

[40] Chen 1908: 22.

[41] Chen 1908: 32.

[42] Chen 1908: 23.

[43] Chen 1908: 25.

[44] Citing Legge 1970: 475.

[45] Citing Chan 1969: 125.

[46] An occasional saying, if lifted from the context, could appear to endorse agnosticism:

The flesh of the victim might be presented raw and as a whole, or cut up in pieces, or sodden, or thoroughly cooked; but how could they know whether the spirit enjoyed it? The sacrificer simply showed his reverence to the utmost of his power (9.3.25).

Yet throughout it is clear that reverence presupposes the continued existence of the deceased: the ancients practiced the rites "to express by them their reverence for Spiritual Beings" (7.1.6). "How well sustained was their reverence! How complete was the expression of their loyal devotion! How earnest was their wish that the departed should enjoy the service!" (21.1.6).

[47] In fact, for each rank in the social hierarchy, once the mandated number of temples was constructed "the ancestor still more remote was left in his ghostly state" (20.5).

[48] Citing Lau 1979: 65.

[49] "Sacrifices should not be frequently repeated. Such frequency is indicative of importunateness; and importunateness is inconsistent with reverence. Nor should they be at distant intervals. Such infrequency is indicative of indifference; and indifference leads to forgetting them altogether" (21.1.1).

[50] Legge 1964: 236 n3.

[51] "When the most honoured, at the close of the sacrifice, did not forget those who were the most mean, but took what was left and bestowed it on them, (it may be seen how) with an intelligent ruler above, there would not be any of the people within his territory who suffered from cold and want. This is what was meant by saying that sacrifices show the relation between high and low" (22.23).

[52] Ching 1993: 153–69.

[53] It was his brand of Confucianism that was taught in the public schools, in most of the private academies, in the Imperial University, and even in the imperial household. And it was his understanding of Confucianism that served as the basis of the prestigious civil service examinations. From the fourteenth century until the early decades of the twentieth century, Chu's teachings constituted a sort of orthodoxy. Indeed, to be fully literate was to be educated in the thought of Chu Hsi (cf. Gardner 1990: ix).

[54] Chan 1969: 133.

CHAPTER 5

Gods and Ancestors: Food Offerings and Communal Meals in Greco-Roman Culture

Summary: The cultural and religious context in ancient Corinth is similar in important respects to contemporary shenism. First, the offering of food to gods and ancestors—and the consumption of food offerings in communal meals—pervade life within the home and social relations outside the home. Secondly, these meals inseparably unite religious and social functions. Thirdly, the effects of social location on ritual interpretation are readily apparent: the philosophical elite tended toward rationalism; the bureaucratic elite, toward pragmatism; and the masses, toward spiritism.

Greco-Roman religion sheds two broad beams of light on 1 Corinthians 8–10.[1] For one, it illumines the context in which the Corinthians lived. Many of the Christians were first-generation converts from idol worship (8:7).[2] They disagreed among themselves about how conversion should affect their lifestyle. We cannot adequately understand their disputes or Paul's response without some familiarity with contemporary ritual and beliefs. The first use of Greco-Roman backgrounds, then, is to clarify the *interpretation* of the biblical text.

Why, for example, might some Christians want to eat in the temple (8:10)? Why might others be reluctant to buy meat from the meat market or to accept an invitation to a meal with a non-Christian friend (10:25–28)? How is it that different groups of Christians would take opposing positions on such a fundamental issue as idolatry (8:1–13)? Answers to such questions lie in pagan practices and beliefs.

The second use of Greco-Roman backgrounds is to guide the contemporary *application* of 1 Corinthians 8–10. Paul wrote against the backdrop of Greco-Roman ritual and beliefs, but when we seek contemporary guidance from the biblical text, we ask our own questions from within a shenist framework. Are the two religions— ancient Greco-Roman polytheism and modern Chinese shenism—

sufficiently similar in practice and interpretation to permit us to apply Paul's teaching directly to our context?

Even a superficial reading of 1 Corinthians 8–10 reveals at least two similarities between Greco-Roman and Chinese customs: worshippers make offerings to idols, and they subsequently eat the offerings in a communal feast. Given these parallels, it is tempting to assume that Paul would promulgate exactly the same guidelines if he were writing directly to us. Yet this would be problematic. These two similarities fall far short of detailed correspondence.

Two thousand years and five thousand miles is too great a distance to cross in a single bound. A detailed comparison of Greco-Roman religion and shenism is crucial for bridging that gulf. To what extent and at what points do Greco-Roman and shenist ritual and beliefs coincide? Where are they different? Are the similarities sufficient to justify invoking the guidelines of 1 Corinthians today? How should the differences affect the contemporary application of Paul's teaching?

The agenda of this chapter, then, is to survey relevant aspects of Greco-Roman religion in order to shed light on the original ramifications of 1 Corinthians 8–10, as well on the contemporary application of this teaching within a shenist context. Because the scope of Greco-Roman religion is broad and the material vast, this survey necessarily focuses on those elements most relevant to shenist belief and practice. While the Olympian gods and their Roman counterparts are most familiar to modern readers, the ancestral cult is most pertinent to this study. Similarly, while the ancient temples are world famous from their archaeological remains, the practices of domestic and social cult are more relevant here.

Consequently, this overview examines Greco-Roman religion from 'the underside,' as it were: the religion of daily life, of home and hearth, of family and ancestors, of social relations with friends and colleagues.[3] The survey turns up extraordinary parallels between Greco-Roman domestic and ancestral ritual and belief, on the one hand, and shenism, on the other.[4]

Roman Domestic Cult[5]

The domestic cult pervaded the home, both architecturally and ritually.[6] From the front doorway through to the back storeroom, gods and spirits were everywhere present in statuary and mural. From first breath to last, Romans honored their patron deities and ancestral spirits, until after death they too joined the tutelary host.

The Architecture of the Domestic Cult

Various patron deities shared supervision over the home and its activities. The guardian of the doorway was Janus, symbolized either by statue or simply by an arch. Vesta ruled the hearth and its fire: sometimes she was represented in painting, in addition to her presence in the flames. In the larder stood the penates *(di penates)*, guardians of the domestic food supply, and thus, of the heart of the home.[7]

The atrium was both the architectural and the social center of the home, and contained the main household shrine. Here *lares familiaris* protected the inhabitants of the household, including slaves.[8] During imperial times, lares were represented as a pair of dancing youth wearing wreaths and tunics, and carrying a drinking horn and a libation plate or pitcher.

In portraiture, the lares commonly flanked the 'genius,' the patron spirit of the *paterfamilias.* The genius served as the procreative power and tutelary spirit for the paternal lineage. The birthday of the *paterfamilias* and his wedding were the chief occasions for worship of this spirit.

One final category of domestic spirit which appeared frequently in the household lararium was *genii loci,* the tutelary deities over the residential location. These were commonly pictured as a pair of snakes, male and female, with a beard and crest to distinguish gender.

Reduced to the lowest common denominator, shrines *(lararia)* required only two basic components: images of deities and a place to set offerings. Shrines took a wide variety of forms: a miniature temple containing statuettes of the gods and set on a podium *(aedicula),* a niche in the wall with statuettes inside and stucco pillars framing the recess *(pseudo-aedicula),* a simple niche with gods, or, in wealthy homes, a separate room or building *(sacellum).*

Thus, architecturally, the ancient domestic cult was both pervasive and conspicuous. The cult of the doorway, the altar in the central public room of the house, the deity of the hearth, and the tutelary spirits of the home would all have been evident to casual visitors, and the cult of larder would be assumed. The various idols and altars signify the integration of cult with the typical routines of daily life: its comings and goings, meals and prosperity, domestic affairs and social life.

This provides important background for the scenario anticipated by the apostle Paul: "If an unbeliever invites you [to a meal], and you wish to go, eat everything served you without scruple" (10:27). A host's religious affiliation would be unmistakable to those entering the home, even before they actually stepped inside. A meal with a non-Christian neighbor or friend would have been a meal in the vicinity of his gods. More than that, since many ancient dining rooms had niches for small altars, or murals of the household spirits, the meal would often have been shared under the watchful eye of domestic deities. Could a Christian accept an invitation under such circumstances?

The Ritual of the Domestic Cult[9]

Domestic ritual confirms the implications of domestic architecture. Literary sources reveal that the worship of gods and ancestors was a central element in family life: each day, at every transition in the family life-cycle, and in various annual ancestral rituals.[10] Again, this survey focuses on the cult of the ancestors because of its relevance to contemporary Chinese shenism.[11]

Rituals of Daily Life

Offerings to the domestic deities and ancestral spirits were a common feature of Roman households.[12] Small offerings were made every morning and evening and during the main meal each day, with somewhat more elaborate offerings thrice a month, on the Calends, Nones, and Ides.

Incense and small grain cakes were the most common offerings in the domestic cult, though a variety of other foods might also be provided, including flowers, honey, cheese, fruit, wine, and milk. Due to their expense, animal sacrifices were reserved for special occasions. For the offering at meals, a small piece of food might be placed on a plate or thrown into the fire for the lares and for Vesta (Ovid *Fasti* 2.633-34; 6.310). Greek practice closed the meal with a libation to the house guardian *Agathos Daimōn.*[13]

Rituals of the Family Life-Cycle

The gods and ancestors were involved in every stage of the individual and family life-cycle. At each stage, the celebrants sought protection and blessing from the household deities.[14]

At the birth of a child, the family would lay a table for the family guardian deity, with the image of the deity reclining on the dining couch (such a ceremony was called a *lectisternium).* Subsequent birthday celebrations were marked by sacrifices of cakes, incense, food, and wine to the protective *genius* or *juno,* as well as by presents for the celebrant and a dinner party with friends (e.g., Persius *Satire* 2.1–2).

Puberty, too, was marked out ritually, at least for boys.[15] The ceremony would normally occur on March 17, during the festival of Liberalia. Relatives and family friends would escort the youth to the Forum, and introduce him to public life. They would also make an offering to Junventas in the temple of Jupiter on his behalf. A dinner for family and friends would conclude the celebration.

A marriage ceremony would begin in the bridal home or in a nearby sanctuary, with the taking of auspices, sacrifice of an animal (a pig, ewe, or ox), and the invocation of one or more patron deities of marriage. A lengthy feast and celebration followed the taking of vows. That evening, the guests conducted the bride to her new home. The next day she took her place as *materfamilias* and assumed responsibility for the household cult.

At death, the corpse was bathed, anointed with perfume, clothed, and laid on a couch for viewing. A coin was placed in the mouth of the deceased to pay the boat fare into the afterworld. Relatives wailed; mourners presented flowers and incense. After a wake of up to seven days, a procession of relatives escorted the body to the graveyard, all the while wailing, tearing their clothes, pouring dust on their heads, and crying out to the deceased. After burial, a pig would be sacrificed and consumed at the gravesite. The mourning period officially ended on the ninth day, with a further sacrifice and funeral banquet at the grave (Lucian *On Funerals* 24).[16] At this time the deceased (called *daimōn,* spirit of the departed) became one of the household lares.

Ancestral Rituals

Like shenists, ancient Romans viewed the family neither as nuclear, nor even as extended, but as linear. That is to say, the family included not only those living at any given moment but also generations past. Consequently, domestic ritual commonly encompassed the dead alongside the living.[17]

As in Chinese religion, so also in Roman, the dead were thought to exist as disembodied spirits *(manes)* in the vicinity of the tomb, and to be in continued need of nourishment. Thus food was placed in the coffin at burial, and offerings were made regularly after internment, especially on significant occasions such as the birth and death dates of the deceased. Commonly graves would incorporate holes or pipes through which food and drink could be poured into the grave. The mausolea of the wealthy contained dining chambers with fixed couches; some even had kitchens. The deceased were also thought to need clothes, which their descendants burned on their behalf (Herodotus 5.92).

Apart from these private celebrations, the civic calendar marked out two annual festivals for honoring deceased ancestors, *Paternalia* and *Lemuria.*

Held annually from 13-22 February, Paternalia was a community-wide festival to honor deceased parents and immediate relatives. Descendants were advised to make offerings and prayers to their ancestors:

> Appease the souls of your fathers and bring small gifts to the extinguished pyres. The ghosts ask but little: they value piety more than a costly gift...A tile wreathed with votive garlands, a sprinkling of corn, a few grains of salt, bread soaked in wine, and some loose violets, these are offerings enough: set these on a potsherd and leave it in the middle of the road [i.e., near the tombs which lined the road]. Not that I forbid larger offerings, but even these suffice to appease the shades: add prayers and the appropriate words at the hearths set up for the purpose (Ovid *Fasti* 2.533–42; cf. 2.565–66).

The festival climaxed on February 22, with a gathering of the extended family to worship the family gods with incense, food offerings, and libations at a communal meal (Ovid *Fasti* 2.617–19). In a description of ancient Roman practice which largely parallels Asian custom, Ogilvie pictures "little groups of mourners making their way...to the big cemeteries on the outskirts of the city, with sprays of flowers and jugs of wine and milk in their hands."[18]

Just as Paternalia has affinities with the Chinese *qing ming,* so Lemuria, held annually on May 9, 11, 13 is similar to Chinese 'hungry ghost' celebrations. In both cultures, the spirits honored at the former are generally benevolent, and the offering is an expression of devotion. The latter, on the other hand, honors neglected and therefore dangerous spirits, and the offering is designed to ward off hostility: "If anyone has not left a friend or kinsman behind him on earth, he goes about his business there as an unfed corpse, in a state of famine" (Lucian *On Funerals* 24.9). In a statement evocative of traditional shenism, Kennedy comments concerning Roman beliefs: "Without the amenities the dead would have a miserable existence and be quite justified in doing whatever possible to convince the living to provide them with the necessities of death. Hence ghosts and haunts."[19]

Implications

Two issues require brief comment: the intended or implied meaning of the rituals and the ramifications of these rituals for Christian converts.

Considerable ambiguity surrounds the significance of these offerings and the motivation underlying them, not merely in contemporary scholarly interpretation but even in ancient attitudes. At least six meanings and motives, not mutually exclusive, receive support in ancient and modern analysis. Ovid captures three in one sentence:

> Offer food, that the lares, in their girt-up robes, may feed at the platter presented to them as a pledge of the homage that they love (*Fasti* 2.631–34).

The offerings serve to feed the ancestors and to express devotion to them, in both ways pleasing them.

These three motives imply two others: to avoid the revenge that spirits take against those who neglect them, and to gain from the reciprocation that spirits grant to those who provide for them. [20] "Appease the souls of your fathers and bring small gifts to the extinguished pyres," Ovid urges (*Fasti* 2.533–34). Toynbee explains: "If duly propitiated [the spirits] were capable of aiding their descendants, but were harmful and spiteful to the living if kinless and neglected."[21] Thus, Ovid recounts that when the distraction of a lengthy war once caused the Romans to overlook *Paternalia,*

> the ancestral souls did issue from the tombs and make their moan in the hours of still night; and hideous ghosts, a shadowy throng, they say did howl about the city streets and the wide fields (*Fasti* 2.547–556).

"From that ominous day," Ovid adds, "Rome grew hot with the funeral fires that burned without the city."

A sixth motive is likely: the satisfaction of communion with the beloved deceased as though they were still present. Interpretation of modern ritual is tenuous; ancient ritual is even more obscure. This uncertainty acknowledged, Toynbee is likely right when he supposes that an offering *to* the ancestors (whether in the home or at the grave) represents a meal shared *with* them.[22] Remarkably, all six motives find parallels in modern analysis of Chinese rituals.

With respect to the ramifications of ancestral rituals for Christian converts, two parallels between ancient Roman religion and contemporary Chinese shenist practice are particularly noteworthy. First, neither culture constructs an unbridgeable gulf between human beings and spirits: the deceased join the household patron spirits and receive veneration from descendants in a perpetual lineage cycle. Secondly, neither distinguishes family celebrations from religious rituals. Offerings to both gods and ancestors play a crucial role in daily life, several times a month, throughout the family life-cycle, and on specially designated ancestral holidays.

Consequently Christian converts would face the same dilemma in Roman times as in contemporary shenist settings. Should a Christian participate in family celebrations (births, coming-of-age ceremonies, marriages, funerals), when those would inevitably include the offering and consumption of sacrifices to gods and ancestors? Those who participate would appear to be joining in the worship of the gods and ancestors; those who refuse would appear to be rejecting their own families and ancestors. A prima facie argument could thus be made either for or against participation.

Roman Communal Meals and Idol Offerings[23]

Much as in shenist culture, food offerings and communal meals were a feature not only of private domestic life but also of normal social interaction in the Greco-Roman world.[24] The formal meal (in Greek, *deipnon;* Latin, *cena)* was a central element in maintaining relations with neighbors, friends, and colleagues.[25] These meals commonly followed and consumed a sacrifice, or at the very least incorporated the offering of token amounts of food and drink to the presiding deities and spirits. Consequently, the consumption of idol offerings was virtually unavoidable in the course of normal social life.

Settings for Communal Meals[26]

Communal meals occurred in a variety of contexts, including domestic, professional, and cultic occasions.[27]

Communal Meals in Private Homes

Generally meals were held in the *triclinium* of a private home (a more formal room than the family area used for daily meals). A number of other venues could also serve the same purpose, from inns and taverns to triclinia attached to temples.[28]

Dinner would normally begin just before sundown, and could last anywhere from three hours to early morning. Generally meals were taken in a reclining position: only children—and in the earlier periods, women—sat to eat. Greek dining rooms typically had seven, nine, or eleven couches, arranged around the walls of a small room, each holding a single guest, with a table alongside for the food. Roman customs generally provided only three couches, each taking up one side of a room and holding up to three diners, with a central table for the food. So meals tended to be intimate, with anywhere from three to eight guests.[29]

Meals divided into two consecutive parts: the meal proper, followed by an extended period of drinking and entertainment (the latter was called *symposion* in Greek, or *convivium* in Latin).[30] The menu commonly consisted mainly of bread and a variety of vegetables, though fish was also common. Meat was a luxury item, generally available only on festive occasions or in the wealthiest homes. Much of the meat served derived from sacrifice.

The transition from the meal proper to the drinking and entertainment segment was marked out ritually. A libation of unmixed wine was poured out to the household spirits or patron deities, while participants sang a paean (e.g., Lucius Apuleius *The Golden Ass* 4.22; Plutarch *Pericles* 7.4).[31] The remainder of the wine would be diluted with water and distributed, and the drinking and entertainment would begin. For the more sophisticated or pretentious, this might entail philosophical discussion (Catullus *Poem* 44; Epictetus *Discourses* 1.26.9; Pliny *Letters* 9.36).[32] More popular entertainments included musicians, story-telling, dancers, and even acrobats (Lucian *The Dream, or the Cock* 11; Lucius Apuleius *The Golden Ass* 4.8; 6.24; Longus, *Daphne and Chloe* 2.30–32; 4.37–38). Drunkenness was a common phenomenon, and sexual immorality—including both male and female prostitution—a frequent accompaniment (Seneca *Epistle* 95.24; Plutarch *Table Talk* 1.620–622).[33]

Communal Meals in Workshops, Trade Guilds, and Clubs[34]

Food offerings were a regular feature not only in private homes, but also in businesses, trade guilds, and private associations. Every trade had a patron deity.[35] Each workshop and store had a god-shelf.[36] Bars, restaurants, and hotels also contained wall- or floor-niches, altars, and cult rooms, mostly in the communal parts of the building.[37]

Apart from the home, clubs were the most important social network in Rome.[38] Some were organized around professional concerns, others around religious and social interests (such as the worship of a foreign deity); funerary clubs existed to provide a decent burial for members. Each club contained images of a guild genius, a patron deity, and the emperor. Monthly meetings were typical, with special celebrations for the calendrical festival of the patron deity. The central activity was a sacrifice to the deity, followed by a communal meal.[39] This might be conducted in the club's meeting quarters, in a restaurant or perhaps in a temple of the tutelary deity.[40]

Communal Meals in Temples

Strictly speaking, worship rituals are not of central concern here, because there is no evidence that the Corinthians were arguing for the right actually to participate directly in worship of other gods. But at least some of them were willing to participate in feasts in the temple.[41] Two features of Greco-Roman cult help to explain why.

For one, temples served as venues for a wide range of functions.[42] They often hosted civic celebrations and political rallies.[43] They served commercial functions, for example, as sites for shops, as meeting places for trade or professional guilds, and even as banks.[44] They were also cultural centers, sponsoring theatrical productions, dances, athletic competitions, zoos and parks, libraries, sculpture, and public lectures.[45] Consequently, a constant stream of visitors poured through the temple grounds, coming sometimes to participate in sacrifice or banquet, other times merely to stroll the gardens or to patronize the surrounding shops.

For the other, a wide variety of civic, social, and family festivities included sacrifice followed by a communal meal, and this combination was most easily arranged in a temple. A sacrifice might be sponsored by a private individual in celebration of a major event in the family-life cycle, by an association or guild in celebration of a patron deity, or by the city in a regular schedule of public festivals (e.g., Horace *Ode* 4.11).[46] Whoever the sponsor and whatever the occasion, a sacrifice generally led to a communal meal (Achilles Tatius *Leucippe and Clitophon* 2.2–3).[47] For this purpose, many temple compounds included dining rooms laid out like those in private homes.[48]

Visiting temples would thus have been a natural and normal part of life. Indeed, to avoid temples altogether would require a virtual retreat from civic, public, and social life.[49] Consequently it comes as no surprise to find that at least some Corinthian Christians were inclined to visit the temple, any more than modern Christians are inclined to go to the theater, bank, gym, library, stadium, shopping mall, museum, parties, marriage counselor, civil court, or restaurant. The greater surprise would be if Christians in Greco-Roman times were able to avoid all such contacts.

The Significance of Communal Meals

Without constructing too sharp or rigid an antithesis, religions can be marked along a continuum from canonical to diffused.[50] Canonical religions are characterized by formal and differentiated structures; they have a canon and professional clergy to regulate faith and practice, and tend to distinguish religious from secular activities. Diffused religions tend toward more informal and integrated struc-tures, commonly prioritizing ritual over belief, with cult suffusing all of life.[51] Greco-Roman religion, like shenism, tends toward the dif-fused end of the spectrum.

This distinction has significant implications for ritual interpreta-tion. Those coming from the context of modernized, rationalized Christianity are inclined to ask, "What did the Greeks and Romans believe? What did their rites mean?" This is problematic at several points.

For one, it grants priority to beliefs and meanings over ritual performance. For another, it assumes an explicit, intellectualized, and articulated meaning.[52] For a third, it presumes a normative meaning, which in turn presupposes a canonical text to affirm that meaning and a priesthood to reinforce it.[53] Zaidman and Pantel observe, to the contrary, that in ancient Greek religion, "rituals were performed without the citizens knowing precisely what they meant," and that "piety was judged to be displayed through participation" rather than through doctrine.[54]

Western New Testament scholarship has largely been insensitive to the nature of diffused religion, not least in the analysis of 1 Corinthians 8–10 (or in the interpretation of shenism).[55] Until re-cently, scholarship has devoted considerable energy to assessing whether Greco-Roman rites were religious or social. Where religion is diffused, rituals are both simultaneously.[56]

This conclusion is supported by recent studies on invitations to private meals and to club banquets, on the functions of ancient guilds and associations, and on the architecture of Corinthian temples.

Invitations to Domestic Celebrations[57]

Chan-Hie Kim analyses twenty-five invitations to meals from the first through the fourth century A.D. Most follow the same basic format; for example,

Chaeremon invites you to dine at a banquet of the lord Serapis in the Serapeum tomorrow, that is, the 15th, from the 9th hour.[58]

Nine invitations in this collection are cultic feasts in honor of a god (Serapis, Isis, or Demeter): most of these are held in a temple, but at least two are set in private homes. All explicitly identify their pur-pose to be a shared meal (to dine) at the table *(kleinē)* of the 'Lord.' Of the remaining invitations, the majority are to family life-cycle celebrations: eleven weddings, one first birthday, and one coming of age.[59] Most of these celebrations are set in the home, but at least two occur in the temple.

The celebration of family occasions in religious contexts—and religious occasions in family contexts—reinforces the interpenetration of religion and culture in Greco–Roman society. The effort to separate religious from social functions, meanings, and locations ends in frustration, and is likely misguided from the beginning.[60]

Invitations to Guild and Club Banquets

Invitations to guild and club banquets confirm the intermingling of religious and social functions. They are also noteworthy for the use of terminology familiar from 1 Corinthians 8–10. An invitation to a club's cult banquet in honor of Zeus of Panamara, and issued by the patron deity, reads in part:

> The god invites [kalei] all men to the altar [or 'feast'] and provides a public and egalitarian table [trapeza; i.e., an equitable distribution of sacrificial offering to participants]...There exists between our cities a kinship to one another and a sharing [koinōnian] of sacred rites—I invite [kalei] you to come to the god and summon also those in your city to share in the festivity in his presence.[61]

Among the noteworthy linguistic parallels with 1 Corinthians 8–10 are kalei ('invites,' cf. 1 Cor 10:27), trapeza ('table [of the god],' cf. 1 Cor 10:21), and koinōnian ('sharing,' cf. 1 Cor 10:16). At the same time, the conjunction of offering ('the god invites,' 'altar'), communal meal ('feast,' 'table') and social celebration ('festivity') confirms the interplay of religious and social functions.

Another invitation in the same collection supports the same point, and repeats some of the same terms, suggesting that this language is conventional.

> The god invites you [kali] to the sacred altar [or 'feast'], which he always provides for all men, especially for those who participate in the sharing [koinōnia] of sacred rites. I summon you to visit the god more frequently in order that you may partake in the festivity in his presence and in common with the cities.[62]

In addition to the verbal similarities, the convergence of sacred worship, communal feast, and social festivity is again noteworthy.[63]

The Functions of Ancient Associations

Official club statutes remain from antiquity, and they reflect both the interplay of religious and social motives, as well as significant parallels with the language of 1 Corinthians 8–10.

A religious association calling itself 'the community *[koinōnia]* of sacrifices' stipulates that the host is to sacrifice a suckling pig as an offering to the Heroines, to set up a table *[trapezan]* for the offerings, to make an offering of a mature animal to the Hero, and to distribute the meat *[krea]* to officiants and participants in set portions.[64] Smith comments:

> Since it was from the god's table that the distribution was made, the table would most probably function as a primary symbol for commensality with the god who would be implicitly interpreted as host and provider of the food. Further, the commensality experienced among the membership with one another could be interpreted as a gift of the god, since it originated at the common table.[65]

Religious devotion and communal celebration are not easily separated.[66]

The intermingling of social and religious functions is nowhere more explicit than in Aristotle's explanation of voluntary associations:

> Some associations *[koinōniōn]* appear to be formed for the sake of pleasure, for example religious guilds and dining-clubs, which are unions for sacrifice and social intercourse (*Nicomachean Ethics* 8.9.5).

Associations, he continues, assemble in order to "perform sacrifices and hold festivals in connexion with them, thereby both paying honour to the gods and providing pleasant holidays for themselves."[67] Given the wide variety of organizational purposes, it is to be expected that guilds and clubs would reflect different levels of religious emphasis and devotion, but all apparently combined both religious and social roles.[68]

The Architecture of Temple Dining Rooms

Archaeological remains of Corinthian temples have sometimes been invoked in support of a distinction between religious and social meals. Gooch, for example, notes that the temple precinct of Demeter and Kore contained over forty dining rooms: given the centrality of meals in the cult, and the location of the dining rooms within the temple compound, meals eaten here would likely be considered unequivocally religious.[69] The temple of Asklepios, on the other hand, shared dining facilities with the public gardens associated with Lerna.[70] Given the peripheral function of meals in the cult of Asklepios, and the dual function of the dining rooms, meals here might conceivably have been religiously ambiguous.[71]

This architectural distinction could explain why Paul appears tolerant of some temple venues in 8:10, but intolerant of others in 10:1–22. Gooch hypothesizes that precincts such as those envisioned in 8:10 might be religiously ambiguous; those assumed in 10:1–22, decidedly cultic.[72] Though initially sympathetic to this line of argument, Gooch subsequently rejects it on the basis of Greco-Roman literature:

> The literary evidence shows time and again that socially significant meals involved explicit religious rites. If such meals involved rites even when held in private homes, it seems most unlikely that there would not be some cultic acts in meals celebrated in cultic settings.[73]

In conclusion, he also rejects the premise of the architectural argument: "Social event and religious events could not be separated in the Greco-Roman world to the same extent as they can be in ours."[74]

In the end, the distinction between religious and social interpretation proves dubious in principle and unworkable in practice.[75] Invitations to meals, procedures at meals, and the settings of meals all reflect the interweaving of religious and social functions and meanings. But this does not mean that all participants viewed the rites in the same way.[76] Greco-Roman religion, no less than shenism, reflects the effects of social location on ritual observance and interpretation.

The Effects of Social Location on Ritual Observance and Interpretation[77]

The case of Julius Caesar provides a classic example of the multiple functions of religion, and their correlation with various social locations. According to Sallust, when debating a proposal to execute prisoners, Caesar declared: "Amid grief and wretchedness death is a relief from woes, not a punishment; that it puts an end to all mortal ills and leaves no room either for sorrow or for joy" (*Catiline* 51.20).[78] Stated simply, death ends human existence.

Yet this theology did not stop Julius from seeking divinization. Dio attributes his assassination to the acceptance of honors due only to gods, including the appellation Jupiter Julius (43.45; 44.6–8). Even

in the absence of theological conviction, divinization serves important—albeit risky—bureaucratic functions.

At the same time, the Roman historian Suetonius describes the
visceral response of the masses: Julius was "numbered among the
gods not only by a formal decree, but also in the conviction of the
common people" (*Julius Caesar* 88). This is an understatement. Appian
records that a grieving mob sought to bury Julius in the temple in the
presence of the gods (*Civil Wars* 2.148). When prevented by the priests,
they stormed back to the forum, cremated his remains on a pyre, and
then erected an altar and subsequently a temple.

The career of Julius Caesar thus provides evidence of elite rationalism, political pragmatism, and populist spiritism.

Poets, Philosophers, and Politicians

Of course, one rationalistic, pragmatic politician and a single
instance of mob hysteria do not substantiate the general tendencies
supposed by the theory of social location. But ancient Roman social
critics do. Both Scaevola and Varro distinguished three stances toward the gods and linked each with a particular social location: the
mythical, found in the poets and among the masses; the physical,
championed by the natural philosophers; and the civil, promoted by
bureaucrats.[79]

With a view to strengthening the moral foundations of the state
ideology, Scaevola and Varro rejected both the mythical and the
physical worldviews. The mythology of the poets portrayed the gods
as unworthy models for imitation; the rationalism of the philosophers
rejected the existence of the gods altogether. The masses inclined
toward the poets rather than the philosophers, Varro worried, but
either was prejudicial to social order (Augustine *City of God* 4.32;
6.5,6).

So Varro advocated a third course: philosophical rationalism
muted by civic pragmatism, intended to encourage the populace to
believe in such gods as would strengthen the social order. Toward
this end he collected and revised the ancient mythology, removing
the more odious elements so people might more readily worship the
gods (Augustine *City of God* 4.31; 6.5,6). The goal underlying this
revisionism was to bind the populace in civil society, and to encourage their subordination to rulers (Augustine *City of God* 4.32; 6.2).

Social Location and Ritual Interpretation

On the whole, Greco-Roman intellectuals portrayed the traditional religions and the masses who practiced them as superstitious. The elite tended toward rationalism, but most eschewed atheism in recognition of the valuable social functions of religion.[80]

Lucian was undoubtedly the sharpest critic of populist beliefs and rituals (e.g., *On Sacrifices* 1–13; cf. *The Lover of Lies, Or The Doubter* 2–10). He dismissed the masses as dolts engaged in idiocy and mocked the idea of reciprocation, as though the gods would sell blessings for the cost of a rooster, wreath, or stick of incense. He ridiculed sacrifice on several grounds, including the idea that gods, like common flies, would feast on the ascending smoke of burnt offerings and spilt blood (cf. Juvenal *Satire* 10.354–55). He mocked the requirement of ritual purity for a priest who would soon be splattered with the gore of sacrifice. He derided temples, as though the gods needed homes, and images, as though any sculptor had actually seen what the gods looked like.[81]

Despite this vituperative, Lucian was a rationalist, not an atheist. He criticized sacrifice on the grounds that gods do not need food; temples, because gods do not need housing; and prayer in the temples, because gods can hear their supplicants wherever they may be (*Demonax* 11, 27). He rejected populist practices not because he denied the gods, but because he felt that populist notions dishonored the gods (cf. Persius *Satire* 2.24–75).[82]

Diogenes Laertius ascribes similar sentiments to the philosopher Epicurus, again reflecting the effects of social location both on the practice and on the interpretation of religion:

> For verily there are gods, and the knowledge of them is manifest; but they are not such as the multitude believe…Not the man who denies the gods worshipped by the multitude, but he who affirms of the gods what the multitude believes about them is truly impious (10.123).

Opposed to populist superstition yet also to atheism, Epicurus, like Lucian, promoted a revisionist faith.[83]

The objective, in part at least, was to preserve the social functions of religion. The Senate met in temples; all civic meetings began by invoking the gods; civic officials served as the priests in the state cult; even emperor worship was fundamentally a matter of social unity across a wide and diverse empire.[84] Civil religion made for stability and its preservation was beneficial to the civil order.

Toward this end, Plutarch criticized atheism for mocking the gods, and superstition for fearing them; true religion lay between these alternatives (*De superstitione* 164e–171f). He disapproved of the populist idols and worship, and commended the efforts of revisionist philosophers and statesmen who portrayed the gods as magnanimous and kindly. Clearly he worked within the same tripartite framework as Varro. His motivation included the preservation of the social functions of religion: "The pleasantest things that men enjoy are festal days and banquets at the temples, initiations and mystic rites, and prayer and adoration of the gods" (*De superstitione* 169d-e).

Cicero is a classic example of a philosopher–bureaucrat who sought to cleanse traditional Roman religion of its more outlandish elements, while preserving its civic functions. Though holding the bureaucratic office of augur, Cicero denied the legitimacy and logic of augury, even wondering aloud how one augur could meet another without laughing at their common charlatanry (*On Divination* 2.24,37,47,48,72; *De Natura Deorum* 1.26). Still, he advocated that the practice be maintained for the stability of the State and as a check on the impulses of the undisciplined masses (*On Divination* 2.12,33).

Despite this cynical perspective, Cicero opposed those philosophers, like Livy (1.19.4–20) and Polybius (6.56.6–12), who went so far as to suggest that "the entire notion of the immortal gods is a fiction invented by wise men in the interest of the state, to the end that those whom reason was powerless to control might be led in the path of duty by religion" (Cicero *De Natura Deorum* 1.42).[85]

Conclusion

At each point of this survey, remarkable parallels exist between Greco–Roman ritual and modern shenist practice. In both cases, the religious commitment of practitioners is evident architecturally to all who enter their homes. In the case of an invitation to dine, there would be no doubt about the host's religious commitments.

In addition, Greco-Roman festivities celebrate many of the same sorts of occasions as their shenist counterparts, with offerings both for gods and for ancestors, daily, monthly, throughout the life cycle, and especially at funerals and on death anniversaries. The parallel extends beyond the occasions being celebrated and incorporates the meaning of the offerings, including veneration, affection, and the notion of ancestors needing food and reciprocating those who provide it or punishing those who do not.

Similarities include the multiple and inseparable functions of sacrificial meals (social, civic, and religious), the lack of a clear distinction between worship and veneration, and the indeterminate significance of the meal location (with social and civic meals held in temple dining rooms, and cultic meals held in private homes or guilds).

With regard to social location, Varro perceived much the same tendencies in Roman society as Weller proposes for Chinese culture.[86] Cicero played the role of social philosopher and civil servant among the Romans, much in the same way as Confucius did among the Chinese. Though largely rationalists, both eschewed populist spiritism, on the one hand, and philosophical atheism, on the other. Both pragmatically adapted traditional ritual in support of society and state.

Of course, the parallels between Greco–Roman religion and shenism are not exact, and there are other dimensions in each cult which lack correlations in the other. But that is both inevitable and beside the point. Religions and cultures separated both by millennia and by continents will always diverge. Under such circumstances what is noteworthy is not the differences, but the extent of the similarities. The correlations hold out hope that the dialogue between the Corinthian church and the apostle Paul will provide guidance for converts from shenism in their relations with family, lineage, culture, and tradition.

But before turning in that direction, one last avenue of background requires brief investigation. Judaism had several hundred years head-start in addressing the pressures on exclusivistic monotheists living among polytheists. Moreover, both Christianity as a whole and the apostle Paul in particular had their formative development within Judaism. So just as Greco-Roman religions provide helpful background for understanding the Corinthian mentality, Jewish backgrounds may illumine Paul's assumptions, thinking, and directives. In fact, at least two recent interpretations of 1 Corinthians 8–10 resolve ambiguities in the biblical text by appeal to the apostle's Jewish heritage.[87] This approach merits consideration and requires evaluation.

Endnotes

[1] The phrase 'Greco-Roman religion' is a misnomer in two regards. First, there was no single religion, but a great variety of them. Secondly, Greek and Roman religions were distinct, though traditional Greek and Roman deities tended to assimilate. The objective here is not to engage in detailed distinctions between various Greek and Roman religions, but to describe features common to Greco-Roman religion generally, particularly the presentation of food offerings to gods and ancestors, and the consumption of these offerings at communal meals. The focus is on basic commonalities, not on fine distinctions.

[2] A few interpreters suppose that opposition to idol offerings in 1 Corinthians 8 derives from Jewish Christians (e.g., Sawyer 1968: 122–30; cf. Witherington 1995: 196 n35). Sawyer argues mainly from the extended contrast between Jew and Gentile in 9:19–22, which he interprets as a chiasm:

A	all (v19)
B	Jew (v20a)
C	under the law (v20b)
C'	without the law (v21)
B'	weak (v22a)
A'	all (v22b).

But given the contrast between C (under the law) and C' (without the law), B (Jew) more likely contrasts with B' (weak). Confirming this, the parallel between B (Jew) and C (under the law) supports a contrasting parallel between C' (without the law) and B' (weak). In that case, the 'weak' would be those without the law. Or quite possibly, given the break in semantic parallelism caused by mention of the 'weak,' this is argument by analogy, and the identity of the weak must be determined by other means.

Witherington (1995: 196 n35) points to Paul's argument from Hebrew Scriptures in 10:1–10 as suggestive of the weak being Jews. But 10:1–10 is directed against the strong, not the weak. Besides, the Hebrew Scriptures are the only canonical authority available to Paul, whether in addressing Jewish or gentile Christians. Since the Church was originally a sect of Judaism, these are equally the early Christian Scriptures.

The most obvious clue of the identity of the weak comes with Paul's description in 8:7, "Some are habituated to idols still now"; this would not fit Jews (cf. Barrett 1968: 194; Newton 1998: 37).

Though he disputes the strength of that argument, Murphy-O'Connor (1978: 554) rightly supposes that gentiles would face greater familial and social pressure to participate against their convictions than would Jews.

³ Bakker (1994: 2; cf. Harmon 1978: 1592) distinguishes between domestic cults (*feriae privatae*) and public cults (*feriae publicae*). The line of demarcation is determined by who officiates at the ritual, and for whom. The rituals of 'public' (or 'civic') religion are performed by individuals appointed to represent the populace as a whole; 'private' (or 'household') religion is the responsibility of domestic units and voluntary networks, such as guilds or other associations. Civic and emperor cults provide crucial background for interpreting the imperial Chinese and early twentieth-century Japanese experiences of idol offerings, but are less relevant for contemporary Chinese shenism. Consequently, due to space constraints, these cults receive little attention here.

Newton (1998: 105–10) provides evidence of the imperial cult in first-century Corinth. Winter (1995 cf. 1994a) argues that the imperial cult in particular was the cause of the dispute reflected in 1 Corinthians 8–10, but nothing in the text requires such a narrow focus. More likely the imperial cult was one dimension of the problem. Thus Chow (1992: 152) concludes that "the imperial cult could account for the problems involved in 1 Corinthians 8–10," yet explicitly qualifies this verdict: "I merely see the case of imperial cult as illustrative, and by no means the only context through which the significance of the Corinthians' participation in meals at an idol's temple can be appreciated" (p 147).

⁴ With occasional exceptions, the primary data cited date mainly from the second century B.C.E. to the second century C.E., and include both Greek and Roman sources. The chronological spread is necessitated by the haphazardness of extant sources, and is justified by broad continuities throughout the period (cf. Gooch 1993: 27; Newton 1998: 185–86; and in an analysis of the Roman emperor cult, Price 1984: 4–5). While specialist concerns about reductionism and false homogeneity are legitimate (e.g., Friesen 1993a: 142–45), there is still a place for the survey, even if by nature it is forced to focus on broad continuities and to overlook subtle distinctions.

The geographical breadth is justified by the interpenetration of Greek and Roman cultures from Hellenistic through imperial Roman times, not least of all in Corinth, a Greek city destroyed by Roman forces in 146 B.C.E. and then refounded as a Roman settlement beginning in 46 C.E. (on the debate over the relative Roman or Greek character of Corinth, see Gill 1993a; Engels 1990: 93–95; Willis 1991; Wiseman 1979: 491–96). Oster (1992: 54–55) warns that "it would be a grave error to suppose that the inhabitants of colonial Corinth lived in a setting which was mono-cultural." Due to strict space constraints the survey below concentrates on Roman cult. This focus does not suppose that Greek cult is irrelevant.

5 Wiencke (1947) provides a comparable survey of the Greek domestic cult from the classical period, and draws attention to a number of similarities between Greek and Roman cult across the centuries: for instance, between the functions of Zeus Patröios and penate (pp 156–57), hermes and lares (p 79), as well as Zeus Ktesios and lar familias (p 169).

6 This section relies on Orr 1972, 1978, and Harmon 1978. Wiencke (1947) provides an excellent survey of the architecture of Greek household religion during the classical period.

7 By imperial times, a certain imprecision had melded the deities of the domestic cult, so that the penates, lares, and Vesta were often viewed and treated collectively. 'Penates' could even refer in a generic sense to the entirety of the domestic deities: not only the lares, Vesta, and penates proper, but also the traditional deities worshipped in the particular home, such as Jupiter, Minerva, Fortuna, Hercules, Bacchus, Mercurius, Venus, Egyptian gods, or the imperial cult (Bakker 1994: 40–41).

8 Even more than 'Zeus' for the Greeks, 'lares' was a generic term for Roman deities, with an epithet delimiting particular jurisdictions. *Lares viales* were guardians of roads and travelers; *lares permarini* looked after ocean voyagers; *lares ludentes* supervised the games; *lares militares* protected soldiers; lares even served as guardians over forests, fields, streets, buildings, and the air. The origin of the lares familiaris is uncertain: one theory suggests that they represent distant deceased ancestors; another, that they were originally field deities.

9 This section draws heavily from Harmon 1978 and Scullard 1981.

10 Gods and ancestors were distinguished, but they both received cult and in parallel forms: Juvenal (*Satire* 13.230) speaks of the guilt-ridden who come under the punishment of the gods, and "dare not vow a bleating victim to a shrine, or offer a crested cock to the Larea; for what hope is permitted to the guilty sick? What victim is not more worthy of life than they?"

11 On domestic worship of the gods, see, for example, Lucian *The Dream, or the Cock* 14.

[12] On the largely comparable daily offerings in Greek households during an earlier period, see Nilsson 1940: 73–75; Gill 1974: 120; and especially Jameson 1949 and Wiencke 1947.

[13] Lucian (*Timon, or the Misanthrope* 7) describes Timon as celebrating festivals to the gods at home: "He is the man who often treated us to perfect sacrifices; the one who had just come into a fortune, who gave us the complete hecatombs [sacrifice of one hundred cattle] and used to entertain us brilliantly at his house during the Diasia [festival of Zeus at Athens]."

[14] The gods and ancestors were also invoked for help—and rewarded for services rendered—during crisis events. Horace *Ode* 3.8 describes worship with flowers, incense, and a burnt offering, followed by a feast and drinking party, in thanksgiving for deliverance from a falling tree; *Ode* 2.7 for return from war; *Ode* 1.37 for military victory; *Ode* 1.36 for safe return from a journey. For other examples, see Juvenal *Satire* 12; Lucian *Zeus Rants* 15; Plautus *Amphitryon* 1.946–48.

[15] For a girl, the rite of passage to adulthood was postponed until the day before her wedding, when she would dedicate childhood toys and garments to Venus or to her household gods.

[16] Catullus (*Poem* 59) portrays a woman who was often seen in the graveyards grabbing the baked meats from the funeral pyre and collecting loaves that rolled down out of the fire. Seneca (*Epistle* 12.8) describes a comic scene involving an eccentric aristocrat who would daily hold his own funeral meal, with the customary feasting and wine, after which his attendants would carry him from the dining room to his bedroom, singing, "He has lived his life! He has lived his life!" Plutarch (*Alexander* 70.1) describes a drinking contest held after a funeral. Kennedy (1987: 231) provides a general description of Roman funeral customs.

[17] Newton (1998: 100–05) surveys secondary sources that provide evidence of the cult of the dead in Corinth. Kennedy (1987: 230) proposes that

> the real problem at Corinth is Christian participation in the pagan funeral rites for members of the family or for friends. It is this perpetual problem of dealing with the care and feeding of the dead that Paul addresses in 1 Cor. 8–10, and not the eating of meats that were slaughtered in pagan temples or offered to pagan gods.

His argument, however, depends on a proposed etymology for *eidōlothuton* which is improbable: he argues that *eidōlon* has "primary association with an image of a deceased member of the family"; and thus, that *eidōlothuton* means "a memorial meal for the dead." Consequently, he takes *eidōleion* in 8:10 as "a tomb triclinium...for the less affluent, the memorial meal would be more like a picnic; the wealthy could afford a complete dining room with adjacent kitchen" (1987: 232–33). He fails to provide, however, any definite evidence from ancient texts that either word was ever used with this specific meaning. Moreover, Paul appears to assume a routine and regular practice, which better fits the numerous and wide uses of temples. The cult of the dead more likely was one aspect of the problem, rather than the sum total. In a later study, Kennedy (1994) surveys the terms for 'idolatry' in the Hebrew Bible and the Septuagint without arguing for such a narrow semantic field or specific referent.

[18] Ogilvie 1969: 76.

[19] Kennedy 1987: 228. While Lemuria was probably also a civic celebration, all that remains is Ovid's account of the private ritual. At midnight the worshipper rose from bed, making a gesture with thumb in the middle of closed fingers for protection in case of an encounter with a spirit in the dark. After washing his hands, he would take black beans, throw them behind him, and repeat nine times, "These I cast; with these beans I redeem me and mine." The spirit is thought to follow behind, gathering the beans. Then the worshipper would again touch water, bang bronze, and another nine times appeal to the ghosts to leave the house: "Ghosts of my fathers, go forth!" (Ovid *Fasti* 5.430–44).

[20] In Lucian's *Timon, or the Misanthrope* (10), Zeus resolves to act on behalf of Timon, "who burned so many fat thigh-bones of bulls and goats on the altar to honour us; indeed, I have the steam of them still in my nostrils!" In *The Double Indictment* 2–3, Lucian has Zeus complain about overwhelming responsibilities, and the danger that if he takes a break from answering prayers,

> our temples will have no wreaths, our wayside shrines no savoury steam, our wine-bowls no drink-offerings, our altars will be cold, and in short there will be general dearth of sacrifices and oblations, and famine [among the gods] will be rife...I should like to ask the philosophers, who say that only the gods are happy, when they suppose we really find leisure for our nectar and our ambrosia in the midst of our countless bothers.

[21] Toynbee 1971: 35.

[22] Toynbee 1971: 62.

[23] Gooch (1993: 27–46) provides a helpful survey of Greco-Roman literary sources pertaining to the social importance of shared meals and the frequent use of offered foods in shared meals.

[24] In an amusing letter whose menu provides some sense of the importance of social meals, Pliny (*Letters* 1.15) castigates a friend who snubbed his invitation to dine:

> How happened it, my friend, that you did not keep your engagement the other night to sup with me? Now take notice, the court is sitting, and you shall fully reimburse me the expense I was at to treat you—which, let me tell you, was no small sum. I had prepared, you must know, a lettuce and three snails apiece; with two eggs, barley-water, some sweet wine and snow (the snow most certainly I shall charge to your account, and at a high rate, as 'twas spoiled in serving). Besides all these curious dishes, there were olives, beets, gourds, shalots, and a hundred other dainties equally sumptuous. You should likewise have been entertained either with an interlude, the rehearsal of a poem, or a piece of music, as you like best; or (such was my liberality) with all three...How agreeably should we have spent the evening, in laughing, trifling, and instruction!

[25] One unmistakable evidence of its centrality—and its widespread abuse—is the frequency with which dinner behavior features in ancient discussions of ethics. See, for example, Xenophon *Symposium*, Plutarch *Table-Talk*, Plato *Symposium*, Lucian *Carousal*, and *Parasite*, as well as Petronius *Satyricon*. Communal meals were also a means of reinforcing relative social position (e.g., Petronius *Satyricon* 21; Juvenal *Satire* 3.140; 5; Pliny *Letter* 2.6; Lucian *The Dream or the Cock* 8–11; Epictetus *Encheiridion* 25.2,4–5; Lucian *Nigrinus* 17; Callus *Poem* 47).

[26] This section relies heavily on Smith 1980: 12–32; 1990: 21–35. Among primary sources, Xenophon provides a thorough description of banquets in his *Symposium*. This material provides an important corrective to an earlier perspective which still lingers, expressed, for example, by Ehrhardt (1964: 279 cf. Witherington 1995: 188) that "the temples of the ancient world...had to supply the need for restaurants, especially in the Greek cities. If a Christian husband for some reason or other wanted to go out for dinner he had, unless he lived in one of the big cities, no other choice."

This is inaccurate. Various types of restaurants and eateries existed, in addition to private dining in the homes of the wealthy.

Stambaugh (1988: 198–208 cf. Meggitt 1994: 137–41) describes three different types of establishment: *caupona, popina,* and *taberna.*

Addressing similar claims concerning meat on sale in the market, Barrett (1965: 48) rightly warns, "The extent to which the Christian shopping in the Corinthian *macellum* would be forced to purchase goods with a religious history behind them must…not be exaggerated." Thus, for example, Cadbury (1934: 141) observes that the presence of entire skeletons of sheep in one shop excavated at Pompeii "suggests that the meat may have been sold on the hoof or slaughtered in the *macellum* as well as sold already butchered or sacrificed in a temple."

[27] Communal meals also occurred within civic settings (e.g., Plutarch *Table Talk* 2.10), but these receive little attention here since they are less relevant to contemporary shenist practice.

[28] Dining practices—including domestic architecture—obviously differed dramatically between the leisure class and the working class, and the bulk of extant literature and archaeological remains naturally derives from the former. Yet elite reflections on common practices reflect a basic continuity across the classes, though lower-class celebrations obviously were characterized by decreased frequency and less extravagance.

[29] Through the use of multiple tables, larger celebrations might include up to twenty-seven or even thirty-six diners. Outdoor dining in the courtyard and gardens of large estates could permit a guest list of several hundreds—or even thousands on big estates—but such numbers were rare.

[30] Plutarch (*Table Talk* 1–9) describes meals held in combination with rites, drinking, word games, and philosophical conversation. Cf. Horace *Satire* 2.2.119–25.

[31] Horace refers to the offering between courses in communal meals. Host and guests would share a chicken or goat "and Ceres, to whom we made our prayer…smoothed out with wine the worries of a wrinkled brow" (*Satire* 2.2.115–25). Later in the same work, he describes another, similar scenario: "When before my own Lar we dine, my friends and I, and feed the saucy servants…after due offering" (*Satire* 2.6.65–66).

[32] Pliny (*Letters* 9.17) sympathizes with a correspondent who complained about raucous entertainment provided at a meal, including a range of buffoons, fools, and prostitutes:

I confess, indeed, I admit nothing of this kind at my own house; however, I bear with it in others…The soft gestures from a wanton, the pleasantries from a buffoon, or the folly from a professed fool, give me no entertainment, as they give me no surprise. It is my taste, you see, not my principles, that I plead against them. And indeed, what numbers are there, think you, who distaste the entertainments which you and I are most delighted with, and consider them either trivial or wearisome! How many are there, who as soon as a reader, a musician, or a comedian is introduced, either take their leave of the company, or if they continue at the table, show as much dislike to this kind of diversions, as you did at those *monsters*, as you call them.

[33] It is a commonplace in New Testament studies that the consumption of idol food and the practice of sexual immorality (e.g., Acts 15:20; 1 Cor. 6:12–20 and 8:1–11:1; Rev. 2:14,20) would converge especially in the temple (e.g., Fee 1987: 455; Witherington 1995: 190, 221). But as Witherington (1995: 193) himself notes, Greco-Roman feasts were notorious for both gluttony and sexual decadence (cf. Slater 1991: 2–3; Booth 1991: 106–7).

[34] This section summarizes and adapts the discussions in Smith 1980: 101–77; Bakker 1994: 56–76; Stambaugh 1988: 209–11; and Meiggs 1960: 310–36.

[35] Dionysus, the god of wine, was naturally patron of bars. Fortuna, as protector of people and localities, brought good fortune to shopkeepers. Hercules, guardian of the house, and Mercurius, god of trade, often appeared in front of shops. Neptunus was protector of those working with water, including fishmongers. Stables would have a shrine to Epona, Celtic god of horses (Apuleius *Metamorphoses* 3.27.1). Daedalus was protector of cabinet-makers. Minerva was popular with a variety of vocations, from the wool industry to shoemakers, carpenters, doctors, teachers, painters, sculptors, and poets (Ovid *Fasti* 3.817-34). Mars was patron of thieves and kidnappers (Lucius Apuleius *Golden Ass* 7.10–11).

Multiple patrons were also common. Among the deities worshipped in the Ostian service industry were the Roman gods Dionysus, Fortuna, Hercules, lares, and genii, as well as the oriental gods Apis, Isis, Isis-Fortuna, and Serapis (Bakker 1994: 73).

[36] Bakker (1994: 56–76) describes one bakery in Ostia which contained a shrine measuring thirteen square meters, built off a corridor containing four wall-niches and an altar. Fifty bronze and silver statuettes were found inside, along with a marble statuette of a lar. Deities represented included Silvanus (the god of property boundaries), the two Dioscures, Fortuna (the goddess of good fortune),

three Egyptian deities associated with the corn supply on which bakeries depended (Annona, Harpocrates, and Isis), a genius, a lar, Alexander the Great, and Augustus. Even Jewish and Christian deities could join the assembly: in one home the lararia included depictions of Alexander the Great, deified emperors, Abraham, Christ, Orpheus, Achilles, as well as the statesman Cicero and the poet Virgil (Bakker 1994: 158).

[37] Bakker 1994: 77–95. Apart from their standard patron deities, hotels also made provision for guests to bring personal deities with them (Apuleius *Apologia* 63).

[38] Stambaugh 1978: 588.

[39] Though held for obvious reasons in the open rather than in a guild, the meal described by Lucius Apuleius (*Golden Ass* 7.10–11) is otherwise representative. Bandits sought the help of Mars in ransoming a kidnap victim and in securing additional gang members, but there was "no manner of beast to make sacrifice withal nor wine sufficient for us to drink." Gang members went to town, and came back with wine and a great number of beasts. After they offered a goat to Mars "to help and be with them," they ate the goat for supper and spent the night drinking. Notably, Longus (*Daphne and Chloe* 2.24,30–32) describes sacrifice to nymphs and Pan in thanks for the safe return of a kidnap victim, so different gods could profit from each side of the exchange.

[40] Stambaugh (1988: 210–11) describes a meeting place *(schola)* for a prosperous builders' guild in Ostia:

> Members entered the central courtyard through a wide entrance from the main street. Facing the entrance across the courtyard was a chapel in which typically statues of the patron deity and the presiding *genius* of the collegium, and also of members of the imperial family, were displayed. Along the east and west sides of the courtyard were rooms arranged with couches to accommodate diners at the collegial meals.

Two features are noteworthy: the prominent display of cult statues, and the association of trade guild with cult banquet.

[41] Initially it is hard for Western interpreters to imagine first-century Christians attending cultic feasts in the temple, so the supposition is that the feasts must have been purely or predominantly social (see especially Willis 1985a: 17–21). Such a distinction, of course, reflects a modern dichotomy between social and religious functions, whereas traditional societies are generally characterized by a unity of religious and social functions. Thus, in the first-century, the temple provided the opportunity to celebrate important social occasions in

the presence of the gods. This connection is weaker, but not absent in the modern West: for instance, many people who do not attend the regular services of the church will still seek its services for weddings and for funerals.

[42] Stambaugh 1978: 554–608.

[43] On critical civic occasions, such as impending military battles, all temples would offer prayer and sacrifice for the welfare of the city (Achilles Tatius *The Adventures of Leucippe and Clitophon* 2.14–15; Plautus *Amphitryon* 1.229–31). Ceremonies called *lectisternium* would find dining couches and tables laid out for the gods to join the banquet (Livy 5.13.6; 11.59.7). With victory, the wealthy would sponsor public banquets in thanks to the gods. Persius (*Satire* 6.48–51) describes such a public festival, which a wealthy citizen sponsored in celebration of the Roman victory over the Germans: "In honour of the Gods and the Genius of our General, I am putting on a hundred pairs of gladiators to celebrate...I am giving the mob a largess of oil and bread and meat."

Routinely, political bodies would hold meetings in temples. The Roman Senate, for example, met in the temples of Jupiter, Castor, or Concordia; military deliberations might be held in a temple of Apollo; civic tribunals also commonly met for litigation on the steps of a temple. So, too, civic officials commonly led sacrifice (Pausanias, *Description of Greece* 1.5.1; Achilles Tatius, *Leucippe and Clitophon* 8.7.6).

[44] Merchants would set up business around appropriate sites, such as clothing and perfume sellers around the temple of Diana. Trade or professional guilds often met at the temple of their patron, such as merchants at the temple of Mercurius, or bankers around the temple of Saturnus, headquarters for the state treasury. Needing security to guard their own treasures, temples could also provide safekeeping for private fortunes and valuables.

[45] Cf. MacMullen 1981: 35. Newton (1998: 110–14) discusses the evidence of cultic associations attached to the Isthmian games.

[46] Greek and Roman animal sacrifices were largely comparable in basic procedure. Both required preparation of the animal and the officiant; both included the ritual slaughter of live animals; both apportioned the vital organs to the gods; both customarily reserved the bulk of the sacrifice for a feast among the worshippers. (For a brief summary of the process employed in Greek sacrifices in the archaic and Hellenistic periods, see Gould 1985: 16–17. For Roman sacrifices, see Ogilvie 1969: 41–51; Stambaugh 1988: 219.)

Not all sacrifices were animal; not all animal sacrifices ended in a feast. Bloodless offerings included breads, cakes, fruits, cooked dishes, vegetables, spices, and wine. These were common in the household cult, but also featured in some temple rituals. In some cults, the animal would be burned in its entirety (Zaidman and Pantel 1992: 37). Among the animals used were goats, cows, dogs, horses, bulls, rams, and boar, depending on the god and the occasion. Beyond this, male gods received male animals, and female, female; deities of the sky received white animals; underworld deities, black (Ogilvie 1969: 43–44). Kadletz (1976) examines in detail the type, sex, and color of animals sacrificed to the major Greco-Roman deities.

[47] Juvenal (*Satire* 15.38–52) describes a festival to the gods accompanied by "grand banquets, with tables set out at every temple and every crossway, and with night-long feasts, and with couches spread all day and all night" lasting up to a week, and including music, dancing, and drunkenness. Herodas (*Mime* 4) provides an extensive description of a temple offering and distribution.

[48] While the occasional cult required that the sacrifice be consumed within the temple compound, more commonly those who could not stay for the feast would be permitted to take their portion home. So, too, the priests' portion and (where offered) an extra portion of meat allotted to the gods might find its way to the public meat market. As a result, much of the meat eaten in the home or purchased in the meat-market would have come from sacrifices (Zaidman and Pantel 1992: 33; MacMullen 1981: 41).

[49] Zaidman and Pantel (1992: 38–39) describe the social isolation faced by Orphics, a vegetarian cult which practiced only bloodless sacrifice, and thus "cut themselves off radically from all civic life, since that presupposed…participation in animal-sacrifice and its culminating distribution of meat." Some Pythagoreans were vegetarian, others ate goat and pig; "in this way they achieved a compromise between an oppositionist religious stance and participation in civic life."

[50] This distinction is common in the literature (see, e.g., Muir 1985: 193–94; Nilsson 1940: 73–80; Ogilvie 1969: 1–2; Zaidman and Pantel 1992: xi–27; Finley 1985: xiv–xx; Gould 1985: 1–9).

[51] Admittedly, the categories must not be absolutized. Thus, Christianity, a canonical religion by this typology, tends to be diffused and informal—at least on the popular level—in any culture where it is vital. Conversely, Greco-Roman philosophers commonly reflected on the meaning and existence of the gods worshipped reflexively by the masses. That is to say, the distinction likely reflects social location (both of practitioner and of analyst) as much as the intrinsic characteristic of the religions involved.

⁵² MacMullen (1981: 103) remarks sardonically: "No one from the past has been good enough to tell us what he really thought he was doing when he wrote *any* religious message upon stone."

⁵³ Muir (1985: 193–94) expresses the consensus among classicists when he rejects all three assumptions:

There was a certain similarity in forms and places of worship—the rituals of sacrifice and libation, for instance, were part of everyone's experience...As for personal belief...no Greek worshipper was required to subscribe to a body of dogma or to accept a number of common doctrines as a precondition of practicing religion.

The paradox is that, although Greek religion seems to lack so many of the things which characterize modern religions and which require degrees of personal commitment and faith from their followers, Greeks were involved with religion to a degree which is very hard nowadays to understand. Some form of religion seems to have penetrated all aspects of life.

In short, Greco-Roman religions were diffused rather than canonical.

⁵⁴ Zaidman and Pantel 1992: 13. Price (1984: 5) speaks similarly of the Roman imperial cult: "There is no point in asking bluntly what someone believes about the after-life, or about the imperial cult. The respondent would probably have no definite, articulate response to make" (cf. pp 5–19, 243–48).

⁵⁵ Newton (1998: 115–257) has done much to redress this neglect, surveying at considerable length the various "ambiguities, boundary definition problems and conceptual differences" affecting the interpretation of images, sacrifices, and communal meals in first-century Greco-Roman society. He concludes, firstly, that interpretations would differ from one person, setting, occasion to the next; and secondly, that social and religious meanings intermingled.

⁵⁶ The consensus maintains that at the very least feasts in honor of the gods were in part religious: at times the invitations identify the god as host; other times murals or statues picture the deity reclining at table (Gilliam 1976: 316–17; Horsley, ed. 1981: 6). Yet even domestic celebrations honored deities with libations and hymns of praise, and a preceding sacrifice would have been common.

⁵⁷ Various invitations are collected in Hunt and Edgar 1970: 400–3; Horsley, ed. 1981: 5–9; Gilliam 1976: 315–24; and Youtie 1948: 9–29.

⁵⁸ Cited in Kim 1975: 393.

⁵⁹ Achilles Tatius (*The Adventures of Leucippe and Clitophon* 2.12; 2.18; 5.14; 8.19) describes sacrifices in the temple in conjunction with

weddings. Longus (*Daphne and Chloe* 4.37–38) describes a wedding which combines offerings, music, dancing, and feasting; cf. Lucian *Toxaris, or Friendship* 25; Lucius Apuleius *Golden Ass* 4.26; 5:3,4; 6:10–11; Plutarch *Alexander* 70.2–3; Seneca, *Octavia* 1.700–25.

   [60] Ancient authors were sometimes quite scathing about the proportion of festivity to worship. Lucian (*Parasite* 15) indicates that most people "drudge all the time except one or two days a month which they celebrate as holidays, and are said to have their good time then." He also has Pan complain that though he protected the people from the barbarian invasion, "they come up only two or three times a year, pick out and sacrifice in my honour a he-goat with a powerful goatish smell, and then feast on the meat, making me a mere witness of their good cheer and paying their respects to me only with their noise" (*The Double Indictment* 10).

   [61] Adapted from Smith 1980: 246; citing J. Hatzfeld, 'Inscriptions de Panamara,' *Bulletin de correspondance hellénique* 51 (1927) 73–74, no. 11.

   [62] Adapted from Smith 1980: 248; citing J. Hatzfeld, 'Inscriptions de Panamara,' *Bulletin de correspondance hellénique* 51 (1927) 74, no. 14.

   [63] Newton (1998: 217, 251–55) rightly remarks that the god is always host or fellow-guest, never victim or food. That is, the invitations provide no evidence of a sacramental interpretation.

   [64] Smith 1980: 250–51; citing Benjamin Meritt, 'A Decree of Orgeones,' *Hesperia* 11 (1942) 283.

   [65] Smith 1980: 111–12.

   [66] Willis (1985a: 17–64 cf. Nock 1964: 24–30) attempts such a distinction between a 'sacramental,' 'communal,' or 'social' interpretation of meals. He concludes that the predominant ethos was one of conviviality and festivity, even to the point of drunken carousing. On this basis he rejects a sacramental connotation, and strongly endorses the social over the communal (Willis 1985a: 46–47; contra Conzelman 1975: 174).

   Willis' conclusion has proved controversial, in large measure because his terminology is misleading. In describing the rites as 'social' he does not intend to deny all religious import to the sacrifices (though he has often been taken in that sense).

   In virtually all meals of Hellenistic groups the gods are invoked in prayers and libations are poured. The gods are also the recipients of the sacrifice which precedes the meal. Some civic festivals featured the visit of the deity as the occasion for a feast. Therefore even in the social understanding of these meals, it is granted that due regard was given, and a portion

allotted, to the deity. Their presence at such meals was assumed (Willis 1985a: 48).

How, then, does the social interpretation differ from the communal?
Only in emphasis:

> The difference, then, between the social and the communal
> interpretations of these meals is where the *focus* is believed to
> lie. The communal view stresses the relationship of the wor-
> shippers to the deity; the social, the relationship between the
> worshippers (Willis 1985a: 49).

In the communal interpretation, the social element exists, but the
religious predominates; in the social interpretation, the religious element exists, but the social predominates.

This supposes that festivity and worship are competing agendas.
Commenting on wild festivities, MacMullen (1981: 39–40) rightly
asks: "Does all this add up to something less than the spirit of worship, to shallowness of feeling, a secular devaluation of once-fervid
beliefs? Or can that only be said if some extraneous standard of
behavior, defining what is and is not 'truly' religious, were imported?"

[67] Similarly, Stambaugh (1978: 591) concludes that temples
"served not only for the worship of the gods...They also served as a
community center and private club, where a good meal could be
found on specified occasions, and where agreeable company could
be found at least once a month."

[68] Given the presence of altars, patron deities, and sacrifices in
cult associations, Meiggs (1960: 327) concludes reasonably:

> For the religious aspect of the trade guilds the evidence is less
> explicit, but it seems clear that it was an integral element in
> their organization. The cult of the guild *genius* and some form
> of imperial cult were common to all guilds, but most if not all
> had also their own patron gods or goddesses.

At times clubs were banned altogether as political destabilizing, except for funerary clubs and collegia which met for religious purposes.
Unsurprisingly, the number of religious associations proliferated rapidly, while to demonstrate their loyalty, clubs conducted rites in
honor not only of the patron deity but also the emperor (Stambaugh
1988: 211; Justinian *Digest* 47.22.1–3). So Roman associations of
various types and at various times likely reflected a wide range of
devotional commitment and emphasis; nonetheless, apparently all
combined religious and social functions.

Even Willis, the most ardent advocate of a predominantly 'social'
interpretation, freely acknowledges the inextricable combination of

social and religious import in guild celebrations: "One cannot accurately distinguish these private associations, trade guilds, or cult-brotherhoods as secular or religious. Both their self-descriptions and their functions overlap these categories" (Willis 1985a: 51).

[69] The excavations of the temple of Demeter and Kore have been described by Bookidis and Fisher (1974, 1972), Bookidis and Stroud (1987), and Bookidis (1993, 1990, 1969).

[70] See, Roebuck 1951: 51–57; Oster 1992: 65–66.

[71] Cf. Gooch 1993: 25–26. It is worth noting, in passing, that perhaps neither of these particular dining facilities was in use when Paul wrote 1 Corinthians. Newton (1998: 91–99) surveys the evidence from the archeological reports.

[72] On second glance, the architectural evidence which Gooch cites actually undermines his argument. He proposes to correlate eating in the dining rooms of Lerna with permissible temple meals (cf. 1 Cor. 8:10), and eating in the temple of Demeter and Kore with prohibited feasting from the sacred table (cf. 1 Cor. 10:21) (1993: 15). Yet he concludes that Lerna was not actually a temple and that Demeter and Kore was. Thus, he unwittingly ends up with prohibited meals in the temple of Demeter and Kore (contra 1 Cor. 8:10), permissible feasting with friends in the ambiguous Lerna compound (cf 1 Cor. 10:27–29), and no parallel to the prohibited eating from the 'table' of the gods (per 1 Cor. 10:21).

[73] Gooch 1993: 82 cf. 102–3. While acknowledging the futility of attempting to distinguish religious and non-religious temple meals, Oster (1992: 65–66) seeks to retain this solution by distinguishing between idolatrous and non-idolatrous activities in the temple. By the former, he means activities that were part of the 'official *cultus*,' and therefore prohibited to Christians. With the latter, he has in mind social and cultural events such as meals and birthday parties, "which would not necessarily involve idolatry," in the sense that they "would not have necessarily involved the believer in active participation in the *cultus*." As we shall see, for Paul, even where there was no direct participation in worship activities, the meal itself might involve 'participation in the *cultus*.'

[74] Gooch 1993: 82.

[75] With respect to theory, the distinction is based on a false disjunction: more religious, less social; more social, less religious. There is no intrinsic correlation—either direct or inverse—between religious fervor and social function, and thus no reason why a given meal or festival could not be maximally religious and maximally

social simultaneously. Thus, Plutarch (*Moralia* 1102A) comments that: "It's not the abundance of wine or the roasting of meat that makes the joy of festivals, but the good hope and the belief that the god is present in his kindness and graciously accepts what is offered."

In practice, the distinction requires subtle assessments of a variety of meals in diverse contexts. The depth of religious sentiment would naturally vary according to the participants, the occasion, the setting (home, guild, temple), and even the stage of the meal (e.g., sacrifice, dining, libation, drinking) (cf. Youtie 1948: 14). This raises questions about the value of generalizations such as:

> It may be granted at the outset that in some cults, on some occasions, some diners had a greater sense of the presence of the patron deity…However, the indications are that cult meals, including the mystery cult meals, were generally regarded fundamentally as occasions for social association and conviviality (Willis 1985a: 49; cf. Conzelmann 1975: 148, 174).

With such wide variation, the appeal to a mean is largely pointless. Moreover, the selection of any mean is inevitably arbitrary: given that an overall average is unattainable for contemporary shenism, it is all the more inaccessible for Greco-Roman religion at such distance and in the absence of living informants.

[76] Allowance must be made for a range of private interpretation. Newton (1998: 242–55) surveys a variety of functions of communal meals, including as markers of socio-economic standing, as opportunities to build friendship and as fulfillment of socio-political obligations. He concludes: "For some, sacrifices were meaningless, for some, simply customary, but for others they involved a recognition of the presence of the god and a recognition that they were in some sort of relationship with that god which could either help or harm them" (p 255).

[77] In this section, discussion broadens beyond domestic religion to include evidence from the traditional cults of deities and from the emperor cults. This is necessitated by the nature of the primary sources. Greco-Roman discussions of preternatural beings generally focus on gods and emperors, rather than on ancestral or other sorts of spirits. Still, it is unlikely that social location influenced the interpretation of the one without corresponding effects on the other.

[78] Similarly, albeit more sardonic, the emperor Vespasian is famous for his death-bed quip: "Alas, I think I am becoming a god" (Suetonius *Vespasian* 23.4).

79   The writings of Scaevola and Varro are no longer extant, but their ideas are known from Augustine (*City of God* 4.27,31,32; 6.5–7) and, to a lesser degree, from Tertullian (*Ad Nationes* 2.1). Momigliano (1987: 58–73) provides a helpful overview of what he calls "the theological efforts of the Roman upper classes in the first century B.C."

80   Cf. Ogilvie 1969: 6; Chow 1992: 152–54.

81   In *On Funerals* 24, Lucian turns his mockery toward funeral practices, again highlighting the effects of social location: "The general herd, whom philosophers call the laity, trust Homer and Hesiod and the other myth-makers in these matters, and take their poetry for a law unto themselves" (24.2). He mocks the belief that spirits "get their nourishment...from the libations that are poured in our world and the burnt-offerings at the tomb" (24.9). He imagines the deceased telling their descendants:

> What, pray, is the use of your pouring out the pure wine? You don't think, do you, that it will drip down to where we are and get all the way through to Hades? As to the burnt offerings, you yourselves see, I think, that the most nourishing part of your provender is carried off up to Heaven by the smoke without doing us in the lower world the least bit of good, and that what is left, the ashes, is useless, unless you believe that we eat dust (24.19).

82   In Lucian's *Timon, or the Misanthrope* (1–7), Timon accuses Zeus of impotence and laziness in failing to ensure justice, for which reason his worship has fallen into neglect. In reply Zeus castigates Timon as "a mouthy fellow and an impudent one. Very likely he is a philosopher, otherwise he would not talk so impiously against us." Subsequently, Zeus breaks two tines from a thunderbolt punishing the sophist Anaxagoras "who was teaching his disciples that we gods do not count at all" (10).

In *Zeus Rants*, Lucian develops an extensive argument between two philosophers disputing and defending the existence of the gods. In the end, he puts the following consolation into the mouth of Hermes: "What very great harm is it if a few men go away convinced of all this [philosophical rationalism]? The people who think differently are in large majority, not only the rank and file of the Greeks, but the barbarians to a man" (53). The social location of disbelief was axiomatic for Lucian.

83   Though considerably milder in tone, the natural historian Pliny (*Natural History* 2.5.14–27) similarly opposed both atheism and polytheism. He disapproved of a wide range of popular beliefs and prac-

tices, including the traditional mythology and the many new divinities, such as deified vices and virtues, individual junos and genii, the
emperor cult, and foreign deities. Yet he was uncertain which would
be worse: to attribute shameful behavior to the gods, or to give no
heed to them at all.

    [84] Liebeschuetz 1979: 1–2, 20, 196; cf. Ogilvie 1969: 1.

    [85] It is not clear whether Cicero opposes such cynical analysis as
inaccurate or as indiscrete. Cicero criticized any aspect of religion
that could undermine the authority and stability of the State, including the inclusion of foreign deities, and the subversion of traditional
festivals, sacrificial regulations, the priesthood, or even augury (*De
Legibus* 2.10–12). He also opposed private initiative in religion, explaining that his disapproval

> really has to do with the condition of the State as well as with
> religion, its object being that private worship may not be
> satisfactorily performed without the assistance of those in
> charge of the public rites; for the people's constant need for
> advice and authority of the aristocracy helps to hold the State
> together (*De Legibus* 2.12.30).

Thus he considered it the responsibility of the civic and intellectual
elite to uphold the traditional cult, including its rites and ceremonies
(*On Divination* 72).

    Cotta, one of Cicero's protagonists, mocked the deification of
humans as "an extension of the franchise," and rejected both popular
mythology and the Stoic deification of nature and natural forces (*De
Natura Deorum* 3.15). Nevertheless, as a leading citizen, pontiff, and
augur, he recognized his commitments:

> I ought to uphold the beliefs about the immortal gods which
> have come down to us from our ancestors, and the rites and
> ceremonies and duties of religion. For my part I always shall
> uphold them and always have done so, and no eloquence of
> anybody, learned or unlearned, shall ever dislodge me from
> the belief as to the worship of the immortal gods which I
> have inherited from our forefathers (*De Natura Deorum* 3.2).

In this matter, Cotta clearly speaks for his fellow augur.

    [86] Weller 1987.

    [87] Tomson 1990; Cheung 1999.

God and the Gods: Idol Offerings and Communal Meals in Jewish Perspective

---

Summary: *The Hebrew Bible and rabbinic traditions insisted on scrupulous avoidance of anything remotely associated with idolatry or idol offerings. At the same time, some evidence remains to suggest that at least a portion of the Jewish social elite reached a degree of accommodation with pagan rites, and that the Jewish philosophical elite sought rapprochement with Greco-Roman philosophical interpretations of religion.*

With the shift to Jewish backgrounds comes a fundamental change in orientation. To this point, the focus has been on the making and consumption of idol offerings, whether in the modern Chinese or the ancient Greco-Roman context. These investigations helpfully illumine why disputes over eating idol offerings are likely to arise among Christian converts: in part because of the prevalence and importance of such meals in polytheistic contexts, and in part because of the range of interpretations given to the offerings. The survey of Jewish literature, on the other hand, serves primarily as background for appreciating Paul's response to the issue.

The Jewish response to idolatry divides into basically three stages.[1] The early canonical strategy was to exclude idols and idolatry from the land. Subsequently, in the face of widespread apostasy, the prophets developed a two-pronged polemic, highlighting the impotence of idols, on the one hand, and their demonic nature, on the other. Once the exile and the foreign occupation of Palestine precluded total separation from idolatry, rabbinic literature formulated guidelines to distinguish prohibited and permissible contacts between faithful Jew and gentile idolater.

Idolatry in the Pentateuch

The prohibition of idolatry is axiomatic in the Pentateuch. To be the people of God is to eschew other gods and idols:

> I am the Lord your God, who brought you out of Egypt, out
> of the land of slavery.
> You shall have no other gods before me.
> You shall not make for yourself an idol in the form of any-
> thing in heaven above or on the earth beneath or in the
> waters below. You shall not bow down to them or worship
> them (Exod. 20:2–5a; cf. Lev. 19:4; 26:1).[2]

Thus, the covenant renewal ceremony just prior to entering the land
closes with a series of ritual curses and blessings. First among the
curses is one against those who carve images or cast idols (Deut.
27:15).

Significant, too, is the reason given for avoiding idolatry: the
Lord is a jealous God, punishing those who dishonor him (Exod.
20:5b). The punishments decreed for idolatry are conquest of Israel
by its enemies, and exile from the land (Deut. 4:15–28; 30:17–18). The
covenant of blessing provides no protection for idolaters (Deut. 29:16–
28).

Given the severity of the consequences that idolatry brings, the
Pentateuch takes care to specify in more detail which behaviors are
prohibited. The Jews are neither to offer sacrifices to other gods
(Exod. 22:20; 34:16; cf Lev. 17:7; Deut. 29:17–18), nor to use foreign
cultic practices in worship of the Lord (Lev. 18:21; 20:2–5; Deut.
12:30–31; 16:21–22). They must not even mention the names of foreign gods (Exod. 23:13). Instead they are to destroy the cultic statues
and altars (Exod. 23:24; 34:13; Num. 33:52; Deut. 7:5,25–26; 12:2–3).
They are also forbidden to intermarry with the peoples of Palestine,
lest they be seduced into worshipping other gods (Exod. 34:15–16;
Deut. 7:2–3). In short, as Israel enters the new land, the basic strategy
for avoiding idolatry is to sterilize the territory, removing every
vestige and memory of the previous gods.

Even before reaching the new land, the people make idols themselves (Exod. 32:1–4) and they engage in cultic sex with Moabite
women (Num. 25:1). God backs up his threat of punishment: in the
first incident more than three thousand die (Exod. 32:27–35); in the
second, twenty-four thousand (Num. 25:4–9). Notably, each account
links idolatry with both feasting and sexual immorality:

> So the next day the people rose early and sacrificed burnt
> offerings and presented fellowship offerings. Afterward they
> sat down to eat and drink and got up to indulge in revelry
> (Exod. 32:6).
> While Israel was staying in Shittim, the men began to indulge
> in sexual immorality with Moabite women, who invited them

to the sacrifices to their gods. The people ate and bowed down before these gods. So Israel joined in worshiping the Baal of Peor (Num. 25:1–3).

Thus, the ban on idolatry incorporates a prohibition against eating food that others have sacrificed to idols: "Be careful not to make a treaty with those who live in the land; for when they prostitute themselves to their gods and sacrifice to them, they will invite you and you will eat their sacrifices" (Exod. 34:15).

Of these principles, three are especially germane to Paul. First, the prohibition against idolatry is fundamental to being God's people. Secondly, the prohibition extends to joining meals which the hosts are celebrating as cultic feasts. Thirdly, God judges those who violate these prohibitions, as he has repeatedly demonstrated. Paul affirms the same three propositions in 1 Corinthians 8–10.

Idolatry in the Rest of the Old Testament

The 'Song of Moses' anticipates widespread apostasy leading to divine judgment (Deut. 31:14–29; 31:30–32:43). Much of the remainder of the Old Testament records the fulfillment of this expectation. Israel's frequent idolatry with the gods of surrounding nations repeatedly results in the threatened destruction (see, for example, 2 Chron. 11–36). First Israel (2 Kings 17:1–23), then Judah (2 Kings 21–22) fall at the hands of their enemies, and are transported into exile. Yet the prophets insist that Israel's real enemy is God, and the cause of their destruction is their adultery with other gods (Hos. 4:12–15; 8:4–6; 10:1–8; 11:1–11).

"Will you steal and murder, commit adultery and perjury, burn incense to Baal and follow other gods you have not known, and then come and stand before me in this house, which bears my Name, and say, 'We are safe'—safe to do all these detestable things?" (Jer. 7:9–10).

"I will smash this nation and this city…The houses in Jerusalem and those of the kings of Judah will be defiled…all the houses where they burned incense on the roofs to all the starry hosts and poured out drink offerings to other gods" (Jer. 19:11–13).

In fact, the entire history of Israel is often recapitulated as a litany of idolatry followed by divine punishment (e.g., Ps. 106:34–43; Ezek. 20:1–49). But the dirge consistently ends on a note of hope. If only Israel will renounce idolatry, God will restore the nation to the land (e.g., Ezek. 11:16–21; 36–37; Zech. 13:2).

Given this lengthy battle against idolatry, the Old Testament naturally contains extensive anti-idolatry polemic. Frequently idols are derided as impotent. Isaiah, for example, mocks:

Half of the wood he burns in the fire;
over it he prepares his meal,
he roasts his meat and eats his fill.
He also warms himself and says,
"Ah! I am warm; I see the fire."
From the rest he makes a god, his idol;
he bows down to it and worships.
He prays to it and says,
"Save me; you are my god" (Isa. 44:16–17).

Jeremiah is equally caustic:

Like a scarrow in a melon patch,
their idols cannot speak;
they must be carried
because they cannot walk.
Do not fear them;
they can do no harm
nor can they do any good (Jer. 10:5).[3]

The impotence of idols is by far the strongest theme in Old Testament polemic (e.g., Lev. 26:30; 1 Sam. 12:21; 1 Kings 16:13,26; 2 Kings 17:15; Ezek. 43:7,9; 1 Chron. 16:26; Ps. 115:4).

Yet on occasion, another perspective emerges: idols represent demons. At the same time, it should be noted that these viewpoints are complementary, rather than contradictory (at least, they appear in tandem within the Old Testament). Thus, for example, Deuteronomy 4:28 portrays the impotence of idols: "You will worship man-made gods of wood and stone, which cannot see or hear or eat or smell." Deuteronomy 32:16-17, on the other hand, characterizes idols as demonic: "They made him jealous with their foreign gods and angered him with their detestable idols. They sacrificed to demons, which are not God…" More pointedly, both polemics appear in proximity within Psalm 106:

They yoked themselves to the Baal of Peor
and ate sacrifices offered to lifeless gods (v 28).
They [Israelites] worshipped their [Canaanites'] idols,
which became a snare to them.
They sacrificed their sons
and their daughters to demons (v 36–37).

On the one hand, idols are lifeless, impotent, man-made figurines; on the other, worship offered them is actually directed to demons.[4]

Both of these features—God's destruction of his people in punishment for their idolatry, and the twofold nature of idols as impotent yet demonic—reappear in 1 Corinthians 8–10.

Idolatry in the Intertestamental Literature

Intertestamental literature adds considerable clarity and texture to the portrait of ancient Judaism's interaction with idolatry. Chastened by the exile, the Israelites steadfastly resist participation in idol worship. Esther (AddEsth 14:17) and Judith (Jud. 10:5; 12:2,9–12), like Daniel before them (Dan. 1:8), go so far as to refuse all food offered them by non-Jewish rulers. So does Tobit, though many of his colleagues in exile are not so scrupulous (Tob. 1:9–12). Even when Antiochus demands the worship of idols on penalty of death, many in Israel refuse not only to worship but even to eat food offerings (1 Macc. 1:41–64).

Implicit in these narratives is the conviction that to eat food offered to idols would be to participate in idolatry. Despite lengthy torture, for instance, Eleazar refuses to eat either pig flesh or idol offerings (4 Macc. 5–7). Seven sons and one mother subsequently follow his example, though refusal means painful execution (4 Macc. 8–17).[5]

The intertestamental polemic against idolatry follows largely the same two lines as its Old Testament precedent. Idols are impotent:

> The greatest fools of all, and worse than infantile, were the enemies and oppressors of thy people, for they supposed all their heathen idols to be gods, although they have eyes that cannot see, nostrils that cannot draw breath, ears that cannot hear, fingers that cannot feel, and feet that are useless for walking (Wis. 15:14–15 cf Bel 5–7; JosAse 13:11).[6]

At the same time, idols represent demons:

> (And those) who worship stones, and those who carve images of gold and silver and of wood and of clay, and those who worship evil spirits and demons, and all kinds of idols not according to knowledge, they shall get no manner of help in them (1 Enoch 99:7).

The latter receives more emphasis in intertestamental literature than in the Old Testament (e.g., Jub. 1:11; 11:4–5; TJud 23:1; TJob 3:3; 1 Enoch 19:1).

In a new development, the anti-idolatry polemic specifically encompasses offerings to the dead:

Good things spread before a man without appetite
are like offerings of food placed on a tomb.
What use is a sacrifice to an idol
which can neither taste nor smell? (Sir. 30:18–19).

In a lengthy diatribe, the Sibylline Oracles combine all three aspects of the polemic:

They decree an image, fashioned of wood, to be mine,
and shaping it with their hands, a speechless idol…
[They make] burnt offerings at meals, as to their own dead.
For they burn flesh and, sacrificing bones full of marrow on
altars, they pour blood to demons…
For they will do these things to the memory of kings and
tyrants, for dead demons, as if they were heavenly beings,
performing a godless and destructive worship (OrSib 8:382–
4,393).

The intertestamental critique of gentile religion finds no discrepancy in mocking idols as impotent, identifying them with demons, and associating them with the deceased.

This perception of food offerings has obvious ramifications for Jewish relations with gentiles.

Separate yourself from the gentiles,
and do not eat with them,
and do not perform deeds like theirs.
And do not become associates of theirs.
Because their deeds are defiled,
and all of their ways are contaminated, and despicable and
abominable.
They slaughter their sacrifices to the dead,
and to the demons they bow down.
And they eat in tombs (Jub. 22:16-18).[7]

Gentile idolatry includes sacrifices both to gods and to deceased humans, and each involves the worship of demons. To avoid contamination, Jews are to avoid close contact with gentiles.

This isolation in turn has significant impact on gentile attitudes toward Jews.

Reverencing God and conducting themselves according to
his Law, they kept themselves apart in the matter of food,
and for this reason they appeared hateful to some…[The
foreign rulers] talked incessantly about how different [the

Jews] were in regard to worship and food, asserting that they
did not fulfill their contracted obligations either to the king
or the armed forces but were hostile and very unsympathetic
to his interests. So it was not small charge they fastened on
them (3 Macc. 3:4–7).

In an environment where there is no clear line between religion,
politics, and social obligation, the Jewish desire to maintain purity of
faith communicates both anti-social isolation and political disloyalty.

Strikingly, 3 Maccabees persists in the prohibition against imperial ritual and social interaction even while recognizing the predominantly socio-political function of the ruler cult. To celebrate his
victory over Antiochus, Ptolemy IV visits the various religious shrines
in the surrounding regions, making offerings as a sign of political
goodwill (1:6–7). When he enters Jerusalem with similar intent, the
Jews refuse him entry to the Holy of Holies (1:9–2:20). The author
quotes Ptolemy:

"When we desired to enter their shrine and to honor it with
resplendent and beautiful offerings, carried away by their
ancient pride, they stopped us from going in, but because of
the benevolence we practice toward all men they were left
untouched by our might. But they plainly exhibited their
hostility to us and, the only ones among all people who offer
lordly resistance to kings and their own benefactors, they
refused to accept anything as genuine" (3:19–21).

Ptolemy goes so far as to grant the Jews the great honor of Alexandrian
citizenship with the right of participation in associated religious rites.
When the Jews rebuff this overture, Ptolemy infers:

"Accordingly, we have adequate proof of our conviction that
these people are in every way hostile to us, and noting in
advance that, if ever a sudden disturbance should be stirred
up against us later on, we would have these impious people
behind our backs as traitors and barbarous enemies" (3:19–
25).

Given the political implications of religious motivations, the emperor
ordered the Jews to be destroyed. Strikingly, though recognizing that
religious exclusivism was misinterpreted as political rebellion and
social antagonism, the author of 3 Maccabees continued to advocate
abstention and isolation.[8]

By way of summary, five principles from the intertestamental
literature are relevant to 1 Corinthians 8–10. First, the sin of idolatry
extends to the consumption of food known to have been previously

offered to idols. Secondly, the polemic against idols is two-pronged: they are both impotent and demonic. Thirdly, the sin of idolatry explicitly extends to the offering of food and to the veneration of the dead. Fourthly, the emperor cult also falls under the ban on idolatry, even though its predominant political functions are openly acknowledged. Finally, the Jews stand firm in these convictions, despite social alienation and political persecution.

Idolatry in the Rabbinic Literature

The rabbinic literature signals a marked shift in the Jewish strategy toward idolatry and idol offerings. The change is not in thrust; the rabbis opposed idolatry no less than Jewish tradition always had. But as foreign occupation made it impossible to keep pagan deities and their worshippers out of territorial Israel, and as exile left the diaspora Jews surrounded by idolatry, the rabbis developed far more detailed guidelines to guide Jewish conduct. In fact, an entire tractate within the Mishnah, *Abodah Zarah,* is devoted to differentiating permitted and forbidden activities.[9]

Indirect Complicity in Idolatry

No longer was the focus on prohibiting Jewish idolatry; that battle had largely been won. For the rabbis the issue shifted to spelling out the precise implications of the unqualified prohibition. The operative question was, "What sorts of activities constitute complicity with idolatry?" The focus shifted from Jewish participation in pagan religious practices to mundane activities by which Jews might inadvertently facilitate gentile idolatry. How careful must a devout Jew be in the effort to avoid indirect involvement with idolatry? Quite careful, as it turned out.

The Mishnah forbade Jews to conduct any sort of business with gentiles near the time of their cultic celebrations. For three days before their festivals, Jews could have no financial dealings with pagans, whether lending or borrowing, paying or receiving payment. Purists extended the prohibition to three days after the festival as well (m*AZ* 1.1–2).

Notably, the Jews were aware of the timing and occasions for the major celebrations of gentile worship. Among the prohibited festivals were Calends (the first day of the Roman month, with the biggest celebration on the first day of the year), Saturnalia (an orgiastic celebration in honor of the god Saturn, from December 17–23), Cratesis (a commemoration of the empire), and celebrations connected with the emperor cult (specifically, commemorations of his birth, ascent to the throne, and death; m*AZ* 1.3). In addition to these civic holidays, the rabbis also prohibited Jewish participation in pagan personal and familial celebrations, such as the day when a gentile shaved off his beard or a lock of hair in coming of age ceremonies, when he returned safely from an ocean voyage, when he was released from prison, or when he gave a banquet for his son. On such occasions, gentiles would typically worship and offer sacrifices to their household deities; consequently, Jews could not conduct business with the family (m*AZ* 1.4).

The Mishnah similarly prohibited Jews from conducting business with gentiles in the presence of their idols. If a town had an idol of a patron deity, Jews could not trade with its populace. Or, at least, if the idol was situated inside the town, they must transact business outside the town; or if the idol was located outside the town, they must conduct business inside (m*AZ* 1.4).

Jews could not patronize any shop decorated in honor of a patron deity (m*AZ* 1.4). Nor could they share facilities constructed for cultic purposes, not even with the purpose of engaging in explicitly non-cultic activities. Thus, they could not live in a house built specifically to be an idol shrine—not even after removing the idols—though they could remove traces of an idol which had been introduced into a home in later renovations (m*AZ* 3.7). They could not use a bathhouse or garden which belonged exclusively to a temple, though they could use one shared between a temple and other owners (m*AZ* 4.3). If a Jewish home shared a wall with a temple, and the wall collapsed, it must be rebuilt as a separate structure (m*AZ* 3.6). If a road led directly and only to a city with a patron idol, Jews could not travel in that direction; but if the road led on further, they could take it (m*AZ* 1.4).

The principle of indirect complicity extended to the presumption of intent. Jews were forbidden to sell gentiles products which generally featured in offerings to the gods, such as white roosters, fir cones, white figs, or frankincense. The significance of this ruling is evident in its elaboration: if the Jewish seller cuts a spur off the rooster, thus rendering it unsuitable for offering to the gods, it may then be sold to Gentiles. Products not characteristically used in offerings could be sold without qualms, unless the gentile purchaser specified an idolatrous intent (m*AZ* 1.5).

By similar logic, Jews could work with gentiles to build a bathhouse, but not a basilica, stadium, or tribunal, for the latter would inevitably include idols (m*AZ* 1.7). Jews were also forbidden to rent to gentiles, for the latter would undoubtedly bring idols into the home (mAZ 1.9). Nor could a Jew serve as a midwife to a gentile, for the children would be raised to worship idols (m*AZ* 2.1).[10]

Two controversial cases sought to avoid the stigma of indirect complicity by distinguishing religious and social functions. In the former, rabbis permitted Jews to use coins, clothing, or utensils—but not food or fruits—found at the Roman idol shrines commonly situated at the intersection of two roads. The justification was that the former would have been placed there for needy travelers, but the latter, in veneration of the idol (m*AZ* 4.2).[11]

For the latter, Rabbi Gamaliel defended attending the bathhouse of Aphrodite as a secular act—despite the conspicuous presence of her idol—on three grounds. First, the bathhouse existed before Aphrodite was introduced: thus, the goddess was merely a decoration for the bathhouse; the bathhouse did not exist to venerate the goddess. Secondly, bathing and urinating in front of the goddess were clearly not acts of veneration. Thirdly, based on Deuteronomy 12:3 ("cut down the idols of their gods"), Gamaliel argued that the prohibition applied only to what gentiles treated as a god, and was thus inapplicable in this instance and context (m*AZ* 3.4).[12]

Food Offerings, Libation Wine, and Common Meals

Many of the rabbinic regulations governed the consumption of food and drink offerings made to idols. Jews could not associate with gentiles on the day when the latter gave a banquet for a son, because such meals regularly incorporated both worship of the gods and the consumption of food offerings (m*AZ* 1.3). The Babylonian Talmud (8a) extended the prohibition in two directions. For one, Jews were forbidden not merely to eat the wedding banquet, but even to attend with their own food and servants. For the other, the blanket prohibition now lasted for a full thirty days, and up to a year if the invitation specified that the banquet was in celebration of a previous wedding.

Among the goods belonging to gentiles which were prohibited to Jews because of their common association with idolatry were libation wines, hides pierced at the heart (in some pagan rituals, the heart would be torn out and offered to the gods), and meat coming out of an idol temple (though meat on its way to the temple was permitted) (m*AZ* 2.3). If a gentile helped an Israelite to move jars of wine, the former could not be left alone with the wine or the Jew was not allowed to use it (m*AZ* 5.3).

The contamination of idolatry passed not only to the food and wine that had been offered, but even to anything touching the offerings. If libation wine fell on grapes, they must be washed before eating, but if they had already split open, they were prohibited. If libation wine fell on figs, they were forbidden if they had absorbed sufficient wine for the flavor to be detected (m*AZ* 5.2). If a small quantity of libation wine fell into a fresh vat, the entire vat was prohibited (m*AZ* 5.8,10). In short, the Mishnah opposes any consumption—no matter how small the quantity—of food or drink previously offered to idols.

The Social Consequences of Jewish Absolutism

Inevitably the rabbinic and broader Jewish policy of avoiding idolatry had significant social consequences and in two directions: first, it prompted the Jews to withdraw from many social activities and civic celebrations which, secondly, led to hostility from the mainstream culture (e.g., Diodorus *Bibliotheca historica* 34.1.2; Josephus *Contra Apion* 2.258).

The people of Ionia, for instance, complained to the Roman emperor that the Jews living among them refused to worship their gods (Josephus *Jewish Antiquities* 12.125–26; 16.27–65). Similarly, Apion asked about the Jews living in Alexandria, "Why, then, if they are citizens, do they not worship the same gods as the Alexandrians?" (Josephus *Against Apion* 2.66). Where there is no separation of religion and society, religious exclusivity implies anti-social or seditious behavior.[13]

Tacitus (*Historiae* 5.5.1–4) notes that this isolation occurred not only on the civic level, but also in the domestic setting. He expressed outrage that the Jews "sit apart at meals" due to their "hate and enmity" toward outsiders. The first lesson they teach converts, he supposes, is "to despise the gods, to disown their country, and to regard their parents, children, and brothers as of little account." The Jewish refusal to eat food previously offered to idols is deemed not only irreligious, but also anti-social, seditious, and unfilial. To the gentiles, Jewish exclusivism was offensive and incomprehensible.

Summary

The specifics are less important than the broader ethos. Overall, four general points emerge from the survey. First, rabbinic Judaism resolutely opposed idolatry and even warned against indirect complicity, such as by providing supplies which gentiles might use in worship or by eating food which gentiles had previously offered to idols.

Secondly, the effort to avoid complicity in idolatry within a religiously diffuse and pluralistic environment raised a great many ambiguities, requiring a detailed response. Within the geographical limits of an independent national Israel, an absolute prohibition sufficed. Within occupied Israel—or in the diaspora—the complexities of application prompted more thorough explication in the effort to distinguish permitted and proscribed activities.

The ethos and tone of the such detailed and extensive regulations could easily be misconstrued. Elmslie cautions:

> Although many of them must seem over-scrupulous or even casuistical, they are the outcome not of a mean and pettifogging spirit but of the attempt rigidly to carry out a high ideal, difficult of attainment...They result from the practical application in daily life of an unbending determination neither to share in heathen rites nor to seem guilty of aiding and abetting the idolater in his worship. That this was a task of immense difficulty is obvious to all who understand the extent to which idolatrous acts entered not only into the religious worship of the ancient world but also into its commercial and political activities.[14]

While the result may seem pedantic or legalistic to a modern interpreter, such an assessment may be as much an expression of contemporary relativism as a reflection on rabbinic absolutism.

Thirdly, in a traditional culture, where religion, politics, and social life are intertwined, any attempt at religious exclusivism leads also to political and social alienation. From the perspective of the dominant culture, such withdrawal is misanthropic and seditious. Mainstream Judaism generally did not seek confrontation with pagan authorities, but accepted it as inevitable. Religious purity was a higher value than political or social integration, even when exclusivism led to virulent persecution.

Fourthly, in describing 'rabbinic' or 'mainstream' Judaism, it should be noted that extant literature largely portrays a unidimensional perspective on Judaism. Segal, for instance, observes that

> we do not know how ordinary Jews, as opposed to strict Pharisees, observed the dietary laws in the first century...There was obviously a range of practice that we cannot precisely reconstruct, since we have to rely on the mishnaic laws, codified a century and a half after Paul, which

represent a prescriptive idealization by the successors to the Pharisees.

His suspicion is that "Jewish practice of the time encompassed every strategy from total abstinence to virtual commensality."[15]

This possibility warrants consideration, partly in the interests of comprehensiveness, and partly in the investigation of the effects of social location on participation. Is there evidence to sustain the distinction which Segal postulates between 'strict Pharisee' and 'ordinary Jew'? Does social location exert a comparable impact on ancient Jewish interpretation and practice, as on ancient Greco-Roman and modern shenist belief and ritual?

Alternative Responses to Idolatry and Idol Offerings

Does the sanitizing effect of the rabbinic era cloak greater diversity within the Judaism of Roman or New Testament times? This question actually entails two others, which are properly distinct and should be handled separately. First, is there evidence of a divergent perspective on idolatry or on the consumption of food offered to idols within Judaism of the first-century C.E. or earlier? Secondly, to the extent that there was divergence, were the competing positions socially located? That is, does the evidence suggest that the political elite, the intellectuals, and the masses (or some other schema) each leaned toward a different strategy in coping with a polytheistic environment?

The Evidence for Accommodation

Pressures from society, culture, and home may have caused some Jews to take a softer stance toward idolatry in the effort to demonstrate political loyalty, social engagement, or filial devotion. Some modern interpreters merely assume that this was the case.[16] Others infer it.[17] A few argue by analogy. Generally, though, the variation recorded in extant sources tends to be limited, allowing no more than that some Jews did attend predominantly social celebrations which at the same time included pagan ritual activity.

Jewish philosopher Philo (*Special Laws* 2.230), for instance, is quite positive about the athletic training provided by the gymnasium, even though cult statues were located there, participants were naked, and Jews were therefore tempted to undergo epispasm to reverse circumcision. He also freely describes his attendance at boxing and wrestling matches (*Every Good Man is Free* 26), at chariot races (*On Providence* 58), at clubs (*On Drunkenness* 20–26,95), and at the theater (*On Drunkenness* 177), even though each of these activities was generally held in conjunction with sacrifice and other cultic ritual.[18]

Remarkably, Philo participates in all these activities despite their cultic associations even while resolutely opposing participation in cultic ritual and sacrifices. Paraphrasing Deuteronomy 13:1–11, he insists that

> if a brother or son or daughter or wife or a housemate or a friend however true, or anyone else who seems to be kindly disposed, urge us to a like course, bidding us fraternize with the multitude, resort to their temples, and join in their libations and sacrifices, we must punish him as a public and general enemy, taking little thought for the ties which bind us to him (*Special Laws* 1.315–16).

The punishment he proposes for such apostates is execution.

Clearly Philo is working with a distinction between direct participation in idolatry, on the one hand, and passive attendance at peripherally cultic or religious activities, on the other. On the same principle, it might be possible to distinguish cultic meals from dinners that happened to include food offered to idols. Unfortunately, Philo does not provide specific guidance on how a Jew who joins a club or guild, or who participates in the gymnasium or in public festivals, can either justify or avoid cultic celebrations and meals. The most specific he gets is to restrict club membership to those associations which promote character rather than carousing (Philo *On Drunkenness* 20–26,95).[19]

The Social Location of Accommodation

Other evidence of accommodation exists, apart from the example of Philo. At the same time, most of it hints at the influence of social location on ritual practice and interpretation. Though the sample is too small to be conclusive, there is at least an intimation that those who wholeheartedly embraced Greco-Roman culture belonged to the bureaucratic elite, while Jewish intellectuals tended to advocate more limited and intellectualized accommodation.[20]

Bureaucratic Accommodation and the Social Elite

In the ancient world, taking part in the normal routines of social life and holding office in local government would normally require participation in the civic cult. From ancient literary and archaeological sources, it is clear that some Jews were fully integrated into pagan life. What is not so clear is the nature of the accommodation they reached with the civic cult.[21]

The best-known example of accommodation comes from 1 and 2 Maccabees. Jason, who had obtained the office of the high priest through bribery, built a gymnasium in Jerusalem. He led the elite youth into a Greek lifestyle. Even the priests neglected their duties out of devotion to the sports competitions (2 Macc. 4:12–15; cf. 1 Macc. 1:11–15). Jason went so far as to send envoys to games at Tyre with funds for a sacrifice to Hercules (though the envoys deemed it unwise, and spent the money instead to equip ships; 2 Macc. 4:18–20).[22] Because of this devotion to Hellenistic culture, notes the author, "heavy disaster overtook them, and those whose ways of living they admired and wished to imitate completely became their enemies and punished them" (2 Macc. 4:16).[23]

The initiative for rapprochement evidently came from the upper social strata. The aim was

complete and final bridge-building with Hellenistic culture and the incorporation of the Jewish upper strata into the privileged class of 'Hellenes,' i.e., those with Greek education For this purpose, everything that separated the Jews from their more progressive neighbours and had earned them the charge of hostility to foreigners had to be pushed into the background.[24]

Of course, it should come as no surprise that the politically ambitious elite were responsive to rapprochement with the new regional powers.[25]

Borgen draws attention to three other possible examples of civic accommodation, three Jewish officials whose position in the Roman bureaucracy would have required them to perform sacrifices.[26] For one, the name of Eleazar, an administrator in Cyrene in the first century C.E., appears alongside two high-priests of Apollon in an inscription honoring a pagan deity. For another, in Acmonia, a single family produced one member who served as a synagogue leader and another who served as high priest of the imperial cult. For the third, in Iasos around 150 B.C.E., an emigrant from Jerusalem (so probably a Jew) was commended for contributing 100 drachmas to a civic festival for Dionysus.

What cannot be determined from the inscriptions, however, is whether these Jews were apostates, or whether they coupled private worship of Jehovah with their public responsibilities to the Roman civic cult. Grabbe notes that

imperial decrees around 200 CE allowed Jews to hold office
but to be exempted from activities which conflicted with
their religion. Before that, however, Jews still seem to have
held office in some cases. One can suspect that they acqui-
esced passively to the pagan ceremonies; that is, they did not
participate actively but were present and witnessed the rites
when required...This suggests that those who held office
were willing to make certain compromises without feeling
that it detracted from their loyalty to Judaism.[27]

This is a reasonable deduction, though, as Grabbe admits, extant
sources are not explicit.

Philosophical Accommodation and the Intellectual Elite

Apart from bureaucratic cooperation with the civic cult, sources
also give evidence of philosophical reinterpretation designed to facilitate social relationships while avoiding syncretism.

Aristobulus, writing in the second century B.C.E., is the first writer
known to have proposed that Greek philosophers such as Socrates,
Plato, and Pythagoras learned from Moses. In demonstration of his
point, he takes two Greek hymns to Zeus and shows that they are
equally applicable to Jehovah (see Eusebius *Preparation for the Gospel*
13.12.7–8).[28]

The Letter of Aristeas, dating from sometime in the first century
C.E., adopts a similar approach. Aristeas, purportedly a high government official in Alexandria, allegedly said to Ptolemy II: "The (same)
God who appointed them their Law prospers your kingdom, as I
have been at pains to show. These people worship God the overseer
and creator of all, whom all men worship including ourselves, O
King, except that we have a different name" (15–16). Despite this
rapprochement, the author remains opposed to idols and to idol food
(134–35). When the king invited the Jews to a formal meal, he did so
on their terms, serving and eating food prepared in accordance with
Jewish law and customs, and asking Eleazar the Jewish high priest to
offer the prayer (181–84).

The message of the letter is clear: "Association with Gentiles can
be compatible with the Torah...but only if the laws of diet, ritual
purity, and abstinence from idolatry are strictly observed."[29] Significantly, Hengel argues that the opposition to idolatry and the use of
Stoic terms for deity (*Dia* and *Zana*) indicate rapprochement particularly with "philosophically educated Greeks."[30]

Some one hundred and fifty years later, Josephus incorporated the Letter of Aristeas intact into his *Antiquities* (12.22). In his apologetic work *Against Apion* (2.168–69), he elaborates:

Pythagoras, Anaxagoras, Plato, the Stoics who succeeded him, and indeed nearly all the philosophers appear to have held similar views concerning the nature of God. These, however, addressed their philosophy to the few, and did not venture to divulge their true beliefs to the masses who had their own preconceived opinions.

The effects of social location are demonstrated three times in this short apologetic.

First, Josephus witnesses to the effects of social location on Gentile beliefs: the philosophers are largely monists; and the masses, polytheists. Secondly, his recognition of this phenomenon influences his own attempts at rapprochement: he aims at the elite, who reject populist idolatry and whose monism can be turned in the direction of theism.[31] Thirdly, in so doing, he manifests the effect of social location in his own person: it is Josephus the intellectual elite who attempts to bridge the gulf between Jew and gentile elite.

Hengel captures the effects of social location on the Jewish literary and philosophical elite:

For Josephus, as for Aristobulus and for Ps. Aristeas, the God of the philosophers is fundamentally also the God of Israel.

Clearly, this was not the predominant attitude of Judaism towards conceptions of God current in the world of Greek culture. The negative, separationist tendency was very much stronger.[32]

At the same time Josephus also seeks rapprochement with the civic bureaucracy. Though the emperor cult is not the focus of this study, it is instructive to note his defense against charges that the Jews foment sedition by their refusal to honor statues of the emperor. Moses, he explains,

forbade the making of images, alike of any living creature…He did not, however, forbid the payment of homage of another sort, secondary to that paid to God, to worthy men; such honours we do confer upon the emperors and the people of Rome. For them we offer perpetual sacrifices…We jointly accord to the emperors alone this signal honour which we pay to no other individual (*Against Apion* 2.75–77).

Jews refuse to offer sacrifices *to* the emperor, but they do make sacrifice *for* him, and accord this honor to him alone.[33] Josephus seeks rapprochement while still obeying the Jewish law.

Summary

While the sample is not large enough to be conclusive, the correlation between social location and degree of accommodation is at
least suggestive. Bureaucrats and social elite had little choice if they
desired to advance or even maintain their position: they had to participate in politically or socially mandated rites. Religious leadership
unsurprisingly reinforced exclusivism and defined orthodoxy. The
literary and philosophical elite sought rapprochement, but they sought
it in a particular direction: not with populist idolatry but with the
Greco-Roman literary and philosophical elite who were simultaneously moving away from idolatry.

Jewish Precedents and the Apostle to the Gentiles

To what extent did Paul's Jewish background condition his perspective on the Corinthian controversy?[34] The traditional scholarly
consensus has been that Paul permitted the eating of food which had
been offered to idols (e.g., 1 Cor. 8:1–7; 10:25–27). On this basis, he is
perceived to have turned radically from his Jewish roots. Barrett's
famous conclusion is representative of this perspective: "In the matter of *eidolothuta*…Paul was not a practicing Jew."[35]

Both parts of that consensus have recently been challenged.
Tomson and Cheung independently argue that Paul resolutely opposes the consumption of any food known to have been offered to
idols.[36] By this reading, Paul does not reject Jewish tradition, but
concurs with it.[37]

This question is not merely of historical interest. If it can be
demonstrated that Paul is essentially in line with Jewish tradition,
then the Mishnah may be invoked to clarify ambiguities which remain in 1 Corinthians 8–10.[38] Thus, Cheung reasons: "Nothing in
Paul's Jewish background would encourage Paul to condone eating
idol food. If Paul was influenced by his Jewish past in any significant
ways, his attitude toward idol food was likely to be negative."[39] In
large part on this grounds, he argues that "Paul considers conscious
consumption of idol food a denial of the Corinthians' allegiance to
Christ and urges them to avoid idol food if, and only if, it is identified
as such."[40]

The most obvious argument against appeal to Jewish background
comes in Paul's exposition of his *modus operandi* (1 Cor. 9:19–22):

Though I am free from all, I have enslaved myself to all,
    in order that I might win the most;
To the Jew I became as a Jew,

in order that I might win Jews;
To those under the law as under the law…,
in order that I might win those under the law;
To those who do not have the law as not having the law…,
in order that I might win those who do not have the law;
To the weak I became weak,
in order that I might win the weak;
I have become all things to all people,
in order that I might by all means save some.

The rabbinic literature knows nothing so bold or categorical as this: any permission to dine with pagans is carefully qualified and circumscribed in order to avoid the slightest possibility or implication of contamination from idol offerings. In contrast, Paul writes simply, "If any unbeliever invites you and you wish to go, eat whatever is placed before you, not evaluating anything on the ground of conscience" (1 Cor. 10:27).

This principle clearly does not lead Paul into active idolatry, for he consistently and vehemently opposes that. Yet might it permit him to share a domestic meal with a Gentile despite a strong suspicion, perhaps even the firm expectation, that the food had previously come from idol offerings? Paul explicates his position at length in 1 Corinthians 8–10. If the answer is to be found at all, it will be located there. If the answer is not found there, it cannot be inferred from Jewish precedents.[41]

Conclusion

In short, Jewish solutions to the problems of idol offerings must not be superimposed onto Paul, but they do provide an important piece of the historical and theological backdrop to understanding 1 Corinthians 8–10. Paul was a Jew ministering under the auspices of what was in his time essentially a sect of Judaism, yet he was appointed an apostle to the Gentiles. Little could be more obvious than the fact that any attempt to bridge these two worlds would be an ambitious project fraught with difficulties and dangers.

'Mainstream' Judaism sought nothing more than commercial co-operation and social tolerance, and prioritized purity as traditionally defined.[42] This required a wall between Jew and Gentile, one low enough to pass goods over in either direction, but high enough to discourage contamination from non-kosher food or idolatry. Even then, the ambiguities were numerous, the debates acrimonious, and the temptations to apostasy considerable (especially for the upwardly mobile or the socially connected).

Overall, the Jewish background illustrates the complexities, ambiguities, and delicacy of rapprochement between exclusivistic monotheism and hegemonistic civil religion in a pluralistic environment. Beyond this, a number of more specific propositions, prohibitions, and practices from Jewish literature provide a helpful comparison or contrast to Paul's teaching in 1 Corinthians 8–10:

(1) the categorical prohibition against idolatry;

(2) the warning that God punishes his people if they commit idolatry, and that the covenant provides them no protection;

(3) the association of sexual immorality with idolatry;

(4) the prohibition against eating food which was known or even likely to have come from idol offerings;

(5) the characterization of idols as both impotent and demonic;

(6) the refusal to participate fully in political and social life due to its idolatrous elements;

(7) the political and social hostility arising from this refusal to participate;

(8) the concern to avoid indirect and unintended complicity in idolatry;

(9) the development of detailed guidelines delimiting the boundaries of idolatry;

(10) the prohibition of specific social and familial celebrations as inevitably idolatrous;

(11) the restriction of commercial traffic between Jews and non-Jews due to concerns over idolatry;

(12) the interpretative significance assigned to intention (and the debate over whose intention is significant);

(13) the attempt to distinguish religious from social or civic intent and functions; and,

(14) the influence of social location on ritual performance (among the social elite) and on ritual interpretation (among the literary and philosophical elite).

This is not to imply that Paul was directly indebted to Jewish sources on any point, much less that his position converges at every point. But if nothing else, these teachings shed light on the general context from which Paul came, and offer some helpful comparisons and contrasts to his teaching, once it is independently reconstructed.

Endnotes

[1] Of course, scholars of historic Judaism rightly complain that this collation and harmonization called 'the Jewish approach to...' fails to see the diversity and discontinuities of ancient Judaism (e.g., Alexander 1983: 244–45; Neusner 1993: 13–15; 1995: 7–13; Dunn 1995: 230). The purpose here is not to construct a comprehensive summary of ancient Jewish response(s) to idolatry, nor to propose dependence between Paul and the rabbis, but simply to bring to the fore a broad consensus which reflects a degree of similarity with Paul.

[2] Unless otherwise noted, Old Testament passages are cited from the *Holy Bible, New International Version ®.* Copyright © 1973, 1978, 1984 by International Bible Society. Used by permission of International Bible Society.

[3] In addition to the impotence of idols, Jeremiah develops a second polemic, focusing on the disloyalty of Israel:

This is what the Lord says:
"What fault did your fathers find in me,
    that they strayed so far from me?
They followed worthless idols
    and became worthless themselves...
Has a nation ever changed its gods?
    (Yet they are not gods at all.)
But my people have exchanged their Glory
    for worthless idols.
Be appalled at this, O heavens,
    and shudder with great horror," declares the Lord.
(Jer. 2:5,11–12)

Both polemics take a naturalistic view of idols: the gods of the nations are impotent figurines. Where they differ is in the particular negative value assigned to idolatry: it is irrational in the first instance, and disloyal in the second.

[4] In this regard, Psalm 96:5 is significant: the Hebrew text refers to the gods of the nations as 'idols'; the LXX, as 'demons.'

[5] Similarly, the story of Joseph and Aseneth guards against any insinuations which might arise from the canonical allusion to their marriage (Gen. 41:45). Joseph purportedly refuses marriage so long as Aseneth worships idols or eats food which has been sacrificed to idols (JosAse 8:5–7). In response, she destroys her idols and throws all her food offerings to stray dogs, refusing even to let her own dogs eat (10:12–13). Repeatedly Aseneth confesses that to eat food sacri-

ficed to idols is defiling, no less so than to worship idols (11:7–9,16; 12:5, 12; 21:13; cf. Philo, *Spec Leg* 1.315–16). The Dead Sea community goes so far as to refuse to eat or drink anything which comes from gentiles (1QS 5:13,16), or even to sell them produce or animals which might be used in sacrifice (*CD* 12).

⁶ Similarly, the Epistle of Jeremiah, a lengthy diatribe against idolatry, includes the refrain, "They are not gods, so have no fear of them" (EpJer 16, 23, 29, 40, 44, 52, 56).

⁷ The Letter of Aristeas reflects a considerably more casual attitude toward relations with Gentiles. Though recognizing the purpose of Jewish food laws in preventing idolatry, Aristeas shows no qualms about eating with Gentiles, though he takes pains to portray Ptolemy as providing foods acceptable to Jewish scruples (139, 180–81).

⁸ A similar event occurred earlier under Antiochus. After sacking Jerusalem, he established a garrison in the city and instituted a cult of Olympian Zeus, including a monthly celebration of his own birthday (2 Macc. 6:7). He ordered the Jews, with all other conquered peoples, to renounce their own religion and to embrace the new cult, on pain of death (1 Macc. 1:41–51; 2 Macc. 6:1–11). Those who refused either fled or were executed (1 Macc. 1:52–64; 2 Macc. 5:11–6:11).

Hengel (1974: 286) explains that Antiochus' motive was probably less religious than political. He sought to establish a syncretistic 'imperial cult' to unite his kingdom. Cooperation signified loyal submission; refusal, political rebellion. But Israelite religion was equally diffused: if for Antiochus religious ritual expressed political loyalty, for the Jews such expression of political loyalty violated religious commitments. Whatever the underlying motives or proposed interpretation—and whatever the penalty for disobedience—to offer sacrifice to pagan deities or even to eat from the sacrifices was an unthinkable sacrilege (1 Macc. 1:62–63; 2 Macc. 6:7–9, 21–28).

⁹ Elmslie (1911) provides helpful commentary on this tractate; cf. Tomson 1990: 154–63.

¹⁰ The slaughter of animals proved more controversial. According to Rabbi Simeon, a Jew might slaughter on behalf of a gentile. But Rabbi Eliezer took exception on the grounds that the intention of a gentile, even if unstated, is always to make an offering to the idols. Rabbi Yose countered that the intention of the one performing the action is determinative, not the intention of the one on behalf of whom the action is performed (m*Hul* 2.7). All agreed, though, that where an idolatrous intention is specified, Jews must not be involved, even indirectly (m*Hul* 2.8).

In line with his overall thesis of "real ambiguities, boundary definition problems and conceptual differences" over idolatry, Newton (1998: 183–85) argues that a "wide range of attitudes existed in Hellenistic Judaism," and that there was "no such thing as an official or universal Jewish attitude." The evidence he cites, however—like that which I survey here—reflects a basic consensus, with differences limited to peripheral details.

[11] Cf. Elmslie 1911: 62–63.

[12] The attempt to delimit idolatrous activities on the basis of intent proved controversial, and prompted considerable debate within the Babylonian Talmud (44b).

[13] Cf. Goldstein 1981: 318; Feldman 1990: 357.

[14] Elmslie 1911: xxiii–xxiv.

[15] Segal 1990: 231.

[16] Sanders (1990: 281) raises "the possibility of another attitude among some Diaspora Jews." He cites no evidence, but merely supposes that the consistent emphasis on abstinence "implies that some were not as strict as the most zealous Rabbi." His 'guess' is that sharing a meal with pagan friends "has a home somewhere in Judaism…We cannot quantify, but we may suppose that Jewish attitudes toward pagan meat varied." Of course, as Neusner (1993: 275–89) caustically observes, scholarship is more reliable where it is based on evidence rather than on guesswork and supposition.

Feldman (1990: 288) rightly warns against arguments from silence: it is just as likely that the record accurately reflects consistent Jewish opposition to idolatry. Lieberman proposes that "the Jews were so far removed from clear-cut idolatry that there was not the slightest need to argue and to preach against it" (1950: 120–21; cf. Feldman 1990: 101–2; Schürer 1979: 81–83). He does not deny that some Jews succumbed to the temptation and renounced Judaism for paganism, but insists that their number was so few and their apostasy so great that the rabbis made little effort to reclaim them. Instead, the rabbis "were concerned with the heathen rites only in so far as they affected the social and commercial contact of the Jew with the gentile" (Lieberman 1950: 120–21).

As surveyed above, the Mishnah and Talmud do reflect the pattern of building a fence around the law, concentrating not on the prohibition of idolatry, but on the avoidance of indirect complicity in gentile idolatry. This emphasis would be curious were active idolatry widespread among the Jews.

[17] Extant sources record ancient decrees directing that food suitable for the Jews be made available to them for purchase in the market (e.g., Josephus *Antiquities* 14.259–61; 14.226; 14.245). "These passages imply," proposes Sanders (1990: 277), "that, at some times and in some places Jews did not have suitable food and drink...We must assume that some transgressed." In support of this inference, Sanders (1990: 281–82) supposes that the prohibition against eating food offered to idols was less seriously applied than that against consuming pork and blood: "I am proposing that some Jews regarded the minor, formal idolatry involved in eating sacrificial meat as less serious than transgressing either of two prohibitions which are among the strongest in the Bible: do not eat pork, shellfish, donkey etc.; do not consume blood."

Both arguments are unsubstantiated assumption. Is there any evidence that Jews really were more tolerant of idol offerings than of pork and blood? Were the biblical prohibitions against pork and blood significantly stronger than the prohibition against idolatry? Nothing in the references from Josephus indicates that the problem specifically concerned meat, let alone that its focus was pork and blood more than idol offerings. Sanders (1990: 278–80) himself goes on to argue that all three could readily have been avoided in most cases. He also admits that the problem in view was likely broader; that is, a general Jewish aversion toward gentile food rather than a restricted focus on particular items. So there is nothing here to indicate or to imply any equivocation on idol offerings.

[18] Borgen (1996: 26) notes that while the rabbis generally prohibited attendance at theater, they had to make provision for occasions when the state required their presence (e.g., *b'AbodZar* 18b; *t'AbodZar* 2.5–7). At the same time, those—such as Josephus and Philo—who sought rapprochement nonetheless opposed participation in cultic celebrations.

[19] Notably, though, his reservations about clubs concern drunkenness rather than libations and food offerings. Unfortunately, the significance of this distinction is inaccessible. Is it because he saw nothing wrong with Jews attending social activities where gods might be honored, provided they did not take an active part in the offerings? Or is it because he could safely assume that no Jews would attend such functions? The evidence does not permit an answer.

[20] What is lacking is concrete information about the ill-defined yet often maligned *am ha-aretz,* the 'common people.' Alexander (1983: 245, n11) notes that the Pharisees, Sadducees, Essenes, and adherents

of the 'Fourth Philosophy' totaled roughly 20,000 combined. "But the Jewish population of Palestine at the turn of the eras is conservatively estimated at 500,000. What sort of Judaism was practiced by the remaining 480,000 Palestinian Jews?"

In the early second century a prayer was prescribed for daily repetition: "Blessed art thou... for not having made me a pagan...for not having made me a woman...for not having made me an *am haaretz*" (Safrai 1987: 803). It is widely assumed that the masses were more lax in obeying the Law generally, and equally in avoiding idol offerings. But as is inevitably the case, the masses are underrepresented in the literature so this assumption cannot be confirmed.

[21] Borgen (1996) proposes a typology of three basic responses: full-blown apostasy, categorical prohibition, and social relations coupled with cultic prohibition. In actual fact, however, his main thrust is to support the existence of what should better be considered a fourth category: those who participated fully in pagan cults yet still considered themselves members of the Jewish or Christian community, though they were vehemently repudiated by Jewish or Christian colleagues. There is little evidence of apostates consciously renouncing Judaism or Christianity (category 1). Rather, they view themselves as dual-religionists (category 4), while absolutists view them as apostates (category 1) (see, e.g., Rev. 2:14,20; Philo *Special Laws* 1.54–56; 1.315–16; Josephus *Antiquities* 4.141–44). Borgen (1996: 23–24) summarizes:

> Some Jews said 'Yes' to participation in pagan cults to such an extent that they became apostates or were treated as apostates by some. Moreover...there also were Jews (see Philo, *Spec.* 1.315–16) and Christians (Rev. 2:14, 20) who attempted to remain Jews and Christians and at the same time compromised to a large extent with the pagan surroundings. They said 'yes,' some in a limited way, but others went as far as participating in pagan worship.

Actually, Revelation does not view the people described in 2:14,20 as compromisers but as apostates.

[22] While the text does not explicitly indicate whether or not Jason introduced a Greek altar to Hercules and Hermes—typically the patron deities of the gymnasium—in the Jerusalem gymnasium, the implication is that he did not. Otherwise the refusal of the envoys to offer the appointed sacrifice to Hercules at Tyre (2 Macc 4:18–20) makes little sense. Presumably Jason recognized the impossibility of introducing the cult in Jerusalem, and likely saw no need. To make an

offering at Tyre, though, was socially mandated and politically astute; it is likely that he saw it in that light rather than primarily as an
act of worship.

The author of 2 Maccabees, however, obviously saw it in a different light, and understood the subsequent sacking of Jerusalem to be
vindication of his assessment. The absence of pagan worship in the
gymnasium would help to account for Jewish tolerance; Maccabean
disapproval reflects rigorous opposition to the spread of Hellenism.

Goldstein (1981: 67) describes six characteristics of Hellenism:
social contact with Greeks, some knowledge of the Greek language,
the spread of rational philosophy, the popularity of Greek literature,
the introduction of Greek education through the gymnasium, and the
increase in Greek architectural structures, such as stadiums, theaters,
and gymnasiums. He notes that none is forbidden in the Hebrew
Bible, so that liberal Jews could argue for their acceptance and rigorists
for their prohibition.

[23] According to Goldstein (1981: 86–87), the Jews in Judea
accepted the Maccabean interpretation and never built another gymnasium, and some extended the prohibition to other Greek structures,
such as the theater and stadium.

[24] Hengel 1974: 73.

[25] The text gives no indication of widespread resistance to accommodation, at least not at first (Hengel 1974: 73). This suggests
that the value judgment assigned by the text was a subsequent reflection, arising from the horrors of the sacking of Jerusalem and the
desecration of the temple, interpreted as divine judgments. Goldstein
(1981: 80) gives voice to the obvious *ex post facto* inference: "Only one
set of great innovations came in the years which just preceded those
disasters: the 'reforms' of the high priest Jason. How could they not
be the cause of God's wrath?"

[26] Borgen 1996: 21.

[27] Grabbe 1995: 63.

[28] This proposition does not lead him to syncretism, however: he
is unwilling to countenance Zeus as a name for God, and takes
Judaism as the benchmark by which to measure Greek philosophy
(cf. Hengel 1974: 265).

[29] Goldstein 1981: 83.

[30] Hengel 1974: 265.

[31] In this respect, Josephus' approach to Greek philosophy anticipates Ricci's appeal to Confucianism by one-and-a-half millennia.

[32] Hengel 1974: 266.

[33] Philo (*The Embassy to Gaius* 349–57) records a similar expedient. The emperor Gaius greeted the delegation, "Are you the god-haters who do not believe me to be a god, a god acknowledged among all the other nations but not to be named by you?" Accused of refusing to sacrifice, the Jewish delegation insisted that they had indeed done so, and extravagantly:

"Lord Gaius, we are slandered; we did sacrifice and sacrifice hecatombs too, and we did not just pour the blood upon the altar and then take the flesh home to feast and regale ourselves with it as some do, but we gave the victims to the sacred fire to be entirely consumed" (356).

This did not satisfy Gaius:

"All right," he replied, "that is true, you have sacrificed, but to another, even if it was for me; what good is it then? For you have not sacrificed to me" (357).

Three relevant points emerge from this incident. Firstly, the initial accusation and the emperor's animosity both reflect hostility toward those who refused to participate in civic religion. Secondly, the Jewish defense reveals a creative attempt to harmonize the demands of exclusivistic monotheism and hegemonistic politics. Thirdly, in contrasting their sacrifice with pagan convention, the Jewish delegation bears witness to the common pagan practice of bringing sacrificial food home for consumption. These Jews, on the other hand, refused to eat the food offerings.

[34] Given the relatively late dating of the rabbinic collections (third century CE and later), care must be taken in the application of these materials to I Corinthians 8–10. While the traditions obviously predate their collection, it is difficult to assess which portions existed in Paul's time in either written or oral form, and, of those, which he was familiar with, dependent on, or reacting to. But if nothing else, the earliest rabbinic sources provide a model of exclusivistic monotheism and illustrate the general environment in which the first-century Christians lived. Alexander (1983) provides more detailed discussion of the use of Mishnah in New Testament interpretation.

[35] Barrett 1982: 50 cf. 49; 1968: 211, 240, 244; Willis 1985a: 231; Murphy-O'Connor 1978: 557. Less flamboyant, but ultimately still slightly overstated is his assessment that:

A quick reading of *Abodah Zarah* suffices to show the repeated investigations *dia tēn suneidēsin* [on account of conscience] that were incumbent upon the devout Jew. Paul is nowhere more un-Jewish than in this *mēden anakrinontes* [judging nothing]. His whole life as a Pharisee had been essentially one of anakrisis, not least into foods (Barrett 1982: 49).

[36] Tomson 1990; Cheung 1999.

[37] Tomson (1990: 217) adds a further twist by appeal to halakha: Paul "does not teach a partial permission to eat idol food. He teaches a rational, halakhic definition of what should be considered an idol offering in uncertain cases and what should not."

Overall, Tomson's thesis is too ambitious and depends on some semantic equivocation. He starts with a broad concept of halakha: "Halakha may be described as the tradition of formulated rules of conduct regulating life in *Judaism*" (Tomson 1990: 19 *emphasis added*). But he cannot even adhere to that: in the end it turns out that halakha appears not only in rabbinic Judaism, but also in the teaching of Jesus, the writings of the apostles, and in the early Church (pp 261–62). He portrays halakha as a literary *genre* (p 19), yet concedes that all extent Christian 'halakha' appears only "in an incidental or fragmentary way" in non-halakhic genre (pp 28–29, 259). Tomson never identifies the particular characteristics of a halakhic text–form; the vagueness makes it easier to assert the presence of halakha in Paul, but harder to prove the point. For the various meanings of the term 'halakha,' see Safrai 1987: 121–22. Cheung (1994: 245–46) draws attention to the shift in meanings within Tomson's analysis.

There is also the problem of distinguishing fortuitous convergence and literary or conceptual dependence. When Augustine offers an example and position identical with Mishnah which predated him, his reasoning "resembles" the principles of halakha, which "is surprising but no actual coincidence. It shows that this particular situation was very common in the ancient world and that Jews and Christians approached it similarly" (Tomson 1990: 209). Yet when 1 Corinthians reflects only general parallels with halakha which was written a century later, "it appears that Paul must have known similar principles" from other Jewish sources (Tomson 1990: 217).

Does halakha appear in 1 Corinthians? Only if it is loosely defined as "formulated rules regarding life" (Tomson 1990: 19). That is to say, like the rabbis, Paul felt obliged to provide concrete guidance for moral conduct and based his directives in part on Scripture. Occasionally both Paul and the rabbis develop the same principle, sometimes perhaps because of a common heritage, other times perhaps simply fortuitously or inevitably (as in the case of Augustine and the Mishnah). This hardly warrants supposing that Paul is following Jewish tradition, literary genre, or text-form.

Nonetheless, Tomson renders helpful service in highlighting halakha. At the very least, these materials illustrate the sorts of issues facing any exclusivistic monotheist in the religiously pluralistic and politically hegemonistic environment of the first-century Roman empire, not least among them being idolatry and food offerings. The halakha also illustrate a favorite Jewish response: absolute prohibition. Finally the halakha reveal that even categorical prohibitions face ambiguities requiring detailed explication. Whether Paul's position converges with the rabbinic consensus can be determined only by careful exegesis of 1 Corinthians 8–10.

[38] Specifically, Paul never explicitly addresses the concrete situation which shenists most commonly face and find most problematic: if they know that some food at a meal in the home has been offered to idols, but no one draws attention to its origin, may they quietly eat or must they resolutely abstain?

[39] Cheung 1999: 81 cf. 297.

[40] Cheung 1999: 296; cf. 162. While arguing that Paul's position derives primarily from Scripture, he adds: "Of course, it is foolhardy to think that Paul could have bypassed centuries of Jewish interpretative traditions and approached the Scriptures with a *tabula rasa.* His understanding of Scripture would have been, to a considerable extent, conditioned by his upbringing and training in Judaism of his day."

To be fair, Cheung (1999: 76–81) recognizes that Paul's position cannot simply be inferred from Jewish prohibitions: the coming of Christ led to decisive changes in circumcision, Sabbath, and dietary laws (e.g. Rom. 14:1–23; Gal. 2:11–13; 3:1–25). At the same time, he rightly insists that the abrogation of food laws in Romans 14–15 cannot simply be extended to permit the consumption of food offered to idols, for Paul treats the two issues separately and differently. Moreover, he does devote considerable space to exegesis of 1 Corinthians 8–10 (pp 82–164).

Nevertheless, where Paul is not explicit, Cheung's argument relies heavily on Jewish precedent. Paul clearly opposes idolatry (e.g., Rom. 1:21–23; 1 Cor. 12:2; 1 Thess. 1:9). But a fundamental issue in the rabbinics is to set the boundaries for what constitutes idolatry. Given Paul's renunciation of his Pharisaic background and its foundational values (Phil 3:4–9), it cannot be assumed that his demarkation of the boundaries would remain unchanged.

[41] Curiously, Segal (1990: 234–35) acknowledges that Paul opposes the Pharisaic position on food laws and commensality with

Gentiles, yet nonetheless supposes that the apostle's warnings against idolatry derive from his background ("He has brought his Pharisaic sensibility into an entirely new environment")! Gooch (1993: 140–1) too supposes that Paul opposed idol food based on his self-understanding as a Jew.

[42] Lieberman 1950: 120–21.

CHAPTER 7

Theology, Rights, and Christian Moral Ethic: Idol Offerings and Communal Meals in Corinthian Perspective

Summary: In 1 Corinthians 8–9, Paul is not setting out his own position, but is refuting the Corinthian justification for participating in cultic feasts. Their argument reflects the effects of social location on ritual interpretation. Read as indirect communication, his reply harmonizes naturally with his argument in chapter 10.

At first glance, 1 Corinthians 8–10 promises to provide the goal of our lengthy quest. After all, where better to uncover the biblical position on eating idol food than in the most detailed discussion of the topic in the entire Bible?

Unfortunately, the passage appears to be fundamentally contradictory. In 8:4 Paul dismisses idols as 'nothing'; yet in 10:20 he characterizes them as demons. In 8:7–13 he apparently takes a permissive stance toward eating idol food, provided that weaker Christians are not harmed; yet in 10:1–22 he categorically prohibits consumption.[1] In addition, the discussion of rights in chapter 9 is something of a digression, interrupting the teaching on idol offerings. A wide range of stratagems have been devised to resolve these problems, including partitioning[2] and various semantic reinterpretations.[3] None proves convincing.

In the end, appeal to an external solution is unnecessary. The appearance of contradiction arises from inattention to the rhetorical context and the development of the argument.[4]

Paul had written the Corinthians an earlier letter, in which he categorically forbid them to associate with a wide range of sinners, including idolaters (5:9–10). This could be taken as prohibiting not only meals in temples but also meals with non-Christian friends and even meat purchased from the market (all the more since the Jews adopted such a stance, and Paul's Jewish roots would have been readily apparent to a predominantly Gentile congregation). Apparently the Corinthians took exception, and replied with a justification of their own position.[5]

In chapters 8–10, Paul responds. Chapters 8–9 are conspicuously marked by a series of affirmations followed by qualifications. The common and reasonable explanation for this feature is that Paul cites or paraphrases Corinthian arguments as though in agreement, but then so severely qualifies the propositions as to restrict or even contradict them.

Read in this way, 1 Corinthians 8–9 employs indirect communication.[6] Given the low regard for Paul among the Corinthian Christians generally, and their opposition to his teaching on this issue, a direct challenge would only exacerbate the tension and cause them to become more obstinate. So, in keeping both with common sense and with ancient rhetorical principles, Paul unfolds his position gradually and progressively.[7] He first responds obliquely and at length to the arguments of the Corinthian strong (8:1–9:27). Next he lays the foundation for his own position (10:1–13). Only then does he offer his verdict on the consumption of idol feasts (10:14–11:1).

In other words, chapters 8–9 provide Paul's rebuttal of the Corinthian argument, rather than an exposition of his own position.[8] Contemporary application, therefore, appropriately prioritizes chapter 10. All the same, the thrust of the two sections is compatible. Read attentively, chapters 8–9 strongly and persistently discourage the consumption of idol food; 10:1–22 prohibits it outright. The two passages differ only in rhetoric method: the former is subtle and indirect; the latter, direct and unequivocal.

The pattern of affirmation, then qualification, makes it possible both to reconstruct the Corinthian position and argument, and to differentiate their argument from Paul's correction. This chapter reconstructs the Corinthian position and the apostle's response in chapters 8–9; the following chapter examines Paul's statement of his own position in chapter 10.

Corinthian Rationale and Pauline Refutation

While the significance of the pattern of affirmation/qualification is widely recognized, considerable debate occurs over the details.[9] What is needed is a method for distinguishing those statements which represent the Corinthian position or argument from those which represent qualifications by Paul.[10]

A Methodology for Reconstruction

The most reliable marker of a Corinthian tenet is the pattern of affirmation followed by a series of qualifying remarks so restrictive that for all practical purposes they amount to an implicit contradiction. Another indicator is the repetition of characteristically Corinthian—and non–Pauline—vocabulary and themes. The most obvious is the elitist appeal to 'knowledge' (*gnōsis*), reflected especially in Paul's frequent sarcastic rhetorical question, "Do you not know?" (3:16; 5:6; 6:2,3,9,15,16,19; 9:13,24; but elsewhere in Paul only once, Rom. 6:16). As the argument develops, other distinctive emphases appear, including the appeal to rights, the assertion of individualism, and the claim to a higher spiritual status.

Other indicators include apparent contradictions (e.g., 'we all have knowledge' 8:1 cf. 'not all have this knowledge' 8:7), the ironic use of key terms (e.g., 'build up' in 8:10; cf. 8:1; 10:23), and the juxtaposition of themes (e.g., the eating of idol food and the surrendering of personal rights in chapters 8–10, or the evaluation of leaders and the place of wisdom in chapters 1–4, and the critique of spiritual pride and the deflation of tongues in chapters 12–14).

Some aspects of the Corinthian argument are easily reconstructed from such markers. Other clues are more allusive and ambiguous. Once the basic outline is sketched, details can be filled in from more subtle clues.[11]

"We all have knowledge" (8:1)

This clause is widely recognized as a Corinthian affirmation.[12] The redundancy of the initial phrase is one indication: "*we know that we all have knowledge.*" In addition, Paul eventually contradicts the affirmation outright: "Not all share this knowledge" (8:7).[13] Moreover, toward the end of the chapter Paul twice refers directly and caustically to the Corinthian claim: "*you who have knowledge* and recline in the temple" (8:10); "the weak is destroyed by *your knowledge*" (8:11). Throughout this epistle, pride in their own perception reflects the Corinthian attitude, one which Paul corrects (ch 1–4) or satirizes (3:16; 5:6; 6:2,3,9,15,16,19; 9:13,24; 10:1).

The clearest indication that Paul is here quoting the Corinthians is his immediate and emphatic disavowal of knowledge in 8:1b–3.[14] Theology alone forms an inadequate basis for determining the proper course of action because it suffers from three liabilities or limitations (8:1b–3). First, it 'inflates' the claimant rather than 'building up' others (8:1c).[15] Secondly, its arrogance reflects actual ignorance of God

(8:2). Thirdly, it is the wrong priority: what matters most is not our knowledge about God, but living in love so that he acknowledges us (8:3).[16]

Thus, Paul initially suggests that his topic is idol offerings, but shifts immediately to a brief yet searing critique of intellectual and theological arrogance in Christian ethics and spirituality. In one form or another, the root "know" appears six times in these three verses, while there is no reference to idol offerings after verse 1a. Specifically, Paul dismisses claims to theological profundity as pretentious, oxymoronic, and misdirected. The relevance of this corrective to the discussion of idol offerings is allusive at this stage, but becomes evident as the argument develops.

"An idol has no reality and there is no God but one" (8:4)

Again the introductory 'we know' and the immediate qualifications (8:5–6) indicate that this quote or paraphrase represents a Corinthian position.[17] Clearly Paul is not entirely in agreement.[18]

The point of 8:5–6 is somewhat elusive because it is allusive, but Paul clearly intends to qualify the categorical denial of idols and other gods in two directions. Objectively, even if they are not actual divinities, these beings do in fact exist:

> for even if there are many so-called gods, whether in heaven or
> on earth, just as there are many gods and many lords (8:5b)...[19]

Subjectively, while Christians do not venerate them either through direct worship or in feasting, the implication is that others do:

> *To us* there is one God, the Father, from whom all things came
> into existence and for whom *we* live, and one Lord Jesus
> Christ, through whom all things came into existence and
> through whom *we* live (8:6).[20]

Paul does not elaborate these qualifications until 10:20–22, where they are found to be decisive in prohibiting participation in cultic feasts.

"Eating commends us to God" (cf 8:8)

Verse 8 marks a slight shift in method: instead of citing and then qualifying the Corinthian position, Paul simply contradicts it.[21] Consequently, the simple expedient of removing the negatives in verse 8 yields the underlying Corinthian viewpoint:

> 'Food commends us to God:
> if we do not eat, we suffer loss;
> if we eat, we gain.'[22]

Those who eat idol food clearly perceive this to be evidence of their strong and divinely accredited faith, while abstention is evidence of ignorance (8:7 cf. 8:10,11) and weak faith (8:7,9,10,11,12).[23] Paul sharply rejects both evaluations:

'Food does not commend us to God:

if we do not eat, we suffer no loss;

if we eat, we gain nothing.'

Contrary to what the Corinthian strong assert, eating idol offerings is no mark of strong faith, and gains no approval from God.[24]

"We have the right to eat" (cf. 8:9)

Continuing in the pattern of 8:8, Paul again alludes to the Corinthian position without quoting it, but their claim can clearly be inferred from his caustic reference to "this right *of yours*" (8:9). The strong insist that they have the right (*exousia*) to eat idol food.

The same attitude is evident both earlier in the letter, and later in this section: the Corinthians repeatedly justify their behavior with the slogan, "all things are permissible (*exestin*)" (6:12a,c; 10:23a,c). Each time Paul adds a restrictive qualification: "not everything is beneficial" (6:12b); "I shall not be mastered by anything" (6:12d); "not everything is beneficial" (10:23b); "not everything builds up" (10:23d). The pattern of blanket assertion followed by careful qualification, and the obvious suitability of such a slogan in justifying participation in cultic feasts, point to this claim as part of the Corinthian rationalization.[25] The corrective on benefiting and edifying others also ties in with Paul's emphasis in these chapters and elsewhere in this letter (cf. 8:1,9–11; 7:35; 10:33; 14:4).

The Corinthian insistence on 'rights' accounts for Paul's extended assertion of his own rights throughout the first half of chapter 9 (9:4,5,6,12).[26] As an apostle (9:1–2), he possesses the right to financial support (9:3–6), a claim supported by a series of nine analogies and arguments (9:7–14). The reason for—and function of—this claim becomes evident in the next portion of their argument and his rebuttal.

"Our example strengthens the faith of the weak" (cf. 8:10)

This line of argument is suggested by an otherwise peculiar feature in these final verses of chapter eight. At first Paul seems to imply that those who eat idol food publicly serve as helpful role models for other Christians: "For if someone sees you who has knowledge eating in a temple, will not his weak conscience be *built up* to eat idol food?" (8:10). But the next verse overturns the portrait: "Thus the weak is *destroyed* by your knowledge" (8:11). Such 'modeling' does not *'build up'* but rather *'beats up' (tuptō)* the conscience of the weak (8:12b). The scathing wordplay between 'build up' and 'destroy'/ 'beat–up' indicates that 8:10 reflects the Corinthian claim.

Paul responds to this argument in two parts: first, in 8:7–13; then in 9:15–27. The earlier paragraph begins with a direct disavowal of the claim in 8:1, "*Not all* have this knowledge" (8:7).[27] The subsequent verses contrast two groups: the weak and the strong.[28] The weak come from an idolatrous background, and have still not shaken cultic associations (8:7b).[29] Their conscience is sensitized (8:7c), and thus defiled if they eat (8:7d).[30]

The strong, in contrast, participate without qualm (8:10,11). Yet their example could cause the weak to do likewise, in violation of their conscience (8:10) and to the destruction of their faith (8:11).[31] To eat under such circumstances is a sin both against the weak and against Christ (8:12). It would be better, then, to renounce not only that meat known to have been previously offered to idols, but even to become vegetarian (8:13). That is, they must not claim their rights if others might be injured, but must renounce them for the sake of others.

Paul elaborates on this theme in the second half of chapter 9. Having substantiated his right to financial support in 9:1–14, he explains that he renounced this prerogative for the sake of the Corinthians, for the progress of the gospel, and for his own salvation (9:15–27). Thus, Paul presents himself as an illustration of the appropriate restriction of individual freedom for the welfare of others.[32] His ministry among and to the Corinthians reflects the same values and models the very behavior that he has just urged of them in 8:9–13.[33]

Summary and Ramifications

Attention to the structure and flow of the argument in chapters 8 and 9 clarifies the Corinthian rationale, the thrust of Paul's response, and the relationship between chapters 8 and 10.

The Corinthian Rationale

The dominant faction among the Corinthians held themselves to be theologically astute, and demanded the right to follow in the direction that truth led them (8:1). The fundamental theological tenets underpinning their consumption of idol offerings were the tandem propositions that there is only one God and that idols have no reality (8:4). If gods and idols really do not exist, then food offered to them is inconsequential; and if Christians worship the true God alone, they are not guilty of idolatry when they eat food offerings.

To this way of thinking, eating idol offerings is not only permissible, but actually advantageous on several counts: it honors the true God, commends the faith of the confident (8:8), and strengthens the faith of the insecure (8:10–12). In addition to these specific benefits, the general principle of freedom in Christ must prevail (8:9): all things are permissible (10:23). On these grounds, the Corinthian strong argued that Paul was wrong to impose restrictions against participation in meals that included food offered to idols.[34]

Various interpreters have appealed with more or less success to a number of other texts for light on the Corinthian rationale and argument; for example, 10:1–6;[35] 10:25–27;[36] and 10:29b–30.[37] Nonetheless, the texts noted above represent a cautious consensus, and suffice to provide a fairly comprehensive outline of Corinthian reasoning.[38] Given the ambiguities, a minimalist reconstruction is prudent.

Paul's Response

In the pattern of indirect communication (*insinuatio*), Paul begins in apparent agreement with the Corinthians, but rapidly corrects their estimation of the importance of theology (8:1–3), the content of their theology (8:4–6), and their claim to the right to act as they wish (8:7–13 cf. 9:1–27). Participation in idol feasts starts out as their apparent 'right' (8:9) only to end up as sin, not only against other Christians but also against Christ (8:12). From having the prerogative to eat any meat—even that which has been offered to idols (8:9–10)— they end up potentially obliged to abstain from all meat (8:13).

Indirect communication was a characteristic of first-century Greco-Roman culture (as of most contemporary Asian cultures). If an audience is ill-disposed toward the speaker, ancient rhetoricians advised, it is best to begin with a point of common agreement, a personal example, or a narration, in order to pave the way for introducing the controversial matter.[39] The purpose is to circumvent the audience's defenses, often with subtle anticipations of subsequent corrections. Beginning circumspectly, a speaker or author often ends by saying directly what was first only implicit (*Ad Herennium* 1.6.9–10; Quintilian 4.1.42; 9.1.29; 9.2.66,69,92; Pseudo-Demetrius 5.287).[40]

Paul employs indirect communication here for some of the same reasons as the rhetorical handbooks advise. His defensiveness throughout the epistle (e.g., 2:1–5; 3:10–11; 4:1–5; 4:18–21; 7:25,40; 14:37–38) and within these three chapters (9:2–3; 10:29) reflects the hostility of his audience. The pattern of affirmation, then qualification, indicates that they are sympathetic to a viewpoint contrary to his own. Those not kindly disposed toward him in the first place may have long since tired of his strident rebukes, firm demands, and open threats (e.g., 1:26–31; 3:1–4; 4:8–13,18–21; 5:1–2; 6:7–11,15–20; cf. 11:17–22; 14:20–25). Determined eventually to warn them in the direst tones, Paul seeks to defuse their opposition and to gain a hearing by finding common ground, or at least by appearing initially to agree with them.[41] He then proceeds cautiously, qualifying their position point by point, until his fundamental disagreement becomes obvious.

The Topic of 8:1–9:27

While Paul initially purports to address the topic of idol offerings ("Concerning idol offerings," 8:1a), and specifically, the consumption of idol offerings ("Concerning the eating of idol offerings," 8:4a), he does not directly do so in this chapter. This is not to suggest that he has lost his train of thought, or that the chapter has no bearing on the issue. To the contrary, 8:1a and 8:4b clearly relate this discussion to the eating of idol offerings. Moreover, in the course of the chapter Paul touches on the nature of idols (8:4–6) and illustrates his point by reference to joining a meal in the temple (8:10–12). Nonetheless, the consumption of idol offerings is not the theme of this chapter. It is merely the presenting occasion and the context of application for the actual theme.

The central focus and purpose of the chapter are provided by the initial slogan in 8:1a, "We all knowledge have." This chapter is concerned with the role played by theology in reaching a verdict on the issue of idol offerings. Its thesis is along the lines: "Christian ethic is characterized not by theological elitism, but by concern for others." The thesis is stated in general terms in 8:1–3; then restated by way of concrete illustration in 8:7–13.

This point needs laboring because its significance is widely— nearly universally—ignored. All too often urgent contemporary questions are allowed to distort the point of the text. Where Christians still face the pressure to eat food offered to gods or spirit beings, or when systematic theologians want to collate the full range of biblical data on the issue, they inevitably come to this text with question already in hand: "May Christians eat food which has been offered?"

Once the question is asked, 8:1–13 is inevitably taken—or rather, mistaken—as providing the answer. After all, 8:1 promises such an answer, and 8:4 repeats the promise. On a quick reading, 8:10 seems to fulfill the promise. The conclusion hastily follows: given that Christians must not eat meals in a temple dining room if others are likely to see and suffer harm as a result, then it is permissible to eat provided no weaker believer is likely to see.

This reading of the text begs the question at two points. For one, the use of chapter 8 to answer either the systematics or pragmatics question misses the actual point of the text. The thrust of this section is carefully, clearly, and consistently marked: the use of knowledge in love and the restriction of individual rights for the welfare of others. The hypothetical temple meal is simply a relevant illustration of the overall principle. While that illustration undoubtedly has implications for the broader issue of consuming idol offerings, inferences must be carefully drawn because they are at best implicit rather than explicit, and thus are more easily misconstrued.

For the other, given that the purpose of the case study—indeed, of the entire chapter!—is to restrict participation in temple meals, it is a significant reach to use the example in defense of participation. Logically, the prohibition of temple meals where others might see and stumble does not necessarily imply permission in cases when others would not be negatively affected. Perhaps the necessary conditions are unrealistic: given that temples are public settings, can those who wish to eat ever be confident that no weaker Christian will see them? Perhaps the condition is only one factor to consider: once Paul directly addresses the issue of eating idol food he may offer additional restrictions. Quite simply, a conditional prohibition does not necessarily constitute a permission where the conditions are not in force, especially when the entire thrust of the argument has been driving toward restricting the behavior.[42]

To infer a permission from the obverse of 8:9 actually misreads the text as though Paul were saying, "You may eat idol meat in the temple unless someone will be scandalized."[43] But this is wrong on both counts: Paul does not here authorize the consumption of idol food; nor is the possibility of stumbling others the circumstance under which the permission is curtailed. To the contrary, Paul implicitly prohibits the consumption of idol food: "Beware lest perchance this authority of yours be a stumbling block for the weak" (8:9), and the possibility of stumbling others provides the ground of the prohibition.

In any event, contrary to common consensus, 1 Corinthians 8–9 does not provide Paul's position on consuming idol food. Instead, his central concerns are to reorient the Corinthian ethic from individualistic self-assertion to communal concern, and to add nuance to their simplistic denial of the reality of idols. Certainly, his correctives carry implications for the eating of idol offerings, but these must be extrapolated with caution, for the simple reason that this issue is only the context or background of these chapters, not the foreground, theme, or purpose.

Reconciling Chapters 8 and 10

The perception that chapters 8 and 10:1–22 are in conflict arises from a failure to recognize the purpose of chapters 8–9. The apparent discrepancy between 8:4 (where Paul seemingly portrays idols as impotent unrealities) and 10:20 (where he portrays them as demonic) resolves when the former is properly seen to be the Corinthian position, which Paul implicitly qualifies in 8:5–6, but does not directly contradict until 10:19–20.[44] Paul's position in both chapters is carefully stated and complementary: idols are lifeless (8:4 cf. 10:19); but the worship offered them is directed toward 'so-called gods and lords' (8:5) which are actually demons (10:20).[45] The only difference is that 10:19–20 is explicit, elaborating the allusions of 8:4–6.

The supposed contradiction between the implied permission of 8:7–13 and the categorical prohibition of 10:1–22 arises from three errors. First, it incautiously reads a permission into the obverse of what Paul actually says in 8:7–13. Secondly, it fails to attend to Paul's purpose in chapter 8: to undermine the Corinthian rationale for eating idol food, not to establish his own position. Thirdly, it overlooks the consistently restrictive intent of these verses.

Every verse in 8:7–13 discourages participation in idol feasts: "their conscience, since it is weak, is defiled" (8:7); "food does not commend us to God: if we do not eat, we suffer no loss; if we do eat, we gain nothing" (8:8); "beware lest somehow this right of yours become a stumbling block to the weak" (8:9); "his conscience, being weak, will be 'built up' to eat" (8:10); "the weak is destroyed by your knowledge" (8:11); "by sinning thus against your brethren and wounding their weak conscience" (8:12); "if my eating causes my brother to stumble, I will never eat meat again, lest my brother be caused to stumble" (8:13). This is the strongest possible discouragement short of an outright prohibition.[46]

As Newton observes, "whilst verse 9 might appear to grant conditional permission to the 'strong' to eat temple meals, yet the overall thrust of 8:7–13 is highly negative, repeatedly underlining the very serious consequences of such eating."[47]

To put the matter plainly, the apparently irreconcilable contradictions result from the failure to attend to the flow of the argument in these chapters. What then is Paul's position on eating food offered to idols? The answer is best sought from texts where the apostle addresses the question directly, rather than by inference from passages where he is addressing other (albeit related) issues and appealing to cultic meals merely by way of illustration. Instead of approaching the biblical text with a preformed question and picking out those verses that seem to provide an answer, it is imperative first to trace the flow of the argument in the passage, and only then to collate its teaching on the topic of interest.

When this is done, it becomes apparent that 1 Corinthians 8 and 9 are not directly indicating how Christians should respond to meals involving idol offerings. Instead, these chapters serve as prolegomena, sketching out a methodology for approaching the question at hand; or, actually, refuting the faulty methodology the Corinthians employed in justifying their practice. Certainly they carry implications for the reconstruction of Paul's position; but they do not directly elucidate his position.

What is a valid basis for determining whether or not a Christian may eat food offerings? The answer of chapters 8–9 is largely negative: not theology alone (8:1–3), and explicitly not an unnuanced affirmation of monotheism (8:4–6), much less the autonomous right of the self-professed elite (8:8–9). Rather theology must be coupled (not juxtaposed) with love (8:1–3). Intrepid monotheism must be coupled with the recognition that idols represent real spirit-beings, even if they are not true gods or lords (8:4–6). Any supposed right to partake is subordinate to the welfare of others (8:7–13). Paul's advice is consistent with his apostolic ministry among the Corinthians (9:1–18). More than that, it is what God requires not just of apostles but of all Christians (9:19–27).

In their entirety, the purpose of chapters 8 and 9 is to reject a narrowly theological and individualistic framework for addressing the question presented by the prevalence of idol offerings in communal meals. These chapters never attempt to construct a comprehensive framework, much less do they provide explicit guidelines. For that we must look to 1 Corinthians 10. But before moving on, one more aspect to the Corinthian position warrants attention; namely, the possibility that social location played a role in the divergent responses to idol food within the church.

The Effects of Social Location on Corinthian Perceptions

The surveys of contemporary Chinese practice, Chinese literary traditions, the Christian missions to China, and ancient Greco-Roman religions, have each highlighted the effects of social location on cult interpretation. In short, while religious practice generally transcends social location, ritual interpretations largely vary according to social location. Specifically, populist interpretations tend toward spiritism; elite, toward rationalism; and political-bureaucratic, toward pragmatism.[48]

The question naturally follows: Are the effects of social location similarly evident in 1 Corinthians 8–10? Here the paucity of evidence poses a fundamental problem.[49] Like forensic technicians examining trace evidence, New Testament scholars have in recent decades been pouring over the minutia of the biblical record in search of details that promise to reveal the social location of the Pauline churches and its effects on their theology and practice. A basic consensus has emerged that Paul's problems in Corinth—including the dispute over idol food—came particularly from the relative elite within the congregation.[50]

If this consensus is well-founded, it would advance a secondary thesis of this monograph. The main proposition stands regardless: Paul addressed an environment much like Chinese East Asia, with rites strikingly comparable and interpretations similarly diverse. These similarities give rise to the hope that his advice to the Corinthian church will provide helpful guidance today. But the parallel would be closer—and the contemporary application of 1 Corinthians 8–10 correspondingly more direct—if it turned out that the Corinthian elite in particular were the ones denying the existence of demons and permitting the consumption of idol offerings, with the non-elite more inclined to spiritistic interpretations.[51] Three lines of evidence suggest that social location likely exerted its influence within the Corinthian church, including in the matter of idol offerings.[52]

The Social Status of the Corinthian Congregation

Paul twice describes the social status of the Corinthian church. In 1:26, he reminds them: "Not many of you are wise according to human standards, not many are powerful, not many well-born" (1:26). Three conclusions follow, especially from the use of 'well-born' (*eugenēs*).[53] First, in context, the Corinthians are clearly claiming an elite status of some sort, whether socio-economic or spiritual (and it is not entirely clear that these two may be neatly distinguished). Secondly, Paul deflates their pretensions by appeal to the less-than-elite social origins of the majority. Thirdly, Paul admits that this argument *ad hominem* is effective against most—but not all—of his antagonists. Some were indeed 'well-born.'

From this, it seems likely that the majority of the trouble-makers were socially ambitious, claiming an elite status they did not possess by virtue of birth. Their precise socio-economic standing remains uncertain, but most seem to be neither ruling class nor impoverished. This supports Malherbe's proposed intermediate wealth.[54]

The second description of the Corinthians' status comes in 4:10, where Paul satirizes their self-elevation and their devaluation of him:

We are fools for Christ, you are wise in Christ;

we are weak, but you are strong;

you are esteemed, but we are dishonored.[55]

The descriptions "wise, strong, esteemed" clearly reflect a Corinthian claim to prestige.[56]

Elite Individuals within the Corinthian Congregation

Apart from these two general comments about the entire Corinthian congregation, the text provides a number of clues pointing to the possibility of individual wealth. Among these are holding office, owning homes, rendering service to the church, and business travel. Whether individually or combined, these references may not be definitive, but they are at least suggestive.

Crispus, an early convert, was a synagogue ruler and as such may have been responsible for upkeep of the property. If so, this would have required considerable private means.[57] Erastus was the city treasurer (Rom. 16:23); this may have necessitated sufficient financial and social standing to support public works projects.[58] The evidence is far from certain on either score, but either interpretation is at least within the realm of possibility.

Several members of the church likely owned their homes. References to the 'households' of Crispus (Acts 18:8) and Stephanas (1 Cor. 1:16 cf. 16:15–17) are suggestive of both home ownership and the possession of slaves, and consequently imply both wealth and social status.[59] Other members host meetings in their homes, including: Gaius (Rom. 16:23); Aquila and Priscilla (1 Cor. 16:19; Rom. 16:3; Acts 18:26); and Titius Justus (Acts 18:7).[60] Home ownership is a likely indicator of at least intermediate wealth.

In addition, Paul refers to a number of people who rendered service to him or to the church, and benefaction would require a measure of disposable income. From Stephanas (1 Cor. 16:15–18), to Phoebe (Rom. 16:1–2), to the collection for the Jerusalem church (2 Cor. 8:4), the support of missionaries and impoverished churches is a regular feature of first-century church life. Though these services may involve sacrificial generosity, they still suggest at least a measure of surplus wealth.[61]

Finally, Paul's various letters refer to a number of the Corinthian Christians traveling from one city to another. While not all travelers are well-heeled, travel generally presupposes an income higher than subsistence level.[62]

These considerations fall short of conclusive proof that the Corinthians either possessed or lacked elite social status. But they provide reasonable evidence of a range of intermediate wealth and social status.[63] Meeks, a prime mover in promoting the consensus, acknowledges the apparent absence of either ruling elite or truly impoverished, yet concludes that "the levels in between...are well represented."[64]

The presence of even a moderate range of stratification makes it possible to test for a correlation between socio-economic status and theological conviction.

Elites and the Controversies at Corinth

A number of the controversies in 1 Corinthians likely reflect the effects of socio-economic stratification.[65] The value placed on wisdom and knowledge (1:18–4:13), for instance, reflects an elitist soteriology. Whether that in turns reflects elite status or is a form of compensation for inferior social status is both moot and largely inconsequential.[66] Whether prestigious or pretentious, the subjects of 1:18–4:13 were clearly intellectually and spiritually elitist.

Litigation (6:1–11) assumes sufficient wealth both to be defrauded in the first place and to seek legal redress in the second.[67] This need not imply membership in the ruling elite.[68] But it does presuppose greater prosperity than mere subsistence.

The association of gluttony with immorality (6:12–20) was presumably not exclusive to the well-to-do, but it was at least a characteristic feature of their formal banquets.[69] Dio (77/78.28–29,33) notes specifically that those able to obtain abundant food and drink as well as male or female consorts included "satraps and princes and, forsooth, vulgarians and flunkies who have become wealthy." The 'temperate man of cultivation,' however, is swayed neither by "fame nor wealth nor pleasures of eating or drinking or copulating" (Dio 77/78.30).

This is a transparent attempt to curb gluttony and sexual immorality on the part of the elite (cf. Philo *Vit* 48–63).[70]

The improprieties involved in the Corinthian celebration of the Lord's Supper (11:17–34) also likely reflect the misconduct of the relatively more prosperous: they are able to arrive early; they bring their own food, engage in the typical banquet behavior of gorging themselves on food and wine, and possess private homes where they otherwise can eat their fill on their own.[71]

Each of these controversies arguably involves a sociological component, alongside the theological.[72] Whether or not that entails elite status outside the church is difficult to assess, but at a minimum it involves elite pretensions within the church.

Elites and the Consumption of Idol Offerings[73]

Several features in chapters 8–10 suggest that social stratification also played a role in the controversy over idol offerings.[74] First, the disparagement of the weak by the 'strong' is indicative of elite pretensions, and possibly also carries socio-economic overtones (as in 1:26–28 and 4:8–13).[75] Secondly, the appeal to *gnōsis* is characteristically elitist.[76] Thirdly, Paul interacts almost exclusively with the strong; that is, with the elite: they are his informants ('we all have knowledge'), his addressees ('be careful lest this liberty of yours'), and apparently his critics (9:1–27).[77]

Undoubtedly the strongest evidence of elitism comes in the social location of the slogan, "All things are permissible" (1 Cor. 10:23; cf. 6:12).[78] This was a common slogan in description of the elite in Greco-Roman literature.[79] Dio (62.2) describes rulers who hold unbridled power: "because it is permissible for them to take all things, they lust after everything." Xenophon (8.1.30) uses similar terms to commend king Cyrus for not abusing his authority. Polybius (3.24.12) uses the phrase to describe the rights of a Roman citizen in Carthage.

Dio provides further parallels with 1 Corinthians. The privilege of unrestricted authority calls for self-control (*egkrateia*), whether on the part of Christians (cf. 1 Cor. 7:9; 9:25), or on the part of the elite, to whom equally 'all things are permissible' (Dio 3.10). Similarly, the ruler for whom it is 'permissible' to take all things must practice 'self-restraint' (Dio 62:2). The logic of this attempt to restrict the indiscriminate and uncontrolled exercise of freedom by the elite is remarkably similar to Paul's admonition to the Corinthians (1 Cor. 9:1–27).

Most striking is the extensive discussion between Dio and an interlocutor over the relationship between freedom (*eleutheria/eleutheros* cf. 1 Cor. 9:1,19), slavery (*douleia/doulos* cf. 1 Cor. 9:19; cf. *exousiazō*,

6:12), and the permissibility of doing whatever one wants (Dio 14). The antagonist first proposes that freedom belongs to those for whom it is permissible to do whatever they wish (Dio 14.13–18). After further probing by Dio, he revises this to propose that freedom is possessed by "the one who has authority [*exousia* cf. 1 Cor. 6:12; 8:9; 9:4,5,6,12,18] to act or not, as he wishes" (Dio 14.14). Further discussion leads to the restriction of the permissible to what is, among other characteristics, 'beneficial' (*sumferon* cf. 1 Cor. 10:23) (Dio 14.16).

The conversation closes with a cornucopia of terms familiar to readers of 1 Corinthians, including 'permissible,' 'wise,' 'foolish,' 'free,' and 'slaves':

> Therefore, for the wise, whatever they wish to do is permissible; but the foolish attempt to do what they wish although it is not permissible; so that it follows of necessity that while the wise are free and are allowed to act as they wish, the ignorant are slaves and do that which is not permissible for them (Dio 14.17).

Relating freedom, knowledge, and the permissible, Dio (14.18) concludes, "Therefore we are forced to define freedom as the knowledge of what is allowable and what is forbidden, and slavery as ignorance of what is allowed and what is not."

Winter concludes: "The free man and the élite in power do not have the restraints of those without social status. They can live by the maxim 'all things are permitted'."[80] Given their rationale, then, it seems likely that advocates of eating idol offerings come from among the elite. This might be a cultural elite, despite their minimal numbers in the Corinthian church (1:26).[81] Or, possibly, the Corinthian 'strong' apply the slogan by analogy, claiming a spiritual elitism resulting from an over-realized eschatology.[82] Whether their claim to status reflects actual gentry rank or mere spiritualizing pretensions, their logic presupposes elite values.

Conclusion

Ample evidence supports the conclusion that the Corinthian church included people of intermediate status and wealth. Compelling evidence indicates that the strong considered themselves to be of higher spiritual status and adopted the conduct and the attitudes toward idol offerings—and toward the 'weak'—which characterized the pagan elite. The elitism of the strong comes to most conspicuous manifestation in their rationale: they claim theological insight (8:1) and disparage non-participants as weak (8:7, 10, 11, 12).

Whether the Corinthian elitism includes a socio-economic dimension or is restricted to spiritual pretensions, whether the claim corresponds to inherited status or is reflective of social climbing, whether it has a basis in social realities or is compensation for low status, these distinctions are not crucial for present purposes. What matters is that the strong ones claim the status of elite within the church, and—consistent with that claim—accept the rationalistic interpretation of the rites characteristic of the pagan social elite.

While conduct and interpretation are inextricably linked—conduct flows out of interpretation—it is fundamentally interpretation at issue in 1 Corinthians 8–10. The strong ones reason that idols are impotent and gods do not exist (8:4); therefore, they may attend feasts held in the temple. For the weak, however, the cultic associations of idolatry are still fresh in mind (8:7); consequently, they cannot in good conscience participate.

Unfortunately, both sides in the contemporary debate over social stratification in Corinth tend to focus on cult participation rather than on ritual interpretation. Theissen argues that the elite would have been under professional and social obligation to eat, while the poor could abstain without suffering any disadvantage.[83] Meggitt retorts that 10:27–29 reflects the presence of both strong and weak Christians at the same feast.[84] Each focuses on participation in, or absence from, the feast.

In chapters 8–10, however, Paul centers his attention firmly on interpretation prior to discussing participation. Is theology sufficient justification for action (8:1–3)? Do the gods exist (8:4–6)? Are idols impotent (8:4–5; 10:19–22)? Does God commend bold faith (8:7–8)? Do Christians have the right to participate (8:9; cf. 9:1–14)? Is it appropriate to exercise that right (8:10–13; cf. 9:15–23)? Has God ever revealed his sentiments on this issue (10:1–13)? What is the significance of participation in a cultic feast (10:15–20a)? Paul's actual verdict on participation in the feasts does not come until 10:20b–22, after he has spent two chapters refuting the Corinthian rationale, and two-thirds of a chapter charting his own.

But that is to anticipate the next chapter. For the moment it is sufficient to note the ample evidence that social location plays a significant role in the Corinthian dispute. Within the Corinthian church, as in Greco-Roman society generally, the elite tend toward rational interpretations of the rites, and the non-elite, toward spiritistic interpretations.

The conflict in Corinth reflects somewhat stronger emotions and antagonisms than exist generally in the Asian Church today, but otherwise the two situations are largely comparable. For each, idol food plays a significant role not only in religious celebrations, but also in normal social relationships. Indeed, while religious celebrations and social relations can be differentiated, in neither culture can they be separated.

Given the opposing pressures of social obligation and Christian commitment, it comes as no surprise to find that Christians in both contexts struggle with the appropriate course of action and disagree over both rationale and conclusion. Now as then, too, the effects of social location on cult interpretation are apparent, with the elite favoring rationalistic interpretations, and the masses, spiritistic understandings. These similarities between ancient Corinth and modern Asia raise the hope that Paul's directives for the first century will resolve the ambiguities of our own time.

Endnotes

[1] Yeo (1995: 75–83, 157–60, 180–83, 209–11) lists a lengthy series of other 'drastic differences' between these two passages, including style, theme, and rhetoric. Mostly his list reflects a methodological formalism (e.g., the prescriptive use of ancient rhetoric), and few are improved by his extensive rearrangements (e.g., the resultant literary transitions are no less rough).

[2] Partitioning rearranges the text, excising and relocating 10:1–22, generally to an earlier and stricter letter from Paul to the Corinthians (e.g., von Soden 1972; Jewett 1978; Yeo 1995). For surveys of various proposals, see Hurd 1965: 43–47; Sellin 1987; and Richter 1996. This solution faces three problems. Firstly, the diversity of proposed rearrangements does not inspire confidence in the method. Secondly, the complete lack of textual support casts suspicion on the entire approach. Thirdly, partition theories must assume that Paul's position on the ever-present problem of idol offerings was still in a state of flux some two decades after his conversion, so that he could flop from a narrow exclusivism (10:1–22) to a redemptive inclusivism (8:1–13; 10:23–11:1) at first challenge (Yeo 1995: 83, 210, 213–14).

[3] While appearing in many variations, all reinterpretation theories propose some semantic distinction between 8:7–13 and 10:1–22 in order to justify the difference in practice endorsed by each. One popular proposal differentiates between eating idol food (8:7–13) and participating in cultic feasts (10:1–22) (Fisk 1989: 62–64; Delobel 1996: 182–84; Belleville 1987: 29; Mitchell 1991: 240). Another contrasts joining idol feasts with participating in cultic sacrifice (Oster 1992: 65–67; cf. Barrett 1982: 52; Newton 1998: 362–64). Unfortunately, neither fits Greco-Roman practice or the biblical text.

[4] Driving many studies is the systematics question: 'Is 8:7–13 consistent with 10:1–22?' Others focus on pragmatics: 'Can Christians eat food offered to idols?' Both tend to concentrate on 8:7–13 and 10:14–22 with little regard for how each unit functions within its larger section and within the entire argument of chapters 8–10. As important as the systematics question—and as urgent as the pragmatics—may be, both are premature and will likely produce skewed judgments without prior consideration of the thrust and development of the entire argument.

[5] Two other origins are sometimes suggested for the conflict, both connected with Peter. Ehrhardt (1964: 177–78) proposes that on his first visit, Paul ate idol food freely. Subsequently Peter admonished him, insisting on the applicability of the decree, to which

Paul then submitted and subsequently wrote 1 Cor. 8–10. Barrett (1982: 53) supposes instead that controversy broke out in Corinth when Peter or his associates visited in an attempt to implement the Apostolic Decree. Both views suppose a rather simplistic understanding of the conflicts within Corinth; namely, that the church was divided into fixed camps whose positions were consistent (and consistently at odds with each other) on each issue. In the multicultural, multireligious, urbanized environment which was Corinth, the surprise would come if only two (or four) perspectives existed, and if they correlated consistently across the various controversies.

⁶ Indirect communication is widely overlooked, due largely to the bias of Western culture on interpretation. In fact, one of the few Western interpreters who recognizes the phenomenon views it with suspicion bordering on disdain:

> Paul's condemnation of the eating of 8:10 only on grounds of its effect on the weak is part of Paul's strategy of persua-sion—put charitably, that Paul in 8:7–13 simply focuses on one problem with such eating, offers one argument against it, and will go on to offer another; or, put less charitably, that Paul wishes not to lose his credibility with the Corinthians at the outset so offers a less offensive (that is, more flattering to the Corinthians) reason for not eating in the idol's temple (Gooch 1993: 83–84).

In actual fact, however, indirect communication is less a matter of duplicity or cowardice than it is a matter of cultural patterns of disagreement and confrontation.

North American society values directness and subordinates relations with others to one's personal (even idiosyncratic) convictions. Aggression is accepted as a matter of course, and assertiveness training is a major industry. But much of the rest of the world values relationships alongside truth, subordinates personal convictions to communal consensus, and expresses disagreement obliquely. In this regard, at least, Greco-Roman culture has more in common with traditional Asian cultures than with modern Western cultures: indirection (*insinuatio*) was a widely advised rhetorical technique (for example, *Ad Herennium* 1.6.9–10; Pseudo-Demetrius 5.287; Quintilian 4.1.42; 9.1.29; 9.2.66,69,92).

⁷ Given the recent popularity of a certain form of rhetorical analysis (e.g., Betz 1975, 1979; Mitchell 1991; Watson 1988; Witherington 1995; Wanamaker 1990; cf. Longenecker 1990), my de-cision not to employ it here requires brief defense.

The use of ancient rhetorical handbooks to analyze New Testament epistles is vulnerable to a number of criticisms. Most damaging of all, modern practitioners tend to construct a single, composite model of rhetorical analysis from diverse ancient models and then impose that in Procrustean fashion on the biblical text.

More concretely, Kern (1998) offers a wide range of objections: rhetoric was designed for specific venues, none of which apply to the meetings held by the early church; ancient rhetoric was a tool used in the construction rather than in the analysis of speeches; letters and speeches were perceived to be two distinct genre governed by differing principles; the apostles were arguably more influenced by Jewish than by Greco-Roman rhetoric; few New Testament authors give any indication of rhetorical training, a fact widely conceded by early Church Fathers professionally trained in rhetoric; even the language of the New Testament (*koine*) fails to meet the standards of ancient rhetoric. Finally, the inability of modern analysts to agree on such basic matters as the species and structure of Galatians, for example, gives little ground for confidence. (Similarly, see Classen 1993; Porter 1993, 1997a, 1997b; Reed 1993, 1997; Stamps 1995).

[8] Similarly, Willis (1985: 66) writes:

1 Corinthians 8 is organized around phrases taken from the Corinthians' arguments setting forth their reasons for their participation in pagan cult meals. These quotations from their letter account for the structure of the chapter, because in each case Paul takes a statement from the Corinthians as his starting place and then responds to it.

Fisk (1989: 59–61) is one of the few interpreters to take 8:1,4,8 as representing Paul's position rather than the Corinthian viewpoint, though he appears to do so reflexively; at least, he provides no explicit justification.

[9] Wong (1994: 28–31) provides a helpful summary. Hurd (1965: 68) charts earlier analyses.

[10] More than any other recent interpreter, Hurd (1965: 114–239) set the precedent for full-scale reconstruction of the Corinthian position. He supposes that every topic in 1 Corinthians 7–16 reflects a Corinthian counterstatement to Paul's earlier letter (1 Cor. 7:1 cf. 5:9), and on this basis reconstructs both previous letters. While reconstruction has proven to be a fruitful avenue of investigation, there is a growing consensus that some controls are needed (see, for example, Lyons 1985; Barclay 1987; Sumney 1990).

[11] In reconstructing the Corinthian position, it seems advisable to limit the data to chapters 8–9, rather than reaching across the entire breadth of the epistle, and for two reasons. For one, as Murphy-O'Connor (1978: 547–48) suggests, the argument defending the consumption of idol food differs markedly from (and is made redundant by) the earlier defense of immorality: if 'food is for the stomach and the stomach for food, and God will destroy both the one and the other' (6:13), then there may be no need to invoke the unreality of idols in defense of participation in cultic feasts.

For the other, in the diverse and pluralistic context which was ancient Corinth, it is inherently unlikely that all the problems in the church would reflect consistent and competing perspectives. The existence of defined factions was a common assumption in a previous age (e.g., a Judaizing Peter-faction, a liberal Paul-faction, a philosophical Apollos-faction, a Christ-faction). It still persists in the attempt to identify a unifying characteristic underlying all the conflicts in Corinth (e.g., gnosticism, Schmithals 1971; 'realized eschatology,' Thiselton 1978). Given the wide diversity of pagan religions and philosophies in the city of Corinth, it may be optimistic to assume that converts coalesced into a few fixed groups (much less one!), each with a single, unifying theological focus.

[12] Smit (1996: 583) is one of the few to dispute the proposal that this verse represents a Corinthian slogan. He argues that it functions as a carefully worded '*captatio benevolentiae*' or section heading. This is a false dichotomy; it could be both.

There is also some ambiguity over whether the initial 'we know that' derives from Paul, or from the Corinthians (so Willis 1985a: 67–68). The phrase commonly introduces a generally accepted fact (e.g., Matt. 22:16; Luke 20:21; John 3:2; 9:31; etc.; BAGD 556). Here, though, it is an indirect rebuke: Paul disarms the Corinthians by appearing to agree with them, only to chip away at the proposition until nothing remains of it.

[13] Because of this contradiction, Murphy-O'Connor (1978: 545) thinks that the 'all' in 8:1 was originally part of the Corinthian slogan. That is to say, the strong really believed that all in the community held to this position; thus, they were not elitist. On this reading, the content of their knowledge was only the affirmation of monotheism (8:4), not its ramifications for participation in cultic feasts. Perhaps, however, 'all' actually reflects Paul's inclusion of himself in the category of the elite as part of his rhetorical strategy of indirection.

[14] These few verses have a remarkable number of variants in quick order. The longer readings all appear to be scribal attempts to

improve the terseness of the apparently original text: *de* (v2) present
in the Western manuscripts; *ti* (v2), *ton theon* (v3) and *hup' autou* (v3),
all absent from p^{46} and Clement. As Metzger (1971: xxvi–xxvii) observes, scribal improvements are commonly marked by superficial-
ity. Assuming an original asyndeton and ellipsis, the effect is far
stronger (though terse):

> If anyone thinks that he knows,
>> he does not yet know
>>> as it is necessary to know.
> If anyone loves,
>> this one is known.

Noting that p^{46} and Clement are the earliest witnesses in Egypt, Fee
(1987: 367) adds: "This latter reading fits the context so perfectly that
it is either the Pauline original or else the work of an editorial
genius." Generally scribes are not known for editorial genius.

[15] The metaphor works as well in Greek as in English:
knowledge and love both yield an increase in size, but the former is
insubstantial and self-absorbed; the latter is solid and other-directed.

[16] Throughout the paragraph Paul contrasts knowledge with
love. There can be no doubt, though, that he considers theology
crucial; what he disparages is knowledge exercised apart from love.
The etymological link between 'know' and 'ac*know*ledge' is an
attempt to capture Paul's pun between 'know' and 'is known.'

[17] Some interpreters take 8:4–6 in totality (with the possible exception of 8:5b) as a Corinthian slogan (e.g., Willis 1985a: 84–87;
contra Conzelmann 1975: 142–45; Hurd 1965: 122). This is less likely,
though still possible. In that case, their claim is that they can eat—
even while others participate as an act of worship—so long as they do
not acknowledge pagan gods. This makes good sense, but it requires
the Corinthians to qualify their own bald assertion. Given Paul's
tendency to represent the Corinthian position through absolute statements which he then qualifies, it seems more likely that 8:4 alone
represents their argument. In that case, they defend participation on
the grounds that the gods do not exist, so by definition eating the
food cannot be idolatrous. Taking 8:5–6 as Pauline qualification, later
strengthened in 10:20, also fits the indirectness characteristic of this
chapter.

[18] According to Mitchell (1991: 241), in 8:4–5 Paul
affirms the theological principles of 'the strong' uncondition-
ally, just as in 10:7 and 14 he will uncompromisingly urge all
the Corinthians to flee from idolatry (not idol meats). He
agrees with the fundamental principles *of both sides,* to which

he adds a proper reminder of their theological unity in the
common baptismal acclamation of one God and one Lord in
8:6.

One could excuse the Corinthians for being confused to discover that
both opposing viewpoints were right, but that each must give way to
the other: this is wonderful ethic in theory, but in practice what is one
to do? Quite apart from practicality, this proposal overlooks the
qualifying effect of 8:5–6, developed at greater length in 10:20–22,
and the highly directive 10:1–30, which corrects the stance of both the
strong and the weak. Moreover, closer examination of 10:7 reveals
that the consumption of idol food is the actual form of idolatry which
Paul prohibits.

[19] Paul's point in verse 5 remains somewhat ambiguous. Perhaps
he simply intends a parallel subjective sense both in verse 5a and in
verse 5b (cf. Murphy-O'Connor 1978: 561). Yet verse 6 also combines
both subjective and objective senses, and 10:19–20 clearly endorses
the objective existence of beings represented by idols. Likely, the idea
of contrasting subjective and objective senses is a modern construct
imposed on the text.

In any event, Paul shows no hesitation in affirming the reality of
spirit beings; he categorically denies the deity—but never the
reality—of other claimants to divinity. Thus, Murphy-O'Connor
(1978: 561 cf. 554) misconstrues Paul in allowing only that "such
'gods' had a subjective existence. They were 'gods' for those who
believed in them," and in supposing that the problem was nothing
more than "the time-lag between intellectual acceptance of truth and
its emotional assimilation." On this score, Conzelmann (1975: 143 cf.
Fee 1987: 370–71) is closer to the mark: "The Corinthians' knowledge
is not sufficient even in the realm of the objective statement. The
formal knowledge of the fact that there is *one* God is not yet insight
into the truth about the powers of the world...Paul himself is
convinced that they do exist. But they are not gods. The explanation
is provided by Gal. 4:8."

[20] Denaux (1996: 603–7) explores various proposed sources for
8:6 (e.g. Stoic monotheism and Jewish-Hellenistic missionary
propaganda) and finds the verbal parallels inexact and the
conceptual parallels unconvincing. Since the literary features fit
Paul's style and the content fits his theology (cf. 1 Thess. 1:9–10), it is
simpler to suppose that Paul wrote the text. Little is at stake in any
event, as the present context controls interpretation (cf. Fee 1987:
374).

[21] Fee (1987: 383–84) offers another option. He proposes that verse 8 is a quotation from the Corinthians, who are applying Paul's teaching concerning dietary laws to idol food. But this proposal does not work. Verse 8 could indeed represent Paul's position on Jewish food laws:

Food does not commend us to God:

if we do not eat 'kosher' food, we are no worse off;

if we do eat 'kosher' food, we are no better.

Then if the Corinthians are arguing analogically, they would be claiming:

Food does not commend us to God:

if we do not eat idol food, we are no worse off;

if we do eat idol food, we are no better.

That appears to be the exact opposite of their position (cf. 8:4,10).

[22] The second half of the verse appears in basically three variants: (1) "Neither if we do not eat, do we lack; nor if we eat do we abound" (p^{46} B 81 *pc* vgst co); (2) a simple reversal in order, "neither if we eat do we abound, nor if we do not eat do we lack" (א A^c 33 *pc* vg^{cl} Tert Cl Or); and, the converse, "neither if we do not eat do we abound, nor if we do eat do we lack" (A*).

Murphy-O'Connor (1979b; cf. 1978: 547) discounts the external evidence and adopts the third reading: "this verse is intended to demonstrate that the eating of idol-meats is not an indictable offence in the eyes of God...The eating of idol-meats was morally neutral, since God did not react one way or the other." (He also explains the abounding and lack in terms of spiritual gifts!). Yet 8:10–12 indicates that the strong were arguing for the positive benefits—not the spiritual neutrality—of eating idol offerings. Moreover, this reading is the easier, and thus more likely to be a scribal improvement, as it casts the statement as a direct quotation from the Corinthians (cf. 8:1,4), instead of as an allusion embedded in Paul's reply. The choice between the first and second readings has little interpretative significance.

[23] The designation 'the strong' appears nowhere in these chapters, perhaps because Paul could not bear even to voice the sentiment. But it is clearly implied by the characterization of others as 'weak.' Since their primary characteristic is the claim to knowledge, the phrase 'know-ers' would be more appropriate, were it not so infelicitous. For a similar rationale, see Murphy-O'Connor 1978: 544; Denaux 1996: 595–97.

Sawyer (1968: 122) supposes that the labels 'strong' and 'weak' derive from Paul, for had the Corinthians used the terms in their letter to him, they would have been confused by his multiple meanings (e.g., 1 Cor. 1:25,26,27; 4:10; 9:22; 11:30). Yet this sort of comparative evaluation reflects Corinthian elitism, not Paul's pastoral theology (8:7,9,10; 9:22; cf. 11:19; 4:8; 5:2,6; Rom. 14:1–2). Thus he is more likely taking over his opponents' terminology and attitude, turning it back on them in irony.

[24] Mitchell (1991: 240–41 cf. Witherington 1995: 199) proposes that this verse represents Paul's compromise position on idol food, rebuking both sides at once: "There is no *personal* advantage to be gained from either point of view (this must fly in the face of those who argued these two positions at Corinth)." But the statement expresses only one point of view, from two different directions: there is neither disadvantage in abstaining, nor advantage in eating.

[25] Interpreters widely assume that the Corinthian slogan reflects the misapplication of Paul's own teaching concerning Jewish food laws (e.g., Mitchell 1991: 242 n319). On the pattern of I Cor. 5:9–11, Winter (1997: 77n1) argues instead that had the Corinthians misunderstood him, Paul would have cited his previous teaching and clarified its meaning. The warnings about sin bringing exclusion from the kingdom of God (e.g., 1 Cor. 6:9) appear to be part of Paul's most basic instruction, so it is unlikely that anyone would confuse his teaching on liberty to be permission for licentiousness. Besides, the Corinthians apparently perceived Paul's previous letter (I Cor. 5:9–11) to be excessively strict, not libertine. While appeal to a Pauline slogan remains possible, this quotation more likely reflects an intentional extension or twisting of his position rather than innocent misunderstanding.

[26] I Corinthians 9 has so little explicit relevance to the issue of idol offerings that it is frequently dismissed as an interpolation by an apparently clumsy editor. Yeo (1995: 77), for instance, defends partitioning on the grounds that "the subject matter of chapter 9 has nothing to do with the eating of idol meat…Paul's refusal to accept material support from the Corinthians is a separate major topical issue that deserves an entirely different treatment rather than being treated as a side issue or a digression about idol food." His solution (1995: 81–82) is to subdivide chapter 9 and parcel it out to three (of a proposed six) separate letters from Paul to the Corinthians.

The proposal that I Cor. 9 is a digression and *therefore* does not fit here is especially curious. Ancient rhetorical handbooks actually advocate the use of digressions; by which they mean extended discussions of subordinate themes, examples, illustrations, and supporting argumentation relevant to the topic under discussion. Digressions, it was felt, hold interest, stir emotions, arouse empathy, clarify ambiguities, and provide a helpful change of pace (e.g., Quintilian 4.3; cf. Kennedy 1984: 24). Thus, Wilhelm Wuellner (1979: 177) concludes that Paul's digressions "are illustrative of his rhetorical sophistication and...serve to support his argumentation."

Given Yeo's concept of thematic unity, it comes as little surprise to find that he also excises the digression concerning love in chapter 13 from between the discussions of gifts in chapters 12 and 14 (Yeo 1995: 81). Curiously, though, he permits the digression on wisdom in 1:18–2:16 to remain between the discussions of competition over apostles in 1:10–17 and 3:1—4:5.

The verbal and thematic links between chapter 9, on the one hand, and chapters 8 and 10, on the other, are more than sufficient to confirm its fit and relevance here (e.g., authority *[exousia]* 8:9; cf. 9:4, 5, 6, 12, 18; 10:23; freedom *[eleutheros]* 9:1, 19; cf. 10:29; all *[pantes]* 8:1, 6[2x], 7; 9:12, 19, 22, 23, 24, 25; 10:1[2x], 2, 3, 4, 17, 23[2x], 25, 27, 31, 33; weak *[asthenās]* 8:7, 9, 10; 9:22; judge *[anakrinō]* 9:3; 10:25, 27; share *[metechein]* 9:10, 12; 10: 17, 21, 30).

[27] Mitchell (1991: 241 n308) rightly—if caustically—comments that "in the face of this unambiguous contradiction, it is intersting that no partition theorists, on the basis of their methodological principle of resolving contradictions, puts these two verses in different letters!"

[28] Cf. Murphy-O'Connor 1978: 548. Hurd (1965: 123–25) disputes the existence of the weak, though he does not express his point very well, and is therefore widely misinterpreted; Murphy-O'Connor (1978: 544) concurs while providing a clearer statement. Hurd's concern is to argue that there is no such established 'group' or 'party' in Corinth (Hurd 1965: 123–24, 147; cf. Fee 1980: 173, 176, 179–80). Unfortunately, he also states that "the really striking fact is that in 8.10–13 and 10.28, 29 the 'weaker brother' is completely hypothetical and indefinite." He (1965: 125) subsequently clarifies what he means by that: "We may presume, as Paul presumed (8.7) that some Corinthians were less secure in their new faith than others. But nowhere is there evidence that they formed a group."

Paul clearly aims mainly at the strong (cf. Fee 1987: 6–10, 361–63). Clearly also, had there been no actual weak in Corinth, Paul's argument in 8:7–13 would have discredited him, and there would be no way to account for the lengthy digression of chapter 9. All that remains uncertain is whether the conflict prompting these three chapters was between the strong and weak in Corinth, or between the strong and the apostle. A decision on this matter does not significantly affect the interpretation of the chapters.

²⁹ In place of 'habit' (*sunētheiai* ℵ* A B P Ψ 33 81 630 1739 1881 *pc* vg^mss sy^hmg co), Western and Byzantine text traditions support 'conscience' (*suneidēsei* ℵ² D F G lat sy). The latter probably results from assimilation to *suneidēsis* in v7b (Metzger 1971: 557). Murphy-O'Connor (1978: 551–52) provides a defense of the former.

³⁰ The precise ground of the defilement is in dispute. The consensus supposes that the harm derives from the weak violating their personal—albeit excessively scrupulous—convictions against the consumption of idol food (e.g., Murphy-O'Connor 1983: 164; Robertson and Plummer 1975: 172; Willis 1985a: 105; Barrett 1968: 194–95). Dawes (1996: 96, 98), however, attributes this interpretation to the imposition of Romans 14–15 on 1 Corinthians 8. He argues instead that the weak are in danger of returning to the worship of their old gods through participation in cultic feasts; that is, the example of the strong promotes syncretism, not guilt feelings). On that reading, 8:7–13 seems rather muted as compared with 1 Cor. 10:1–22, but Dawes attributes this to Paul's rhetorical strategy of first responding "to those 'having knowledge' on their own grounds," before introducing a second and more decisive reason for refraining (p 92).

But if Paul is responding to those having knowledge *on their own grounds* then he could only be highlighting the subjective guilt felt by the weak, for the strong admit to no objective idolatry. Moreover, were Paul intending that consumption is idolatrous for those who suppose that the gods exist, he would be vulnerable to the proposal by the strong that the weak should be educated in the practical implications of monotheism, so that they might participate freely.

³¹ Murphy-O'Connor (1979a: 80–82) proposes a scenario which is far more detailed than the text actually provides, but which parallels the experience of many modern converts to Christianity from shenism. The weak

> could not justify their reluctance to participate on the grounds that they were now Christians, because other believers had no such scruples. Hence, they were forced to choose between following their instincts or giving the impression that they wanted to have nothing more to do with well-loved family or friends. They could not do the latter, and so were compelled to eat meat which revolted them.
>
> The arguments of the Strong did not touch the Weak, but the social pressure generated by the former was another matter.

The biblical text actually seems to suppose a more direct connection between the conduct of the strong and the imitating behavior of the weak in violation of their own convictions (8:10). But the scenario which Murphy-O'Connor envisages is appropriate to the Greco-Roman context and resonates with the experience of modern converts from shenism, even though he begins with the assumption that "the concrete problem which occasioned this section is of very limited interest" (1979a: 77).

³² Paul likely also intends a component of defense, especially considering 9:3 (cf. Yeo 1995: 76; Mack 1990: 60–64; contra Witherington 1995: 204; Mitchell 1991: 243–44, and nn 324, 327, 329). Both Mitchell and Yeo disallow mixed genre: for Mitchell, chapter 9 must be solely exemplary because 1 Corinthians is deliberative, not forensic; for Yeo, chapter 9 must be an interpolation since it is forensic, while chapters 8 and 10 are deliberative. Notably, classicist George Kennedy (1984: 19) treats mixed genre as a matter of course: "In a single discourse there is sometimes utilization of more than one species." Mack (1990: 34, 61) goes even further, proposing that one section can have differing *de facto* and *de jure* genre: he suggests that chapter 9 is actually epideictic disguised as forensic. Without denying a subordinate element of apologetic (cf. 2:1–5; 4:1–21; 11:2,17; 14:18), the overall role of chapter 9 in the extended argument is as an exemplum (Willis 1985b; cf. Murphy-O'Connor 1979a: 85, 93; contra Fee 1987: 362, 392–94, though see also 437–40, where he allows an exemplary role).

³³ This connection is supported by numerous semantic and thematic links between 9:19–23 and 8:9–13. Contextually, 'to win' (9:20a, 20b, 21a, 22a) is the equivalent of 'to save' (9:22b), and thus contrasts with 'to destroy' (8:11). Thematically, the aim of winning people to Christ (9:20–22) is complementary to safeguarding the faith of those in Christ (8:9–13). Semantically, the potential negative effect on the 'weak' is expressed in the two passages with a variety of contextual synonyms: 'hindrance' (*egkopā,* 9:12), 'obstacle' (*proskomma,* 8:9), 'offence' (*aproskopos,* 10:32) and 'cause to stumble' (*skandalizō,* 8:13 [2x]).

Yet the most obvious link between chapter 9 and 8:9–13 comes through the parallel rationale which Paul offers for renouncing rights. Expressed negatively, he goes to considerable lengths to avoid hindering the gospel (9:12). Positively, he restricts his rights in order to win as many people as possible to Christ (9:19–22). This rationale provides a clear parallel to his advice in 8:9–13.

³⁴ Hurd (1965: 126 cf 147) is right to insist: "The slogans from the Corinthians' letter indicate that the Corinthians were not merely

asking for information, but that they were aggressively defending their enlightened position."

[35] In 10:1–11, Paul constructs a parallel between the experiences of the wilderness generation and Christian sacraments: the wilderness generation had 'sacramental' signs of God's favor, comparable to Christian baptism and communion (10:1–5); nevertheless, they came under judgment for idolatry, among other sins (10:7–10); this serves as a warning to Christians not to commit comparable sins (10:6,11). From this, many interpreters infer not only that the Corinthians were presumptuous, but that their presumption was grounded in the sacraments. On this view, Paul wrote specifically to counter their sacramentalism (e.g., Barrett 1968: 220; Conzelmann 1975: 167; Fee 1980: 180). A growing chorus protests that Corinthian sacramentalism is neither implied in the text nor required by the logic of the argument (e.g., Hurd 1965: 143; Willis 1985a: 139–41, 154, 159–60; Murphy-O'Connor 1979a: 93; Mitchell 1991: 250–54; and less convincingly, Sandelin 1997: 165–82).

[36] Hurd (1965: 145–46) supposes that these scenarios represent two more objections which the Corinthians raised to Paul's previous prohibition of idolatry.

> The probability that these…were objections originating from Corinth becomes a virtual certainty when it is remembered that this pair of difficulties reflects the normal, day–to–day life of the Gentile Christian. Thus it was not Paul, but the Corinthians, who by their letter posed the problem of the Christian use of idol meat.

Such questions were certainly inevitable. But the assumption that this issue would have occurred only to the Gentile Corinthians and not to the Jewish Paul is most curious: Jewish literature provides extensive and detailed guidance in the avoidance of idol meat, including in the market place and at meal with pagan friends.

Smit (1996: 590) instead attributes the section to Paul's rhetorical strategy of counter-balance:

> Such a negative argument asks for a positive counterpoise. From a rhetorical point of view it is really wise that Paul, having severely excluded participation in temple meals, concludes by pointing out everything which is positively permitted. For the Corinthians addressed this makes the painful rejection easier to forget.

Perhaps so. But again, any pagan or Jew would have realized the need for some elaboration in assessing how scrupulous a Christian must be in the effort to avoid food offered to idols. This discussion is already anticipated in 9:19–23; it is not a rhetorical afterthought.

[37] The rebuke of 10:29b–30 is a notorious crux: "For why is my freedom judged by another person's conscience? If I partake with gratitude, why am I maligned over something for which I give thanks?" Neither the identity of the accused or of the accuser is immediately apparent. Of the numerous proposals, two are germane to the reconstruction of the Corinthian argument.

Perhaps Paul is responding to criticism of his evangelistic lifestyle. His submission to Jewish scruples when with Jews, but eating more freely with non–Jews (9:19–23) would have seemed hypocritical. In addition, by eating freely with non-Jews, Paul would inevitably have eaten idol offerings, even if unknowingly. This would leave him open to accusations of idolatry from the scrupulous (cf. Murphy-O'Connor 1978: 570), and hypocrisy from those whom he was restricting (cf. Fee 1987: 486–87).

Alternatively, despite the first-person pronoun, Paul may be anticipating the strong's objection to his counsel. In 8:13 Paul switches from the second-person pronoun to the first–person, yet clearly continues to direct his remarks at the Corinthians. Similarly, 10:29b–30 may serve as a response to anticipated objections from the strong, reassuring them that their sense of moral propriety is not subject to the scruples of the weak (even if their actions are!), and/or as rebuke to the weak for standing in judgment on others.

[38] Fee (1987: 362, 393), Willis (1985a: 110–11) and Hurd (1965: 146) provide similar summaries, with minor differences.

[39] The appeal to ancient rhetorical handbooks does not imply that Paul formally studied in a school of rhetoric or that he ever read a handbook. The texts were descriptive, deriving principles from effective speeches. So it is sufficient to suppose that the handbooks reflect a culture where indirection was a common rhetorical strategy, especially in the face of hostility. By way of illustration, contemporary manuals on cross-cultural communication commonly note the directness of American culture and the indirectness of many Asian cultures. Yet when an American speaks directly, or an Asian circumspectly, this is no evidence that either has read the manuals.

[40] Murphy-O'Connor (1979a: 82) overlooks the use of indirect communication and consequently misreads the significance of Paul's methodology here:

> The Strong had tried to force-feed the 'conscience' of the
> Weak with knowledge. Paul did not believe that conscience

could be educated by such direct methods since emotional factors were such an important component. In consequence, he does not try to bully the consciences of the Strong by intellectual arguments. He contents himself with setting up the real situation so clearly that they can draw the correct conclusions for themselves.

Actually, Paul does eventually 'bully' the conscience of both the strong (10:1–22) and the weak (10:23–30). He just does not begin that way, and he does not permit them to bully each other.

[41] The specific strategies which *Ad Herennium* (1.6.9–10) advises for overcoming opposition are also relevant. When the audience is sympathetic to an opposing viewpoint, the manual recommends that the rhetor begin with the opponents' strongest argument. This seems to be what Paul is doing through the pattern of affirmation followed by qualification. When the audience is alienated from the speaker, *Ad Herennium* advises excuses or deflection. If not exactly these, Paul provides something similar in the extensive self-justification of 9:1–23.

[42] Perhaps a mundane illustration serves to drive home the point. If a teacher warns students that cheating on an exam will result in failure, this does not imply that refraining from cheating will result in a passing grade. Other conditions apply, though they may be explained not under the policy on cheating, but as part of the course requirements. So the presence of weaker Christians may require abstention from the meal, thus illustrating the appropriate restriction of freedom, without necessarily implying that their absence permits consumption.

[43] Thus, e.g., Fisk 1989: 67; Oster 1992: 65. Fisk (1989: 67) supposes that in 8:1–13 and 10:23–11:1, "while the emphases are different, the basic message is almost identical:

8:1–13   Eat idol meat UNLESS SOMEONE WILL BE SCANDALIZED.

10:23–11:1 EAT IDOL MEAT unless someone will be scandalized."

[44] Fisk (1989: 59), for example, fails to distinguish between Corinthian slogan and Pauline qualification and argues:

Paul first denies the spiritual reality and potency of idols in no uncertain terms (8:4). And because these idols are lifeless and impotent, it follows that food set before them is clean in God's sight (8:8). And since the food (*brōma*) is declared harmless (v. 8), eating (*brōsis*) must also be insignificant, *in and of itself* (8:4,13). The flow of Paul's thought is as follows:

Impotent Idol —> Uncontaminated Idol Meat —> Unaffected Customer

In attributing this position to Paul, Fisk (1989: 61–64, 68) inadvertently sets up a contradiction between 8:4–13 and 10:1–22, which he then attempts to resolve. This complex manoeuver is unnecessary if 8:4 and 8:8, like 8:1, represent the Corinthian position. If so, then in 10:1–22 Paul disagrees not with himself, but with them.

⁴⁵ The wording of 10:19–20 demonstrates that Paul intends it explicitly as a reply to the Corinthian slogan of 8:4:

8:4 "an idol is *nothing*"

10:19–20 "What do I mean? That an idol offering is *something* or that an idol is *something?* Yet that which they offer, they offer to demons and not to God."

⁴⁶ Fisk (1989: 62) overlooks this lengthy list of restrictive comments and concludes: "evidence within chap. 8 suggests strongly that Paul did NOT view those dining in the temple as morally culpable (unless they scandalized someone else)."

⁴⁷ Newton 1998: 313. Hurd (1965: 148) argues that the exhortation to 'build up' the weak would not have required the Corinthians to change their behavior even if the weak actually existed (which he doubts): "The Corinthians could well argue that radical behaviour could be lovingly calculated to educate and strengthen newer Christians." This is likely what they did argue *before* Paul wrote; it is hard to see how they could have argued it after they read his letter.

⁴⁸ Once again I freely acknowledge that this schema provides something of an over-simplification: the correlation with social location is a tendency, rather than an immutable law; and arguably more than three rubrics are justifiable, especially with regard to the details. Particularly noteworthy, in the ever-present domestic context, a familial interpretation commonly comes to the fore: offerings serve above all to honor the deceased in much the same way as when they were still living. That is, the deceased are still viewed as members of the family, as much as preternatural spirits. But the basic pattern appears to be supported by the evidence.

⁴⁹ Meggitt agrees with the consensus position on few points, but this is one of them: the evidence is "fragmentary, random, and often opaque" (1998: 100; cf. Meeks 1983: 72).

⁵⁰ E.g., Judge 1960; Theissen 1982; Meeks 1983; Chow 1992; Clarke 1993; Malherbe 1983: 29–59; Marshall 1987; Mitchell 1993; Winter 1994a,b; Witherington 1995. This consensus explicitly aims to overturn the earlier assumption that Paul and his churches drew largely from the impoverished lower classes (e.g., Deissmann 1957 [1927]: 235–44; 1978 [1922]: 9). Unhappily, in academic theology, a consen-

sus rarely lasts long. Meggitt (1998) has recently launched an all-out
assault on this view.

[51] Much of the controversy arises unnecessarily because of a
failure to define terms. Theissen (1982) speaks too vaguely of elite in
the church at Corinth, without specifying exactly what he has in
mind. Meggitt (1998: 99) assumes that he is referring to a ruling elite
and retorts:

> The Pauline Christians *en masse* shared fully the bleak mate-
> rial existence which was the lot of more than 99% of the
> inhabitants of the Empire...Statistically this is unremarkable.
> To believe otherwise, without clear evidence to the contrary,
> given the near universal prevalence of poverty in the first-
> century world, is to believe the improbable.

There are two problems in his assessment.

First, in disallowing any intermediate wealth between ruling elite
and impoverished masses, Meggitt likely collapses the economic
realities, as his own subsequent argument demonstrates. On the one
hand, he insists that "the non-élite, over 99% of the Empire's
population, could expect little more from life than abject poverty"
(Meggitt 1998: 50). Constantly in fear of unemployment, unable to
take for granted daily sustenance, reliant upon government grain
dole, with thread-bare and patched clothes, the fortunate few housed
in overcrowded slums while the rest slept under bridges or in
shanties; "the non–élite of the cities lived brutal and frugal lives,
characterized by struggle and impoverishment" (Meggitt 1998: 73;
cf. 5n17, 41–73, 96). Yet every time Theissen cites evidence of
disposable income, Meggitt denies that it is evidence of elite status
because the populace at large could afford a variety of non-essential
expenses, such as meat (pp 111–12), the public baths and other leisure
pursuits (p 116), the support of missionaries (p 117), home ownership
(pp 120–21), litigation (pp 123–24), slave ownership (pp 129–32),
benefactions (pp 132–33), and travel (pp 133–34). In his
characterization of general economic conditions within the Roman
empire, he makes no provision for a range of intermediate wealth; in
his refutation of the consensus view, he relies heavily upon it.

Secondly, some proponents of the consensus do clarify what they
have in mind, in a way which respects the sort of evidence which
Meggitt cites. Malherbe, (1983: 86), for example, with appeal to
Roman historian Ramsay MacMullen (1974: 89–90, 99), provides a
more nuanced portrait:

> The property requirements for membership in the senatorial
> and equestrian orders were of such magnitude that those

orders constituted far less than one-fifth of 1 percent of the total population of the Empire. While there was no middle class as we understand it, statistically there was one. 'Between the top and bottom, taking into a single glance the entire empire, a range of intermediate wealth made up the aristocracy of small cities.'...Between the municipal aristocracy and the impoverished was a heterogeneous group that cannot be called a middle class. Although small tradesmen rarely acquired great fortunes, 'people who started with some minor skill or minor sum of money could indeed rise to relative affluence.'

Relative wealth and status variations apparently existed within the vast tracts which constituted the Roman non-elite. This is all that is required to sustain the existence of socio-economic stratification in the church at Corinth

[52] In theory, a fourth line of evidence is available: the social circumstances of Corinth can be extrapolated from the wider economic condition of the Roman Empire. Unfortunately, the general economic condition of the empire is a matter of considerable dispute among specialists in ancient Roman history, so it is not surprising that non-specialists differ.

Theissen (1982: 100–5) largely accepts the 'modernist' perspective, proposing that Corinth would have experienced rapid economic development following its refounding as a Roman colony in 44 B.C.E. Homes were more grand; civic construction projects were numerous; the Isthmian games resumed; trade, banking, exports, and the provincial seat of government all contributed to the general economic well-being; Paul's skill as a craftsman provided a measure of personal financial independence; and the availability of space for congregational gatherings reflects the presence of prosperous homeowners.

Meggitt (1998: 41–73), on the other hand, adopts a 'primitivist' perspective, insisting that the economy of the Roman Empire "remained weak and rudimentary, with little or no growth" (p 42). The economy was marked by subsistence farming, workshop-industries, little long-distance trade beyond luxury goods, the absence of a strong work-ethic, cronyism and nepotism, and a huge gulf between the few elite and the teeming masses.

[53] Meggitt too readily dismisses the force of this verse. '*Eugenēs*,' he writes (p 104), was

apparently the most socially precise of the three words. It was
undoubtedly employed to signify noble birth by the élite of the
Graeco-Roman world, but there is also quite clear evidence of
its arrogation. Epigraphic sources show that in the period
under examination, *eugenēs* and its cognates became applied
to individuals who were clearly not members of the ruling
class by any objective criteria.

On this basis he denies it "any role, however minor, in describing the
social make-up of the Pauline congregations" (Meggitt 1998: 106).

It is certainly legitimate to insist that since the term is
polysemous, its precise nuance cannot be inferred apart from the
context. But to deny it any relevance on this ground is an enormous
leap. At the very least, the popularity of the term confirms its socio-
economic flavor, and thus its attraction for the socially ambitious and
pretentious (which is actually sufficient for present purposes).

[54] Meggitt (1998: 105) himself grudgingly concedes the point:
      [These terms] are indeed socially descriptive, [though] it is
      impossible to be certain what exactly they describe. By itself
      Paul's words in 1 Cor. 1:26 can tell us nothing concrete about
      the social constituency of the congregation...except that a
      small number were more fortunate than the others. How much
      more fortunate it is impossible to determine.

Comparative wealth and prestige are enough to substantiate
Malherbe's thesis, and to undermine Meggitt's portrait of the Roman
and Corinthian non-elite as universally impoverished.

[55] Origen (*Against Celsus* 3.48) cites this text to refute Celsus's
disparagement of the church as solely lower-class. In so doing, he
grants the claim more legitimacy than the apostle Paul does.

[56] Because 4:8–10 includes categories that are not socio-economic
('already you have begun to reign,' 4:8), Meggitt (1998: 106–7) denies
that it provides any evidence of elite social status. To him, the verse
reflects "the Corinthians' sense of spiritual (rather than social) self-
importance" (Meggitt 1998: 106). This creates a false dichotomy. The
combination of socio-economic and theological terms does not mili-
tate against socio-economic elitism, but simply adds a second, spiritual component to their social pretensions.

Inadvertently Meggitt (1998: 107) actually supports a socio-
economic reference to these descriptions.

      Paul is contrasting the bleak nature of his daily life as an
      apostle with the Corinthians' exalted, heavenly, pretensions,
      in order to highlight the absurdity of their claims, and to bring

them back to earthly reality. His words do not tell us anything
at all about the Corinthians' socio-economic location.

If the description emphasizes Paul's low status and his economic
deprivation, then it is difficult to avoid the conclusion that the contrast presupposes a relatively higher socio-economic status for at
least some Corinthians. In contrasting Paul's socio-economic priva-
tion with Corinthian spiritual elitism, Meggitt constructs a double
false dichotomy. The antagonists in Corinth appear to have viewed
the apostle as *both* socioeconomically *and* spiritually inferior; and
themselves, conversely, as *both* socioeconomically *and* spiritually
superior.

[57] Cf. Theissen 1982: 73–75. Meggitt (1998: 141–43) resorts to
argument from silence: conceding that literary and epigraphic evidence credits some officials with the restoration and upkeep of the
synagogue, he insists that not all officials necessarily performed such
a function. True enough, but some definitely did, and this counts for
something.

[58] Theissen 1982: 75–83; cf. Clarke 1993: 46–56; 1991: 146–51;
Gill 1989. Meggitt (1998: 135–41; cf. 1996) argues that the evidence is
insufficient to equate the Erastus of Romans 16:23 with the Erastus
known from inscriptional evidence to have contributed to public
works projects in Corinth, and that the precise bureaucratic position
and function of a 'city-treasurer' (*ho oikonomos tēs poleōs*) is uncertain.

[59] Theissen 1982: 83–87.

[60] Theissen 1982: 89–91, 105. Meggitt (1998: 120–21) dismisses
this line of argument by questioning its underlying assumptions: the
homes might be rented rather than owned; they might be shacks or
tenements rather than single-family dwellings; the number of Christians in the Pauline circle may not have been large or may not have
gathered all together in one place. Here again, though, one might
hope for concrete evidence rather than argument by exception.

[61] Cf. Theissen (1982: 87–91, 96–97) makes allowance for both a
measure of disposable income and a degree of sacrifice; Meggitt
(1998: 132–33) affirms the latter and doubts the former.

[62] While developing this argument, Theissen (1982: 91–92) nonetheless recognizes that the evidence is inconclusive: "We must necessarily be cautious in drawing conclusions about the social status of
people who travel. Business trips can be made by dependent workers; others who travel are simply sailors, companions of the wealthy,
and so forth." Meggitt (1998: 134) goes considerably further in
discounting this evidence: "All but the enslaved or the sick could
journey at their own volition."

⁶³ Since virtually all those named by Paul fulfill one or more of these four criteria, Theissen (1982: 95) concludes: "The great majority of the Corinthians known to us by name probably enjoyed high social status." Meggitt (1998: 134) reaches the opposite conclusion: "Given the weakness of these...criteria we can immediately rule out the possibility that a number of individuals mentioned by Paul in his epistles can be reasonably classed with the élite or prosperous in society."

The contrasting conclusions are in large measure the result of a divergence in the standards of assessment. In each case, Theissen concedes that his interpretation is at best possible, not definite (1982: 75, 87, 88, 91, 97), but this is enough to convince him (1982: 83, 87, 91). Meggitt demands a much higher standard of proof, accepting only that evidence which is incapable of alternative interpretation.

⁶⁴ Meeks 1983: 72–73.

⁶⁵ Proponents of the consensus appeal to socio-economic factors to explain an ever-increasing number of the controversies, with varying degrees of success (e.g., Theissen 1982: 121–43; Gill 1990, 1993b; Chow 1992; Clarke 1993). Meggitt (1998: 107–18) again takes aim at each proposal. Both sides tend toward overstatement. Proponents of the consensus sometimes fail to distinguish between the possible and the plausible; Meggitt tends to be dissatisfied with the plausible, demanding instead conclusive proof, which is a rather high standard for ancient, and piece-meal evidence.

⁶⁶ Theissen (1982: 97) argues for elite social status; Meggitt (1998: 113–16) for compensation.

⁶⁷ Cf. Theissen 1982: 97; Winter 1994b; Gill 1993b: 330–31; Mitchell 1993.

⁶⁸ Cf. Meggitt 1998: 122–25.

⁶⁹ Cf. Booth 1991; Winter 1997: 82–84.

⁷⁰ On the correlation between gluttony and sexual immorality, see Booth 1991.

⁷¹ Cf. Theissen 1982: 96, 145–74; Gill 1993b: 332. Meggitt (1998: 118–22, 189–93) denies any evidence of social divisions in this text, but to do so, he must suppose that no feast is involved. Instead, greedy participants wolf down the communion elements, and Paul's comments about gluttony and drunkenness are simply sarcastic hyperbole.

⁷² Several other controversies less likely reflect elite influence. Perhaps those who opposed Paul included prosperous members of the congregation miffed by his refusal of patronage (9:1–23) (Theissen

1982: 138). Gill (1990; 1993a: 331–32) proposes that the wearing of a head covering during prayer was particularly characteristic of elite males, but Meggitt (1998: 125–26 cf. Oster 1988) provides evidence that the non-elite did similarly, even during domestic ritual in private homes. Clarke (1993: 73–88; cf. Chow 1992: 140–41) speculates that the case of incest (5:1–13) may reflect an attempt by the son to preclude his step-mother remarrying, lest he have to share his inheritance, but Meggitt (1998: 149–53) rightly objects that this has no basis in the biblical text or in Roman laws governing either inheritance or incest.

[73] The assertion of a sociological component to the controversy is not, of course, to diminish the theological element (cf. Theissen 1982: 122–23). To the contrary, the influence of sociological factors should not come as any surprise for the simple reason that cultic meals are inherently social events, and in a largely undifferentiated society—and even in contemporary American society after two-hundred years of self-conscious disestablishment—social celebrations often include a religious component (even if it is commonly limited to civil religion).

[74] Advocates of the consensus offer far more arguments than these few (cf. Theissen 1982: 121–43). Meggitt (1998: 107–18) denies them all. Due to space constraints, this survey selects the more convincing lines of argument.

[75] Cf. Theissen 1982: 124–25. Meggitt (1998: 107–8) disputes this correlation on the grounds that Paul uses 'weak' in different senses throughout this letter (cf. 9:22; 11:30; 12:22), and that the terms are qualified differently in 1:27 ('the weak things of the world') and in 8:7–13 ('weak conscience'). The verbal and thematic links between 1:26–28 and 8:7–13 carry more force, he allows. Both passages reflect Corinthian spiritual elitism: in the former, they disparage Paul's preaching; in the latter, they disparage those who do not join idol feasts. Paul responds differently in each case: in the former, he reminds them of their humble socio-economic origins; in the latter, he appeals to their sympathy for other Christians. Social status clearly plays a subordinate role in the former, and there is no reason to deny it a comparable role in the latter (unless it can be argued that there were several groups in Corinth claiming to be elite on different grounds and over different issues).

[76] Cf. Theissen 1982: 132–37. Meggitt (1998: 113–16) rightly objects to Theissen's anachronistic appeal to Gnosticism in defense of this proposition. He also disputes socio-economic elitism on the

grounds that sects and cults often serve a compensatory role, claiming spiritual elitism to make up for low socio-economic status: even if "such people held leadership positions *within* the church it does not follow that they held such positions *outside* it" (Meggitt 1998: 116–17). Once again, for present purposes, elite pretensions are no less significant than actual elite status.

[77] Theissen 1982: 137–40. He also argues that meat would be more likely to carry religious overtones for the poor, because they had access to this luxury only through public distributions in conjunction with religious rites on important civic occasions. The wealthy could afford meat on numerous occasions, so consumption would not carry the same associations (Theissen 1982: 125–29). Meggitt (1998: 108–12) insists, however, that the non-elite would have had access to meat more commonly and in decidedly non-sacral contexts; for example, from eateries of low quality and worse repute, from street vendors, or even from the public baths. In any event, against Theissen, it could equally be argued that the social elite would more often come under obligation to participate in cultic feasts, due both to their wider circle of associates and to their more prominent position in the civic structure.

[78] Malherbe (1995) provides a lengthy survey of the philosophical discussion of *exousia* ('freedom' or 'authority'). He supposes that the Corinthian justification has affinities with Stoic thought (pp 235–38), and that Paul responds in kind (pp 243–54). All the same, he is careful to explain that

> the philosophic traditions do not constitute a 'background' against which Paul is to be viewed. Paul is rather to be seen as working within a milieu in which issues that engaged him and his converts were already widely discussed. As his readers appropriated some elements from that discussion to describe their Christian existence, so did Paul, and his mode of self-expression, although in this instance triggered by the Corinthians, was as natural to him as any other that he employed (p 255).

[79] For this argument, see Winter 1997: 80–81.

[80] Winter 1997: 80.

[81] Theissen 1982: 138.

[82] Cf. Thiselton 1977: 510–26.

[83] No city official, Theissen (1982: 129–32) reasons, could maintain his position while rejecting invitations to meals which included sacrificial food. For the poor, however, Christian communion feasts

would more than offset any dietary deprivation resulting from their withdrawal from social clubs and trade guilds.

In actual fact, idol offerings ran throughout all levels of Greco-Roman society, so people of every class would have come under pressure to participate, from elite rulers in the civic cult, to working-class tradesmen in the guilds, to private citizens in neighborhood associations and networks, to converts living in pagan homes. It is this social pressure—not dietary concerns—which would have posed the biggest obstacle to abstaining.

[84] Meggitt 1998: 112–13. That is to say, in Meggitt's estimation, the informant must have been one of the Christian weak because the 'conscience' of a pagan would not raise an issue over idol food. The problem with this interpretation is that the informant used the respectful term *hierothuton* ('sacred offering'); the usual Jewish and Christian term was the pejorative *eidōlothuton* ('idol offering'). It is reasonable enough to suppose that the pagan was familiar with the values of his Christian friend. While distinctively Christian values might not have been widely known at this early date, Jewish values were, and to pagans, Christianity would likely have seemed to be a Jewish sect.

CHAPTER 8

Cultic Feasts and Social Meals:
Idol Offerings and Communal Meals in
Pauline Perspective

Summary: In 1 Corinthians 10 Paul renders his verdict on the consumption of idol offerings. He distinguishes two contexts: feasts held in conjunction with an offering, and meals with no apparent ceremonial component. The former are prohibited as idolatrous; the latter are generally permissible.

In 1 Corinthians 10 Paul shifts from refuting the Corinthian rationale and position to explaining his own.[1] Throughout the chapter, Paul's agenda is to delimit the boundaries of the prohibition against idolatry.

At no point is there any hint that the Corinthian Christians were actively participating in the worship of idols or were sponsoring offerings, much less that they were arguing for the right to do so. What is at issue is participation in feasts either held in conjunction with sacrifices or incorporating food previously offered to idols. The central question that Paul addresses is: How far does the prohibition against idolatry and idol food extend? Or, in other words, how far must Christians go in the effort to avoid indirect complicity in someone else's idolatry?

In an attempt to preclude imposing a pre-set agenda from systematics or pragmatics on to the biblical text, this chapter proceeds by tracing the development of the argument within the chapter. Only once the structure and thrust of the argument are clear is it feasible to reconstruct Paul's position and rationale on the consumption of food offerings.

Thematic Development in Chapter 10

Chapter 10 divides readily into basically three paragraphs: the judgment of the wilderness generation and its immediate ramifications for the Corinthian church (10:1–13); a prohibition against participation in cultic feasts (10:14–22); and, a permission to eat freely when the meal has no apparent connection with an offering (10:23–30). While Paul never provides an abstract principle to govern application, his scenarios reflect a distinction between participation in cultic meals and eating food which has no current—but may have prior—associations with idolatry.

Thematic Development in 10:1–13

Paul's point is again indirect, at least initially.[2] He begins with what is beyond dispute and non-threatening—the biblical record of wilderness transgressions and judgments (10:1–5)—in order to address what is controversial and sensitive: the behavior of Corinthian Christians (10:6–10).[3] He argues by analogy, recounting the experience of the exodus generation, rather than immediately and directly confronting the Corinthians.[4] To reduce further the sting of his warning, Paul mingles first- and second-person plural pronouns ('we' and 'you'), but in the concluding summary his concern is demonstrably for them rather than for himself (10:11–13).[5]

10:1b–5. Two features stand out in this paragraph. One is the stark contrast between the numerous repetitions of 'all' throughout the first two strophes, and 'most' in the concluding strophe: all enjoyed divine blessing; most suffered divine judgment. The other notable feature is the explicit parallel that Paul draws between the wilderness experience and Christian sacraments.

By virtue of both their identity and their experience as the people of God, the members of the wilderness generation are "forefathers" of the Corinthians (10:1). The wilderness generation enjoyed signs of divine blessing comparable to the Christian sacraments: baptism (in the cloud and the sea; 10:2) and communion (spiritual food in the form of manna and spiritual drink in the form of water from the rock, 10:3–4). Yet despite being the people of God, recipients of his grace and participants in the sacraments, the majority died outside the promised land under the judgment of God (10:5). As recipients of sacramental grace, the wilderness generation were forefathers of the Corinthians. By implication, they may equally be forefathers with respect to judgment. The next paragraph makes that warning explicit.

10:6–11. The concept of types provides Paul with not only the theme of this paragraph, but also its structure. Two statements of correspondence bracket the paragraph, forming an inclusion: "these events occurred as types for us" (10:6); "these things happened to them as types" (10:11). The intervening material develops the parallel, exhorting Christians to avoid the sins of the wilderness generation: idolatry, sexual immorality, testing God, and grumbling.

Two features of this list draw particular attention to the prohibition against idolatry. For one, it receives pride of place as the first specific item in the list. For the other, it is one of two exhortations in the second person plural ('you') rather than the first person ('let us').

More subtle yet more significant is the explanatory clause that supports the prohibition against idolatry. Each of the other three subordinate clauses supports its respective prohibition by warning of the consequences that befell those who transgressed: they died (10:8b); they were killed by the serpents (10:9b); they were destroyed by the destroying angel (10:10b). The prohibition against idolatry is supported, instead, by a description of the form taken by the idolatry (10:7b): 'the people sat down to eat and drink and rose up to play.' This is the only one of the four to include a description of the sin or to omit mention of the punishment inflicted.[6]

What may initially appear to be a trifle is demonstrably significant. A glance at the Old Testament incident and text highlights the implications of Paul's citation. Exodus 32:6 describes the incident of the infamous golden calf:

So the next day the people rose early and sacrificed burnt offerings and presented fellowship offerings [on an altar before the golden calf]. Afterwards they sat down to eat and drink and got up to indulge in revelry.

Strikingly, though appealing to this passage because of its prohibition against idolatry, Paul omits the explicit reference to sacrificial rites and offerings (Exod. 32:6a), focusing instead on the mention of eating, drinking, and revelry (Exod. 32:6b).

This is all the more notable since subsequent references in Exodus 32 focus on the making of the idol and the offering of sacrifice, not on the meal and orgy that followed (Exod. 32:8,24,31). Significantly, also, Exodus 32 records the punishment inflicted by the Lord. Yet Paul omits this information, breaking the parallelism with the other three sins in his list, in order to highlight the description of the form taken by the idolatry. In both respects Paul omits and selects portions of the Old Testament account to emphasize the point that God judged the wilderness generation for participating in a cultic meal (without reference to actual worship).

Clearly the content of his citation reflects the issue under debate at Corinth. The Christians are not directly worshipping idols or advocating actual participation in cultic rites. Rather, they are joining feasts held in conjunction with idol offerings, and justifying their participation on the grounds that they worship God alone and that idols are not real beings. Paul prepares for his rebuttal by referring to the judgment of the wilderness generation, omitting reference to their direct acts of idolatry, and focusing instead on their culpable consumption of food and drink in the cultic celebration. Implicitly, to join meals held in conjunction with worship is to commit idolatry, even without direct involvement in the worship. Paul will elaborate this point explicitly in 10:14–22.

10:12–13. This short paragraph supplies a generalizing conclusion, bridging the gap from wilderness generation to Corinthian church. At the same time, these verses seek to condition the Corinthian perspective, preparing for the upcoming exhortations on the consumption of food offered to idols.

Paul explicitly places those sins which he has just described— and by anticipation those activities which he is about to proscribe— under the category of temptations that cause people to fall. Those whom he is about to correct are at risk of sin: this time it is the strong—rather than the weak as in 8:9–13—who are susceptible (10:12). Nonetheless, these temptations need not result in a fall. They are typical of the human condition, not unique, and God limits their power over his people, providing a way of escape so that they can endure (10:13). God does not deliver them through sacraments if they indulge in sin; rather, he provides an avenue of escape so that they need not sin.

With these repeated warnings and assurances in rapid succession, Paul implicitly exhorts his readers to resist idolatry, sexual immorality, testing Christ, and grumbling.[7] Anticipating Corinthian opposition to his position on idol offerings, Paul constructs a framework in which they have only two options: to accept his directives or to succumb to temptation and sin. In this way his aim is that they will be predisposed to accept his position. By the time they realize where Paul is actually heading and the specific temptation that he has in mind, it will be too late to protest. Again this is indirect communication: its intention is far more apparent in retrospect than along the way.

Thematic Development in 10:14–22

As he shifts into application, Paul differentiates three distinct contexts for meals: cultic celebrations (10:14–22), food purchased from the market (10:25–26), and meals taken with non-Christian hosts (10:27–30). The length and vigor of Paul's response indicate that his main concern is with cultic meals. Moreover, only this section joins with the polemic against idolatry in 10:1–13; the subsequent applications to market and to dining invitations develop afresh out of the maxims of 10:23–24.[8]

A Ban on Christian Participation in Pagan Cult Meals

While Paul begins by urging the Corinthians to flee idolatry (*eidō-lolatria*, 10:14), the focus of the passage remains fixedly on eating and drinking rather than on worshipping, and on the substances eaten and drunk rather than on the act of offering them to the gods. Even where he mentions cultic rituals, the purpose is to highlight the ramifications of the ritual for consumption. The reason is quickly evident: his aim is to demonstrate that joining a feast held in conjunction with an offering—even without participating in the actual worship—is an act of idolatry.[9]

The argument invokes two analogies: Christian communion (10:16–17) and Jewish sacrifice (10:18). Paul's point is that consumption of an offering to a pagan deity—no less than a meal in honor of God or Christ—involves fellowship in two directions simultaneously: with the deity to whom the offerings are presented and with the worshippers making the offering.

Thus, in Christian communion, the cup and bread are a sharing [*koinōnia*] in the blood and body of Christ, which simultaneously unites those who share the meal (10:16–17). Notably, in verse 16 these effects are portrayed not as the immediate results of an act of worship, but as mediated through eating and drinking: "the cup of blessing which we bless...the bread which we break." Verse 17 is even more forceful, as it omits any reference to blessing or prayer, but focuses solely on the element and its consumption: "The many are one body, for they all share from the one loaf." In a cultic context, spiritual effects are conveyed through the foods to those who consume them, even if they do not actually participate in the worship.

In further support of the proposition that participation in a cultic feast conveys spiritual effects, Paul cites Jewish sacrificial practice and interpretation: "Consider ethnic Israel: are not those who eat the sacrifice sharers [*koinōnos*] in the altar?" (10:18). Joining the cultic feast entails participation in the sacrificial rites. Again there is no mention of offering the sacrifice or of taking part in overt worship; eating the food itself carries cultic significance.[10]

Paul immediately defends his position against an obvious objection from the skeptical strong at Corinth. His judgment that eating and drinking are idolatrous could convey the impression that he takes idols to be potent spiritual powers, or food and drink offerings to be somehow contaminated. He denies both inferences: "What am I saying? That idol food is anything or that an idol is anything?" (10:19). The Corinthian strong are right to insist that idols are not real gods (8:4) and that idol offerings remain simply food, untransformed by the rites (cf. 10:26). Nevertheless, they are wrong in concluding that participation in the feast is without meaning; to the contrary, it carries cultic significance.[11]

Paul proceeds to put the point more sharply: pagan sacrifices are actually offered not simply to dead idols but rather to malevolent demons:

The things which they sacrifice, they offer to *daimōn* and not to God; I do not want you to be sharers [*koinōnos*] in *daimōn* (10:20).

Once again, it is only pagans who engage in the actual worship ('*they* sacrifice'); nonetheless, Christians who share the feast are implicated in the idolatry ("I do not want you to be sharers in *daimōn*"). Yet an advance in the argument comes in the identification of idols with demons. Joining the feast involves something more loathsome than simply worshipping non-gods; it actually entails the worship of demons.

This assertion depends on a pun. In Greek, *daimōn* is a generic term, much like 'spirit' in English.[12] Broadly speaking, all beings who might receive offerings could be called *daimōn*, including gods, nature spirits, and ancestors. More narrowly, the patron spirit of the household—known generically as *ho agathos daimōn*, 'the good *daimōn*'—was a common recipient of offerings at meals and on other occasions, both within the private home and in public ritual.[13] By their own definition pagans presented their offerings to *daimōn*, whether broadly or narrowly conceived. At the same time, Paul surely intends a Christian perspective: these *daimōn* are demons. From this orientation, the offerings become sinister. Paul draws the correlation between cultic feasts and demon worship not just once, but four times in this verse and the next.

The idolatrous associations of eating and drinking are reinforced as Paul absolutizes the previous statement. In verse 20 he phrases his teaching as a personal preference: "*I do not want* you to be sharers in *daimōn*." He now repeats the statement as an absolute prohibition:

"You *cannot* drink the cup of the Lord and the cup of *daimōn*. You *cannot* share the table of the Lord and the table of *daimōn* (10:21)."[14] They stand in danger of committing this heinous act, it is worth pointing out once again, not by making the offering, but by eating and drinking the offerings.

The next verse outlines the consequences of participating in cultic feasts (or, in other words, fellowshipping with demons).[15]

Shall we make the Lord jealous?

Are we stronger than he? (10:22)

This warning is clearly an allusion to the Decalogue, with its prohibition of idolatry on the grounds that God is a jealous God (see especially Deut. 32). The warning recalls 10:1–13 and forms an inclusion binding these two sections: God destroyed the Israelites for engaging in a meal held in honor of a pagan deity; dare the Corinthians think that they shall escape if they do likewise?

Defining Characteristics of Cult Meals

By associating pagan, Christian, and Jewish ritual meals, Paul again constructs a framework that leaves the Corinthians no room for disagreement. If they reject his interpretation of pagan cult meals, they must also reject the Jewish interpretation of sacrifice and the Christian interpretation of the eucharist. If the pagan cultic feast is just another meal, so are Jewish sacrificial feasts and Christian communion (10:15–18).

By equating idolatry with demon worship (10:20), Paul seeks to make the feast as repulsive to the Corinthians as it is abominable to God (10:21–22). They should no more join a pagan cult meal than they would engage in demon worship. It is difficult to conceive how the apostle could have made this point more emphatically.

While there can thus be no doubt about either Paul's meaning or his intensity, an ambiguity remains that has crucial effects for the application of this prohibition: When is a meal cultic, and when is it merely social? What are the defining characteristics of a cultic meal?

Paul does not answer the question directly, but his discussion does provide a number of indications: the appeal to the wilderness idolatry (10:7); the parallels with Christian eucharist (10:16) and with Jewish sacrifice (10:18); the reference to pagan sacrifice (10:20); the mention of cup and table (10:21); and, the repeated mention of *daimōn* (10:20 [2x]; 10:21 [2x]).

These indicators, at the very least, portray meals as cultic when they are held in conjunction with an offering. This is the point, for instance, of Paul's citation of the wilderness idolatry: the Israelites sacrificed burnt offerings and presented fellowship offerings and then sat down to feast (Exod. 32:6). The meal is cultic because it not only consists of sacrificial offerings, but because it occurs in conjunction with the act of offering. Thus, Exodus 34:11–17 prohibits Israelites from joining meals which the prior inhabitants of the land hold in conjunction with sacrifice.

The appeal to the Christian eucharist is similar (10:16). While there is no sacrifice, ritual is nonetheless present in the blessing of the cup and the breaking of the bread. In that context, Paul later argues, a eucharistic meal is a cultic act, not a private dinner (1 Cor. 11:20–22).

The analogy with Jewish cultic meals (10:18) points in the same direction. Fellowship offerings are sacrificed to the Lord and then consumed in feast (Lev. 3:1–17; 7:11–18; 19:5–8; Deut. 14:22–27). Because the food derives from the altar and is consumed in conjunction with the act of offering, all who eat share in the altar (1 Cor. 10:18).

So too, then, by analogy, a meal held in conjunction with pagan sacrifice is cultic: "What they sacrifice, they offer to demons…I do not want you to be sharers in demons. You are not able to drink…the cup of demons. You are not able to share…the table of demons" (10:20). Christians share in demons by joining a meal held in conjunction with pagan sacrifice.

Significantly, Greco-Roman interpretation reinforces the cultic associations of meals based on offerings. The scholiast to Plutarch (*Fragment* 95) explains the significance of offering sacrifice before eating a meal:

> By first offering to the gods a portion of what we are going to eat, we make all the rest of it holy. For laying out the table [*hai trapezōseis*] for the gods follows the same procedure: first the offering, then the meal.[16]

Sacrificial ritual serves as a model for both the procedure and the meaning of the offering at meals: first a portion is set apart (or burned in the fire) for the gods, then the participants eat. As a result, it is not just the offered portion that is sanctified, but the entire meal. All who share in the daily meal—just like all who share in the cultic feast—participate in the cultic associations of the offering.

Similarly, the emperor Julian (*Orations* 5.176d) describes sacrifices "suitable to share with [*koinōnein*], and to place on the table of [*trapezoun*], the god." The chief qualification is that the food must be such as the people themselves eat, and they must not eat what they do not share in sacrifice with the gods. In the sacrifice, by offering on the sacred table a portion of what they eat together, the people share the feast with the god.

Some sacrificial ritual brings this point home graphically. For certain occasions, the image of the god would be placed on a standard dining couch alongside a table with food portions, in a ceremony known as a *lectisternium*. This implies, Gill notes, that "the god was thought of as himself being present at the meal in some way."[17] All those who join in the feast share in the cultic associations of the sacrifice.

The parallel between eating at the table of demons and drinking from their cup supports this analysis (10:21). In Greco-Roman meals, a small portion of the food was commonly offered on the household altar or set aside on the table in front of the altar, and the rest was consumed in the first course. Then a small portion of the wine was poured out as a libation, with a paean sung to household deities, and the remainder was diluted and drunk during the second portion of the meal.

For Paul, sharing the cup, no less than sharing from the table, is a cultic act, even apart from participation in the worship or offering.[18] The act of worship extends not only to those who participate in the actual offering of a sacrifice, but also to those who join in the accompanying feast.

Ramifications of the Ban on Participation in Pagan Cult Meals

In 10:1–22, Paul directs his efforts against Christian participation in pagan cult meals. He senses no danger of Corinthian Christians actively participating in the offering of sacrifice or worship. From all reports, there is no threat from that direction: the strong in Corinth were convinced monotheists (8:4–6); the weak, for whom pagan worship was still vital, resolutely opposed even indirect contact with their former deities (8:7–8). So Paul's burden is to dissuade the strong from participating in feasts held in conjunction with pagan offerings.

Given the association of offerings with a wide variety of meals, this would be no easy task. Temple feasts, of course, were inevitably associated with sacrifice, so Christians could not attend any meal in the temple.[19] Since sacrifice played a prominent role in civic celebrations, as well as in the meetings of trade guilds, ethnic associations, and clubs generally, Christians could not join meals in these venues either. The restriction would apply not only to those feasts held specifically to honor deities or emperors, but would also include what moderns consider predominantly social occasions, such as births, coming-of-age ceremonies, weddings, funerals, or thanksgiving feasts. In each of these architectural and social settings, meals were customarily joined with sacrifice, and were therefore out of bounds to Christians.

The prohibition likely extends to the social meals of the elite and to daily domestic ritual. In such contexts, simple offerings were more common than full-fledged sacrifices. Yet Paul's term for sacrifice, *thuÇ* (10:20), can refer equally to the offering of food or drink to the gods without the slaughter of a sacrificial victim; the word may even have originated in the domestic ritual.[20]

Moreover, the prohibited category of *daimÇn* would encompass the offering to *agathos daimÇn*, the tutelary deity of the household and beneficiary of the wine offering at formal meals. This reference is reinforced by the extension of the prohibition beyond idol food to include 'the cup,' even more, 'the cup of *daimoniÇn.*' So in 10:14–22 Paul apparently prohibits any communal feast or domestic meal which accompanies—or is accompanied by—an offering to the gods.

The prohibition extends further still. Beyond gods, the category of *daimÇn* incorporates spirits, ancestors, and all other sorts of preternatural beings. As noted in the survey of Greco-Roman religion, the domestic and ancestral cults were pervasive in both the architecture and the daily life of the home, as well as during calendrical celebrations and throughout the family life-cycle. As a result, even those rabbis liberal enough to permit Jews to eat with Gentiles nevertheless excluded any meal held to celebrate important familial, calendrical, or life-cycle occasions, on the grounds that the food would have derived from a sacrifice. Paul does not go quite this far, as he explains in 10:23–30. Nonetheless, his restriction would preclude Christian participation in any meal held in evident connection with either an animal sacrifice or a simpler offering, whether to gods or to ancestors.

Thematic Development in 10:23–30

Just as 10:14–22 develops out of the scriptural exposition in 10:1–13, so the applications of 10:25–30 follow from the maxims of 10:23–24. The placement and brevity of this section indicates that it is secondary to Paul's main concern of prohibiting idolatry. Yet the careful composition and stylistic emphases demonstrate that it is not an inconsequential afterthought. To the contrary, the passage provides crucial guidance in matters not covered by 10:1–22, and an important safeguard in preventing overscrupulous application of the prohibition against cultic meals.[21]

10:23–24. These verses comprise a series of compact, artistic, and forceful aphorisms that state the same basic point three times in slightly different terms. Appropriate Christian ethic considers not simply what is permissible but also what is helpful to others (10:23a); not only what is permissible, but also what builds up others (10:23b); not what is in one's own interests, but what advances the interests of others (10:24).[22] Two case studies illustrate the application of these directives.

10:25–26. In the first scenario Paul imposes no restrictions on the consumption of meat from the market.[23] Though the origin of any particular item would have been uncertain, much of what was available for purchase from the market would have derived from temple sacrifices, either as originally part of the priest's portion or as remainders from the sacrificial feast. Nonetheless, Paul offers two reasons why it may be freely eaten. For one, conscience is irrelevant (10:25 cf. 8:7–13). For the other, "the earth belongs to the Lord, along with its abundance" (10:26 citing Ps. 24:1).

The citation from Psalm 24:1 is particularly germane, as verses three and four of the same psalm prohibit those who worship idols from entering the presence of the Lord:

> The earth is the Lord's, and everything in it,
> the world, and all who live in it;
> for he founded it upon the seas
> and established it upon the waters...
> Who may ascend the hill of the Lord?
> Who may stand in his holy place?
> He who has clean hands and a pure heart,
> who does not lift up his soul to an idol.
> (Psalm 24:1–4)

Significantly, Paul places the purchase of meat from the market under the permission of Psalm 24:1 rather than under the prohibition of 24:4.

All food ultimately derives from the Lord, so in the absence of any apparent connection with idolatrous rites, all is permitted (10:26). With the exclusion of conscience from consideration, no one is susceptible to stumbling, so the welfare of others is not at risk, and the maxims of 10:23–24 do not apply. This logic recalls the Corinthian argument in 8:4, albeit now applied to a different context.

10:27–30. The second scenario similarly imposes no initial restrictions on eating with friends and neighbors, apart from personal preference. When invited to dinner by a non-Christian host, those Christians who wish to accept may do so and they may eat freely; conscience is no consideration (10:27).

Yet if someone at the table draws attention to the prior cultic history of some dish on the menu, the Christian should abstain "for the sake of the informant and for the sake of conscience" (10:28).[24] This caveat links all four elements from the introduction in 10:23–24: free exercise of prerogatives, where conscience is not involved; restraint of prerogatives, where someone might be adversely affected.

The interplay between rights and conscience, individual prerogatives and the welfare of others, continues in the elaboration and clarification that follows (10:29–30). At first glance, and probably intentionally, 10:28 appears to suggest two separate reasons for abstaining from food known to have been previously offered to idols: "for the sake of the one who informed you and for the sake of conscience." The reference to conscience could appear to offer a second and independent motive: for the sake of the one who informs and for the sake of one's own conscience (now that the origin of the food is known). The ambiguity sets a trap for the scrupulous in Corinth: they would likely presume that Paul is supporting their convictions. It also affords him the opportunity to clarify—and thus to emphasize—his point.[25]

Paul guards against misunderstanding with an immediate clarification: the conscience in view belongs not to the one who is prepared to eat, but to the (probably pagan) informant who presumes that the Christian would not want to eat (10:29a).[26] The two reasons thus turn out to be one (a rhetorical device called 'hendiadys'): "for the sake of the one who informed you; that is to say, out of concern for his convictions on the matter." Notably, Paul never asserts that the eating is wrong *per se*; what is wrong is to violate someone else's expectations of proper Christian ethic.

In this instance, both the weak and the strong are wrong: the former for prohibiting the latter from eating; the latter for insisting on the right to eat. In such a case, participation or abstention is a matter to be decided not on the basis of personal conviction, but on the grounds of the welfare of others. Against the weak, the food is fully permissible, provided no one is harmed. Even once the host points out the source of the food, the Christian still need have no scruples about the food *per se*.

> Why should my freedom be judged by another person's conscience? If I partake with gratitude, why am I slandered on the basis of what I thank God for? (10:29–30)

Christians retain their freedom—they reserve the right to participate in the meal—even if for the sake of the pagan, they decide to forgo the right.[27]

Those who feel that a Christian should never wittingly eat leftovers from idol offerings cannot impose their convictions on those who lack such compunctions. While Paul requires Christians to avoid the meal for the sake of others, he does not call for a shift in their moral judgment: their assessment that the food is permissible is apparently justified.[28] Before they knew the origin of the food, they had every right to eat; in fact, Paul counseled them to eat without question or reservation (10:27). Even now that they know its origin, Paul does not revoke their freedom to eat on this ground. If those with no qualms decide not to exercise their personal prerogatives—and in some circumstances they must—they do so not out of moral conviction or obligation, but out of compassion. To eat is not intrinsically wrong; it is wrong merely because it is unhelpful to others who happen to be present (cf. 10:23–24).

Paul hones the point: to castigate anyone who eats food of unknown derivation—or even food which derived from a prior sacrifice but is currently removed from any apparent cultic setting, framework or ethos—is to be guilty of slander: "If I participate with gratitude, why am I slandered on the grounds of what I say grace over?" (10:30).[29]

Outside of a cultic context, then, a Christian may simply give thanks and eat. Where the immediate source of the food is unknown, its ultimate source takes precedence (cf. 10:26; 8:4). Where the source is declared, the food itself apparently remains acceptable, though eating it is not, since it violates the expectations which outsiders have of Christians (cf. 10:23–24; 8:7–13).

Thematic Development in 10:31–11:1.

This paragraph concludes the entire discussion of idol offerings, presenting little that is new, but drawing together the various threads of all that precedes in a highly stylized structure.[30] "So whether you eat or drink" (cf. 8:4,7,8,10,13; 9:3; 10:3,7,16,18,21,25,27,28), "do all for the glory of God" (cf. 10:5,20–21), "give no offense" (cf. 8:9,13), "whether to Jew or to Gentile" (cf. 9:20–21), "or to the church of God" (cf. 8:7–13), "just as always and in all things, I try to please everyone in every way" (cf. 9:22), "seeking not my own benefit" (cf. 10:23a), "but that of the many, so that they might be saved" (cf. 9:22). Paul ends by making his function as a role-model explicit: "Become imitators of me, just as I am an imitator of Christ" (11:1 cf. 9:3–27). In this way 10:31–11:1 encapsulates the predominant themes and key words of the three chapters, and thus serves as an argument for their unity.

Conclusion

In its most succinct form, the issue that Paul addresses is: *the consumption of idol offerings.*[31] Each of these three terms merits elaboration.

The *Consumption* of Idol Offerings

Two points warrant comment under this rubric. First, the issue of contention between the Corinthians and their apostle is the consumption—not the making—of offerings. No evidence suggests that any Christians in Corinth were syncretists, at least not in self-perception or in intention. Those advocating participation in cultic feasts argued from the premise that idols are impotent and that other gods do not exist (8:4–6).

With such presuppositions, there can be no intention of worship. Nor is there any suggestion that the Corinthian Christians initiated or sponsored offerings to the gods.[32] They argued merely for the right to participate in communal feasts regardless of the setting of the feast, the associations of the meal, the intentions of the other participants, or the origin of the food.

Paul consistently directs his reply to this same issue. At no point does he explicitly prohibit either the worship of other gods or the presentation of sacrifice to them. Evidently he perceives no threat from this direction. Moreover, were participation in worship or sacrifice at issue, a simple prohibition with scriptural citations would have sufficed. The extent and complexity of his argument reflects the effort to demonstrate that participation in a communal feast could also be tantamount to idolatry. This focus is most evident in his selective citation of Exodus 32:6 (1 Cor. 10:7). His point is that the sin of idolatry (1 Cor. 10:14) attaches not only to the actual presentation of offerings to idols (Exod. 32:6a), but also to participation in feasts typically held in conjunction with the offerings (1 Cor. 10:7,16-21; cf. Exod. 32:6b).

Secondly, the issue involves the consumption of both food and drink, not simply the eating of idol meat. Current discussion erroneously fixates on meat offered to idols. Paul, however, refers to food generally and also to drink (e.g., 1 Cor. 10:7,16,21,31). This reflects the Greco-Roman practice of offering various sorts of food as well as wine to the gods. More to the point, the inclusion of drink alongside food means that Paul's teaching applies beyond formal temple sacrifice and encompasses also common practice at formal meals, with an offering of food prior to the dinner and an offering of wine between the meal and the subsequent symposium. The prohibition against both eating from the table and drinking from the cup of *daimͼn* would therefore encompass not only formal cultic celebrations but also many communal meals.[33]

The Consumption of *Idol* Offerings

Again important both for accuracy in the first-century setting and for relevance in the twenty-first century is the delineation of what constitutes an idol within 1 Corinthians 8–10. Western biblical scholarship—generally far removed from the traditional practice of idol worship—gives little attention to this issue of definition. Anthropological analyses are preoccupied with constructing typologies and thus with differentiating gods, spirits, and ancestors. While these rubrics are helpful for analytical purposes, they do not clarify the Christian perspective.

Paul establishes boundaries for the Christian worldview with his description of idols as '*daimͼn*' (10:20). Given first-century Greco-Roman practice and terminology, '*daimͼn*' incorporates all three categories of shenist preternatural beings—gods, spirits, and ancestors—as well as a fourth which is no longer honored in shenist practice, the cult of deceased emperors.

The Consumption of Idol *Offerings*

Paul establishes the boundaries between permissible and forbidden activities in terms of sacrificial offerings (10:19–20). This is significant in three respects.

First, for Paul, the decisive factor is the act of offering, not the motives underlying either the offering or the subsequent meal.[34] Among other purposes, Greek and Roman offerings served to appease the spirits, to demonstrate respect toward ancestors, and to commune with them. Greco-Roman meals fulfilled both cultic and social functions. Moreover, the functions and meanings of both offerings and meals tended to vary with the social location of the worshipper. Yet in contrast to the historic and current debate over shenist rites, Paul makes no attempt to distinguish worship from veneration, or the idolatry of traditionalists from cultural customs perpetuated by elite revisionists. The making or consuming of an offering to preternatural beings (or to idols) is itself problematic, whatever the underlying motivation, intention, interpretation, or social location of those making the offering.[35]

A second consequence of defining the problem in terms of making an offering is that cultic significance extends beyond explicitly and distinctly cultic buildings.[36] By and large, contemporary academic discussion is preoccupied with the reference in 8:10 to a temple venue. Yet neither in the first-century Roman world nor in twenty-first century Asia is the temple the only—or even the most common—site for making or consuming offerings to gods, spirits, or ancestors.

Ancient venues stretched from temples and shrines, to hotels and restaurants, to private clubs and homes. So in 10:21, Paul prohibits eating from the cultic *trapeza* (10:21), the table placed alongside an altar and used for holding the offering and carving the sacrifice, and found widely outside the temple.

Consequently, today, the prohibition against idolatry applies equally to any context where a meal is held in conjunction with a sacrifice or offering, whether the food be eaten inside a temple, a civic building, a public square, a trade guild, an ethnic association, a hotel or club, or even a private home.[37]

Thirdly, in focusing on the act of offering, Paul shifts attention from the prior history of the food ('food offered to idols') to the present context of the meal: food eaten in conjunction with the offering of sacrifice or worship. This is his focus throughout the argument: 'the cup of blessing *which we bless'* (10:16a); 'the bread *which we break'* (10:16b); 'those who eat *the sacrifice* are sharers *in the altar'* (10:18). The offered substance is 'nothing'; the idol is 'nothing' (10:19); what is decisive is the act of offering: 'the things *which they offer, they offer* to demons and not to God' (10:20). It is the immediate role of the beverage in the worship or sacrifice—not its prior history—which renders it either 'the cup of the Lord' or 'the cup of demons' (10:21a). It is the conjunction of meal with sacrifice or worship which marks it as 'the table of the Lord' or 'the table of demons' (10:21b). For Paul, the issue is participation in cultic feasts, not the prior history of some item on the menu.

The distinction between cult meals and food previously offered to idols arises from the contrasting advice in the scenarios of 10:14–30. Paul prohibits idolatry, which he defines to include not only the making of offerings, but also joining meals held in conjunction with sacrifices or offerings (10:14–22). But apart from an immediate connection with sacrifice, all food is considered to derive from God, regardless of its possible history (10:26).

Where there is no evident connection with an offering, all food may be enjoyed, even at a pagan's house, where the likelihood of a sacrificial origin is strong (10:27). The one exception—when someone draws attention to the origin of the food (10:28a)—is no real exception: the reason for restraint is not to avoid idolatry, but simply to avoid violating the informant's sense of moral propriety (10:28b–29a). The freedom to eat remains (10:29b); the food may be eaten with thanksgiving, Paul stresses twice (10:30a,c). In fact, to criticize someone who so eats is to commit slander (10:30b). So Paul's concern is not with the previous history or the origin of the food, but with the immediate conjunction of meal and offering.

Provided they do not join a cultic feast, Christians may eat for the glory of God (10:31). Which is to say, they may eat freely, so long as they are not an obstacle to the salvation of Jew or Greek, or to the stability of other Christians (10:32).

By this logic, while among Jews they must assiduously avoid not only food previously offered to idols, but also any other violation of Jewish food laws (cf. 9:20). Among gentiles, they will eat without exception or inquiry (cf. 9:21), provided the feast is not held in conjunction with a sacrifice or offering (for in that case, they must not join the feast at all).[38] Like Paul, the Corinthians are to be guided not by their own freedoms or convictions, but, on the one hand, by the absolute prohibition against participation in idol feasts, and on the other, by the expectations of non-Christians and the desire to see as many saved as possible (10:33–11:1; cf. 9:19–22).

These are the only two constraints Paul lays down: to participate in the worship of God alone, and to live in whatever way will further the cause of evangelism. He prohibits Christians from joining cultic meals but offers no other dietary restriction. To lay down any position on Jewish food laws would be to impede evangelism: to affirm food laws would alienate gentiles; to abrogate food laws would alienate Jews. Since food is now irrelevant to God (8:8), Paul lays down the one food law which will facilitate evangelism: eat according to the customs of host and companions (9:19–22; 10:31–11:1), with the one exception of not participating in cultic meals (10:14–22).

So while Paul introduces the topic as 'idol offerings' (8:1) and particularly 'the consumption of idol offerings' (8:4), he actually reframes the issue in terms of participation in cultic meals (10:1–22). Why does he introduce the topic in this somewhat misleading way? Because this is how the Corinthians raised the issue (8:1). For them, the issue pertains to the origin of the food; for him the problem is the

context of the meal. This distinction necessitates a thorough reap-
praisal of current academic discussion and populist practice, both of
which largely conceptualize the issue in terms of the history of the
food rather than the context of the meal.

Endnotes

[1] Chapter 10 begins rather abruptly. Despite the verbal connective, 'for' (*gar*, 10:1), 10:1 takes off in a significantly new direction from chapter 9. Paul supplies only a minimal thematic anticipation at the end of chapter 9: the danger of disqualification from eschatological reward (9:24–27). From this allusive reference, divine judgment on idolatry becomes the central theme of 10:1–13, followed by exposition of the boundaries of idolatry.

[2] At the same time, the tone of 10:1 is ironic, even sarcastic. To people proud of their theological profundity (cf. 8:1, 4a), Paul taunts, "I do not want you to be ignorant."

[3] Conzelmann (1975: 165) supposes that Paul here cites early Christian tradition, but the collation of sins so precisely fits the Corinthian situation that he likely composed it for this purpose. Certainly such composition is not beyond the rhetorical capability he has demonstrated to this point. Just as certainly, scholarly enthusiasm for diachronic analysis has until recently encouraged interpreters to find historical trajectories at the slightest hint.

[4] Because Paul's argument expounds Scripture, it is tempting to describe it in terms of Jewish exegetical patterns. Ellis (1978: 156 n36) analyses 10:1–13 as an "implicit midrash"; Meeks (1982: 65 n2) calls it a homily "for convenience's sake." Since the argument thoroughly fits its present context, any prior existence is of secondary importance (cf. Fee 1987: 442).

[5] The first line gives a hint of what is to come in the reference to the wilderness generation as 'our fathers' (10:1b). Yet even this is teasingly ambiguous. Given that the Corinthian church was probably predominantly gentile, '*our* fathers' could allude to the extraordinary privilege which gentiles receive as they are incorporated into the people of God (cf. Rom. 4:12, 16–18; 8:15). At the same time, an ironic twist is equally likely: in prophetic rebukes, the phrase 'your fathers' typically correlates the wickedness of the prophet's generation with the sinfulness of the wilderness generation (e.g., Jer. 3:25; 7:14–18; 16:12–13; 23:27; 44:9–10; Ezek. 20:4, 18, 27, 30, 36 cf. Matt. 23:30–32; Luke 11:47–48; Acts 7:52). As the argument develops, Paul clearly has something similar in mind: 'Do not be like your fathers, or you will suffer their fate!' In this instance, paternity is defined by sinful conduct rather than by divine grace, and is thus grounds for chagrin rather than for pride.

[6] Koet (1996: 610) notices this phenomenon but makes little of it, as he supposes that the punishment is inferred in the death of the

twenty-three thousand in 10:8c (the twenty-three thousand purport-edly represents Paul's intentional assimilation of the three thousand in Exod. 32:28 with the twenty-four thousand of Num. 25:9).

⁷   Mitchell (1991: 250–54; cf. Witherington 1995: 218) offers an idiosyncratic interpretation of this passage in the effort to demon-strate that 'concord' is the unifying theme of the entire epistle. As she sees it, the sins of 10:6–11 (idolatry, immorality, tempting Christ, grumbling) are all manifestations of factionalism, "the quintessential 'human' affliction which now threatens the Corinthian community" (p 252). Unfortunately for this interpretation, the list of sins in 10:6–11 does not include factionalism, nor did the punishment originally fall on the wilderness generation for factionalism. Mitchell finds this theme in Philo and Josephus and then imposes it on Paul. The broader theory would be more convincing if the word 'concord' appeared even once in the letter. Even so, the imposition of a single theme runs roughshod over the obvious shifts of topic throughout the letter. The exhortation of 1:10 convincingly provides the thesis for 1:10–4:21, but hardly for the entire epistle.

⁸   Paul's tone moderates significantly as he turns to the hub of the controversy over idol food. He exchanges the caustic tone and sarcastic introit of 10:1 ('I do not want you to be ignorant') for terms of affection and respect: 'my beloved' (10:14); 'I speak to discerning people' (10:15a); 'evaluate for yourselves what I say' (10:15b). His content shifts correspondingly from the dire warnings of 10:1–13 to expressions of paternal concern and gentle appeal in 10:14–22. At the same time, his position remains unequivocal and non-negotiable. Stylistically, rhetorical questions serve to overwhelm resistance by underlining the incontestability of his logic and the irrefutability of his conclusion. Thus, the change in tone reflects a shift in persuasive strategy rather than a moderation of passion or a change in position.

⁹   As Gooch (1993: 105) observes, "Paul is very clear that partici-patory consumption of a meal sacred to another God is idolatry and carries judgment."

¹⁰   First-century Jewish philosopher Philo (*Special Laws* 1.221) pro-vides a similar interpretation of Jewish sacrificial meals: "[God] caused the convivial company of those who made sacrifice to be sharers [*koinōnon*] of the altar and diners at the same table" (my translation). Philo agrees that Jewish sacrificial meals entail sharing in two direc-tions: in the altar, representing the cult ritual, and in the table, repre-senting the meal together. Paul's contribution, arising out of the situation in Corinth, is to propose that both effects derive from the act

of eating, even for those who do not participate in offering the sacrifice.

[11] Murphy-O'Connor (1979a: 98) finds the motivation for 10:19 in a slightly different, but related, direction: the Corinthians

had denied the reality of idols (8:4), and it would be natural for them to protest that there was no analogy between the eucharist or Jewish sacrifice and pagan temple meals. Hence, Paul at once insists that the validity of the analogy does not depend on acceptance of the view that an idol is capable of efficacious action.

On this view, Paul is insisting that the analogy remains valid, even though Christian eucharist and Jewish sacrifice invoke a true God, while pagan sacrifice is offered to impotent idols. This would, indeed, be a natural objection, but it does not appear to be the one which Paul anticipates: in 10:19 he is defending his understanding of idols as spiritual beings rather than defending the legitimacy of the analogy between God, Christ, and idols.

Elsewhere, Murphy-O'Connor (1978: 556–57) misses the point in concluding that "on the issue of whether the eating of idol-meat was right or wrong in itself Paul certainly adopts the conclusion of the Strong (x, 19, 25, 27)." In opposition to the strong, Paul insists that participation in cultic meals is wrong 'in itself' even though both food and idols are nothing 'in themselves.'

[12] On the meaning of *daimōn,* see Förster 1964: 1–20; Burkert 1985: 179–82, 329–32; Nilsson 1940: 165–70, 283–91; MacMullen 1981: 79–82.

[13] See above, chapter 5.

[14] Again Paul uses repetition, word order, and synonymous parallelism for emphasis:

You cannot / the cup of the Lord / drink / and the cup of *daimōn.*

You cannot / the table of the Lord / share / and the table of *daimōn* (10:21).

[15] Paul employs terseness, rhetorical questions, and sinister implication to underline the seriousness of this transgression:

Shall we make the Lord jealous?

Are we stronger than he? (10:22)

[16] Adapted from Sandbach 1969: 95.

[17] Gill 1974: 137.

[18] Newton (1998: 362–71) attempts to reconcile the permission of 8:7–13 with the prohibition of 10:1–22, by distinguishing between

eating idol food and joining in cultic sacrifice. His argument hinges on 10:21, which forbids participation in the 'table' (*trapeza*) of pagan gods. In Greco-Roman cult, he explains, temple offerings were divided into three portions: one part was burned on the altar; another, the *trapezomata,* was placed on the table of the god and eventually went to the officiants; the largest share went to a feast for the attenders. So when Paul forbids the Corinthians to eat from the *trapeza* (10:21), he is prohibiting consumption of the officiants' portion—which is an indirect way of forbidding Christians from officiating at the sacrifice. The distinction is between "specific people who were personally involved in the sacrificial procedure, rather than simply those who reclined and ate" (Newton 1998: 367).

He adds two subordinate arguments. For one, 10:19, like 8:5-6, underlines the insignificance and nothingness of *eidolothuta* and of *eidola* so the problem cannot be with the eating of food which has been offered. For the other, 10:20 refers for the first time directly to the making of the offerings (*thuousin*) and explicitly forbids Christians from becoming participants (*koinonous,* 10:20) in them. This purportedly indicates that the problem is Christian participation in the offering of sacrifices.

These arguments fail to convince. With regard to the first, within Greco-Roman cult *trapezomata* describes offerings made to the god by placing them on the table (*trapeza*), whatever their ultimate use. Though sometimes officiants ate them, this practice was not so fixed that the term developed a technical use, or took on the connotation 'sacrificial offering to the gods, eaten by officiants.' *Trapezomata* was simply one of many designations (including *theomoiria, hiera moira, to paratithemena,* and *tithemena*) for "portions of meat from the sacrificial animal... which were assigned to the god—usually on his *trapeza*—at the *thusia*" (Gill 1974: 124). Sometimes the table held just the god's portion of the sacrifice; commonly, though, the entire sacrifice was placed there for carving and distribution among all those participating in the banquet (Dow and Gill 1965: 109). In the latter case, all participants—not just the sponsors of the sacrifice—would arguably be 'sharers in the table'.

With regard to the dismissal of idol food as 'nothing,' on any reading of the text, the problem is neither the food nor the idol *per se.* But this point does not necessarily permit Christians to eat idol food any more than it permits them to worship idols.

Finally, the prohibition against Christian participation in the offerings (10:20) does not imply that some were directly engaged in acts of veneration: it is only the pagan 'they' who make the offerings (*thuousin*). Christians participate by joining the cultic feast.

[19] Fisk (1989: 63–64; cf. Delobel 1996: 182–83) supposes that chapter eight permits *eidÇlothuta,* "theologically and morally 'neutral'" temple meals; 10:1–22 prohibits *eidÇlolatria,* "blatantly idolatrous" temple meals.

The linguistic evidence does not support this conceptual distinction. The term *eidÇlothuta* appears not only in chapter eight, but also in 10:19. There it elaborates the exhortation to avoid *eidÇlolatria* (10:14). Given that 10:15–18 are arguments by analogy with Christian communion and Jewish sacrifice, 10:19 is actually the first direct exposition of the thesis sentence in 10:14.

> Flee idolatry [*eidÇlolatria*] [10:14]...
> What am I suggesting? That idol offerings [*eidÇlothuta*] are anything or that an idol is anything? No, but the things which they sacrifice, they offer to demons and not to God. I do not want you to become sharers with the demons. You are not able to drink the cup of the Lord and the cup of demons; you cannot share the table of the Lord and the table of demons (10:19–21).

Idol offerings (*eidÇlothuta*) are sacrifices presented to pagan gods, and then consumed at meal; they fall under the ban on idolatry *(eidÇlolatria).* This would encompass every meal in the temple precinct, and a good many outside.

[20] LSJ 1968: 813; Thyen 1991: 161.

[21] The identity of the addressees in these verses is uncertain. Since conscience is a problem for the weak, many interpreters assume they are in view here, but this requires a sudden change of addressee. Consequently, others argue that Paul is still addressing the strong (e.g., Fee 1987: 477 n10; Witherington 1995: 226–27). Yet that raises the problem of explaining why those with no convictions against eating the food would raise questions of conviction. Perhaps there is no need to choose one over the other. The weak need the admonition, lest the preceding two chapters confirm them in all their convictions; the strong need the reassurance, lest the preceding two chapters prove too difficult to accept. Or perhaps Paul is rounding out his own position rather than addressing one group or the other; if so, it is not necessary to infer a rapid series of unmarked changes in addressee.

[22] The contrast is expressed in terms reminiscent of chapters 8 and 9. The maxim of 10:23 opposes what is 'permissible' (*exestin,* a cognate of 'rights', *exousia* cf. 8:9; 9:4, 5, 6, 12, 18) with what is 'helpful,' which is defined in terms of what 'builds up' others (*oikodomeÇ* cf. 8:10). Once again, communal welfare stands over against personal prerogatives.

[23] On the location of the market in Corinth, see Gill 1992b; Cadbury 1934.

[24] Plutarch *(Convivial Questions* 696E*)* describes a meal in which the cultic origin of the food was shared knowledge among the diners: "the cock, that [the cook] had set before the diners though it has just been slaughtered as a sacrifice to Haracles, was as tender as if it had been a day old."

[25] In ancient rhetoric, this was a common rhetoric device, called 'epanorthosis': phrasing a remark in an unsuitable fashion, so that it might immediately be elaborated.

[26] Though certainty is unattainable, two features point to this informant being a pagan host or fellow-guest. First, the term employed is the respectful *hierothuton* ('sacred offering') rather than the typical Judeo-Christian pejorative *eidolothuton* ('idol offering') (cf. Borgen 1996: 36). Secondly, any Christian could simply be referred to Paul's preceding words permitting consumption.

The most common objection is to ask why the conscience of any pagan would be sensitized to eating idol food (e.g., Meggitt 1998: 112–13; Murphy-O'Connor 1979a: 101), especially if 'conscience' bears the sense which Pierce (1958) advocates, namely, 'bad feelings concerning past action' (cf. Murphy-O'Connor 1978: 570; contra Jewett 1971). Obviously under that definition of conscience, the informant could not be a non-Christian, but the meaning of conscience is controverted.

All that the text requires is for the pagan to expect Christian guests to have scruples about eating offered food, and to volunteer the information out of respect for Christian scruples. Given the widespread gentile familiarity with Jewish scruples, and the origin of Christianity as a sect of Judaism, this scenario does not stretch credulity (cf. Fee 1987: 484–85). Moreover, 10:32 expressly warns against causing gentile (and Jewish) non-Christians to stumble.

[27] As Barrett (1968:244) explains: "His conscience, though there may be occasions when he does not take advantage of the liberty it allows him, remains always his own, and free, and is not called in question by the judgements of others." This interpretation corresponds with Paul's perspective on Christian freedom and rights elsewhere in the letter. To eat food at a friend's house—as to receive support for apostolic ministry—is a right before God (10:25–27 cf. 9:3–14). Christians may choose voluntarily to surrender a right for the welfare of other (10:28–29a cf. 9:12, 15). Nonetheless, the right remains, and no one has the authority to stand in judgment over such decisions (10:29b–30 cf. 4:3–5).

[28] Gooch (1993) misses the centrality of context in Paul's exposition. Consequently, he concludes that the harm resides in the food itself: Paul "understands food to hold deadly contagion" (p 86); "Paul sees the partnership (which can lead either to God's blessing or God's rejection) inherent in food" (pp 86–87); "food itself is a vector of contagion" (p 87 cf. 57); "idol food [is] dangerous" (p 93); "Paul's position at root was that idol-food was dangerous and was to be avoided" (p 126). This is so central to his analysis that it becomes the title of his work: *Dangerous Food.*

Oddly, other times Gooch correctly perceives that with either idol food or the eucharist it is *consumption* of the food *within the ritual context,* not the food item *per se,* which is significant:

> Participatory consumption of a meal sacred to another God is idolatry and carries judgment…Food with a sacred past was acceptable (if it was simply for sale in the market) (p 105).

> If a meal was accompanied by any rite sacred to another God, whether that meal was in a temple, at the homes of friends or relatives, or in their own households, obedient Christians would refuse to eat (p 108).

> Paul is thinking of eating that is consciously sacred to the *daimonia* or Lord it honours (p 77).

On a single page, Gooch first supposes that Paul considers "idol-food…dangerous," but then proposes that "Paul did not eat in any context connected to idolatrous rite" (p 95). Is the danger in the food or in the connection of food to rite?

The conundrum dissolves by the simple expedient of distinguishing food *per se* from food consumed in connection with a cultic celebration. Gooch is able to avoid such a distinction only through verbal gymnastics:

> Paul believed idol-*food* to carry the contagion of demons in the same way that the *meal* of the Lord infects with the Lord's blessing (p 57 *emphasis added*).

Which is it: does idol *food* itself carry contagion just as the *eucharistic elements* themselves convey blessing, or is it participation in the *cultic meal* which brings judgment just as participation in the *eucharistic meal* brings blessing?

Two features of Paul's exposition disallow Gooch's analysis. First, were the problem food *per se,* Paul could simply prohibit it across the board. Instead, he describes various scenarios and shapes his advice to fit the specifics of the context. Secondly, whether he permits or prohibits the food, he explicitly and repeatedly clarifies that the food itself is not at issue: idol food is inconsequential (10:19); all food comes from God (10:26). What God disallows is the offering of sacrifice (10:20), participation in cultic meals (10:21), or the construction of obstacles which stumble or confuse others (8:7–13; 10:28–30).

[29] Paul employs a pun here which is difficult to capture in idiomatic English. "If I participate with gratitude [*haris,* grace], why am I slandered on the grounds of what I say grace [*eu**haristō*]* over?" (10:30).

[30] Hurd (1982: 128–29) supposes that "1 Cor. 10.23–11.1 is a point by point restatement and summary of the argument of 1 Cor. 8 and 9," but many of his proposed parallels are forced (e.g., 8:3 cf. 10:24; 8:8 cf. 10:27).

[31] As Barrett (1965: 40) comments, "the question [is] whether it is or is not proper for a Christian to eat food that has at some stage in its history passed through a pagan rite and been offered in sacrifice to an idol."

Two qualifications are necessary. This may not be an accurate statement of the issue as it was presented to Paul. Perhaps the presenting issue was narrower than this. But some such comprehensive statement is necessary in order to encompass the wide range of his discussion. Secondly, as Fee (1980: 179–81) insists, the Corinthians may have presented this issue to Paul not in the form of a question, but in the form of an argument.

[32] Contra Newton 1998

[33] Contra Oster 1992.

[34] This mitigates against the central thesis of Tomson (1990) that Paul—like the later rabbis—argues from intent, specifically, from the intent of the gentile practitioner. The Corinthian strong argue from intent, but from their own intent, not the intent of pagan practitioners (1 Cor. 8:4). On his part, Paul imposes the conventional Judeo-Christian interpretation of cultic meals on pagan feasts (10:16–18), without regard to the intent of either pagan or Corinthian Christian. Tomson (1990: 208–16) relies heavily on a purported but dubious equivalence between the rabbinic concept of 'intent' and the Pauline concept of 'conscience.' Whatever the value of this purported parallel, in the final analysis, Paul allows conscience scant role in the decision.

[35] Murphy-O'Connor (1979a: 97) writes that "Paul...believed that social gestures had an objective significance which was independent of the intention of those who made them." While the use of the terms

'social' and 'objective' are regrettable, the basic point is valid: participation in sacrifical rites and accompanying meals has an inherent meaning, whatever the intention of the offerers and participants, a meaning established by analogy with the eucharist. As Murphy-O'Connor (1979a: 98) also notes: "If the Strong participate in pagan temple banquets, their physical gesture brings them into a 'common union' with idols and with those who worship them. Whatever be their intention, their physical stance brings them into the category of 'idolaters'." Only at one point does this statement need correction: Paul does not limit cultic meals to a temple context.

[36] Gooch (1993: 108) rightly comments: "If a meal was accompanied by any rite sacred to another God, whether that meal was in a temple, at the homes of friends or relatives, or in their own households, obedient Christians would refuse to eat."

[37] Contra Witherington 1993.

[38] The proviso not to cause Christians to stumble is largely redundant: there should no longer be any controversy for Christians on the grounds of conscience, because Paul has just spent three chapters setting specific parameters, thus rendering conscience redundant.

CHAPTER 9

Standing Firm against the Foe: Idol Offerings and Communal Meals in the Early Church

Summary: Paul's stance on idol food is essentially in harmony with Acts 15 and Revelation 2, though the latter are stricter due to their social contexts. The mainstream of the early Church maintains that stricter stance, due again to its social context.

While 1 Corinthians 8–10 provides the most thorough treatment of idol offerings in the New Testament, two other passages address the issue briefly: Acts 15:19,29 (cf. 21:25) and Revelation 2:14,20.[1] These warrant consideration not only in the interest of comprehensiveness, but also for the additional light they shed on first-century Christian practice, and for their implications today.

In addition, subsequent generations had to implement biblical teaching in daily interaction with an idolatrous society. The cumulative experience of the early Church thus provides an important case study by which to assess the New Testament guidelines.

The Consumption of Idol Offerings in Acts and Revelation

Both Acts 15 and Revelation 2 prohibit the consumption of idol offerings in terse and categorical terms. Consequently, majority scholarly opinion argues, these two passages cannot be reconciled with the permissiveness of 1 Corinthians 8–10.[2] Minority opinion argues in the opposite direction, inferring that the prohibitions of Acts 15 and Revelation 2 support a restrictive reading of 1 Corinthians 8–10.[3]

A decision between these alternatives rests, of course, as much on the interpretation of 1 Corinthians 8–10 as on the meaning of Acts 15 and Revelation 2. Still, the additional texts raise two questions: Does the New Testament provide a consistent response to the consumption of food offerings? If not, does any divergence reflect conflicting values, or is it attributable to some other factor?

Idol Offerings and the Inclusion of Gentiles in Acts 15

The Jerusalem council affirmed that gentile believers—unlike Jewish believers—would not be required to be circumcised or to keep the Law in order to be saved (Acts 15:1,5,8–11; 21:20–24). Instead, the conference placed only four restrictions on gentile freedom: idol food,[4] sexual immorality, strangled animals[5] and blood (15:20 cf. 15:29; 21:25). The prohibitions are unqualified, so the Apostolic Council may be more restrictive than Paul, but if so, not by much. In fact, what is most striking is the degree of support which the Pauline mission to the gentiles receives from the Council.[6]

The entire tenor of the discussion is remarkably supportive of Pauline theology. For instance, when some believers from a Pharisaic background claim that gentiles must be circumcised and must obey the Mosaic Law in order to be saved (15:1,5), Peter rebuts them with a speech (15:7–11) that could have come straight from Paul:

God chose for the gentiles to hear the gospel message through me and to believe [cf. Rom. 1:13–15; Gal. 2:7–9]. And God who knows the heart bore them witness by giving the Holy Spirit to them just as to us [cf. Rom. 8:16; Gal. 3:2–5]. He made no distinction between us and them, cleansing their hearts by faith [cf. Rom. 2:6–11; 3:22–24]. Why then do you test God by putting a yoke on the necks of the disciples which neither our fathers nor we were able to bear [cf. Gal. 3:10–12]? Through the grace of the Lord Jesus, we believe and are saved, just as also they [cf. Gal. 2:15–16].

Paul would dispute nothing in this speech; at the same time, it is Peter, not Paul, who both initiates and defends the ministry to gentiles.

Similarly, James reinforces the central point of Peter's speech by stressing the divine initiative in the outreach to the gentiles (15:14) and cites the prophets in confirmation (15:15–18). Paul is largely silent in the account, with only a passing allusion to his report of the dramatic signs that accompanied his ministry (15:12). In Acts 15, then, the admission of uncircumcised gentiles to the church comes at God's initiative, with the support of James and Peter.[7] Consequently, as Cheung observes, "instead of a source of opposition, Jerusalem now becomes the authoritative patron of the Gentile mission."[8]

Neither would Paul object in principle to Council restrictions on gentile conduct.[9] Four items is a very modest demand compared to the lengthy vice lists which appear in many of Paul's letters (e.g., 1 Cor. 5:9–11; 6:9–11; 10:1–13; Gal. 5:19–21).[10] Moreover, Paul explicitly makes avoidance of vice a condition for salvation (1 Cor. 6:9; 10:6–10; Gal. 5:21), whereas the Apostolic Decree more circumspectly concludes simply, "You do well if you keep yourselves from these things" (15:29).[11] The admonition is mild by Paul's standards and could hardly have offended him.[12]

Nor would these four particular demands trouble him. The prohibition against sexual immorality features regularly in his own vice lists (1 Cor. 6:18; Gal. 5:19; Eph. 5:3; Col. 3:5; 1 Thess. 4:3). He is also resolutely opposed to feasts held in conjunction with idol offerings (1 Cor. 10:14–22).[13] The restrictions pertaining to eating blood and meat from strangled animals are somewhat puzzling, but not only with respect to Paul: the usual method of Greco-Roman sacrifice and animal slaughter involved bleeding the beast, so unsurprisingly, this prohibition appears nowhere else in the New Testament.

The references to blood and strangulation are the best clue to the background and intent of these prohibitions. The four restrictions are largely comparable to those in Leviticus 17 and 18, where they appear in the same order as in Acts 15:29.[14] Notably, the stipulations of Leviticus 17 and 18 are required both of Jews and of gentiles living among them (Lev. 17:8,10,12,13,15; 18:26), a situation comparable to that resulting from the influx of gentiles into the Jewish Church.[15] Even under the Law, then, gentile converts continue to relate to the Law as gentiles, not as Jews.[16] This verdict adds little burden to them, while assuaging legitimate Jewish fears of immorality.[17] More to the point, it is a conclusion with which Paul could easily agree, and an irony at the expense of the Judaizers which he would fully enjoy.

With regard to the prohibition against idol food, Paul is certainly more detailed, but he does not differ in basic position: Christians must not participate in cultic feasts; they may freely eat food of unknown origin from the market or at a pagan home; they may not eat food explicitly identified as an idol offering. The only place where any discrepancy might exist is in the case of food known to have been offered to idols, but served in a non-cultic context, without anyone calling attention to its prior history or ascribing any special significance to the dish. The blanket prohibition in Acts 15 would seem to exclude consumption of any food known to have been offered; Paul could possibly be read to permit it. Even this proposed discrepancy is at best possible, not certain. It rests, in part, on an inference from Paul: he does not explicitly permit the consumption of any food known to have been offered to idols. It rests, in part also, on the ambiguity resulting from the brevity of the Jerusalem decree.

Either way, a categorical prohibition would have been adequate for Jewish Christians, who as Jews could continue living comfortably within primarily Jewish social and ethnic circles, where idol offerings were carefully prohibited. But the apostle to the gentiles—not to mention the gentiles whom he evangelized—did not have the luxury of remaining within a Jewish enclave. In such a context, a blanket prohibition would not provide sufficient nuance for converts; they required more detailed guidance. So it is just as likely that Paul intends 1 Corinthians 8–10 to explain how far the Council prohibition extends. Bauckham concurs:

> Even Paul's discussion of *eidÇlothuta* in 1 Corinthians can be read, not as a rejection of the decree's first prohibition, but as Paul's interpretation of it. In 1 Corinthians 10:25,27 he defines situations in which it does not apply, while in 10:6–22 he strongly endorses it in the situation where he holds that it does apply.[18]

Paul provides the necessary direction, arguably within the parameters established by the formulation of the Jerusalem decree, though not by authority of the council but because his understanding of Scripture leads him to a similar position. Surely not everyone at the council would have accepted his proposals. At the same time, in the absence of concrete evidence, it is tendentious to suppose that the council or its apostolic leaders would have rejected those proposals.

Idol Offerings and the Emperor Cult in Revelation 2[19]

The book of Revelation addresses the problem of idol offerings within the context of emperor worship in Asia Minor.[20] Since the veneration of rulers is not a pressing issue within contemporary Chinese contexts, this section only briefly surveys the imperial cult in Asia Minor, before assessing the compatibility of Revelation 2 and 1 Corinthians 8–10.

The Emperor Cult in Asia Minor[21]

The imperial cult was largely parallel in structure and practice to the traditional Greco-Roman cults of divinities.[22] Comparable honors, temples, priests, festivals, and sacrifices characterized each.[23] More than that, the emperors were actually incorporated into the divinity cults, celebrated at the traditional festivals, housed within the same temples (or in separate temples constructed along the same pattern), and fêted at the same sacrifices (as well as at separate, parallel sacrifices).[24]

The imperial cult was a feature not only of the religious and political landscape, but also of the local and regional social scene. The cult included a regular cycle of city-wide (and also provincial) processions, sacrifices, gladiatorial and animal fights, games, and feasts. Images and offerings were on display not only in the temple, but also in the civic square, in associations, in clubs and collegia, and in the theater, as well as in stadia and gymnasia. During civic festivals, the image of the emperor would be carried through the streets, and residents would offer sacrifice outside their homes as the procession passed.[25] Status as a *neokoros* ('temple warden') brought pride to a city, and was a source of sometimes aggressive competition between provincial rivals.[26]

What is less clear is the significance of all this. Was the imperial cult fundamentally an expression of political loyalty rather than religious conviction?[27] Did people truly believe the emperor to be divine?[28] Is there a single, simple answer?[29] Is this line of investigation even legitimate?[30]

Leaving aside some of the conundrums still hotly contested within the professional guilds of ancient historians, several conclusions are reasonably certain. First, as with the cults of the gods and the home, the veneration of the emperor was pervasive and participation virtually unavoidable, across all classes, at least in the province of Asia Minor. Secondly, the emperor cult, again as Greco-Roman religion in general, defies any neat distinction between religion, on the one hand, and politics, culture, or social relations, on the other.[31] Thirdly, a basic ambivalence existed concerning the status and identity of emperors: they both were—and were not—gods.[32]

Fourthly, social location again comes into play, and at two levels: function and interpretation.[33] With regard to function, sponsoring the imperial festivals was one of the ways by which the civic and provincial elite expressed and reinforced their dominant position.[34] With regard to interpretation, "in the sophisticated circles of philosophers, courtiers, and historians, cynical skepticism about the divinity of a human emperor was readily available."[35]

Response to Emperor Cult in Revelation 2[36]

Prominent church members in Pergamum and Thyatira advocated the consumption of idol food (2:14, 20). The elder John does not identify their motivation, apart from the indication that these teachers—like Balaam and Jezebel before them—were serving Satan by corrupting the Church (2:14,24). But whatever their explicit rationale, the incentives encouraging participation in the emperor and divine cults are readily apparent.[37]

More was at stake than social integration and a sense of communal belonging; life and livelihood were also at risk.[38] In its earliest years, the church—as a sect of Judaism—was exempt from participation in Roman cults. But with the separation from Judaism (2:9; 3:9), and with the increased proportion of gentile members, that immunity would have ceased.[39] To worship other gods in addition to the traditional Greco-Roman deities and the emperor was readily permitted; to refuse traditional worship was understood to be criminally antisocial and politically subversive, and could be treated with the severest consequences (cf. Rev. 6:9–11; 7:9–14; 11:3–11; 12:11; 13:7; 16:6; 17:6; 18:24).

There is no ambiguity or nuance in John's response. Though they be leaders or prophets in the congregation, these teachers are akin to the duplicitous Balaam (Num. 25:1–9; 31:6) or the malevolent Jezebel (1 Kings 16:31; 2 Kings 9:22). Their counsel will lead the church into judgment and ruin. Consequently, if they do not repent, Jesus will come quickly to destroy them and their followers (Rev. 2:14, 22–23). Only those who avoid such sins will be saved (Rev. 2:17, 26).

For present purposes, the primary question is whether or not this response is compatible with Paul's position. The continuities between Revelation 2 and 1 Corinthians 8–10 are widely ignored, but noteworthy.[40] First, the presenting situation in each case is the presence within the church of some advocating full participation in idol feasts (1 Cor. 8:1, 4, 8–10 cf. Rev. 2:14, 20).[41] Secondly, both Paul and John threaten these people with the same consequence: divine destruction (1 Cor. 10:1–22 cf. Rev. 2:16,22–23). Thirdly, both ground the prohibition against idol food in the same Old Testament passage (Num. 25:1–9 cf. Rev. 2:14, 20; 1 Cor. 10:8). Fourthly, both reject revisionist and rationalistic interpretations of cult which were available in the wider culture and advocated in the local church, and which could otherwise justify Christian participation in cultic meals (1 Cor. 8:4–13; cf. Rev. 2:14, 20). So all four—problem, solution, argument, and rationale—are compatible.

The only possible divergence comes from Paul's caveat permitting the purchase of meat from the market and the consumption of food at a neighbor's without regard to its prior history (1 Cor. 10:23–30). Would John concur with this permission?[42] Given his categorical prohibitions, possibly not.[43] But terseness makes it impossible to be certain.

Christians and the Emperor Cult in Roman Perspective[44]

The elder John apparently carried the day against those he typifies as Jezebel and Balaam, for the Christian stance on emperor worship soon became so notorious as to draw the attention of Roman civic bureaucrats. Sometime around C.E. 112, Pliny, a Roman governor over part of Asia Minor (Bithnyia-Pontus), sought advice from the emperor Trajan on dealing with Christians. This letter sheds further light on the early Christian stance toward the consumption of idol offerings.

As governor, Pliny investigated anonymous complaints against Christians. Unaware of any precedent, he sought advice from the emperor concerning how far to go in the effort to uncover them, and what sort of punishment to inflict. His practice had been to provide three opportunities to renounce Christ. Those who persisted in refusing were executed, for obstinacy if for no other reason (*Ep* 10.96.3–4).[45] Those who denied Christ were released once they had fulfilled three requirements: praying before the images of the gods, offering wine and incense before the statue of the emperor, and reviling the name of Christ. These, he explains, no genuine Christian would do (10.96.5–7).[46]

So far Pliny's understanding of the Christian stance on idolatry concurs with the consensus position of Acts 15, 1 Corinthians 10, and Revelation 2. It is in describing the effects of his policy that Pliny enters the realm of biblical ambiguities. The cult, Pliny notes, had infected a great many people, not only in the towns, but also in villages and outlying areas (*Ep* 10.96.9–10). As a result, the temples were almost entirely deserted, the rites had lapsed, and significantly, scarcely anyone could be found to buy meat from sacrificial victims in the market.[47] He is pleased to report that his interrogations and executions had reversed those destabilizing trends.

While the stance of Christians in Pliny's time cannot simply be read back into Revelation 2 (or Acts 15), his letter does at least indicate that early in the second century some Christians in Asia Minor were stricter than Paul explicitly required.[48] The apostle advises Christians to purchase food from the market freely and without inquiry; according to Pliny, Christians in his province were more scrupulous. Evidence from the early Church Fathers confirms the popularity of this stricter stance.

The Consumption of Idol Offerings in the Early Church Fathers

The stance of the early Church Fathers is undisputed: they universally and categorically prohibit consumption of idol food.[49] What is in question is how far their position correlates with—or depends on—1 Corinthians 8–10. Are the Fathers in harmony with Paul?[50] To the extent that they are not, how is the discrepancy to be explained: Were the Fathers unaware of the apostle's teaching? Did they find his position unacceptable or untenable? Did they misunderstand his argument, due to its subtlety and indirection? Or is there some other explanation for any difference?[51]

The earliest texts prohibit idol offerings without qualification or elaboration. For instance, the *Didache*, an early second-century catechism, supplies a single categorical prohibition: "Be diligently on guard against idol food, for it is the worship of dead gods" (6.3 *own translation*).[52] Similarly, the Syriac version of the *Apology* of Aristides lauds the moral standards of Christians, including their refusal to eat "food which is consecrated to idols" (15.2). The strength of each prohibition implies rejection of any food known to have been offered to idols; neither text reflects familiarity with 1 Corinthians 8–10.[53]

Writing in the mid-second-century, Justin indicates that some Christians were still eating idol food, and rationalizing it much the same way as the Corinthians did. Initially he insists that gentile Christians endure persecution rather than "either worship idols, or eat meat offered to idols" (*Dialogue* 34:8). His antagonist, Trypho, counters that many who profess Christ "eat meats offered to idols, and declare that they are by no means injured in consequence" (35:1). Justin rejoins (quoting Matt. 7:15 and 1 Cor. 11:19) that such people are heretics. Given this perspective, and the determination to endure persecution, it is evident that he would not tolerate consumption of any food known to have been offered to idols.

In the latter half of the second century, Irenaeus (*Adv Haer* 1.6.3; 1.24.5; 1.26.3; 1.28.2; 2.14.5) takes aim at even more extravagant opponents. Claiming to be spiritually superior and immune to carnal defilement, his antagonists engage in sexual immorality, use magic, attend gladiatorial contests, and freely eat idol food. They insist that such activities are a matter of 'indifference,' neither causing God any concern nor defiling those who participate (1.6.3; 1.24.5; 1.26.3; 1.28.2; 2.14.5). Their logic is reminiscent of the Corinthian strong (cf. 1 Cor. 6:12–13; 8:1,4), but the only specific allusion to Scripture comes in Irenaeus' appeal to the prohibitions of Revelation 2 (1.26.3).[54] Given the depth of his sentiment, it is unlikely that he would countenance consumption of any food known to have been offered to idols.

Tertullian, ministering between the second and third centuries, is the first Church Father to appeal explicitly to the range of New Testament teaching on idol food.[55] He invokes 1 Corinthians 10:21 to explain why Christians neither worship gods and ancestors nor eat food offered to them: "We cannot partake of God's feast and the feast of devils" (*Shows* 13).[56] Lest his point be misunderstood, Tertullian follows Paul in clarifying that the idol has no reality, but that the homage offered to idols is actually rendered to demons.[57]

At the same time, he goes further than Paul in two respects. For one, he supposes that demons actually dwell in the images and idols (*Shows* 13). For the other, he is significantly more restrictive with respect to marketplace food: the apostle Paul "'delivered...the keys of the meat-market,' permitting the eating of 'all things' with...the exception of 'things offered to idols'" (*Fasting* 15.5). In effect, this reads the permission of 1 Corinthians 10:25 in terms of the prohibitions of Acts 15:20,29 and Revelation 2:14,20.[58]

Roughly contemporaneous with Tertullian, Clement of Alexandria also cites 1 Corinthians 8–10 often and to much the same end. He finds four grounds for abstaining from the consumption of idol offerings, one negative and three positive: not out of fear, for demons are impotent (cf. 8:4–6; 10:19); but by reason of personal conscience (cf. 10:28b–30), out of aversion to demons (cf. 10:20), and from deference to weaker Christians (cf. 8:7,9–13) (*Instructor* 2.1.8–10).

Significantly, the second reason misreads Paul, who takes pains to clarify that his concern is for the conscience not of the Christian participant but of observers (10:29–30 cf. 8:7–13).[59] Like Tertullian, Clement also resolves the issue of marketplace food by subordinating the permission of 1 Corinthians 10:25 to the prohibition of Acts 15:20,29 (*Stromata* 4.15 [97.3]).[60] At the same time, he makes Paul more explicit—and likely more restrictive—than the apostle originally intended.[61]

Writing in the first half of the third century, Origen makes three notable contributions on this issue.[62] First, as the student of Clement, he unsurprisingly views the welfare of the weak and the demonic nature of idols as two parallel reasons for abstaining.[63] Secondly, he integrates Acts 15 and 1 Corinthians 8–10, appealing to the latter to explain the grounds for the prohibitions in the former.[64] Thirdly, his ability to harmonize Acts 15 seamlessly with 1 Corinthians 8–10 is due in part to his highly restrictive interpretation of 1 Corinthians 10: he insists that Christians avoid any food even suspected of having been offered to idols.[65] At the same time, his appeal to Romans 14 in order to justify the extended prohibition demonstrates that 1 Corinthians 10:14–30 does not itself demand such scruples.[66]

Novatian, writing around the middle of the third century, briefly addresses the topic of idol food in the course of a diatribe against Jewish food laws. Arguing that Christians are free from Jewish regulations concerning circumcision, sabbath, and unclean foods, he warns that this liberty does not extend to foods offered to idols.

> It must be very greatly guarded against in the use of food, and we must be warned lest any should think that liberty is permitted to that degree that even he may approach to what has been offered to idols. For, as far as pertains to God's creation, every creature is clean. But when it has been offered to demons, it is polluted so long as it is offered to the idols; and as soon as this is done, it belongs no longer to God, but to the idol. And when this creature is taken for food, it nourishes the person who so takes it for the demon, not for God, by making him a fellow-guest with the idol, not with Christ (*Jewish Meats* 7).

Novatian thus proposes that the act of offering food to an idol nullifies its divine source and attaches demonic pollution which is then conveyed to those who eat the food. This clearly goes beyond—even contradicts—Paul's view that the sacrifice does not affect the character of the food (1 Cor. 10:19) and that Christians may eat freely from the market or at a friend's home (1 Cor. 10:25,27) precisely because the food comes from God (1 Cor. 10:26).[67]

This survey could go on at much greater length, but the general trend and consensus of the early Church is beyond doubt. Three additional Church Fathers deserve a brief look, though, because each contributes some distinctive feature which fills out the picture.

In the first half of the fourth century, Eusebius wrote an apologetic tract defending Christianity over against both Judaism and paganism. While shedding no new light on Christian responses to idol food, this work provides helpful confirmation of two points discussed previously. First, Eusebius describes the predicament in which Christians found themselves by renouncing the worship of pagan deities while in turn being renounced by mainstream Judaism. He quotes the common charge against the Church:

> Must it not be a proof of extreme wickedness and levity lightly to put aside the customs of their own kindred, and choose with unreasoning and unquestioning faith the doctrines of the impious enemies of all nations? Nay, not even to adhere to the

God who is honoured among the Jews according to their customary rites, but to cut out for themselves a new kind of track in a pathless desert, that keeps neither the ways of the Greeks nor those of the Jews? (*Preparation* 1.2.5c).

To break from ancestral traditions was considered the epitome of impiety: both Jewish and gentile converts to Christianity did so, thus confirming public disapprobation of this new religion.

Secondly, Eusebius confirms the customary division of Greco-Roman religion in terms of three distinct social contexts:

They divide their whole system of theology under three general heads, the mythical treated by the poets in tragedy, and the physical which has been invented by the philosophers, and that which is enforced by the laws and observed in each city and country...the political, or state-religion (*Preparation* 4.1.130a–b).

The first and second are malleable by poet or philosopher; the third is

legally ordained by their rulers to be honoured and observed, this, say they, let neither poet nor philosopher disturb; but let every one, both in rural districts and in cities, continue to walk by the customs which have prevailed from old time, and obey the laws of his forefathers (*Preparation* 4.1.130d).

Eusebius rejects each of these perspectives in turn: the poets' mythology, the philosophers' rationalism and the Roman civic cult.

In the latter half of the fourth century, John Chrysostom expounded 1 Corinthians 8–10 in a series of homilies remarkable for their clarity, sensitivity to nuance, and attention to authorial intent (*Homilies on First Corinthians* 20–25).[68] Collating the three chapters, Chrysostom tabulates seven reasons from chapters 8 and 10 for renouncing cultic feasts:

Because of their unprofitableness, because of their needlessness, because of the injury to our brother, because of the evil-speaking of the Jew, because of the reviling of the Gentile, because we ought not to be partakers with demons, because the thing is a kind of idolatry (25.3).

At the same time, he emphasizes the opposing danger of excessive scrupulosity and, with Paul, encourages Christians to eat food from the market and to share meals with friends (25.1).[69] Still, though he does not directly address the issue, Chrysostom clearly assumes that Christians will not knowingly eat idol food.[70]

Finally, a letter to Augustine (A.D. 354-430) reveals that some early Christians, at least, went into great detail in the effort to define the boundaries of the prohibition against idol food (*Letter* 46).[71] If Christians buy meat from the market, thinking that it was not offered, then wonder whether it might have been offered, before finally deciding it was not, may they eat the food or not (46.8)? If someone lies in claiming that a piece of meat was offered to idols, then admits it was not actually offered, and the Christian believes the latter rather than the former, is the meat permitted (46.10)? If a Christian attends a meal at someone else's house, is informed that the meat was offered to idols and abstains, and then unwittingly buys some of the same meat at the market or is served it elsewhere, does he or she sin in eating, if ignorant of its origin (46.17)?[72]

In his reply, Augustine (*Letter* 47.3,4,6) does not dismiss these questions as pettifoggery or legalism, but replies in kind. Generally, Christians may eat freely, since 'the earth is the Lord's, and the fulness thereof' (quoting 1 Cor. 10:25–26). Eating food known to have been offered to idols is a sin, but not eating from a sacrifice unwittingly. Nor do Christians sin if they eat food which they think has probably not been offered to idols, even if they previously thought that it had been. Moreover, if a starving traveler happens upon food in a temple, he or she may eat it so long as it was either certainly or probably not offered to idols.

While Augustine's answers are more detailed than most, the basic thrust is compatible with the consensus of the early Church: as a baseline, eat freely; carefully avoid anything that is known or likely to have been offered to idols; in ambiguous circumstances, eating is permitted.

Conclusion

To a greater or lesser extent, then, Paul's position is unique in the early Church. At the very least, he grants explicit permission to eat market food—and to accept pagan hospitality—without question (10:25–27), a concession which appears nowhere else in extant sources. Moreover, while he discourages consumption of food identified as derived from idol offerings, he grounds the restriction in the expectations of others, not in the prior history of the food (10:28). He may even intend to permit consumption of food known to derive from idol offerings, so long as the meal is held outside the cultic context and carries no cultic significance, and provided its origin is not an issue to anyone else at the meal (10:29–30). Given the uniqueness of his liberality at these points, can his position be harmonized with Acts, Revelation, and the early Church, or are they irreconcilable?

The Apostolic Decree is vague in the fine points of execution, but at the very least the advocates of Jewish Christianity would undoubtedly have disputed Paul's liberal attitude toward marketplace food and dinner invitations. The more important question is whether or not Peter and James would have tolerated this slim sliver of flexibility. The answer is lost in history.

Tension between 1 Corinthians 10:25–30 and Revelation 2 is no more explicit, yet even more likely. Given that Christians were facing martyrdom for their refusal to participate in public festivals and cultic meals, it is hard to believe that they would have adopted a patient tolerance toward marketplace food or dinner invitations. Before the political threat arose, Paul had prioritized peaceable evangelistic initiatives; with the Church in jeopardy, the elder John circled the wagons for the dual purpose of self-definition and survival. The differences between them may not be unbridgeable: had their contexts been similar, their approaches might have coincided exactly.[73] But given that their contexts never did converge, full concurrence seems unlikely.

In subsequent centuries, abstinence from idol food became a defining mark of orthodoxy, and consumption, proof of heterodoxy. Could Christians buy idol meat on sale at the market? Pliny indicates that they would not; Tertullian, Clement, and Origen insist that they must not. Other fathers, such as Justin, Irenaeus, and Minucius Felix, express such antipathy toward idol food that even in the absence of an explicit regulation, their views of market food can reasonably be inferred. Only Augustine demonstrates any flexibility, and even he prohibits the consumption of any food known to have been offered to idols.

Is this what Paul actually intended, that Christians could buy meat from the market and eat freely at a neighbor's *so long as they did not know that the food had been offered to idols*? Cheung and Tomson are convinced, and they may well be right.[74] Certainly the entirety of early 'orthodoxy' is on their side. Nevertheless, this goes beyond what Paul explicitly states, and beyond what he even necessarily infers, as is demonstrated by the fact that those Fathers who advocate such a stance look to Acts 15 and Revelation 2 (e.g., Clement), or even to the discussion of Jewish food laws in Romans 14 (e.g., Origen).[75]

The Church Fathers employ a topical-canonical exegetical method, without sufficient attention to the differences in historical circumstance and presenting occasions between Acts 15, 1 Corinthians 8–10, and Revelation 2. Through such harmonization, the diversity within Scripture collapses into uniformity: Paul's unique approach is the victim; Acts 15 and Revelation 2, the victor. Confidence in the Fathers is further undermined by their occasional misinterpretation of Paul; for example, on the role of conscience (e.g., Clement), or on the source and nature of the harm which besets those who eat (e.g., Novatian).

The Fathers also miss Paul's deeper values at two points. For one, they overlook his underlying distinction between cultic feasts and meals at which some of the food might derive from food offerings. This likely again represents the imposition of the conceptual framework of Acts 15 and Revelation 2 ('food offerings') onto the interpretation of Paul ('cultic meals'). For the other, the Fathers overlook the tension in Paul between purity and evangelism. Instead, they prioritize purity above all else.

That is not to imply that Paul stands opposed to the rest of the canon and to four centuries of Church history. Rather, it is to affirm a range of responses, a continuum reflecting a diversity of contexts and presenting occasions. At the core, unanimity—even uniformity—is evident: Christians must not under any circumstances participate in cultic feasts; they must not eat food offerings in the presence of idols or in the context of worship. But on the peripheries, diversity is apparent: To what extent must Christians go in order to ensure purity? May they eat food from the market? May they join pagan friends at meal?

For the Judaizers of Acts 15, a simple prohibition against idol food suffices; neither their social context nor their evangelistic strategy demands any nuance. Of course, this solution is too vague for gentiles, or for the apostle to gentiles. What exactly constitutes 'idol food'? Food which was at some time in its history possibly or likely offered to idols? Or only that food which is eaten in conjunction with the offering and worship? Is it idolatrous for Christians to eat with non-Christians? The Jerusalem Council did not address these issues because neither their social relationships nor their evangelistic strategy brought them into close contact with idol worshippers.

But the apostle to gentiles could not afford the luxury of social exclusivism. Like the Judaizers, he resolutely opposes participation in cultic meals (1 Cor. 10:14–22), fully observes Jewish scruples when eating with Jews (1 Cor. 9:20), and respects Christian scruples when associating with them (1 Cor. 9:22). At the same time, he happily accepts hospitality from gentiles on their own terms in the hopes of winning them to Christ (1 Cor. 9:21). To those who insinuate that he lacks conviction, Paul insists merely that his convictions lay in a different direction: toward evangelism (1 Cor. 9:19–23; 10:31) and the glory of God (1 Cor. 10:31), rather than toward seclusion.

The elder John wrote within yet a different social context. Militant imperialism would accept nothing less than full submission to the emperor, and the offering of sacrifice to him. The Church was obliged to entrench in order to survive. Paul explicitly opposed such sacrifice, and there is little reason to suppose that his social tolerance could have long endured once the relations between society and church became adversarial. With the persistence of that adversarial relationship until the conversion of Constantine, it comes as little surprise to find that the Church fathers consistently adopted the isolationism of the elder John over the social engagement of the apostle Paul.

Two conclusions, then, arise from this survey of biblical and historical data. First, 'orthodox' elements within the Church have always prohibited participation in cultic meals, including the consumption of food in the presence of idols or in conjunction with offering or worship. This position is assumed or affirmed from the days of the Jerusalem Council, through 1 Corinthians 8–10 and Revelation 2, and throughout the history of the early Church. Apostolic verdict has consistently held such meals to be idolatrous, punishable by divine judgment.

Secondly, coupled with this essential agreement, the Church has adopted a continuum of positions on more peripheral matters, such as market meat or meals with pagan friends and associates. Where concern for purity reigned supreme (e.g., among the Judaizers of Acts 15), socialization was restricted. Where the objectives of purity and evangelism were held in tension (e.g., 1 Corinthians 10), market meat and social meals were permitted in the interest of relationships to facilitate evangelism. Where the Church was oppressed by an autocratic regime demanding obeisance (Revelation 2 and the early Church), relational evangelism was precluded and a defensive antagonism developed as a survival mechanism.

Both the unanimity and the continuum provide crucial direction for the Church today.

Endnotes

[1]   Paul's argument in Romans 14–15 shares some of the same terminology and logic; Cranfield (1979: 691–93) provides a helpful discussion, including a list of similarities between the two passages. The similarities have led some interpreters to appeal to Romans 14–15 in order to shed light on 1 Corinthians 8–10 (e.g., Conzelmann 1975: 137). Nonetheless, the issues are different. In Romans 14–15 the conflict between 'weak' and 'strong' (rather than 'knowledgeable') is over the broader issue of Jewish dietary laws ('clean,' 'unclean') and calendrical observances, rather than specifically over food offered to idols (cf. Dunn 1988: 799–802). There the scrupulous are designated 'weak in faith' rather than 'weak in conscience.' The most obvious difference, though, is that in Romans 14–15, "there is no indication…that Paul saw any harm at all in the practice of the strong in itself, apart from its effect on the weak" (Cranfield 1979: 692).

[2]   Barrett (1982: 52) is representative of a wide stream of thought: "In permitting the eating of *eidÇlothuta,* Paul allows what elsewhere in the New Testament was strictly forbidden." Similarly, Brunt (1978: 266) writes: "There is no doubt that Acts 15 cannot be neatly harmonized with what we learn from Paul in…1 Cor. 8–10." In both cases, the contradiction arises from the erroneous assumption that Paul freely permits consumption of idol food.

[3]   With reference to Acts, Cheung (1999: 181) writes: "If Luke's account is historically accurate, it will be an early and important witness to Paul's negative attitude towards idol food. It will pose tremendous difficulty for the traditional understanding of Paul's stance in this matter." Similarly, with respect to Revelation, he concludes: "All in all, Revelation gives us no reason to believe that Paul was understood to condone eating idol food. If he was understood to take a liberal attitude toward idol food, it is strange that the church in Ephesus (where he labored hard) rejected outright the Nicolaitans and their teaching regarding idol food while those churches on which he seemed to have less influence took a more tolerant attitude" (p209).

[4]   The reference to idolatry in 15:20 is rather vague: 'the defilement of idols.' The two repetitions of this prohibition clarify its significance, however: 'idol offerings' (*eidÇlothuton* 15:29; cf. 21:25).

Witherington (1998: 462–63) argues that the prohibition is directed not against the consumption of idol offerings in private residence or at the market, but only against joining feasts held within the temple precinct. This definition perfectly harmonizes Paul, the Apostolic Decree, and Revelation 2: "Here as in Acts and Paul it was understood that the prohibitions involved staying away from pagan temples" (p466). This solution depends on his dubious distinction between *eidÇlothuton* (food sacrificed to an idol and eaten in the temple) and *hierothuton* (food sacrificed to an idol and eaten outside the temple).

It also assumes improbably that all four activities in Acts 15:20 "were known or believed to transpire in pagan temples" (p464 cf. 461, 463). While conceding that immorality was a common feature of the symposia in private feasts, Witherington proposes that *porneia* in Acts 15 more likely refers to sacral prostitution (p463). Greco-Roman sacrifice commonly bled the animals, rather than strangling them; Witherington offers only one exception, and that from the magical papyri (p464). For the drinking of blood, he refers to the occasional Roman practice of the priest—not the worshippers—tasting the blood of the sacrifice (p464). He deflects all these discrepancies with the caveat that the Decree addresses what Jews 'believed' to be happening in pagan temples; thus, "it is frankly irrelevant how frequently such things actually did transpire in pagan temples" (p463 n421; cf. 464). With this last concession he implicitly concedes the error of his interpretation; the only remaining question is whether the error is attributable to the Jerusalem Council or to Witherington himself.

⁵ Some Western manuscripts (most notably the uncial D) omit the reference to strangulation; one early manuscript, p⁴⁵, omits the reference to sexual immorality. The external evidence overwhelmingly favors a four-fold prohibition (cf. Metzger 1971: 429–35). Recently Head (1993: 438–42) has argued convincingly on the basis of the remaining Western variants in Acts 15 that "the Western text must be understood as a thoroughgoing attempt to address the question of Gentile Torah-observance in a more decisive manner than the Alexandrian text allows" (p442).

⁶ Acts portrays Paul as concurring with the decree, even delivering it on behalf of the Jerusalem church (Acts 15:22,25,30; 21:26). That portrait is widely suspect in New Testament scholarship. Given the conventional interpretation of 1 Corinthians 8–10, it is commonly assumed that Luke falsely portrays Paul as agreeing to restrictions on freedom which he would never have accepted. Barrett, for example, writes: "Notwithstanding Acts it is difficult to believe that Paul was present when the Decree was drawn up" (1982: 58 n41); similarly, "Nothing is more striking than that Luke can make Paul himself part-author of the Decree" (1982: 59, n53). In fact, however, any Lukan harmonizing serves to bring the Jerusalem apostles into line with the Pauline mission, not the other way around.

Given Paul's failure to refer to the decree in 1 Corinthians 8–10, Conzelmann (1975: 138) finds it unlikely that either apostle or church knew of it: "If the decree had been known, Paul could not...have passed over it." Yet this is the same apostle who explicitly cites the sayings of Jesus only infrequently.

For surveys of various interpretations of Paul's relationship to the Decree, see Wenham 1993: 226–43; Brunt 1978: 258–66; Hurd 1965: 250–59. For present concerns, compatibility is the issue, not familiarity.

7   Bauckham (1995:452) notes that Acts 15 develops two lines of argument to support the inclusion of gentiles: (1) charismatic phenomena as evidence of God's approval on gentile converts; and, (2) an halakhic argument from Scripture.

8   Cheung 1993: 151.

9   Nor would he have rejected the restrictions on Jews in Acts 21:20–25, where James calls them to live in harmony with the Jewish law, while gentiles need do no more than observe the four prohibitions. Paul already observes this guideline: "To Jews, I became like a Jew, in order to win Jews; to those under the Law, as under the Law, though I myself am not under the Law, in order that I might win those under the Law" (1 Cor. 9:20). Similarly, he urges both Jews and gentiles to retain their ethnic identities and customs (1 Cor. 7:18–20)

10   Similarly, Borgen (1996: 243–51) argues that 15:20 should be understood in the same terms as the shorter (and longer) vice lists in Paul; that is, as part of the typical Jewish and Christian instruction of proselytes.

More speculative is his attempt to account for textual variants in Acts 15 and for subsequent conflicts over gentile obligations by arguing that the council decision left unresolved what *would* be required of gentiles, beyond the provision that circumcision *would not* be expected. Acts 15:20, he proposes, is not an exactly worded decree but a 'sample catalogue' subsequently developed in different directions (e.g., as a dietary, ritual, or ethical code) by various participants in the council.

11   The mildness of the Council demand is accentuated by the inclusion bracketing the initial paragraph of this unit. The Pharisaic party initially demanded circumcision and obedience to the Law as conditions for salvation: "Unless you are circumcised in keeping with the tradition of Moses, you cannot be saved" (15:1). The paragraph closes with Peter decrying any conditions for salvation beyond faith (15:11). The initial verse also forms a broader inclusion with 15:29, bracketing the entire discussion: beginning with circumcision as a

condition of salvation, the account ends with the four prohibitions as sound advice.

¹² Cf. Bockmuehl 1995: 96–97.

¹³ Murphy-O'Connor (1978: 557–58) supposes that Paul largely agreed with the strong, and that his 'radical antinomianism,' his rejection of law as passe, and his view of apostolic authority allowed him to ignore the Apostolic Decree because it contradicted his own decision that the eating of idol-meats was legitimate. His entire analysis is made redundant by the realization that Paul strongly disputed the position of the strong and significantly restricted the consumption of idol meat.

¹⁴ Cf. Bauckham 1995: 458–59. Callan (1993) develops a some-what more complex—and correspondingly less persuasive—version of this position, finding the origin of the decree in Pentateuchal laws that fulfill three criteria: they apply to resident aliens, they are introduced by the idiom 'any man,' and they include a warning of judgment. Bockmuehl (1995) speaks more generally of antecedents, which he finds in the continuum of biblical and post-biblical halakha for resident aliens (e.g., Gen. 1–11; Lev. 17–18; Ezek. 33:23–26).

Witherington (1998: 464–65) objects that the parallels are insufficient to establish the dependence of Acts 15 on Lev. 17–18: the LXX does not use either *eidÇlothuton* or *porneia*, nor does it refer specifically to strangulation or to the consumption of idol offerings.

Nonetheless, the parallels are close enough and sustained enough to be suggestive: sacrificing to goat idols outside the camp (Lev. 17:1–9) cf. eating idol food (Acts 15:29a); eating blood (Lev. 17:10–12) cf. eating blood (Acts 15:29b); eating meat from animals killed in hunt or found dead (Lev. 17:13–16) cf. eating strangled animals (Acts 15:29c); various forms of unlawful sexual intercourse (Lev. 18:1–28) cf. sexual immorality (Acts 15:29d). The differences may be attributable to James updating the activities of Leviticus 17 and 18 with contemporary equivalents. Or perhaps the proposal from James reflects his own version of the common Jewish discussions of ethical requirements for gentiles (cf. Bockmuehl 1995).

¹⁵ Witherington (1998: 464–65) objects to this link in part because Lev. 17–18 applies to gentiles living in the midst of Israel, whereas in Acts 15 the focus is on Jews living in the Diaspora. Callan (1993: 290; cf. Kuhn 199 : 730–31) draws attention to the application of these texts within post-biblical Jewish writers—including the LXX—to converts to Judaism. Bauckham (1995: 458–59) draws particular attention to the link with the eschatological expectations on gentile converts living 'in the midst' of Israel (cf. Amos 9:11–12; Jer. 12:16; and Zech. 2:11).

[16] Cf. Fitzmyer 1989: 194–95; Bauckham 1995: 452–53.

[17] For the early Church, this is not a compromise, as is widely supposed, but a theological deduction based on exegetical argument: as Bauckham (1995: 462) observes, "the same exegetical case which demonstrates conclusively that Gentile Christians do not have to keep the Law also shows that they do have to observe these four prohibitions" (cf. Bockmuehl 1995: 94; contra Marshall 1980: 243).

[18] Bauckham 1995: 470. Tomson (1990: 217) supports this conclusion by appeal to Jewish moral ethics: Paul "does not teach a partial permission to eat idol food. He teaches a rational, halakhic definition of what should be considered an idol offering in uncertain cases and what should not."

[19] The study of ancient Roman emperor worship is a vast field in its own right, characterized by significant recent advances in understanding (e.g., Price 1984, 1987, 1997; Friesen 1993a). Unhappily, space constraints preclude giving the topic due consideration. Given the focus on contemporary shenism, the Greco-Roman domestic cult necessarily receives higher priority. Were the focus on the Chinese imperial period or on Japanese state shinto during the first half of the twentieth century, the study of emperor veneration in Revelation would feature more prominently.

[20] The contexts of Revelation and 1 Corinthians 8–10 are not entirely different. Emperor worship was likely one element among others in the situation prompting 1 Corinthians 8–10 (cf. Winter 1994c: 94–95), just as the worship of gods also likely played a role in the crisis of Revelation (e.g., Aune 1997: 1xiv; Thompson 1990: 131; Millar 1972: 145–53; Price 1984: 124–25, 221). By and large, though, 1 Corinthians is broader in scope, while Revelation focuses on problems related to the veneration of emperors.

[21] This section largely summarizes the work of Price 1984, 1987, with occasional caveat from Friesen 1993a (who, for example, objects to treating the emperor cult as a unified whole, rather than as a number of somewhat different cults; see pp142–45).

[22] For sheer breadth of coverage, the emperor cult outdid the gods, whose patronage generally tended to be localized. Of the seven cities in Revelation 2–3, all had the imperial cult, six had at least one imperial temple, five had an imperial altar, and five had a resident imperial priest. Ephesus was especially notable, as it contained four imperial temples, a massive altar, an imperial portico and four gymnasia honoring the emperor, along with statues in public locations, from the theater and the council house to the gates and the streets.

Yet while Ephesus may have exceeded most other Asian cities in scale, it was otherwise typical in kind. Pergamum had imperial cult, temple, altar, and priest; Thyatira was lacking only the temple (Price 1984: xxii–xxv). Consequently, the emperor's "name or image met the eye at every turn" (Price 1984: 136).

[23] Price 1984: 3, 234–35; 1987: 77–80.

[24] Sacrifices included the full range of activities associated with the cult of deities. Celebrations could be private or public, and might be sponsored by individuals, by representatives of the entire city or even by provinces. Private sacrifices could be as simple as libations and ritual cakes, though public sacrifice normally included incense and animal slaughter. Price (1984: 210–11) describes a presumably 'typical' procession from the temples of Ascelpius and Hygeia, gods of health, to the imperial shrine for the sacrifice of a bull on behalf of emperors present and past, and thence to the main square for a second sacrifice, before ending in the theater with incense offerings to Augustus, Livia, and Tiberius.

[25] Price 1984: 101–32, 188–91.

[26] Price (1984: 128–29) notes that Pergamum, Smyrna, and Ephesus jointly shared the lead position in a procession at a provincial celebration, due to competing claims for the honor.

[27] Ferguson (1970: 95), for example, flatly declares that "so far as the government at Rome was concerned, the object of the imperial cult was political." Similarly, Bowersock (1972: 182; cf. 1980) claims that, "If we look at participation in the imperial cult in the provinces on the part of the local élite, it is clear that social and political roles are chiefly at issue." Fishwick (1978: 1253) makes the same point, from the under side:

> The impression given by the vast bulk of the surviving evidence is in fact of a purely mechanical exercise, a conventional gesture affirming membership in the state and sympathy with its aims, a duty to be hurriedly performed before turning to the particular worship in hand.

This leads to the blanket judgment that "the impersonalities of state-religion could not satisfy the religious needs of the individual" (Ferguson 1970: 99; cf. Fishwick 1978: 1253; Krill 1978: 43–44). In contrast, Sordi (1983) provides an extended argument in support of the proposition that the Roman persecution of Christians was initially and primarily grounded in religious issues and concerns.

[28] Roman society already had ample precedent for cross-overs from the realm of mortals to divines (or vice versa), in the demi-gods, heroes, and lares (cf. Hopkins 1978: 200–1).

²⁹ No single interpretation can likely cover the full spectrum of responses to the imperial cult. Hopkins (1978: 216) describes ancient Roman beliefs:

> There was a wide spectrum of values, beliefs, and attitudes. At a rational level, several of them were probably incompatible, yet in fact held by the same people simultaneously. Indeed, people often pick values, beliefs, and attitudes from a common social stock and give them different emphasis and expression according to the demands of social circumstances.

A comparable range of responses characterizes contemporary Chinese folk religion.

³⁰ Price (1984) objects to this approach on multiple grounds. For one, it erroneously assumes a disjunction between religion and politics (pp15–16); Price vigorously insists that religion and power functioned together in "a web of power" (pp xi cf. 233–48). Secondly, it prioritizes the beliefs and emotions of individuals over the ritual performance of the group, and conscious articulation over ritual evocation (pp 7–11). Of course, it could in turn be objected that Price's characterization of the emperor cult primarily in terms of power relations reflects a contemporary reductionistic and functionalist bias against belief in the transcendent.

³¹ Price (1984: 230) writes: "Modern scholars wrongly tend to divide what was a single Greek semantic field into two, and to distinguish between religious and secular aspects. The Greeks did not do this." This holds true both for individual rituals and for the cult as a whole. Thus, for example, the sacrifice-and-feast complex cannot be divided into religious and social components; the entire complex and its various parts blended religious and social functions.

³² Even the most expansive contemporary interpreters are reluctant to affirm unequivocally that the ancients 'worshipped' the emperor, preferring instead to speak of 'homage' (e.g., Hopkins 1978: 223; cf. Fishwick 1978: 1252–53). In comments that apply equally to contemporary shenism, Hopkins (1978: 231) writes that "most people may have been hazy about what [the affirmation of imperial divinity] meant; only sophisticated litterateurs would have thought about it, and even then perhaps not clearly."

Price (1984: 18 cf. 19) criticizes the distinction between worship and homage as a 'Christianizing framework,' imposing an outside perspective, rather than analyzing Greco-Roman religion on its own terms and within its own categories. He argues that in architecture, statuary, sacrifice, and address, the imperial cult generally treated emperors the same way as it treated gods, while nonetheless maintaining a measure of distinction between them (pp133–233).

Friesen (1993a: 150–166) turns the same critique back on Price, insisting that "ancient imperial sacrifices should not be understood as a way of indicating who was divine and who was human"; rather, the cult defined and reinforced relationships of power. Yet is it purely coincidental that power relations and hierarchies are standard analytical categories of postmodern, Western social critique, or is Friesen also imposing an etic framework on the imperial cult?

[33] Price is oriented more toward ritual participation, and this causes him to understate the effect of social location on cult interpretation:

> Greek philosophers had long been engaged in a complex attempt to articulate their relationship to popular religious traditions. Their criticisms of these traditions included criticisms of animal sacrifices, but on the whole the philosophers supported traditional institutions…The crucial point is that the criticisms of the philosophers, though searching, were not innovative in the field of ritual and that as a result traditions were upheld (1984: 228).

For Price, the 'crucial point' is that philosophical reinterpretation did not lead to innovation in ritual practice or to decrease in ritual participation. For present purposes, what is notable is the converse: that the continued participation of elites depended on ritual reinterpretation.

[34] Price (1984: 122–23) notes that "to be an imperial priest was a mark of distinction," while "to be a provincial high priest was the pinnacle of achievement."

[35] Hopkins 1978: 216. Bowersock provides the most extensive and vigorous argument for elite rationalism, though he likely overstates the case: "No thinking man ever believed in the divinity of a living emperor…and though he could conceive of the deification of a deceased emperor, he could never consider an imperial *theos* one of 'the gods'" (1972: 206; cf. Hopkins 1978: 217, n26).

Price (1984) consistently plays down the effects of social location on ritual interpretation, insisting that "the cults did not have a different meaning for the élite as against the populace and in particular that the élite was not generally skeptical" (p101). Nonetheless, he acknowledges that,

> the local élites who organized the cults had access to complex philosophical ideas about the gods which were not available to the masses, and one might argue…that the ceremonial therefore could not be understood in the same fashion by the two groups (p116).

So he seems willing to concede the effects of social location as expounded here, provided it does not imply that

> only the official view held by the élite is significant, and that
> others with a 'false' view were alienated from the rituals.
> Ritual can be the basis for various evocations for different
> groups, which can all be 'valid.' Within the Greek city the
> ceremonies were appreciated by all (p116).

Thus, his actual concern appears to be to deny, first, that elite control
led to populist alienation (pp107–14), and secondly, that only elite
interpretations are 'valid' (p116). While Marxist interpretation commonly presumes class tension, and rationalism is often elitist, the
theory of social location does not inherently imply either, but affirms
simply that the rites serve different functions for the various classes.

[36] Aune (1997: lxiv–lxv, cxx–cxxii) sunders the epistolary materials of chapters 1–3 from chapters 4–21, attributing the latter to conflict with the emperor cult, but the former to conflict exclusively with
the synagogue. On this view it is difficult to account for the author's
continued vituperative against Pergamum as the place "where Satan
has his throne," or "where Satan lives" (Aune himself attributes these
descriptions to its role in "*Roman opposition* to early Christianity,
which the author of Rev. 2–3 perceived as particularly malevolent in
that city"; Aune 1997: 184 *emphasis original*; cf. p 194). Even less is
there any sensible way to account for the Christian predilection toward participation in cultic meals (2:14,20). Furthermore, Beale (1998:
262) points out numerous verbal connections between the exhortations to the churches (2:13,19,20; 3:2–4) and the subsequent condem-
nations of the beast (e.g., 13:9,14; 14:11–12), concluding that "this
connection with later chapters was consciously intended." The links
between 2:20–23 and ch 18 are especially notable. Collins (1984: 84–
87) more reasonably proposes four areas of social tension for Christians: synagogue, pagan society, Rome, and class; de Silva (1992: 287)
modifies these into four sociological categories.

[37] Jones (1980: 1022) attributes the conflict particularly to the
imperial cult: "From the perspective of early Christianity, the worst
abuse in the Roman Empire was the imperial cult. Honors which
should be reserved for God alone could not be bestowed upon men."
This is overstated: in his handling of Christians, Pliny (*Ep* 10.96)
places the cult of the emperors alongside the cult of deities as the
ground of persecution.

On the other hand, Thompson (1990: 131) proposes that "the
imperial cult was not a central issue in either official or unofficial
attitudes toward Christians" (cf. de Silva 1992: 278; Hopkins 1978:

227 n37). This too is overstated. Revelation directs considerable vit-
riol against the worship of the beast from the sea (Rev. 13:1–17; 14:8–
12; 15:2; 16:2; 19:20; 20:4), and "Asia was on the cutting edge of
imperial cult activity" (Friesen 1993b: 34).

These considerations raise a question about the merit of comparisons such as, "In the persecutions of the Christians the cult of the
emperor was less important than the cult of the gods" (Price 1984:
221; cf. 125, 222; Aune 1997: lxiii–lxiv). Both were important factors; it
makes little difference which was the more important. Sordi (1983:
171–79) provides a nuanced assessment.

[38] Historically interpreters have sought evidence of official persecution in or from Rome, and have focused especially on persecutions attributed to Domitian (for a critical assessment, see Thompson
1990: 95–115; Aune 1997: lxiv–lxix). But there is little outside evidence of official pogroms during the first century. Consequently,
most interpreters currently look for the answer in local circumstances
within Asia Minor (e.g., Thompson 1990: 130; Collins 1984: 84–107;
Price 1984: 197–98; Friesen 1993a: 142–52; 1993b; Wilken 1984: 48–67;
Beale 1998: 7–9, 12–16).

Less persuasive is the proposal that the pressure came particularly from participation in trade guilds (de Silva 1992: 278, 289–94;
Beale 1998: 241–42, 249; Beasley-Murray 1981: 89–90; Collins 1984:
88, 132), on the mistaken assumption that the guilds exercised the
regulatory and protective functions of mid-twentieth-century trade
unions (cf. Aune 1997: 186; cf. MacMullen 1974: 18–19).

[39] Interpreters commonly focus on the break with Judaism as the
cause for coming under pressure to participate in emperor worship
(e.g., Thompson 1990: 130; de Silva 1992: 279, 289–90; Beale 1998: 8,
31, 240). The gentile origin of much of the church would likely have
been more problematic: religion was tied to ethnicity, and it is not
clear that political authorities would permit gentile Christians to
abdicate their obligations to the emperor.

[40] The parallels between Rev. 2 and the Apostolic Decree are
more widely noted, and include the dual prohibition of idolatry and
sexual immorality as well as the decision to impose no other 'burden'
(*baros)* on gentiles (Rev. 2:24 cf. Acts 15:28).

[41] Perhaps not only the opponents' position, but also their rationale is the same in each instance. Thus, in Rev. 2, Beale (1998: 265 cf.
32, 249) reconstructs the justification of those participating in idol
feasts in terms reminiscent of I Cor. 8, but in the absence of any
explicit evidence, this parallel cannot be confirmed. Among his other
proposals, the most intriguing is the possible defense that "Christians

sacrificing...to Caesar could be understood in the same manner as the sacrifices in the Jewish temple in honor of the emperors as rulers (which did not at all imply that the emperors were gods)" (cf. Josephus *Against Apion* 2.76–77; Philo, *Embassy to Gaius* 357).

[42] Beale (1998: 248, 251, 261) need not address this question because he accepts the argument of Witherington (1993), that *eid-Çlothuton* refers to eating idol offerings "in the context of idolatrous worship." By this reckoning, Revelation 2:14, 20 prohibits the same sort of activities as 1 Cor. 10:1–22.

Unfortunately, Witherington's argument is far from conclusive. Moreover, as evidence of a cultic context in this passage, Beale (1998: 248) draws attention to the parallels with Balaam and Jezebel, "both of which concern blatant idolatry." Yet while Revelation certainly opposes the consumption of idol offerings in idolatrous contexts, it cannot be assumed that it would permit consumption of food from the market or served at a neighbor's home without inquiries about its origin.

[43] Aune (1997: 186), like Beale, assumes too much, albeit in the opposite direction:

Though it is not completely clear precisely what is involved, it would appear that actual participation in sacrificing and eating victims in Greek temples is less likely than participating in the ritual banquets associated with public holy days and festivals or buying sacrificial meat from the market and eating it at home.

At least in Pauline conception, participating in ritual banquets during festivals is in a different category from buying meat in the market or eating it at home. Of course, the elder John may well consider them all alike as idolatrous, yet this cannot simply be assumed.

[44] For a discussion of Pliny's letter and a variety of other Roman commentaries on Christianity, see Benko 1984; cf. 1980: 1055–1118; Wilken 1980: 100–25; Sordi 1983: 59–65.

[45] Benko (1980: 1075–76) discusses some possible motivations for the prosecution of Christians.

[46] Pliny's differentiation between praying before the gods and making offering to the emperor suggests that he perceives a certain distinction between gods and emperors as objects of veneration. Abstention from both, however, reflects the Christian perception that the two activities are in fundamental continuity. The juxtaposition of dishonoring Christ with honoring gods and emperor further implies that the Christian stance on each was grounded in the same consideration; namely, that the former, no less than the latter, is cultic.

⁴⁷ This text (along with another from a 'Life of Aesop') raises the possibility that shoppers in the market could differentiate meats of cultic and non-cultic origin, contrary to what Paul implies. Alternatively, perhaps Christians in Pliny's time inquired of the butcher, whom Paul similarly assumes would be aware of the origin of his stores. Isenberg (1975: 273) rightly concludes that this issue "still awaits its proper solution."

⁴⁸ Cheung (1999: 223) resists this conclusion, arguing that Paul never explicitly permits eating known idol food from the market. That is true enough, and a legitimate objection to Gooch (1993: 125 n13), who claims that "idol–food sold in markets is Paul's one unequivocal allowance (1 Cor. 10:25). This is a stark indication of the extent to which Paul's attempted accommodation of the Corinthians' position was disregarded." Nevertheless, Paul does invite the Corinthians to eat anything sold in the market without investigation; Pliny's Christians are carefully selective. The two approaches are difficult to reconcile. Cheung (1999: 223–28) adduces evidence of links between Paul and the Christians of Bithnyia (where Pliny was governor), but acknowledges that they are too few to establish the point.

⁴⁹ Brunt (1978: 257) writes: "The main trend is one of unqualified opposition to food offered to idols." Though agreeing with Brunt on little else, Cheung (1999: 176) concurs on this point.

⁵⁰ The answer to this question clearly depends as much on the interpretation of 1 Corinthians 8–10 as on the Fathers. Those who suppose that Paul was permissive must account for the subsequent and near universal prohibition. Thus, Brunt (1985: 121) argues that "Paul's approach to the question of food offered to idols is unique in early Christianity. While at no point is his approach explicitly rejected, it is first ignored and later misunderstood."

Those who advocate a restrictive interpretation of 1 Corinthians 8–10, find support for their position in the exclusivism of the early Church:

> The early Christian unanimity on the prohibition of idol food makes the accepted scholarly view that Paul condoned it seem quite unlikely. If he did he would not just have been the first, but in effect the only early Christian authority to defend this position. Indeed it would be a miracle, resulting from pure misunderstanding, that First Corinthians was preserved at all by the early Church in its extant form (Tomson 1990: 185; cf. Cheung 1999: 278–82).

The role of the early Church in text preservation precludes dismissal of this argument as anachronistic.

⁵¹ Given the extent of the data, the survey which follows is illustrative and concise, rather than exhaustive or detailed. Böckenhoff (1903) and Cheung (1999: 165–291) conduct more thorough surveys. For briefer treatments, see also Brunt 1978: 269–75; Hanson 1980; and Gooch 1993: 121–27. Contreras (1980) surveys Christian attitudes toward paganism more broadly.

⁵² The verb 'bear' (*bastazç*) may reflect familiarity with Acts 15:10 (or with a common underlying tradition; cf. '*baros*,' Acts 15:28; Rev. 2:24). The grounds of the prohibition ('for it is the worship of dead gods') may also be a variation on Paul's argument that pagan sacrifices are actually offered not to God but to demons (1 Cor. 10:20). Because the parallels are imprecise, Tomson (1990: 180) takes them to be independent versions of the same tradition.

⁵³ In addition to the categorical prohibition, Aristides 15.2 also includes the 'Golden Rule.' Both features are reminiscent of the 'Western' version of Acts 15.

⁵⁴ Cheung (1999: 245–46) notes that the Valentinian Gnostics commonly cite Paul in their defense, but do not appear to have done so on this issue, as Irenaeus does not attempt to correct their exegesis. Thus it is likely that neither orthodox nor heretic understood Paul to be indifferent to the question of sacrificial meat (contra Brunt 1978: 256).

⁵⁵ From Acts 15, he insists that the abrogation of most of the Law demonstrates that the remaining prohibitions are in force in perpetuity (*On Modesty* 12.3–4). While not citing Revelation 2, he does quote 21:8 with its warning that idolaters will be condemned (*On Modesty* 19.25).

⁵⁶ Tertullian also addresses the social consequences of this prohibition. The Christians' refusal to participate in religious ceremonies, the Saturnalia, cultic feasts, spectacles, burning incense to gods, and temple donations led to accusations of being anti-social. He (*Apology* 42) replies:

> How in all the world can that be the case with people who are living among you, eating the same food, wearing the same attire, having the same habits, under the same necessities of existence?…So we sojourn with you in the world, abjuring neither forum, nor shambles [meat market], nor bath, nor booth, nor worship, nor inn, nor weekly market, nor any other places of commerce. We sail with you, and fight with you, and till the ground with you.

⁵⁷ Minucius Felix, a contemporary of Tertullian, employs a similar rationale to defend Christian refusal to participate in activities
with cultic associations. His antagonist, Octavius, argues that by
abstaining from pagan shows, processions, public banquets, sacred
games, burial customs, foods offered to idols, and libation wine,
Christians indicate their fear of the gods (*Octavius* 12.5). In terms
reminiscent of 1 Corinthians 10:26, Felix retorts that Christians acknowledge God as the giver of food and drink; they abstain not as a
"confession of fear," but "less anyone should think either that we are
submitting to demons, to whom libation has been made" (*Octavius*
38.1). Felix also refers briefly to the social location of cult interpretation: stories about the gods are endorsed by the ignorant and by
poets, and disdained by pagan philosophers (*Octavius* 22).

⁵⁸ Cheung (1999: 259–60) supposes that this understanding of
market food characterized both 'orthodox' and 'heretic' during
Tertullian's time. The latter had to defend a number of his positions
against opponents who cited 1 Corinthians (e.g., on attending the
theater, citing 1 Cor. 9:24–27 [*Shows* 2.1–3]; and on manufacturing
idols for sale, citing 1 Cor. 7:20 [*Idolatry* 5.1–2]). Had an alternative
interpretation of 1 Corinthians 8–10 existed, Cheung reasonably infers, Tertullian would likely have refuted that also.

⁵⁹ Elsewhere Clement extends the application of Paul's teaching
into new areas. To discourage gourmandism and gluttony, he selects
an array of prooftexts from 1 Corinthians 8–10 and Romans 14 (in
order of citation, 1 Cor. 10:20; 8:7, 8; 10:21; 9:4; 8:13; 10:27; Rom. 14:3,
6; 1 Cor. 8:13; 9:4; 8:4, 6, 11–12; 5:11; Rom. 14:21, 20).

⁶⁰ The Pseudo-Clementine *Homilies* (7.4, 8) also collate Acts 15
with 1 Corinthians 10, associating "food offered to idols" (Acts 15: 20,
29) with "the table of demons" (1 Cor. 10:20). This aversion to idol
offerings comes as no surprise in literature representing Jewish Christianity.

⁶¹ Assessment of Clement's interpretation is conditioned by a
prior decision concerning Paul's meaning. Thus, Brunt, convinced
that "Paul is basically indifferent to the question of sacrificial meat"
(1978: 256; cf. 1985: 115) concludes that "by Clement's time Paul's
argument in 1 Cor. 8–10 is not understood and his views are interpreted in light of the Apostolic Decree" (1978: 271 cf. 1985: 117).
Cheung, on the other hand, arguing that Paul counsels Christians to
"avoid any food if, and only if, you know that it is idol food" (1999:
162), takes Clement as confirming his interpretation: "Clement appears to understand Paul's position to be this: buy any food you want

in the market without questioning, as long as you do not know that it is idol food, but any food that is specified as idol food is off limits" (1999: 266–67).

Given that I understand Paul differently from either Brunt or Cheung, it is perhaps unsurprising that I also evaluate Clement differently. With regard to Paul's basic position, Clement rightly understands him to be essentially prohibitive, and in harmony with Acts 15. With respect to Paul's rationale, Clement rightly takes the welfare of the weak and the demonic associations of idol worship as two complementary reasons for abstaining. On both counts he is a more accurate guide to Paul's meaning than is Brunt, yet not because of any intrinsic superiority of ancient Church Fathers over modern interpreters, but because his interpretation finds greater support within the argument of 1 Corinthians 8–10.

Nevertheless, while the central thrusts of 1 Corinthians 8–10 and Acts 15 concur, the ambiguity in detail remains: in approving the purchase of meat from the market and the participation in feasts at pagan homes regardless of the origin of the meat, is Paul more lenient than the Decree? Clement harmonizes the two by appealing to the categorical prohibition in Acts 15 to infer a restriction in 1 Corinthians 10:25–28a, but one might just as well read the permission of 1 Corinthians into the terseness of Acts 15. Or perhaps the two passages represent divergent strategies at this point.

Where the canonical text is ambiguous, Clement cannot be invoked to resolve the uncertainty, and for several reasons. For one, to do so would be anachronistic. For another, Clement misreads Paul on at least one related matter (the role of conscience), and uses 1 Corinthians 8–10 to advocate austerity, if not asceticism. In addition, he pays scant attention to the flow of Paul's argument, treating the various statements as proof-texts instead of as a continuous argument. Furthermore, the appeal to Acts 15 as an interpretative grid for 1 Corinthians 10 is tendentious. The very fact that Clement must appeal to Acts 15 to ban Christians from buying idol meat on sale in the market demonstrates that 1 Corinthians 10:25–27 is ambiguous.

[62] A fourth point is worth noting in passing: Origen stresses that the danger facing Christians who join idol feasts does not come from demons: "Christians have nothing to fear, even if demons should not be well-disposed to them; for they are protected by the Supreme God, who is well pleased with their piety, and who sets His divine angels to watch over those who are worthy of such guardianship, so that they can suffer nothing from demons" (*Against Celsus* 8.27).

⁶³ His opponent Celsus finds Paul's argument contradictory. The specific point of contradiction, however, differs somewhat. Celsus works with the neutral, Greco-Roman sense of *daimÇn*, which affects his understanding of the contradiction: if the gods are nothing (1 Cor. 8:4), then it does no harm to eat offerings; if they are demons (1 Cor. 10:20), then they are God's creatures, and should be venerated with sacrifice (*Against Celsus* 8.24).

Origen replies that though the gods are nothing, to use things offered to idols is injurious to other Christians (1 Cor. 8:7, 9–13); moreover, since the sacrifices are made to demons, Christians must abstain because it is not possible to partake both from the table of the Lord and from the table of demons (1 Cor. 10:21). He concludes, "it will be evident to any one who carefully considers what has been said, that even if idols are nothing, nevertheless it is an awful thing to join in idol festivals" (*Against Celsus* 8.24).

⁶⁴ Celsus argues that if Christians must abstain from sacrifices because they are offered to demons, they should equally abstain from all food, water, and even air, which are also under the control of demons (*Against Celsus* 8.28). In reply, Origen cites Acts 15 to permit all foods except idol offerings, strangled animals, and blood (8.29). He invokes demons to explain all of these prohibitions:

> That which is offered to idols is sacrificed to demons, and a man of God must not join the table of demons. As to things strangled, we are forbidden by Scripture to partake of them, because the blood is still in them; and blood, especially the odour arising from blood, is said to be the food of demons. Perhaps, then, if we were to eat of strangled animals, we might have such spirits feeding along with us. And the reason which forbids the use of strangled animals for food is also applicable to the use of blood (8.30).

⁶⁵ Origen writes:

> But as for us who know that some things are used by demons, or if we do not know, but *suspect*, and are in doubt about it, if we use such things, we have used them not to the glory of God, nor in the name of Christ; for not only does the suspicion that things have been sacrificed to idols condemn him who eats, but even the doubt concerning this; for 'he that doubteth,' according to the Apostle, 'is condemned if he eat, because he eateth not of faith; and whatsoever is not of faith is sin' [Rom. 14:23] (*Matthew* 10.12 *emphasis added*).

Notably, in extending the ban to food which is even suspected to have been offered, Origen is stricter than Celsus understands Christians to be: Celsus complains that Christians abstain from public feasts held in conjunction with idol festivals, which is to say, "when they are looking upon a slain victim" (*Against Celsus* 8.24,28).

⁶⁶ Origen is notable also for the reassuring sentiment that "it would require a whole treatise to set forth fully all that is contained on this subject in the Epistle to the Corinthians" (*Against Celsus* 8.24).

⁶⁷ The *Apostolic Constitution* 7.2.20–21, a compilation of ethical and ecclesiastical materials dating from the end of the fourth century, likewise dismisses Jewish food laws, but insists on abstention from idol food because it is offered to demons. This clearly reflects dependence on 1 Cor. 10, but adds nothing to what is covered in other Church fathers.

⁶⁸ Thus, for example, Chrysostom recognizes that proper understanding of the text requires reconstruction of the original occasion (20.4). Like modern commentators, he distinguishes those verses which represent the Corinthian position (he includes 8:1 and 8:4) from those which represent Paul's position. In contrast to a great many interpreters, he has no difficulty with the phrasing of 8:8 (20.9). He perceives the connection between chapters 8 and 10, proposing that concern for the welfare of the weak and antipathy toward demons are complementary—rather than mutually exclusive—reasons for abstaining from idol food (20.11; 21.2; 25.2). He also avoids the contemporary reductionism that quibbles over whether chapter 9 is an exemplum or an apology, finding elements of each (21.1). He rightly proposes that Paul's actual position on eating idol food does not come until 10:20–22 (24:6). On top of all this, he repeatedly comments on Paul's circumspection and indirect argumentation (20.1–3, 10; 21.1).

⁶⁹ Chrysostom draws attention to the predicament facing Paul due to the presence of both strong and weak. The apostle must prove simultaneously

> that one ought to abstain from this kind of banquet, and that it hath no power to hurt those who partake of it: things which were not greatly in agreement with each other. For when they were told that they had no harm in them, they would naturally run to them as indifferent things. But when forbidden to touch them, they would suspect, on the contrary, that their having power to do hurt occasioned the prohibition (20.4).

The challenge facing Paul was how to dissuade the strong from attending cultic feasts without reinforcing the fears of the weak.

[70] This is the implication of his reassurance designed to avoid excessive scrupulosity: "if thou eat in ignorance and not knowingly, thou are not subject to the punishment: it being thenceforth a matter not of greediness, but of ignorance" (25.1 paraphrasing 1 Cor. 10:25–30).

And again, "he that eateth, if in ignorance, may be rid of anxiety" (25.1). The forgiveness of those who unwittingly eat idol food implies the punishment of those who knowingly participate. So, too, Chrysostom takes for granted that Christians would not knowingly eat: "He who makes scrupulous enquiry doth so as being in dread; but he who, on hearing the fact, abstains, abstains as out of contempt and hatred and aversion" (25.1).

[71] With respect to the Roman ancestral cult, in another letter Augustine (*Letter* 29.9) criticizes the Christian practice of feasting at the graves of the dead as a carryover from paganism. On this practice, see Brown 1981: 26–29.

[72] Reminiscent of the Mishnah, Publicola also addresses the issue of indirect contamination. May Christians eat produce from a threshing-floor or press if they know that pagans have offered some of it to their gods (46.6)? May they, under threat of starvation, eat food left in an idol temple (46.11)? May they drink from a well into which someone has thrown a sacrifice? From a well in the compound of a deserted temple? Of a functioning temple (46.14)? May they eat vegetables or fruit grown in a garden belonging to a temple, a priest, or an idol (46.18)? Publicola asks similar questions concerning idolatry more generally: May Christians use wood from an idol grove (46.7)? May they use public baths in which pagans have offered sacrifice? May they use baths on a feast day, if the pagans are still there? If the pagans have already left (46.15)? May they hire a sedan chair after pagans have used it to go to the temple (46.16)?

[73] Barrett (1982: 56) contrasts the liberalism of Paul with the strictness of the early Church, which "retreated into a narrow religious shell. Jewish Christianity (in this matter) triumphed, though Jewish Christians became less important in the church." At the same time, he concedes:

> For this unfortunate step there was one piece of justification, in that refusel to eat *eidÇlothuta* became on at least some occasions of persecution the touch-stone of loyalty to the Christian faith and of the rejection of idolatry. It must be acknowledged, and would have been acknowledged by Paul,

that in these circumstances the only proper Christian attitude was to abstain.

The latter explanation is more convincting that the former: increasing restrictiveness is more likely the result of persecution than of a Judaizing tendency, especially given that many gentile converts had reservations toward idol food (cf. 1 Cor. 8:7).

[74] Cheung 1999: 162, 280, 297; Tomson 1990: 185, 208, 219.

[75] Tomson (1990: 186) notes two basic interpretations of 1 Corinthians 10:25 among the fathers. Some, such as Clement and Tertullian, take for granted that Paul implicitly intended the exclusion of idol food. Others, such as Chrysostom and Ambrosiaster, assume that food of unspecified provenance is permitted so long as its origin is uncertain. Either way, the fathers concur in prohibiting food which is known to have come from idol offerings.

CHAPTER 10

Glorifying God, Respecting Culture: Biblical Reflections on Cultic Meals in Chinese Culture

Summary: Paul's teaching on idol offerings requires Christians to differentiate cultic and non-cultic celebrations. The distinction is largely feasible, and is assisted by recent developments within shenism.

To bring the biblical text to bear on a contemporary issue is to build a bridge from the first-century Mediterranean world to twenty-first-century East Asia. The width of the chasm should not be exaggerated: on this issue, at least, contemporary shenist culture is closer to the New Testament world than contemporary Western culture is to either. Cultic meals and ancestor veneration are prominent features of both shenism and Greco-Roman culture, serving comparable functions within each, amidst similar ambiguities of intention and interpretation. Nonetheless, a gap of two thousand years and five thousand miles cannot be crossed in a single stride.

Like a bridge, Christian ethics must be securely anchored at two ends. On one side is the biblical text; on the other, the modern context. Only that moral reasoning which is grounded in exegesis of the biblical text and informed by analysis of the human context can lay claim to the mantle of 'Christian ethics.' In this instance, construction of the bridge began from the bank of contemporary context (ch 1–4), and then work shifted to the bank of biblical text (ch 5–9). This chapter aims to complete the middle span, linking biblical text with modern context.

A Brief Recap

In his recent introduction to New Testament ethics, Richard Hays divides the interpretative process into four components: descriptive, synthetic, hermeneutic, and pragmatic.[1] This provides a suitable structure for reviewing the conclusions reached thus far.

The Descriptive Task

Description entails close examination of the relevant biblical texts; in this instance, pre-eminently 1 Corinthians 8–10 (ch 7–8). This study reached two main conclusions: one methodological, the other substantial.

The methodological conclusion is that 1 Corinthians 8–9 provides Paul's response to the Corinthian justification for participating in idolatrous feasts, rather than an exposition of his own position (ch 7). Not until 10:1–11:1 does Paul set out his own stance (ch 8). Two ramifications follow: first, the indirect but insistent restrictions of 1 Corinthians 8 are compatible with the strident prohibitions of 1 Corinthians 10. Secondly, out of respect for Paul's rhetoric and intention, contemporary application must prioritize 1 Corinthians 10.

The substantial conclusion reaches beneath the three scenarios of 10:14–30 in search of the underlying analytical framework. Paul's varied verdicts reflect an implicit distinction between cultic feasts and social meals. At the same time, this distinction must not be abstracted and applied apart from its biblical parameters, for it is those parameters which clarify the nature of the distinction.

The difference lies in the proximity of meal to offering. Feasts held in conjunction with pagan cult are prohibited as idolatrous, whoever the recipient of the cult (whether deities, spirits, or deceased ancestors), and whatever the motive or interpretation of the participants (whether worship, veneration, or merely social interaction). Non-cultic meals, on the other hand, have no evident connection with either worship or offering, and are not only permitted but gently encouraged. In other words, for Paul the distinction between cultic and non-cultic meals depends largely on what participants *do*, and is not susceptible to individual intention or to the influence of social location on ritual interpretation.[2]

The Synthetic Task

Synthesis explores the degree to which biblical teaching as a whole is unified or in tension; in this instance, whether Paul's teaching is compatible with the Old Testament and Judaism, on the one hand (ch 6), and with Acts 15 and Revelation 2, on the other (ch 9).

Like the Old Testament generally, Paul holds to a twofold view of idols: they are simultaneously impotent, at one level, and demonic, at another. As a corollary, this correspondence resolves the purported contradiction between 1 Corinthians 8:4–6, which dismisses idols as nothing, and 10:20–21, which characterizes them as demonic (ch 6). That dual characterization long preceded Paul, and neither he nor the Old Testament authors felt it to be intrinsically contradictory.

At the same time, in contrast to (at least later) mainstream Judaism, Paul counsels behavior guaranteed to result in unwitting—yet easily preventable—consumption of idol offerings, whether from the market (10:25), or at the homes of non-Christian neighbors (10:27–28).

This greater latitude does not reflect a devaluing of moral purity, nor does it dismiss mainstream Jewish standards as persnickety. Rather, it balances two concerns: the absolute obligation to avoid idolatry (10:1–13), and the yearning to see many saved (9:19–23; 10:31–32). As apostle to the gentiles, Paul cannot remain cloistered within a Jewish community, but must engage the pagan world. He does not compromise on biblical prohibitions against idolatry, but only on Jewish inclinations toward social separation. Nonetheless, the disparity means that Jewish sources cannot be used to clarify ambiguities in Paul's position.

Paul stands in greater harmony with Acts 15 and Revelation 2, at least in basic thrust: all three categorically prohibit participation in cultic meals. Yet they likely differ on peripheral issues: Should Christians inquire about food at the market? Should they decline invitations to meals with non-Christian friends? The brevity of Acts 15 and Revelation 2 precludes a definitive answer, but it seems likely that at least the Judaizers would have advocated a stricter interpretation of the Decree, and that the elder John had little tolerance for rapprochement as the Church in Asia Minor fought for its very survival. Yet it is a foible of Western predilection for systemization to demand uniformity as a measure of compatibility.

The Hermeneutical Task

Hermeneutics seeks to bridge the temporal and cultural gap between biblical and contemporary contexts. This entails a search for parallels or analogies between the world of Scripture and our own world.[3]

In this instance, the parallels are of two sorts. For one, in both practice and interpretation, contemporary shenism (ch 2) and ancient Chinese traditions (ch 4) are remarkably similar to ancient Greco-Roman domestic religion (ch 5). For the other, the rationale of modern accommodationists (ch 2) finds close parallels in the interpretations of Greco-Roman philosophers and bureaucrats (ch 5), and in the argument of the Corinthian strong (ch 7). Parallels include the conjunction of offering and meal, the occasions and functions of meals, as well as the correlation between interpretation and social location.[4] The extensive similarities afford greater certainty and higher authority in application.

At the same time, Scripture speaks to the consumption of idol food in three somewhat distinct contexts: the incorporation of gentile believers into a previously Jewish Church (Acts 15), emperor veneration (Rev. 2:14,20), and social and domestic cult (1 Cor. 8–10). Of the three, the occasion prompting 1 Corinthians 8–10 is arguably the closest to the contemporary shenist context. The ethno-religious controversy of Acts 15 would be relevant in the evangelization of Muslims, given the importance of *halal* foods, but is less germane to the evangelization of Chinese. The politico-religious conflict of Revelation 2 was relevant to imperial China or to Japan during the first half of the twentieth-century, but has little bearing on contemporary Asian cultures. The tensions over idol food within contemporary shenist cultures are largely socio-religious in nature, as they were in ancient Corinth.

The Pragmatic Task

The question driving pragmatics is, "How shall the Christian community shape its life in obedience to the witness of the New Testament?"[5]

The early Church addressed this question (ch 9), as did both seventeenth-century Roman Catholic missions and nineteenth-century Protestant missions (ch 3). Threatened by persecution, the early Church reinforced the categorical prohibition against idolatry in the effort to preserve its own identity and character. The Roman and Protestant missions, in contrast, provided two alternatives—accommodation and exclusivism—each reflecting the social location of the missionaries and their target audiences. These two alternatives persist still, and they still reflect the effects of social location, not only on shenist practitioners but also on Christian evangelists and converts.

The pragmatic question remains unresolved today: in part, because the necessary primary sources and secondary literature have only recently accumulated to the point of critical mass; in part, because both shenist practice and Christian convictions modify over time and so require periodic reevaluation and renegotiation; and, in part, because a continually renewing stream of converts must face the issue for themselves and within their families. The pragmatic task is the focus for the rest of this chapter.

The Pragmatics of Christian Exclusivism in a Shenist Context

When may Christians participate in domestic feasts, and when must they abstain? Paul supplies two sorts of guidelines: an aphorism and a set of regulations. The aphorism comes at the end of his discussion. For Paul, the bottom line is:

Whether, then, you eat or drink or whatever you do, do all things for the glory of God.

Do not cause offense, whether to Jew or to Greek or to the church of God…(10:31–32).

These maxims encapsulate two tensions: first, glorifying God while respecting culture; and secondly, avoiding affront to such diverse and often opposing cultures as Judaism, paganism, and Christianity.[6] The aphorism sets the tone and the parameters for concrete application. Yet while helpful as an internal gyroscope, it is rather vague to guide day-to-day decisions. For that purpose, Paul's earlier regulations and the underlying distinction are more helpful.

Those regulations provide essentially three guidelines by which to distinguish cultic from non-cultic meals. First, participation in a feast held in conjunction with an offering is itself idolatrous, even for those who take definite steps to distance themselves from the act of offering. That very act of offering—regardless of interpretation or social location—renders the meal off-limits to Christians. Thus, the ban extends beyond explicitly cultic feasts and encompasses many predominantly social occasions incorporating offerings to gods, spirits, or ancestors. As a corollary, though, this suggests that the prior history of the food is largely inconsequential; what matters is the current context of the meal.

Secondly, the prohibition extends to meals associated with any category of *daimҪn*, from gods and spirits, to deceased ancestors and living rulers. Paul allows no distinction between offerings or meals which worship gods, venerate emperors, or express filial piety toward deceased relatives. Whomever the intended recipient, and whatever the intended meaning, offering-based meals are idolatrous.

Thirdly, the connection with offering transcends architectural location. That is to say, whether the offering and meal are held in temple, public stadium, private association, trade guild, or private home, is inconsequential. What matters is the association of table with altar, and of meal with offering.

These three guidelines do not resolve every ambiguity arising from shenist meals, but they do provide clear guidance in most cases.

Cultic Meals

While the theoretical distinction between cult and culture is straightforward, its application is complicated somewhat by the progress of secularization within Chinese culture. Bloomfield observes rightly that all of the major festivals in the Chinese year were originally cultic, but few remain expressly so today.[7] All the same, the spread of secularization has been uneven: large segments of traditional expression remain untouched. Elsewhere, practices have been simplified or modified. In some areas, originally cultic interpretations have been hollowed of all religious significance. In a diffused religion, without canon to establish custom or adjudicate meaning, without clergy to enforce standards, both practice and interpretation vary widely from one dialect, clan, or family to the next. No blanket rule can encompass all occasions or all people.

Nonetheless, some basic commonalities exist. Some festivals remain essentially and irremediably cultic, both in practice and in interpretation. On these occasions, Christians have little choice but to abstain from both celebration and meal. The following list and descriptions are representative and illustrative, not comprehensive. Other cultic feasts exist, but their character can be identified by application of the same principles.

Hungry Ghost Festival

This festival is unavoidably cultic in practice. 'Hungry ghosts' are spirits of the deceased who have no one to provide for their ongoing needs; it is for this reason that non-relatives must supply food, money, and clothing. The feast closing the month is held under the auspices of a temple. Pigs, chickens, and ducks, along with cognac, cigarettes, and candy, are first publicly offered to the presiding deities and spirit guests, and then served at dinner or divided into portions for sponsors to take home. The festival ends with the burning of a paper effigy of the god of hell, symbolically returning him and the ghosts to purgatory for another eleven months.[8]

The festival also remains largely cultic in interpretation. The offerings are widely motivated by the need to appease the spirits so that they do not harm the living. While Western rationalists may dismiss the motivations as superstitious, many Chinese—even secularists and Christians—take precautions to avoid demonic attack during the seventh month.

Given Paul's strictures against participation in cultic feasts, Christians rightly avoid not only making the offerings, but also joining the closing meal or bringing portions of the offerings home. This they can do relatively easily, because of the particular characteristics of the occasion: it does not venerate family ancestors; it is transparently cultic; it is celebrated under the auspices of the temple rather than the home. Consequently, abstention from this festival is often uncontroversial.

At the same time, as part of the Hungry Ghost offerings, hawker centers (the outdoor equivalent to shopping-mall food courts) commonly set up special tables for the spirits where food offerings are laid out. In more traditional areas, shops may set out representative goods—ranging from bags of rice to CD players and standing fans—to be blessed by the temple and then returned to the shop for sale.[9] Under Paul's guidelines governing market food, Christians may eat at the hawker center or purchase goods from the shops, even though some unidentified items may derive from the offerings. The prohibition of food identified as deriving from idol offerings would, however, apply in the case of any items expressly identified as blessed by the gods.

Death Rituals and Commemorations

Hungry Ghost festival venerates other people's ancestors; funeral rites, death anniversaries, and Qing Ming venerate one's own. The parallel confirms that the latter are no less cultic than the former: both venerate the preternatural spirits of the deceased. The distinction explains why ancestral celebrations are more problematic. They celebrate relatives and lineage ancestors, rather than strangers. Participation in the ancestral rites and meals runs the risk of offending God; non-participation, of offending family.[10]

Some Christians justify participation by distinguishing the worship of gods and spirits from the veneration of ancestors. Yet this is at odds with Paul's guidelines at two points. For one, he takes exception to any offering or meal to *daimÇn* (10:20), a category encompassing all sorts of preternatural beings, ancestors no less than gods. For the other, he defines cultic meals by analogy with Christian communion, not by the interpretation of the practitioner (10:16–17). From a Christian perspective the distinction between worship of gods and veneration of ancestors is unpersuasive: any offering to preternatural beings—and any meal held in conjunction with an offering—is problematic.

Thus, memorial meals conjoined with ancestral offerings—whether on the forty-ninth day of funeral rites, on subsequent death anniversaries, or in the cemetery on Qing Ming—are intrinsically cultic. At the very least, this prohibits funeral and gravesite meals.[11]

Once the meal is separated from the site and act of offering, however, ambiguity sets in. More traditional families may make an offering at the gravesite and have a formal meal at home, eating in veneration of the ancestors, sometimes even supposing the offerings to convey blessing to those who eat. Though locally and temporally separated, the meal is nonetheless conceptually conjoined with the offering. Such meals are prohibited to Christians.

More secularized families may also make offerings at the gravesite, yet reheat the leftovers along with dishes cooked fresh for the next meal, eating both indiscriminately simply because that makes more sense than discarding edible food.

The appropriate response in the above scenario is not clear-cut, because Paul never addresses a situation where (some of) the food is known to derive from idol offerings, but the meal is remote from the offering. On the one hand, he prohibits consumption where an informant indicates the cultic origin of the food (10:28). On the other, that prohibition appears designed to respect the expectations of the informant; it is apparently not otherwise demanded by the prior history of the food (10:27,29–30 cf. 10:19). Given the ambiguity of this scenario, consensus among Christians may be unattainable. Likely some will abstain out of fear of committing idolatry; others will participate out of fear of needlessly offending family. Either response is defensible where at least some of the food is known to have derived from offerings, but where the meal is distant temporally, locally, and conceptually from the act of offering.

Other families visit the gravesite or columbarium, yet make the offerings and celebrate the feast in the home. In this third scenario, the meal may be explicitly joined to the act of offering by time, place, substance, or significance; if so, it is off-limits to Christians. If, however, the meal is held some considerable time after the offering and in another room of the house, if the meal carries no symbolic significance for the family, and if offered and non-offered items are served indiscriminately, Christians may arguably participate.

For Paul, it is the convergence of offering and meal which is problematic, whether both occur in the ancestral hall of the temple, at the gravesite, or at home. It is not primarily the site, but the convergence of offering and meal, which constitutes the event as cultic. This association exists whenever the meal is linked—whether by location, time, or significance—to the offering. Whatever symbolic significance is assigned to the meal—whether veneration or blessing—it is equally problematic.

Other Cultic Meals

These contemporary scenarios are, of course, representative rather than exhaustive. Other feasts may have direct connection with offerings; other meals hold symbolic significance for participants. Some occasions are intrinsically and invariably cultic; for example, meals celebrating the birthday of the gods. Other occasions vary in significance according to the practices of the particular family; for example, meals held on the first and fifteenth of the month, or during wedding and birthday celebrations. The same guidelines apply to all these scenarios: if the food is offered to gods, spirits, or ancestors, and the meal is held in conjunction with the offering, the ban is in effect (10:14–22).

Either due to the nature of the occasion or to the orientation of the particular family, some cultic meals are central to family life. Abstention may express callous disregard and rupture important relationships. If a Christian holds firm, parents and siblings often make the necessary accommodation, and provide non-offered food so that all may participate together. This may ultimately glorify Christ: at the very least, it proclaims the biblical message that God alone is to be venerated. Other times, the cost in hostility and bitterness is high, and the name of Christ is stigmatized rather than honored.

Under such circumstances, rather than totally abstain from important family celebrations, many Christians adopt the expedient of joining the meal but declining offered items. This strategy may be defended on two grounds. First, while it runs afoul of one characteristic of cultic meals (the meal occurs within a cultic context), it avoids the other (the consumption of food offerings) (10:16,18,20). That is sufficient to avoid violating the prohibition against idolatry. Secondly, this strategy pursues both of Paul's dual priorities: it seeks to avoid idolatry while remaining engaged with non-Christian family and friends (9:19–23; 10:27).

Of course, casual observers may misinterpret this expedient, and shenist relatives may not be mollified by the concession. But that is likely the very position in which Paul found himself with the Corinthians. In any event, his counsel that they seek positive relationships with non-Christians justifies the expedient (9:19–23; 10:32–11:1), while the threat of judgment permits no further concession.

Ambiguous Meals

Lunar New Year is problematic, in part because of its cultural importance, and in part because of its ambiguities. Its centrality in family life is demonstrated by the return home of family members working or studying overseas. Its ambiguities are caused not only by modernization and secularization, but also by variations both in practice from one dialect group to the next, and in interpretation from one family to the next.

The centerpiece of the festivities is the reunion feast on New Year's Eve. Is the meal prohibited as cultic or permitted as ambiguous? That verdict may vary from family to family.

The most traditional families explicitly invite the ancestral spirits to the table, set extra plates, serve them food, and treat them as participants in the meal.[12] Under such circumstances, Paul's strictures against joining cultic meals clearly preclude Christian participation: the food is offered; the meal is rendered cultic by the participation of preternatural beings.

Often, however, the only cultic element in the entire celebration is the act of offering. The matron of the home alone presents the offering; after this, ancestors play no further role in the festivities. The meal takes place in a separate room of the house, removed both temporally and locally from the offering at the altar. Since the offered portions are taken to the kitchen and combined with non-offered portions, table guests know that some of the food has certainly been offered, but have no way of knowing which portions.

Since they do not know which portions are offered, many Christians feel obliged to avoid all the food, or at least those delicacies commonly presented to the ancestors (for example, roast pork, duck, chicken, and buns). Such a stance leads to acrimony and quarreling at what is culturally intended to be a time of harmony and tranquility. To preserve the peace in subsequent years, many mothers will set aside specific portions before offering the rest to the ancestors, so that Christian family members can join the feast without fear of contamination.

Ironically, this characterizes the Christian as confrontational and unfilial, and forces the shenist into the role of peace-maker. This inverts Paul's evangelistic strategy. Instead of the Christian becoming all things to all people in order to save some (9:22), the shenist must flex to accommodate Christian family members. Moreover, in a culture that values filial devotion above all ethical values, shenist parents are forced into a subordinate role. On top of it all, to secularists, Christian abstinence often comes across as superstitious.

Sometimes the Christian stance is fueled by fear of contamination or demon possession; other times, by fear of transgressing biblical prohibitions against idolatry. Neither reason precludes participation under the specified circumstances. Paul never implies any risk of demon possession through eating food offerings; instead, warns solely about the danger of divine judgment (10:6–12,14–30). The meal arguably fulfills neither of the cultic criteria: the offered portions are not identifiable; the meal is not directly conjoined to the worship. Where the previous history of any particular item is unknown, and where the meal is simply a joyous reunion of the immediate family without immediate connection to offering or worship, it is arguably legitimate to invoke Paul's permission: "Whatever is put before you, eat, without evaluation on account of conscience" (10:27).

Permissible Meals

A number of traditional festivals were originally cultic, but pose less problem for two reasons. They have largely lost any spiritistic associations, and they do not prioritize family or communal meals.

The dragon boat festival, for instance, likely had its origin in animistic ritual.[13] Yet today its dragon boat races serve solely to encourage tourism, and those shenists who offer the rice dumplings to ancestors do so only because they are a holiday treat, not because they carry special import. The dumplings do not form the core of a communal meal, and only a small fraction of household dumplings would ever appear on the idol shelf. So Christians typically need have no reservations about celebrating this festival, or joining a festive meal associated with it.

Similarly, while worship of the moon goddess was once an important feature of the lantern festival, it is now rather rare. Shenists still commonly offer mooncakes to ancestors, but like rice dumplings, these are merely delicacies. They do not form the core of a communal meal, and most mooncakes would never sit on the ancestral shelf. Consequently, Christians rarely feel any compunction about joining family celebrations of this occasion.

Beyond these specific occasions, leftovers from any cultic feast may be stored in the refrigerator, along with oranges and other fruits from the daily offerings. Shenists make no attempt to distinguish these foods from non-offered portions. Rarely, if ever, does anyone consider the leftovers to convey blessing; the ancestors are not considered to be present when the foods are consumed. Since the setting is non-cultic, and the origin of any particular item generally uncertain, these foods may be eaten without qualm.

The context is somewhat more problematic, however, when a hostess takes oranges down from the ancestral altar to serve to guests. In this scenario, common enough in shenist homes, the origin of the fruit and its previous function as an offering is apparent to all. Yet informants invariably explain that fruit taken directly from the altar bears no special significance; the hostess simply cannot be bothered to go to the kitchen to take another piece of fruit when some lies conveniently at hand in the living room. Under such circumstances, to decline the fruit would convey the impression that Christians are superstitious and fear harm from the spirits. So an argument can be made both for and against consumption: the food item is clearly offered, but the context of consumption is simple, non-cultic, hospitality.

Rejecting Cult, Affirming Culture

The distinction between cult and culture is not entirely straightforward, not even with the case studies Paul provides.[14] Some ambiguities remain. Nonetheless, the overall framework captures Paul's sentiments and is increasingly feasible within modern Asian society.

Distinguishing Cult and Culture

The attempt to differentiate cultic from cultural practices often results in divergent conclusions among Christians, sometimes even among family members and over a single feast. The ambiguity may produce considerable tension, both for the individual who is obliged to assess each situation, and between Christian relatives and friends who—whether because of differing contexts or because of differing interpretations of similar contexts—adopt conflicting stances. In such an environment, the unqualified prohibitions of Acts 15:20,29 and Revelation 2:14,20 prove popular.

But even categorical prohibitions cannot produce total clarity or uniformity. Despite ever more extensive discussion, for instance, the rabbinic literature never resolved all ambiguities and differences of opinion. More than that, a certain diversity is inherent in Paul's approach, given that he varied his lifestyle and diet according to his context (1 Cor. 9:19–23). While it may be little comfort to contemporary audiences, there are indications that the Corinthians were themselves disconcerted by his lack of uniformity.

The matter may be stated more sharply. Ambiguity and contextual variation arise from underlying tension central to the Christian calling. The simultaneous pursuit of both holiness and evangelistic impact (1 Cor. 9:19–23; 10:1–13) requires a certain measure of subtlety and a tolerance for sometimes competing goals. The only way to ensure consistency, harmony, and uniformity is to sacrifice one of these goals to the other. That forces a choice between an exclusivistic sub-world and a syncretistic melting pot. Consistency is obtained at the cost of core Christian values.

Paul on Cult and Culture

The negative tenor of 1 Corinthians 10:14–30 is a function of the presenting issue. May Christians participate in cultic meals? Most emphatically not! Nevertheless, Paul's overall approach toward culture is generally positive.

His broader attitude is evident, first of all, in his rephrasing of the presenting issue. The Corinthians approached him with a dispute over the issue of idol offerings. May Christians eat, or should they not? Each side advocated a categorical stance. Reconfiguring his answer in terms of cultic meals, Paul is able to repudiate the social inclusivism of the strong as idolatrous, while resisting the social exclusivism of the weak. He does not seek accommodation; that is, he does not offer a compromise, tolerating minor idolatries in order to secure a measure of cultural acceptance. Rather, he stands absolutely against idolatry while promoting social interaction with Greco-Roman religionists, largely on their terms rather than on his own.

Regard for culture also constitutes a core element of Paul's worldview. He appeals to a number of fundamental assumptions to support his position on cultic meals: the uniqueness of God, the demonic identity of other 'gods,' the impotence of idols, the role of God as creator and as judge, the sacred character and spiritual effects of cultic meals, as well as the cultic significance of sacred altars and of offerings to preternatural beings, regardless of intent. Among these fundamental tenets, he also advocates reaching people through the avenue of culture (10:31–32; cf. 8:9–13; 10:23–30; 7:17–24). Alongside rejection of idolatry, respect for culture is a fundamental part of his worldview.

Cultural integration is not a legitimate grounds for idolatry; nor may culture set the parameters by which Christians define idolatry. But apart from these caveats, culture is to be respected—even adopted—not only as an channel for evangelism, but equally in its own right. This is precisely the approach that Paul models: in the effort to reach gentiles, he steps out of the confines of his native Jewish culture and follows the conventions of despised gentile culture (9:19–23). This principle is fundamental to his mission and to his apostolic self-understanding.

Overall, then, from his reconfiguration of the issue, through his worldview to his lifestyle, Paul supports contemporary attempts to preserve what is cultural while avoiding what is cultic. The difference is sometimes improperly conceived or inappropriately applied, and is on occasion difficult to discern. Nonetheless, the basic distinction is biblically justifiable, and socially indispensable.

In essence, Paul's solution is that whatever is not cultic—whatever is not directly and evidently linked with an offering to preternatural beings—is permissible. In fact, the point could be stated more strongly: whichever cultural symbols and practices are not prohibited as idolatrous should be respected and advocated in their own right, and, where possible, exploited as avenues for culturally appropriate and sensitive evangelism.

Chinese Clans on Cult and Culture

The effort to distinguish cult from culture receives support from shenist circles; specifically, from the manual of rites produced by the Singapore Federation of Chinese Clan Associations.[15] The Federation attributes the decline in the observance of festivals and rites in part to "confusion between Chinese traditional practices and religious practices."[16] To facilitate the participation of all Chinese, whatever their religious persuasion, the Federation proposes to disentangle the religious and cultural elements in traditional ritual.[17]

Recognizing, for instance, that Christians are generally unwilling to make food offerings, the manual recommends observing a moment of silence prior to the lunar New Year feast.[18] Similarly, seeking to retain the Hungry Ghost festival as a memorial to deceased friends and relatives, the manual suggests replacing offerings to the deceased with donations for the destitute and elderly.[19]

The Federation has considerable prestige and stature as a *de facto* negotiator for the traditional and shenist community. It has proposed a modest truce with Christianity (and with secularism), a truce not in the religious domain, but only in the domain of culture. Its bilingual manual could provide Christian converts a helpful authority in negotiations with shenist parents. The proposal is a commendable attempt to reinforce cultural commonalities, without soft-pedaling religious differences, and as such deserves more careful consideration from the Church than it has received thus far.

The Church should not ignore this opportunity for social and cultural—and explicitly not religious—rapprochement. If this manual were to gain acceptance among shenists, Christian converts will be able to celebrate family occasions and traditional festivals without compromising their faith, jeopardizing other believers, or offending shenist relatives.

The proposal need not threaten the religious distinctives of Christianity, though it could reduce the appearance of cultural foreignness. Nor does the proposal need to impede evangelism; in fact, the reduction of family conflict and the assimilation to Chinese culture could actually facilitate the conversion of the older generation, which thus far has been largely resistant to the gospel. More important, concessions to Chinese culture—albeit not to shenist religion—are fully consistent with the modus operandi of the apostle Paul (1 Cor. 9:19–23).

Endnotes

¹ Hays 1996: 3–7.

² Notably, also, his argument rests not on the standard missiological foundations of participant observation, personal interviews, or emic perspective; but on biblical precedent (the wilderness experience, as recorded in Exodus 32), apostolic authority (selective citation of Exod. 32:6), and analogy with Christian eucharist.

³ Hays 1996: 298–300.

⁴ Western interpreters must resort to remote analogies in the application of 1 Corinthians 8–10. Thus, for example, Hays (1996: 303) himself writes:

> A moment's reflection will suggest that Paul's advice to the Corinthians can in turn become a metaphor for our own struggle to resist the temptations of idolatry. (In our case, the idols may tempt us with 'national security' or sexual fulfillment or tokens of social status rather than with meat.) If and when that metaphorical transfer occurs, the Word leaps the gap from Corinth to America.

He describes these analogies or metaphors as "incongruous conjunctions of two images—or two semantic fields—that turn out, upon reflection, to be like one another in ways not ordinarily recognized." The construction of parallels between Greco-Roman domestic religion and modern shenism still involves analogy and metaphor. Yet the gap is considerably narrower and the parallels markedly closer.

⁵ Hays 1996: 313.

⁶ Glorifying God and respecting culture are often treated as opposing poles of a continuum, with exclusivism on the one end and syncretism on the other. Those who grant greater weight to honoring God may give culture scant regard; those highly sensitive to culture may equivocate on biblical prohibitions against idolatry. Paul, however, prioritizes both concerns simultaneously.

⁷ Bloomfield 1983:49.

⁸ Even during Hungry Ghost month, however, a rare communal meal may be non-cultic. When I lived in a high-rise apartment complex, the residents' committee sponsored a communal feast during seventh month. As far as I could ascertain, there was no cultic element, no sacrifice, offering, altar, or worship. The logic seemed merely to be that the seventh month is the culturally mandated season for a communal feast among loose associates (Lunar New Year being largely restricted to family and close friends). Given the absence of any cultic

element, and the importance of relationships in evangelism, Christians could possibly justify attending such a feast. On the other hand, since it was specifically billed as a seventh-month feast, attendance could imply acceptance of the more traditional version of Hungry Ghost festival.

[9] I owe this observation to Rev. Wong Fong Yang of Batu Pahat, Malaysia.

[10] Since funeral rites as a whole are too numerous and diverse for consideration, the focus here is on the role of meals within the broader context of the rites. Chua (1998) provides a helpful evaluation of funeral ritual and appropriate Christian response; cf. Ro, ed. 1985; Tong 1988.

[11] It does not, of course, prohibit the light refreshments—such as peanuts and soft drinks—commonly served at wakes and funerals. These are generally not offered to ancestors, but are provided simply as a polite gesture to guests.

[12] Wong 1994:77.

[13] Committee on Chinese Customs and Rites 1989:51.

[14] It bears careful statement that I am not perpetuating the traditional and widely disparaged differentiation between cultic and cultural elements within a single feast or an extended festival. That is to say, any single cultic celebration includes social dimensions, and the two are inseparable. That is precisely why participation in the meal is prohibited. Were the two separable, Paul could simply have advised the Corinthians to avoid the cultic elements, while participating in the cultural aspects of the festival. That is actually the solution they advocated ('avoid worship; eat the feast'), and which he rejected.

The distinction I am drawing—that which appears to underlie Paul's permissions and prohibitions—is between events with a cultic element (i.e., those which conjoin social activities with worship or offering), and those without any cultic element. The former are prohibited in toto; that is, both their cultic and their social dimensions are banned.

[15] Committee on Chinese Customs and Rites 1989: see above, ch 2.

[16] To quote:

Very often Buddhist and Taoist practices are mistaken as traditional Chinese customs and dismissed as religious or folk beliefs. The result is that the meaning and significance of the particular Chinese festival is also discarded. In fact Chinese festivals and Chinese customs and rites cut across religious boundaries (Committee on Chinese Customs and Rites 1989: 5).

The handbook also attributes the decline in part to "Western influences and the predominance of the English language" (p11). This is a common misdiagnosis. Just prior to this statement, the handbook listed a number of other factors, including ignorance of the customs, perception of the customs as religious and superstitious, variations in the customs from one dialect group to another, the complexity of the customs, the irrelevance of the agrarian customs in an urban society, and inadequate justification for perpetuation of the customs (pp5–9). Multiple explanations are more satisfying than single causation. Besides, the characterizations 'Westernization' and 'English education' are a widespread mislabeling of the process of modernization, which has been an anti-traditional force in the West no less than in the East. The process looks like 'Westernization' only because modernization overtook the West several decades before it assaulted Asia.

[17] The manual observes:

Readers will also note that we have not emphasised the religious aspects [of the various rites]...This has been done deliberately because we believe that the basic Chinese customs and rites should not be restricted to any particular religion. This core of Chinese rituals may be observed by all Singaporeans, whatever their religious affiliations. For example, the customs and rituals related to Chun Jie (Chinese New Year) can be practiced whether one is a Christian, Buddhist, Taoist, atheist, or agnostic (Committee on Chinese Customs and Rites 1989: 9).

[18] Committee on Chinese Customs and Rites 1989: 39, 49.

[19] Committee on Chinese Customs and Rites 1989: 67.

Bibliography

Primary Sources

Except as otherwise noted, quotations of primary sources derive from the following editions or translations.

Apocrypha:
The New English Bible with the Apocrypha. 1971.

Chinese Classics:
Legge, James, trans. 1960. *The Chinese Classics.* 5 vols. Hong Kong: Hong Kong University Press.

Dead Sea Scrolls:
Vermes, G., trans. 1987. *The Dead Sea Scrolls in English.* 3rd ed. London: Penguin.

English Bible, Old Testament:
New International Version. 1984.

Greco-Roman Literature:
Loeb Classical Library.

Greek New Testament:
Aland, Kurt, et al, eds. 1993 *Novum Testamentum Graece.* 27th ed. Stuttgart: Deutsche Bibelstiftung.

Patristics:
Roberts, Alexander, and James Donaldson, eds. 1989. *Ante-Nicene Fathers: Translations of the Writings of the Fathers down to A.D. 325.* 10 vols. Reprint. Grand Rapids: Eerdmans.

Schaff, Philip, ed. 1988–89. *A Select Library of the Nicene and Post-Nicene Fathers.* First series. 14 vols. Reprint. Grand Rapids: Eerdmans.

Schaff, Philip, and Henry Wace, eds. 1986–88. *A Select Library of the Nicene and Post-Nicene Fathers.* Second series. 14 vols. Reprint. Grand Rapids: Eerdmans.

Pseudepigrapha:
Charlesworth, James, ed. 1983–85. *The Old Testament Pseudepigrapha.* Garden City, NY: Doubleday.

Rabbinics:
Danby, Herbert, trans. 1933. *The Mishnah.* Oxford: Oxford University Press.

Epstein, Isidore, ed. 1935–48. *The Babylonian Talmud.* 35 vol. London: Soncino Press.

Abbreviations of apocryphal, intertestamental, rabbinic, and patristic sources follow the guidelines provided in the 'Instructions for Contributors,' *Journal of Biblical Literature* 117 (1998): 555–79.

Secondary Sources

Abbott, Walter, gen ed. 1966a. "Constitution on the Sacred Liturgy [Sacrosanctum Concilium]." Pp. 137–78 in *The Documents of Vatican II: All Sixteen Official Texts Promulgated by the Ecumenical Council 1963–1965.* New York: Guild Press.

———. 1966b. "Declaration on the Relationship of the Church to Non-Christian Religions [Nostra Aetate]." Pp. 660–68 in *The Documents of Vatican II: All Sixteen Official Texts Promulgated by the Ecumenical Council 1963–1965.* New York: Guild Press.

———. 1966c. "Decree on the Missionary Activity of the Church [Ad Gentes]." Pp. 584–630 in *The Documents of Vatican II: All Sixteen Official Texts Promulgated by the Ecumenical Council 1963–1965.* New York: Guild Press.

Alexander, Philip. 1983. "Rabbinic Judaism and the New Testament." *ZNW* 74: 237–46.

Aune, David. 1997. *Revelation 1–5*. Dallas: Word.

Bauer, Walter, William Arndt, F. Wilbur Gingrich, and Frederick Danker. 1979. *A Greek-English Lexicon of the New Testament and Other Early Christian Literature*. Chicago: University of Chicago Press.

Bakker, Jan. 1994. *Living and Working with the Gods: Studies of Evidence for Private Religion and Its Material Environment in the City of Ostia (100–500 A.D.)*. Amsterdam: J. C. Gieben.

Barclay, John. 1987. "Mirror-Reading a Polemical Letter: Galatians as a Test Case." *JSNT* 31: 73–93.

Barrett, C. K. 1982. "Things Sacrificed to Idols." Pp. 40–59 in *Essays on Paul*. Philadelphia: Westminster.

———. 1968. *The First Epistle to the Corinthians*. London: Black.

Bauckham, Richard. 1995. "James and the Jerusalem Church." Pp. 415–80 in *The Books of Acts in its First Century Setting. Volume 4: Palestinian Setting*, ed. Richard Bauckham. Grand Rapids: Eerdmans.

Beale, Gregory. 1998. *The Book of Revelation*. Grand Rapids: Eerdmans.

Beasley-Murray, George. 1981. *Revelation*. London: Marshall, Morgan & Scott.

Bell, Catherine. 1989. "Religion and Chinese Culture: Toward an Assessment of 'Popular Religion.'" *History of Religions* 29: 35–57.

Belleville, Linda. 1987. "Continuity or Discontinuity: A Fresh Look at 1 Corinthians in the Light of First-Century Epistolary Forms and Conventions." *EQ* 59: 15–37.

Benko, Stephen. 1984. *Pagan Rome and the Early Christians*. Bloomington: Indiana University Press.

———. 1980. "Pagan Criticism of Christianity during the First Two Centuries A.D." *ANRW* 2.23.2: 1055–1118.

Berger, Peter. 1969. *The Sacred Canopy: Elements of a Sociological Theory of Religion.* Garden City, NY: Doubleday.

Betz, Hans. 1979. *Galatians: A Commentary on Paul's Letter to the Churches in Galatia.* Philadelphia: Fortress.

———. 1975. "The Literary Composition and Function of Paul's Letter to the Galatians." *NTS* 21: 353–79.

Blodget, H. 1890. "The Attitude of Christianity toward Ancestral Worship." Pp. 631–54 in *Records of the General Conference of the Protestant Missionaries of China Held at Shanghai, May 7–20, 1890,* eds. W. J. Lewis et al. Shanghai: American Presbyterian Mission Press.

Bloomfield, Frena. 1983. *The Book of Chinese Beliefs: A Journey into the Chinese Inner World.* London: Arrow.

Bockmuehl, Markus. 1995. "The Noachide Commandments and New Testament Ethics with Special Reference to Acts 15 and Pauline Halakhah." *RB* 102: 72–101.

Böckenhoff, K. 1903. *Das apostolische Speisegesetz in den ersten fünf Jahrhunderten: Ein Beitrag zum Verständnis der quasi-levitischen Satzungen in älteren kirchlichen Rechtsquellen.* Paderborn: Ferdinand Schöningh.

Bookidis, Nancy. 1993. "Ritual Dining at Corinth." Pp. 45–61 in *Greek Sanctuaries: New Approaches,* eds. Nanno Marinatos and Robin Haegg. London: Routledge.

———. 1990. "Ritual Dining in the Sanctuary of Demeter and Kore at Corinth: Some Questions." Pp. 86–94 in *Sympotica: A Symposium on the Symposion,* ed. Oswyn Murray. Oxford: Clarendon.

———. 1969. "The Sanctuary of Demeter and Kore on Acrocorinth: Preliminary Report 3: 1968." *Hesperia* 38: 297–310.

Bookidis, Nancy, and Joan Fisher. 1974. "The Sanctuary of Demeter and Kore on Acrocorinth: Preliminary Report 5: 1971–1973." *Hesperia* 43: 267–307.

————. 1972. "The Sanctuary of Demeter and Kore on Acrocorinth: Preliminary Report 4: 1969–1970." *Hesperia* 41: 283–331.

Bookidis, Nancy, and R. S. Stroud. 1987. *Demeter and Persephone in Ancient Corinth*. Princeton: American School of Classical Studies.

Booth, A. 1991. "The Age of Reclining and Its Attendant Perils." Pp. 105–20 in *Dining in a Classical Context*, ed. W. J. Slater. Ann Arbor: University of Michigan Press.

Borgen, Peder. 1996. "'Yes,' 'No,' 'How Far?': The Participation of Jews and Christians in Pagan Cults." Pp. 15–43 in *Early Christianity and Hellenistic Judaism*. Edinburgh: T&T Clark.

Bowersock, G. W. 1980. "The Imperial Cult: Perceptions and Persistence." Pp. 171–82 in *Jewish and Christian Self-Definition. Volume Three: Self-Definition in the Graeco-Roman World*, eds. Ben Meyer and E. P. Sanders. London: SCM.

————. 1972. "Greek Intellectuals and the Imperial Cult in the Second Century A.D." Pp. 179–206 in *Le culte des souverains dans l'empire romain*, ed. Willem den Boer. Geneve: Vandoeuvres.

Brown, Peter. 1981. *The Cult of the Saints: Its Rise and Function in Latin Christianity*. Chicago: University of Chicago Press.

Brunt, J. C. 1985. "Rejected, Ignored, or Misunderstood? The Fate of Paul's Approach to the Problem of Food Offered to Idols in Early Christianity." *NTS* 31: 113–24.

————. 1978. "Paul's Attitude toward and Treatment of Problems involving Dietary Practice: A Case Study in Pauline Ethics." Unpublished PhD dissertation. Atlanta: Emory University.

Burkert, Walter. 1985. *Greek Religion*. Cambridge: Harvard University Press.

Butcher, Beverly. 1996. "Ancestor Veneration within the Catholic Church." *Tripod* 16.92: 15–24.

Cadbury, H. J. 1934. "The Macellum of Corinth." *JBL* 53: 134–41.

Callan, Terrance. 1993. "The Background of the Apostolic Decree (Acts 15:20,29; 21:25)." *CBQ* 55: 284–97.

Chan, Wing-Tsit. 1969. "Religions of China." Pp. 97–227 in *The Great Asian Religions: An Anthology*, eds. Chan Wing-tsit, Isma'il Ragi al Faruqi, Joseph Kitagawa, P. T. Raju. London: Macmillan.

Chen, Ivan, trans. 1908. *The Book of Filial Duty. Translated from the Chinese of the Hsiao Ching.* London: John Murray.

Cheung, Alex. 1999. *Idol Food in Corinth: Jewish Background and Pauline Legacy.* Sheffield: Sheffield Academic Press.

———. 1993. "A Narrative Analysis of Acts 14:27–15:35: Literary Shaping in Luke's Account of the Jerusalem Council." *WTJ* 55: 137–54.

China Centenary Missionary Conference Committee. 1907. Ancestor Worship Resolutions. Pp. 604–24 in *China Centenary Missionary Conference Records: Report of the Great Conference Held at Shanghai, April 5th to May 8th, 1907.* Shanghai: Conference Committee.

Ching, Julia. 1993. *Chinese Religions.* Maryknoll, NY: Orbis.

Chow, John. 1992. *Patronage and Power: A Study of Social Networks in Corinth.* Sheffield: Sheffield Academic Press.

Chua, Daniel. 1998. *Feeding on Ashes: A Biblical Evaluation of Chinese Ancestral Worship.* Kuala Lumpur: Kairos.

Clammer, John. 1985. *Singapore: Ideology, Society, Culture.* Singapore: Chopmen.

Clarke, Andrew. 1993. *Secular and Christian Leadership in Corinth: A Socio-Historical and Exegetical Study of 1 Corinthians 1–6.* Leiden: Brill.

———. 1991. "Another Corinthian Erastus Inscription." *TynB* 42: 146–51.

Classen, C. Joachim. 1993. "St. Paul's Epistles and Ancient Greek and Roman Rhetoric." Pp. 265–91 in *Rhetoric and the New*

Testament: Essays from the 1992 Heidelberg Conference, eds. Stanley Porter and Thomas Olbricht. Sheffield: JSOT Press.

Collins, Adele. 1984. *Crisis and Catharsis: The Power of the Apocalypse.* Philadelphia: Westminster.

Committee on Chinese Customs and Rites. 1989. *Chinese Customs and Festivals in Singapore.* Singapore: Singapore Federation of Chinese Clan Associations.

Contreras, Carlos. 1980. "Christian Views of Paganism." *ANRW* 2.23.2: 974–1022.

Conzelman, Hans. 1975. *1 Corinthians: A Commentary on the First Epistle to the Corinthians.* Philadelphia: Fortress.

Covell, Ralph. 1986. *Confucius, The Buddha, and Christ: A History of the Gospel in Chinese.* Maryknoll: Orbis.

Cranfield, C. E. B. 1979. *The Epistle to the Romans.* Edinburgh: T&T Clark.

Dawes, Gregory. 1996. "The Danger of Idolatry: First Corinthians 8:7–13." *CBQ* 58: 82–98.

Deissmann, Adolf. 1978. *Light from the Ancient East: The New Testament Illustrated by Recently Discovered Texts of the Graeco-Roman World.* Grand Rapids: Baker.

———. 1957. *Paul: A Study in Social and Religious History.* New York: Harper & Row.

Delobel, Joel. 1996. "Coherence and Relevance of 1 Cor. 8–10." Pp. 177–90 in *The Corinthian Correspondence*, ed. R. Bieringer. Leuven: University Press.

Denaux, A. 1996. "Theology and Christology in 1 Cor 8,4–6. A Contextual-Redactional Reading." Pp. 593–606 in *The Corinthian Correspondence*, ed. R. Bieringer. Leuven: University Press.

de Silva, David. 1992. "The Social Setting of the Revelation to John: Conflicts Within, Fears Without." *WTJ* 54: 273–302.

Dow, Sterling, and David Gill. 1965. "The Greek Cult Table." *American Journal of Archaeology* 69: 103–14.

Dunn, James. 1995. "Judaism in the Land of Israel in the First Century." Pp. 229–61 in *Judaism in Late Antiquity. Part Two: Historical Synthesis*, ed. Jacob Neusner. New York: Brill.

———. 1988. *Romans.* 2 vols. Word: Dallas.

Ehrhardt, A. 1964. *The Framework of the New Testament Stories.* Manchester: Manchester University Press.

Ellis, E. Earle. 1978. *Prophecy and Hermeneutic in Early Christianity.* Grand Rapids: Eerdmans.

Elmslie, W. A. L. 1911. *The Mishna on Idolatry 'Aboda Zara, Edited with Translation, Vocabulary and Notes.* In *Texts and Studies: Contributions to Biblical and Patristic Literature*, ed. J. Armitage Robinson. Vol. 8.2. Cambridge: Cambridge University Press.

Engels, D. 1990. *Roman Corinth: An Alternative Model for the Classical City.* Chicago: University of Chicago Press.

Fee, Gordon. 1987. *The First Epistle to the Corinthians.* Grand Rapids: Eerdmans.

———. 1980. "*Eidolothuta* Once Again: An Interpretation of 1 Corinthians 8–10." *Bib* 61: 172–97.

Feldman, Louis. 1990. "How Much Hellenism in Jewish Palestine?" Pp. 263–91 in *Origins of Judaism. Vol 1. Part 1. Normative Judaism*, ed. Jacob Neusner. New York: Garland.

Ferguson, John. 1970. *The Religions of the Roman Empire.* Ithaca: Cornell University Press.

Finke, Roger, and Rodney Stark. 1992. *The Churching of America, 1776–1990: Winners and Losers in Our Religious Economy.* New Brunswick, N.J.: Rutgers University Press.

Finley, M. I. 1985. "Foreword." Pp. xiii–xx in *Greek Religion and Society*, eds. P. E. Easterling and J. V. Muir. Cambridge: Cambridge University Press.

Fishwick, D. 1978. "The Development of Provincial Ruler Worship in the Western Roman Empire." *ANRW* 2.16.2: 1201–53.

Fisk, Bruce. 1989. "Eating Meat Offered to Idols: Corinthian Behavior and Pauline Response in 1 Corinthians 8–10 (A Response to Gordon Fee)." *TrinJ* 10: 49–70.

Fitzmyer, Joseph. 1989. *Luke the Theologian*. Mahwah, NJ: Paulist.

Förster, Werner. 1964. *"DaimÇn." TDNT* 2.1–20.

Friesen, S. 1993a. *Twice Neokoros*. Leiden: Brill.

———. 1993b. "Ephesus—Key to a Vision in Revelation." *BAR* 19.3: 24–37.

Gardner, Daniel, trans. 1990. *Learning to be a Sage: Selections from the Conversations of Master Chu, Arranged Topically*. Berkeley: University of California Press.

Gardner, Paul. 1994. *The Gifts of God and the Authentication of a Christian: An Exegetical Study of 1 Corinthians 8:1–11:1*. Lanham, MD: University Press of America.

Gill, David. 1993a. "Corinth: A Roman Colony in Achaea." *BZ* 37: 259–64.

———. 1993b. "In Search of the Social Élite in the Corinthian Church." *TynB* 44: 323–337.

———. 1992a "Behind the Classical Façade: Local Religions of the Roman Empire." Pp. 85–100 in *One God, One Lord: Christianity in a World of Religious Pluralism*, eds. Andrew Clarke and Bruce Winter. 2nd ed. Grand Rapids: Baker.

———. 1992b. "The Meat Market at Corinth (1 Cor 10:25)." *TynB* 43.2: 389–93.

———. 1990. "The Importance of Roman Portraiture for Head-coverings in 1 Corinthians 11:2–16." *TynB* 41: 245–60.

———. 1989. "Erastus the Aedile." *TynB* 40: 293–301.

———. 1974. "*Trapezomata*: A Neglected Aspect of Greek Sacrifice."
    HTR 67: 117–37.

Gilliam, J. F. 1976. "Invitations to the *Kline* of Sarapis." 1.315–24 in
    Collectanea Papyrologica: Texts Published in Honor of H. C. Youtie,
    ed. A. E. Hanson. Bonn: Rudolf Habelt.

Goldstein, Jonathan. 1981. "Jewish Acceptance and Rejection of
    Hellenism." In *Jewish and Christian Self-Definition. Volume Two:
    Aspects of Judaism in the Graeco-Roman Period*, ed. E. P. Sanders.
    London: SCM.

Gooch, Paul. 1993. *Dangerous Food: 1 Corinthians 8–10 in Its Context*.
    Waterloo, ON: Wilfrid Laurier University Press.

Gould, John. 1985. "On Making Sense of Greek Religion." Pp. 1–33
    in *Greek Religion and Society*, eds. P. E. Easterling and J. V. Muir.
    Cambridge: Cambridge University Press.

Grabbe, Lester. 1995. "Hellenistic Judaism." Pp. 53–83 in *Judaism in
    Late Antiquity. Part Two: Historical Syntheses*, ed. Jacob Neusner.
    New York: Brill.

Hanson, R. P. C. 1980. "The Christian Attitude to Pagan Religions
    up to the Time of Constantine the Great." *ANRW* 2.23.2: 910–73.

Harmon, D. P. 1978. "The Family Festivals of Rome." *ANRW* 2.16.2:
    1592–1603.

Hays, Richard. 1996. *The Moral Vision of the New Testament: A
    Contemporary Introduction to New Testament Ethics*. New York:
    Harper Collins.

Head, Peter. 1993. "Acts and the Problem of Its Texts." Pp. 415–44 in
    *The Book of Acts in its First Century Setting. Volume 1: The Book of
    Acts in its Ancient Literary Setting*, ed. Bruce Winter and Andrew
    Clarke. Grand Rapids: Eerdmans.

Hengel, Martin. 1974. *Judaism and Hellenism: Studies in Their
    Encounter in Palestine during the Early Hellenistic Period*.
    Philadelpia: Fortress.

Hodges, Lewis. 1922. "Non-Christian Religious Movements in China." Pp. 27–31 in *The Christian Occupation of China: A General Survey of the Numerical Strength and Geographical Distribution of the Christian Forces in China*, ed. Milton Stauffer. Shanghai: China Continuation Committee.

Holtom, D. C. 1963. *Modern Japan and Shinto Nationalism: A Study of Present-Day Trends in Japanese Religions*. New York: Paragon.

Hopkins, Keith. 1978. *Conquerors and Slaves: Sociological Studies in Roman History*. Cambridge: Cambridge University Press.

Horsley, G. H. R., ed. 1981. "Invitations to the *Kline* of Sarapis." Pp. 5–9 in *New Documents Illustrating Early Christianity*. Vol. 1. Sydney: Macquarrie University Press.

Hung, Daniel. 1983. "Mission Blockage: Ancestor Worship." *EMQ* 19.1: 32–40.

Hunt, A. S., and C. C. Edgar, trans. 1970. *Select Papyri*. LCL. Cambridge: Harvard University Press.

Hunter, James D. 1983. *American Evangelicalism: Conservative Religion and the Quandry of Modernity*. New Brunswick: Rutgers University Press.

Hurd, J. C. 1965. *The Origin of 1 Corinthians*. London: SPCK.

Isenberg, M. 1975. "The Sale of Sacrificial Meat." *Classical Philology* 70: 271–73.

Jackson, James. 1907. "Ancestral Worship." Pp. 215–46 in *China Centenary Missionary Conference Records: Report of the Great Conference Held at Shanghai, April 5th to May 8th, 1907*. Shanghai: Conference Committee.

Jackson, Peter. 1989. *Buddhism, Legitimation, and Conflict: The Political Functions of Urban Thai Buddhism*. Singapore: Institute of South East Asian Studies.

Jameson, Michael. 1949. "The Offering at Meals: Its Place in Greek Sacrifice." Unpublished PhD dissertation. Chicago: University of Chicago.

Jewett, Robert. 1978. "The Redaction of 1 Corinthians and the Trajectory of the Pauline School." *JAARSup* 46: 389–444.

———. 1971. *Paul's Anthropological Terms: A Study of Their Use in Conflict Settings*. Leiden: Brill.

Johnson, David. 1985. "Communication, Class and Consciousness in Late Imperial China." Pp. 34–72 in *Popular Culture in Late Imperial China*, eds. David Johnson, Andrew Nathan, and Evelyn Rawski. Berkeley: University of California Press.

Johnson, David, Andrew Nathan, and Evelyn Rawski. 1985. "Preface." Pp. ix–xvii in *Popular Culture in Late Imperial China*, eds. David Johnson, Andrew Nathan, and Evelyn Rawski. Berkeley: University of California Press.

Johnstone, Ronald. 1983. *Religion in Society: A Sociology of Religion*. Englewood Cliffs, NJ: Prentice-Hall.

Jones, D. L. 1980. "Christianity and the Roman Imperial Cult." *ANRW* 2.23.2: 1023–54.

Jordan, David. 1972. *Gods, Ghosts and Ancestors: The Folk Religion of a Taiwanese Village*. Berkeley: University of California Press.

Judge, E. A. 1960. *The Social Pattern of Early Christian Groups in the First Century*. London: Tyndale.

Kadletz, Edward. 1976. "Animal Sacrifice in Greek and Roman Religion." Unpublished PhD dissertation. Seattle: University of Washington.

Kelley, Dean. 1977. *Why Conservative Churches Are Growing: A Study in Sociology of Religion*. New York: Harper & Row.

Kennedy, George. 1984. *New Testament Interpretation through Rhetorical Criticism*. Chapel Hill: University of North Carolina Press.

Kennedy, C. A. 1994. "The Semantic Field of the Term 'Idolatry'."
Pp. 193–204 in *Uncovering Ancient Stones*, ed. Lewis Hopfe.
Winona Lake, IN: Eisenbrauns.

———. 1987. "The Cult of the Dead in Corinth." Pp. 227–36 in *Love
and Death in the Ancient Near East*, eds. J. H. Marks and R. M.
Good. Guilford, CT: Four Quarters.

Kern, Philip. 1998. *Rhetoric and Galatians: Assessing an Approach to
Paul's Epistle*. Cambridge: Cambridge University Press.

Kim, Chan-Hie. 1975. "The Papyrus Invitation." *JBL* 94: 391–402.

Kim Myung-Hyuk. 1985. "Historical Analysis of Ancestor Worship
in the Korean Church." Pp. 163–77 in *Christian Alternatives to
Ancestor Practices*, ed. Bong Rin Ro. Taichung, Taiwan: Asia
Theological Association.

Koet, Bart. 1996. "The Old Testament Background to 1 Cor. 10,7–8."
Pp. 607–15 in *The Corinthian Correspondence*, ed. R. Bieringer.
Leuven: University Press.

Krill, Richard. 1978. "Roman Paganism Under the Antonines and
Severans." *ANRW* 2.16.1: 27–44.

Kuhn, Karl. 1968. *"Pros~lutos." TDNT* 6.730–44.

Kuo, Eddie, and Tong Chee Kiong. 1995. *Religion in Singapore*.
Census of Population 1990 Monograph No. 2. Singapore:
Department of Statistics.

Latsch, Marie-Luise. 1985. *Traditional Chinese Festivals*. Singapore:
Graham Brash.

Lau, D. C. trans. 1979. *The Analects of Confucius*. Harmondsworth:
Penguin.

Legge, James. 1877. "Confucianism in Relation to Christianity: A
Paper Read before the Missionary Conference in Shanghai on
May 11th, 1877." Shanghai: Kelly & Walsh.

———. 1852. *The Notions of the Chinese Concerning Gods and Spirits.*
Trans. William Boone. Hong Kong: Hong Kong Register Office.

Leo, Juat Beh, and John Clammer. 1983. "Confucianism as Folk
Religion." Pp. 175–78 in *Studies in Chinese Folk Religion in
Singapore and Malaysia*, ed. John Clammer. Singapore:
Contributions to Southeast Asian Ethnography.

Lewis, W. J., ed. 1878. *Records of the General Conference of the
Protestant Missionaries of China held at Shanghai, May 10–24, 1877.*
Shanghai: Presbyterian Mission Press.

———. 1890. *Records of the General Conference of the Protestant
Missionaries of China Held at Shanghai, May 7–20, 1890.* Shanghai:
American Presbyterian Mission Press.

Liddell, Henry, Robert Scott, et al. 1968. *A Greek-English Lexicon.*
Oxford: Clarendon Press.

Liebermann, S. 1950. *Hellenism in Jewish Palestine. Studies in the
Literary Transmission, Beliefs and Manners of Palestine in the 1st
Century BCE–IV Century CE.* New York: Jewish Theological
Seminary of America.

Liebeschuetz, J. H. W. G. 1979. *Continuity and Change in Roman
Religion.* Oxford: Clarendon Press.

Lin, Chi-Ping. 1985. "Ancestor Worship: The Reactions of Chinese
Churches." Pp. 147–61 in *Christian Alternatives to Ancestor
Practices*, ed. Bong Rin Ro. Taichung, Taiwan: Asia Theological
Association.

Lin Ting Kwong, Ho Kong Chong, Tong Chee Kiong. 1990. "A
Multivariate Approach to Studying Chinese Customs and Rites
in Singapore." *Southeast Asian Journal of Social Science* 18.2: 70–84.

Ling, Trevor. 1993. "Singapore: Buddhist Development in a Secular
State." Pp. 154–83 in *Buddhist Trends in Southeast Asia*, ed. Trevor
Ling. Singapore: Institute of Southeast Asian Studies.

Longenecker, Richard. 1990. *Galatians.* Dallas: Word.

Lowe, Chuck. 1997. "Christianity and Social Context: Foundational Principles." Pp. 1–30 in *Ministry in Modern Singapore: The Effects of Modernity on the Church*, eds. Wong Chan Kok and Chuck Lowe. Singapore: Singapore Bible College.

Luckmann, Thomas. 1967. *The Invisible Religion: The Problem of Religion in Modern Society*. New York: Macmillan.

Lyons, George. 1985. *Pauline Autobiography: Toward a New Understanding*. Atlanta: Scholars.

Mack, Burton. 1990. *Rhetoric and the New Testament*. Minneapolis: Fortress.

MacMullen, Ramsay. 1981. *Paganism in the Roman Empire*. New Haven: Yale University Press.

———. 1974. *Roman Social Relations 50 B.C. to A.D. 284*. New Haven: Yale University Press.

Malherbe, Abraham. 1995. "Determinism and Free Will in Paul: The Argument of 1 Corinthians 8 and 9." Pp. 231–55 in *Paul in his Hellenistic Context*, ed. Troels Engberg-Pedersen. Minneapolis: Fortress.

———. 1983. *Social Aspects of Early Christianity*. Philadelphia: Fortress.

Marshall, I. Howard. 1980. *The Acts of the Apostles*. Grand Rapids: Eerdmans.

Marshall, Peter. 1987. *Enmity in Corinth: Social Conventions in Paul's Relations with the Corinthians*. Tübingen: J. C. B. Mohr.

Martin, David. 1978. *A General Theory of Secularization*. New York: Harper & Row.

Martin, William 1890. "The Worship of Ancestors—A Plea for Toleration." Pp. 619–31 in *Records of the General Conference of the Protestant Missionaries of China Held at Shanghai, May 7–20, 1890*, eds. W. J. Lewis et al. Shanghai: American Presbyterian Mission Press.

———. 1901. *The Lore of Cathay or the Intellect of China*. Edinburgh: Oliphant, Anderson & Ferrier.

Meeks, Wayne. 1983. *The First Urban Christians: The Social World of the Apostle Paul*. New Haven: Yale.

———. 1982. "'And Rose Up to Play': Midrash and Paraenesis in 1 Corinthians 10.1–22." *JSNT* 16: 64–78.

Meggitt, Justin. 1998. *Paul, Poverty and Survival*. Edinburgh: T&T Clark.

———. 1996. "The Social Status of Erastus (Rom. 16:23)." *NovT* 38: 218–23.

———. 1994. "Meat Consumption and Social Conflict in Corinth." *JTS* 45: 137–41.

Meiggs, Russell. 1960. *Roman Ostia*. Oxford: Clarendon.

Metzger, Bruce. 1971. *Textual Commentary on the Greek New Testament*. London: United Bible Society.

Millar, Fergus. 1972. "The Imperial Cult and the Persecutions." Pp. 145–75 in *Le culte des souverains dans l'Empire Romain*, ed. W. den Boer. Geneva: Vandoeuvres.

Mitchell, Alan. 1993. "Rich and Poor in the Courts of Corinth." *NTS* 39: 562–86.

Mitchell, Margaret. 1991. *Paul and the Rhetoric of Reconciliation*. Louisville: Westminster.

Momigliano, Arnaldo. 1987. *On Pagans, Jews, and Christians*. Middletown, CT: Wesleyan University Press.

Mott, John, ed. 1913. *The Continuation Committee Conferences in Asia 1912–13*. New York: Continuation Committee.

Muir, J. V. 1985. "Religion and the New Education: The Challenge of the Sophists." Pp. 191–218 in *Greek Religion and Society*, eds. P. E.

Easterling and J. V. Muir. Cambridge: Cambridge University Press.

Murphy-O'Connor, Jerome. 1983. *St. Paul's Corinth: Texts and Archaeology*. Wilmington: Glazier.

——. 1979a. *1 Corinthians*. Wilmington, DE: Michael Glazier.

——. 1979b. "Food and Spiritual Gifts in 1 Cor 8:8." *CBQ* 41: 292–98.

——. 1978. "Freedom or the Ghetto" (*I Cor.*, VIII,1–13; X,23–XI,1). *RevBib* 85: 543–74.

Neusner, Jacob. 1995. *Rabbinic Judaism: Structure and System*. Minneapolis: Fortress.

——. 1993. *Judaic Law from Jesus to the Mishnah: A Systematic Reply to Professor E. P. Sanders*. Atlanta: Scholars Press.

Newton, Derek. 1998. *Deity and Diet: The Dilemma of Sacrificial Food at Corinth*. Sheffield: Sheffield Academic Press.

Nilsson, Martin. 1940. *Greek Folk Religion*. New York: Columbia University Press.

Nock, Arthur. 1964. *Early Gentile Christianity and Its Hellenistic Background*. New York: Harper and Row.

Noll, Ray, ed. 1992. *100 Roman Documents concerning the Chinese Rites Controversy (1645–1941)*. San Francisco: Ricci Institute for Chinese-Western Cultural History.

Noyes, H. V. 1890. "How Far Should Christians Be Required to Abandon Native Customs?" Pp. 609–19 in *Records of the General Conference of the Protestant Missionaries of China Held at Shanghai, May 7–20, 1890*, eds. W. J. Lewis et al. Shanghai: American Presbyterian Mission Press.

Ogilvie, R. M. 1969. *The Romans and Their Gods in the Age of Augustus*. New York: Norton.

Ohlinger, F. 1890. "How Far Should Christians Be Required to Abandon Native Customs?" Pp. 603–9 in *Records of the General Conference of the Protestant Missionaries of China Held at Shanghai, May 7–20, 1890*, eds. W. J. Lewis et al. Shanghai: American Presbyterian Mission Press.

Orr, D. G. 1978. "Roman Domestic Religion: the Evidence of the Household Shrines." *ANRW* 2.16.2: 1557–1591.

———. 1972. "Roman Domestic Religion: A Study of the Roman Household Deities and Their Shrines at Pompeii and Herculaneum." Unpublished PhD dissertation. College Park, MD: University of Maryland.

Oster, R. E., Jr. 1992. "Use, Misuse and Neglect of Archaeological Evidence in Some Modern Works on 1 Corinthians (1 Cor. 7,1–5; 8,10; 11,2–16; 12,14–26)." *ZNW* 83: 52–73.

Pierce, Charles. 1955. *Conscience in the New Testament*. London: SCM.

Porter, Stanley. 1997a. "Paul of Tarsus and his Letters." Pp. 533–85 in *Handbook of Classical Rhetoric in the Hellenistic Period 330 B.C.–A.D. 400*, ed. Stanley Porter. New York: Brill.

———. 1997b. "Ancient Rhetorical Analysis and Discourse Analysis of the Pauline Corpus." Pp. 249–74 in *The Rhetorical Analysis of Scripture: Essays from the 1995 London Conference*, eds. Stanley Porter and Thomas Olbricht. Sheffield: Sheffield Academic Press.

———. 1993. "The Theoretical Justification for Application of Rhetorical Categories to Pauline Epistolary Literature." Pp. 100–22 in *Rhetoric and the New Testament: Essays from the 1992 Heidelberg Conference*, eds. Stanley Porter and Thomas Olbricht. Sheffield: Sheffield Academic Press.

Price, Simon. 1997. "Rituals and Power." Pp. 47–71 in *Paul and Empire: Religion and Power in Roman Imperial Society*, ed. Richard Horsley. Harrisburg: Trinity Press.

———. 1987. "From Noble Funerals to Divine Cult: The Consecration of Roman Emperors." Pp. 56–105 in *Rituals of Royalty: Power and Ceremonial in Traditional Societies*, eds. David

Cannadine and Simon Price. Cambridge: Cambridge University Press.

———. 1984. *Rituals and Power: The Roman Imperial Cult in Asia Minor.* Cambridge: Cambridge University Press.

Redfield, Robert. 1956. *Peasant Society and Culture.* Chicago: University of Chicago.

Reed, Jeffrey. 1997. "The Epistle." Pp. 171–93 in *Handbook of Classical Rhetoric in the Hellenistic Period 330 B.C.–A.D. 400,* ed. Stanley Porter. New York: Brill.

———. 1993. "Using Ancient Rhetorical Categories to Interpret Paul's Letters: A Question of Genre." Pp. 292–324 in *Rhetoric and the New Testament: Essays from the 1992 Heidelberg Conference,* eds. Stanley Porter and Thomas Olbricht. Sheffield: Sheffield Academic Press.

Ricci, Matteo. 1953. *China in the Sixteenth Century: The Journals of Matthew Ricci: 1583–1610,* ed. Nicola Trigault. New York: Random House.

Richter, Hans-Friedemann. 1996. "Anstössige Freiheit in Korinth: Zur Literarkritik der Korintherbriefe." Pp. 567–75 in *The Corinthian Correspondence,* ed. R. Bieringer. Leuven: University Press.

Ro, Bong Rin. 1985. "Preface." N.p. in *Christian Alternatives to Ancestor Practices,* ed. Bong Rin Ro. Taichung, Taiwan: Asia Theological Association.

Ro, Bong Rin, ed. 1985. *Christian Alternatives to Ancestor Practices.* Taichung, Taiwan: Asia Theological Association.

Robertson, Archibald, and Alfred Plummer. 1975. *The First Epistle of St. Paul to the Corinthians.* Edinburgh: T&T Clark.

Roebuck, Carl. 1951. *The Asklepieion and Lerna.* Vol XIV in *Corinth: Results of Excavations Conducted by the American School of Classical Studies at Athens.* Princeton: The American School of Classical Studies.

Ross, Andrew C. 1994. *A Vision Betrayed: The Jesuits in Japan and China 1542–1742*. Maryknoll: Orbis.

Rule, Paul. 1986. *K'ung-tzu or Confucius? The Jesuit Interpretation of Confucianism*. Sydney: Allen & Unwin.

Safrai, Shmuel. 1987. "Halakha." Pp. 121–209 in *The Literature of the Sages*. Philadelphia: Fortress.

Sandbach, F. H., trans. 1969. *Plutarch's Moralia*. Vol. 15. Fragments. Cambridge: Harvard University.

Sandelin, Karl–Gustav. 1997. "Does Paul Argue against Sacramentalism and Over-Confidence in 1 Cor. 10.1–14?" Pp. 165–82 in *The New Testament and Hellenistic Judaism*, eds. Peder Borgen and Soren Giversen. Peabody, MA: Hendrickson.

Sanders, E. P. 1990. *Jewish Law from Jesus to the Mishnah: Five Studies*. London: SCM.

Sawyer, William. 1968. "The Problem of Meat Sacrificed to Idols in the Corinthian Church." Unpublished PhD dissertation. Louisville: Southern Baptist Theological Seminary.

Schmithals, Walter. 1971. *Gnosticism in Corinth: An Investigation of the Letters to the Corinthians*. Nashville: Abingdon.

Schreiner, Thomas. 1998. *Romans*. Grand Rapids: Baker.

Scullard, H. H. 1981. *Festivals and Ceremonies of the Roman Republic*. Ithaca: Cornell University Press.

Segal, Alan. 1990. *Paul the Convert: The Apostolate and Apostasy of Saul the Pharisee*. New Haven: Yale.

Sellin, Gerhard. 1987. "Hauptprobleme des Ersten Korintherbriefes." *ANRW* 2.25.4: 2940–3044.

Slater, W. J., ed. 1991. *Dining in a Classical Context*. Ann Arbor: University of Michigan.

Smit, Joop. 1996. "1 Cor. 8,1–6: A Rhetorical *Partitio*. A Contribution to the Coherence of 1 Cor. 8,1–11,1." In *The Corinthian Correspondence*, ed. R. Bieringer. Leuven: University Press.

———. 1992. "Argument and Genre of 1 Corinthians 12–14." Pp. 211–30 in *Rhetoric and the New Testament: Essays from the 1992 Heidelberg Conference*, eds. Stanley Porter and Thomas Olbricht. Sheffield: JSOT Press.

Smith, Dennis. 1980. "Social Obligation in the Context of Communal Meals: A Study of the Christian Meal in 1 Corinthians in Comparison with Graeco-Roman Communal Meals." Unpublished ThD dissertation. Cambridge: Harvard Divinity School.

Smith, Dennis, and Hal Taussig. 1990. *Many Tables: The Eucharist in the New Testament and Liturgy Today*. Philadelphia: Trinity.

Smith, Henry. 1989a. "Ancestor Practices in Contemporary Hong Kong: Religious Ritual or Social Custom?" *AJT* 3: 31–45.

———. 1989b. "Christianity and Ancestor Practices in Hong Kong: Toward a Contextual Strategy." *Missiology* 17:1 27–38.

———. 1987. "Chinese Ancestor Practices and Christianity: Toward a Viable Contextualization of Christian Ethics in a Hong Kong Setting." Unpublished Ph.D. dissertation. Fort Worth, TX: Southwestern Baptist Theological Seminary.

Sordi, Marta. 1983. *The Christians and the Roman Empire*. London: Croom Helm.

Stambaugh, J. E. 1988. *The Ancient Roman City*. Baltimore: Johns Hopkins University.

———. 1978. "The Functions of Roman Temples." *ANRW* 2.16.1: 554–608.

Stamps, D. L. 1995. "Rhetorical Criticism of the New Testament: Ancient and Modern Evaluations of Argumentation." Pp. 129–69 in *Approaches to New Testament Study*, eds. Stanley Porter and David Tombs. Sheffield: Sheffield Academic Press.

Stark, Rodney. 1996. *The Rise of Christianity: A Sociologist Reconsiders History.* Princeton: Princeton University Press.

Stauffer, Milton, ed. 1922. *The Christian Occupation of China: A General Survey of the Numerical Strength and Geographical Distribution of the Christian Forces in China.* Shanghai: China Continuation Committee.

Suksamran, Somboon. 1993. "Buddhism, Political Authority, and Legitimacy in Thailand and Cambodia." Pp. 101–53 in *Buddhist Trends in Southeast Asia*, ed. Trevor Ling. Singapore: Institute of Southeast Asian Studies.

Sumney, Jerry. 1990. *Identifying Paul's Opponents: The Question of Method in 2 Corinthians.* Sheffield: JSOT Press.

Tan, Teik Beng. 1988. *Beliefs and Practices among Malaysian Chinese Buddhists.* Buddhist Missionary Society: Kuala Lumpur.

Theissen, Gerd. 1982. *The Social Setting of Pauline Christianity: Essays on Corinth.* Philadelphia: Fortress.

Thiselton, A. C. 1978. "Realized Eschatology at Corinth." *NTS* 24: 510–26.

Thompson, Leonard. 1990. *The Book of Revelation: Apocalypse and Empire.* Oxford: Oxford University Press.

Thyen, Hartwig. 1991. "Thusia." *EDNT* 2:161–63.

Tomson, Peter. 1990. *Paul and the Jewish Law: Halakha in the Letters of the Apostle to the Gentiles.* Minneapolis: Fortress.

Tong, Chee Kiong. 1987. *Dangerous Blood, Refined Souls: Death Rituals among the Chinese in Singapore.* Unpublished PhD dissertation. Cornell: Cornell University.

Tong Chee Kiong, Ho Kong Chong, Lin Ting Kwong. 1992. "Traditional Chinese Customs in Modern Singapore." Pp. 78–101 in *Asian Traditions and Modernization: Perspectives from Singapore*, ed. Yong Mun Cheong. Singapore: Times Academic Press.

Tong, Daniel. 1988. *Ancestral Veneration.* Singapore: Christian Library.

Toynbee, J. M. C. 1971. *Death and Burial in the Roman World.* Ithaca: Cornell University Press.

von Soden, Hans. 1972. "Sacrament and Ethics in Paul." Pp. 257–68 in *The Writings of St. Paul,* ed. Wayne Meeks. New York: Norton.

Waley, Arthur, trans. 1938. *The Analects of Confucius.* New York: Random.

Wanamaker, Charles. 1990. *The Epistle to the Thessalonians.* Grand Rapids: Eerdmans.

Watson, Burton, trans. 1963a. *Hsün Tzu: Basic Writings.* New York: Columbia University.

———. 1963b. *Mo Tzu: Basic Writings.* New York: Columbia University Press.

Watson, Duane. 1988. *Invention, Arrangement and Style: Rhetorical Criticism of Jude and 2 Peter.* Atlanta: Scholars.

Weber, Max. 1964. *The Sociology of Religion.* Boston: Beacon.

Wee, Vivienne. 1977. "Religion and Ritual among the Chinese of Singapore: An Ethnographic Study." Unpublished MSocSci thesis. Singapore: University of Singapore.

Weller, Robert. 1987. *Unities and Diversities in Chinese Religion.* MacMillan: London.

Wenham, David. 1993. "Acts and the Pauline Corpus: II. The Evidence of Parallels." Pp. 215–58 in *The Book of Acts in its First Century Setting. Volume 1: Ancient Literary Setting,* eds. Bruce Winter and Andrew Clarke. Grand Rapids: Eerdmans.

Wiencke, Matthew. 1947. "Greek Household Religion." Unpublished PhD dissertation. Baltimore: Johns Hopkins University.

Wilken, Robert. 1984. *The Christians as the Romans Saw Them*. New Haven: Yale University Press.

———. 1980. "The Christians as the Romans (and Greeks) Saw Them." Pp. 100–25 in *Jewish and Christian Self-Definition. Volume One: The Shaping of Christianity in the Second and Third Centuries*, ed. E. P. Sanders. London: SCM.

Willis, Wendell. 1991. "'Corinthusne deletus est?'" *BZ* 35: 233–41.

———. 1985a. *Idol Meat in Corinth: The Pauline Argument in 1 Corinthians 8 and 10*. Chico: Scholars Press.

———. 1985b. "An Apostolic Apologia? The Form and Function of 1 Corinthians 9." *JSNT* 24: 33–48.

Winter, Bruce. 1997. "Gluttony and Immorality At Élitist Banquets: The Background to 1 Corinthians 6:12–20." *Jian Dao* 7: 77–90.

———. 1995. "The Achaean Federal Imperial Cult II: The Corinthian Church." *TynB* 46.1: 169–78.

———. 1994a. "Civic Rights: 1 Corinthians 8–11:1." Pp. 165–77 in *Seek the Welfare of the City: Citizens as Benefactors and Citizens*. Grand Rapids: Eerdmans.

———. 1994b. "Civil Litigation: 1 Corinthians 6:1–11." Pp. 105–21 in *Seek the Welfare of the City: Citizens as Benefactors and Citizens*. Grand Rapids: Eerdmans.

———. 1994c. "The Imperial Cult." *The Book of Acts in Its First Century Setting. Volume 2: The Book of Acts in Its Greco-Roman Setting*, eds. David Gill and Conrad Gempf. Pp. 93–103. Grand Rapids: Eerdmans.

———. 1990. "Theological and Ethical Responses to Religious Pluralism—1 Corinthians 8–10." *TynB* 41: 209–26.

Wiseman, J. 1979. "Corinth and Rome I: 228 B.C.–A.D. 267." *ANRW* 2.7.1: 438–548. Berlin: Walter de Gruyter.

Witherington, Ben III . 1998. *The Acts of the Apostles: A Socio-Rhetorical Commentary.* Grand Rapids: Eerdmans, 1998.

———. 1995. *Conflict and Community in Corinth: A Socio-Rhetorical Commentary on 1 and 2 Corinthians.* Grand Rapids: Eerdmans.

Wong, C. S. 1987. *An Illustrated Cycle of Chinese Festivities in Malaysia and Singapore.* Singapore: MPH.

Wong, Fong Yang. 1994. *Freedom and Consideration.* Kuala Lumpur: Kairos.

Wuellner, Wilhelm. 1979. "Greek Rhetoric and Pauline Argumentation." In *Early Christian Literature and the Classical Intellectual Tradition*, ed. W. R. Shoedel and R. L. Wilken. Paris: Editions Beauchesne.

Yang, C. K. 1961. *Religion in Chinese Society: A Study of the Contemporary Social Functions of Religion and Some of Their Historical Factors.* Berkeley: University of California Press.

Yates, M. T. 1878. "Ancestor Worship." Pp. 367–387 in *Records of the General Conference of the Protestant Missionaries of China held at Shanghai, May 10–24, 1877*, eds. W. J. Lewis et al. Shanghai: Presbyterian Mission Press.

Yeo, Khiok-Khng. 1995. *Rhetorical Interaction in 1 Corinthians 8 and 10: A Formal Analysis with Implications for a Cross-Cultural, Chinese Hermeneutic.* Leiden: E.J. Brill.

Youtie, H. C. 1948. "The Kline of Sarapis." *HTR* 41: 9–29.

Zaidman, L. B., and P. Schmitt Pantel. 1992. *Religion in the Ancient Greek City.* Cambridge: Cambridge University Press.

Names Index